T0255358

Lecture Notes in Computer Science 3660

Commenced Publication in 1973
Founding and Former Series Editors:
Gerhard Goos, Juris Hartmanis, and Jan van Leeuwen

Editorial Board

Michael Beigl   Stephen Intille
Jun Rekimoto   Hideyuki Tokuda (Eds.)

UbiComp 2005: Ubiquitous Computing

7th International Conference, UbiComp 2005
Tokyo, Japan, September 11-14, 2005
Proceedings

 Springer

Volume Editors

Michael Beigl
University of Karlsruhe
Institute for Telematics, TecO (Telecooperation Office)
Vincenz-Priessnitz-Straße 1, 76131 Karlsruhe, Germany
E-mail: michael@teco.uni-karsruhe.de

Stephen Intille
Massachusetts Institute of Technology
1 Cambridge Center, 4FL, Cambridge, MA 02142, USA
E-mail: intille@mit.edu

Jun Rekimoto
Sony Computer Science Laboratories, Inc.
3–14–13 Higashi-gotanda, Shinagawa-ku, Tokyo, 141–0022, Japan
E-mail: rekimoto@csl.sony.co.jp

Hideyuki Tokuda
Keio University
5322 Endo, Fujisawa, Kanagawa 252-8520, Japan
E-mail: hxt@sfc.keio.ac.jp

Library of Congress Control Number: 2005932242

CR Subject Classification (1998): C.2, C.3, D.2, D.4, H.4, H.5, K.4

ISSN   0302-9743
ISBN-10   3-540-28760-4 Springer Berlin Heidelberg New York
ISBN-13   978-3-540-28760-5 Springer Berlin Heidelberg New York

Springer is a part of Springer Science+Business Media

springeronline.com

© Springer-Verlag Berlin Heidelberg 2005
Printed in Germany

Typesetting: Camera-ready by author, data conversion by Boller Mediendesign
Printed on acid-free paper   SPIN: 11551201   06/3142   5 4 3 2 1 0

Preface

The 7th International Conference on Ubiquitous Computing (UbiComp 2005) marked the first time that this premier venue for original research contributions in ubiquitous computing was held in Asia. The Tokyo, Japan venue reflects the desire of the UbiComp community to make this conference series an international event that showcases the increasing amount of high-quality ubiquitous computing research that is taking place worldwide. As the field of ubiquitous computing has matured, the UbiComp Conference has gained significance worldwide, not only among researchers, but also with industry and general society.

This interest in the potential of ubiquitous computing to impact our lives has resulted in the creation of many new research programs in academia and industry. These efforts have, in turn, led to mass media coverage of efforts and, in some regions of the world, large-scale government-initiated collaborative efforts to explore the potential of these emerging technologies. These trends are reflected in the rise in the number of submissions to UbiComp 2005. This year the conference received 230 full papers, submitted almost equally from Asia (~100 submissions), North America and South America (~60 submissions) and Europe(~60 submissions), with the remainder being received from Australia and Africa. From among many high-quality submissions, the technical program committee accepted 22 papers. These papers were chosen based solely on the quality of their peer reviews using a double-blind review process.

The papers submitted to UbiComp 2005 showcase the diverse nature of ubiquitous computing research. Submissions covered topics such as human-computer interface (HCI), systems, context recognition and use, communications, and social implications and applications of computing. Methodologies included real-world deployments, laboratory experiments, ethnographic analysis, qualitative and quantitative evaluation, and theoretical explorations. The majority of the submissions covered more than one topic area and clearly filled a gap between more established research fields. Topics such as location systems and their applications, case studies and user interfaces, algorithms for recognition of context, and novel devices received the most attention by authors this year.

The Program Committee (PC) and reviewer pool was selected to provide the multi-disciplinary expertise required to evaluate original contributions in these research areas. We were fortunate to have an outstanding group of international researchers volunteering their time and expertise. The high quality of this conference was the result of their hard work and dedication to the advancement of the field. Due to the high number of submissions and the peer-review-process, PC members had to review an exceptionally large number of papers. Each PC member was responsible not only for reviews but also for monitoring the review process and facilitating discussion among external reviewers. External reviewers also had an unusually high review load with an average of six full papers. The comments of these experts provided feedback for the submission authors and helped the Program Committee in their final selection decisions. We thank both the PC members and the external reviewers for delivering excellent and constructive reviews.

We would also like to extend our gratitude to the General Chair of the conference, Hideyuki Tokuda, who made this event possible and who helped with organizing the Program Committee meeting. Other members of our community also made outstanding contributions. Among them, Christian Decker supervised the pre-printing process of these proceedings, Albrecht Schmidt helped with the logistics of the Program Committee meeting (while simultaneously running Pervasive 2004), and Matthias Kranz and Rainer Fink provided valuable technical support during the meeting.

Our final word of thanks goes to all the 663 authors who submitted full papers to this conference. Presenting research work in a paper requires a great deal of effort. We hope that these authors were rewarded with insightful reviews and an enjoyable conference program.

July 2005   Michael Beigl, Stephen Intille, Jun Rekimoto

UbiComp 2005 Paper Review Process

The review process for UbiComp 2005 was very similar to the process used for UbiComp 2004 and was divided into 6 phases.

Phase 1: Program Committee (PC) Assignment and Reviewer Nomination

All papers submitted were assigned to a lead Program Committee member (PC) and a secondary PC reviewer, both selected from the Program Committee (PC). Care was taken that both PC members assigned did not have any conflict of interest with the paper and that the PC members had the appropriate expertise to review the paper. These two PC members in turn nominated two additional reviewers from a reviewer pool suggested by members of the PC and vetted by the PC chairs. PC and external reviewer paper loads were balanced by the PC chairs.

Phase 2: Quick Reject

To allow us to concentrate review efforts on papers with the best chances of being accepted, an additional quick reject phase was added before the review process. Papers where both PC members concurred that the paper was either wildly "out of scope" or "of unacceptably low quality to be accepted" were nominated for "quick reject" after a short discussion phase. In cases where at least two PC chairs also agreed, the papers were returned to the authors with just two reviews.

Phase 3: Reviews

PC chairs then processed all the papers that were not quick-rejected and allocated external reviewers based on the selections suggested by the PC members in Phase 1. A large effort was made to balance reviewing load across external reviewers. Because many papers crossed several research fields, care was taken to assign an expert for every area addressed in the paper. Reviewers were also carefully chosen to preserve anonymity and avoid institutional conflicts of interest. When necessary, reviewers could ask for additional reviews to be carried out. Papers received an average of five reviews in total – two from PC members and 3 from external reviewers.

Phase 4: On-line Discussion

After all of the reviews were received, the lead PC member for each paper coordinated an electronic discussion among the reviewers to reach a consensus as to the technical merit of the paper. When necessary, the reviewers could ask for additional reviews to be carried out to clarify certain aspects of the paper.

Phase 5: PC Meeting

A single PC meeting was held on May 8 in Munich, Germany. Attendance was a condition of acceptance to serve on the PC, and almost all of the PC members attended the meeting. At the meeting the committee examined all the papers that scored above a threshold (roughly corresponding to borderline weak reject) as well as some other papers with unusually high score spans. Each paper was discussed and rated. The final program was selected solely based on the criteria of scientific excellence.

Phase 6: Shepherding

To help authors with accepted papers interpret their reviews, all of the papers were allocated shepherds selected from the PC. These PC members guided the authors through the final revisions of their papers. Acceptance of papers was conditional on approval from the shepherds. This process helped considerably to improve the clarity of written presentation of work in a number of cases, and it ensured that the papers in these proceedings were revised to reflect the extensive feedback provided to the authors by the PC.

Conference Organization

Organizers

Honorary Conference Chair

Yuichiro Anzai   President, Keio University (Japan)

Conference Chair

Hideyuki Tokuda   Keio University (Japan)

Program Chairs

Michael Beigl   TecO, University of Karlsruhe (Germany)
Stephen Intille   MIT (USA)
Jun Rekimoto   SonyCSL (Japan)

Demonstration Chairs

Marc Langheinrich   ETH Zurich (Switzerland)
Yasuto Nakanishi   Tokyo University of Agriculture and
                          Technology (Japan)

Poster Chairs

Elaine M. Huang   Georgia Institute of Technology (USA)
Tsutomu Terada   Osaka University (Japan)

Video Chairs

Masayoshi Ohhashi   KDDI R&D Labs (Japan)
Atau Tanaka   SonyCSL Paris (France)

Workshop Chairs

Yoshito Tobe   Tokyo Denki University (Japan)
Khai N. Truong   Georgia Institute of Technology (USA)

Doctoral Colloquium Chair

Gabriele Kotsis   University of Linz (Austria)

Student Volunteers Chair

Yoshihiro Kawahara   The University of Tokyo (Japan)

Treasurer Chair

Kazunori Takashio   Keio University (Japan)

Local Arrangements Chair

Masateru Minami   Shibaura Institute of Technology (Japan)

Publicity Chair

Koichi Kurumatani   AIST (Japan)

Publications Chair

Christian Decker   TecO, University of Karlsruhe (Germany)

Webmaster

Michael Beigl   TecO, University of Karlsruhe (Germany)
Daisuke Maruyama   Keio University (Japan)
Shunsaku Yamazaki   Keio University (Japan)

Sponsors

Gold Sponsors   KDDI R&D Labs
                    NTT DoCoMo
                    NEC
Silver Sponsors   Fuji Xerox
                    Fujitsu
                    Intel
                    Microsoft
Bronze Sponsors   Crossbow
                    IBM
                    Mitsubishi Electric
                    Uchida
                    NTT
                    DNP
                    Ubitec
                    Panasonic
                    Toshiba
                    Hitachi
                    CiscoSystems
                    Ubiquitous Networking Forum

Program Committee

Gregory Abowd	Georgia Institute of Technology (USA)
Christian Becker	University of Stuttgart (Germany)
Gaetano Borriello	University of Washington and Intel Research Seattle (USA)
Roy H. Campbell	University of Illinois at Urbana Champaign (USA)
Nigel Davies	Lancaster University (UK)
Paul Dourish	University of California (Irvine (USA)
W. Keith Edwards	Georgia Institute of Technology (USA)
Alois Ferscha	University of Linz (Austria)
Geraldine Fitzpatrick	University of Sussex (UK)
Masaaki Fukumoto	NTT DoCoMo (Japan)
Hans Gellersen	Lancaster University (UK)
Scott Hudson	Carnegie Mellon University (USA)
Gabriele Kotsis	University of Linz (Austria)
John Krumm	Microsoft Research (USA)
Anthony LaMarca	Intel Research Seattle (USA)
Marc Langheinrich	ETH Zurich (Switzerland)
Tom Rodden	University of Nottingham (UK)
Ichiro Satoh	National Institute of Informatics (Japan)
Bernt Schiele	Darmstadt University of Technology (Germany)
Chris Schmandt	Massachusetts Institute of Technology (USA)
Albrecht Schmidt	University of Munich (Germany)
Itiro Siio	Tamagawa University (Japan)
Mirjana Spasojevic	Hewlett-Packard Labs (USA)
Yasuyuki Sumi	Kyoto University (Japan)
Yoshito Tobe	Tokyo Denki University (Japan)
Allison Woodruff	Intel Research (USA)
Michiaki Yasumura	Keio University (Japan)

Reviewers

Ken Anderson	Intel Research (USA)
Paul Aoki	Palo Alto Research Center (PARC) (USA)
Jakob Bardram	University of Aarhus (Denmark)
John Barton	IBM Research (USA)
Martin Bauer	Universität Stuttgart (Germany)
Michael Beigl	University of Karlsruhe (Germany)
Genevieve Bell	Intel Corporation (USA)
Alastair Beresford	University of Cambridge (UK)
Mark Billinghurst	University of Canterbury (New Zealand)
Philippe Bonnet	University of Copenhagen (Denmark)

Barry Brown	University of Glasgow (UK)
Matthew Chalmers	University of Glasgow (UK)
Luigina Ciolfi	Interaction Design Centre, University of Limerick (Ireland)
Sunny Consolvo	Intel Research Seattle (USA)
Andy Crabtree	University of Nottingham (UK)
Christian Decker	TecO, University of Karlsruhe (Germany)
Anind Dey	Carnegie Mellon University (USA)
Carl Ellison	Microsoft (USA)
Kenneth Fishkin	Intel Research Seattle (USA)
Christian Floerkemeier	ETH Zurich (Switzerland)
James Fogarty	Carnegie Mellon University (USA)
Adrian Friday	Lancaster University (UK)
Kaori Fujinami	Waseda University (Japan)
Dipak Ghosal	University of California, Davis (USA)
William Griswold	UCSD (USA)
Mike Hazas	Lancaster University (UK)
Jeffrey Hightower	Intel Research Seattle (USA)
Paul Holleis	University of Munich (Germany)
Lars Erik Holmquist	Viktoria Institute (Sweden)
Jason Hong	Carnegie Mellon University (USA)
Eva Hornecker	Interact Lab, University of Sussex, Falmer (UK)
Eric Horvitz	Microsoft Research (USA)
Tom Igoe	NYU / ITP (USA)
Mizuko Ito	Keio University (Japan)
Sadanori Ito	ATR (Japan)
Natalie Jeremijenko	UCSD (USA)
Rui Jose	University of Minho (Portugal)
Eiji Kamioka	National Institute of Informatics, Tokyo (Japan)
Nicky Kern	TU Darmstadt (Germany)
Boriana Koleva	University of Nottingham (UK)
Yasuyuki Kono	NAIST (Japan)
Gerd Kortuem	Lancaster University (UK)
Matthias Kranz	University of Munich (Germany)
Christian Kray	Lancaster University (UK)
Antonio Krüger	University of Münster (Germany)
Michael Kreutzer	TU Darmstadt (Germany)
Albert Krohn	University of Karlsruhe (Germany)
Shoji Kurakake	NTT DoCoMo R&D Center (Japan)
Spyros Lalis	University of Thessaly (Greece)
Mik Lamming	HP Laboratories Palo Alto (USA)
Scott Lederer	UC Berkeley (USA)

Darren Leigh	Mitsubishi Electric Research Laboratories (USA)
Lin Liao	University of Washington (USA)
Cristina Lopes	University of California, Irvine (USA)
Paul Luff	King's College London (UK)
Paul Lukowicz	UMIT (AT)
Carsten Magerkurth	Fraunhofer IPSI (Germany)
Scott Mainwaring	Intel Research (USA)
Jennifer Mankoff	Human Computer Interaction Institute, Carnegie Mellon University (USA)
Natalia Marmasse	IBM Research, Israel (Israel)
Emmanuel Munguia Tapia	Massachusetts Institute of Technology (USA)
Tatsuo Nakajima	Waseda University (Japan)
Chandrasekhar Narayanaswami	IBM T. J. Watson (USA)
Mark W. Newman	Palo Alto Research Center (PARC) (USA)
Nobuhiko Nishio	Ritsumeikan University (Japan)
Nuria Oliver	Microsoft Research, Redmond (USA)
Joseph Paradiso	MIT (USA)
Kurt Partridge	PARC (USA)
Shwetak Patel	Georgia Institute of Technology (USA)
Donald Patterson	University of Washington (USA)
Alex Pentland	MIT Media Lab (USA)
Rosalind Picard	MIT Media Lab (USA)
Claudio Pinhanez	IBM Research, TJ Watson (USA)
Ivan Poupyrev	Sony CSL (Japan)
Nissanka Priyantha	Massachusetts Institute of Technology (USA)
Aaron Quigley	University College Dublin (Ireland)
Kay Römer	ETH Zurich (Switzerland)
Philip Robinson	TecO, University of Karlsruhe (Germany)
Yvonne Rogers	Indiana University (USA)
Michael Rohs	ETH Zurich (Switzerland)
Manuel Roman	DoCoMo Laboratories San Jose (USA)
Mark Rouncefield	Lancaster University (UK)
Enrico Rukzio	University of Munich (Germany)
Kathy Ryall	Mitsubishi Electric Research Labs (USA)
Karsten Schwan	Georgia Institute of Technology (USA)
James Scott	Intel Research Cambridge (UK)
Abigail Sellen	Microsoft Research (UK)
Steven Shafer	Microsoft Research (USA)
Louis Shue	Institute for Infocomm Research (Singapore)
Ian Smith	Intel Research Seattle (USA)
Mathias Stäger	Werarable Computing Lab, ETH Zurich (Switzerland)
Anthony Steed	University College London (UK)
Peter Steenkiste	Carnegie Mellon University (USA)

Oliver Storz	Lancaster University (UK)
Peter Tandler	Fraunhofer IPSI (Germany)
Hiroyuki Tarumi	Kagawa University (Japan)
Khai Truong	Georgia Institute of Technology (USA)
Brygg Ullmer	Louisiana State University (USA)
Harald Vogt	ETH Zurich (Switzerland)
Jay Warrior	Agilent Laboratories (USA)
Mark Weal	University of Southampton (UK)
Torben Weis	Berlin University of Technology (Germany)
Daniel Weld	University of Washington (USA)
Andy Wilson	Microsoft Research (USA)
Keiichi Yasumoto	Nara Institute of Science and Technology (Japan)
Tobias Zimmer	TecO, University of Karlsruhe (Germany)

Table of Contents

CarpetLAN: A Novel Indoor Wireless(-like) Networking and Positioning System

Masaaki Fukumoto[1] and Mitsuru Shinagawa[2]

[1] NTT DoCoMo Multimedia Labs.
3-5, Hikari-no-oka, Yokosuka-shi, Kanagawa-ken, 239-8536 JAPAN
fukumoto@mml.yrp.nttdocomo.co.jp
[2] NTT Microsystem Integration Labs.
3-1, Morinosato Wakamiya, Atsugi-shi, Kanagawa-ken, 243-0198, JAPAN
shina@aecl.ntt.co.jp

Abstract. CarpetLAN is a novel indoor wireless(-like) broad-band networking and positioning system. It uses the floor surface and the human body as an Ethernet-cable, and weak electric fields as the transmission media. Portable and wearable devices can connect to the network while the user stands or walks on the floor; connection speed is 10Mbps. Home and office appliances can also access the network if they are just put on the floor. CarpetLAN also provides an indoor positioning function, which is urgently needed for realizing "ubiquitous" communication. This electric field based transmission system yields ultra-micro communication cells, so the positions of humans and appliances can be detected with about 1 meter accuracy.

1 Introduction

In the last ten years, the time we spend accessing the network in our daily life has been greatly expanded by the miniaturization of information devices and improvement of wireless networking systems. In the near future, people will "wear" many devices at all times and utilize networked information and processors as their own knowledge and brain. The "ubiquitous" world will start to emerge, which means all surrounding objects as well as humans and computers will be connected to the network, and we can grasp all events and situations around the world in real-time.

Nowadays, many buildings and rooms already have networking systems. However, for realizing the ubiquitous world, every human and all surrounding objects in the location should be connected to the network constantly. In this case, it is unrealistic to connect all items with cables because it is too much of a bother and destroys mobility. Thus, the "last 1 meter (/foot)" is the important issue of how to connect people and objects to the each room's network outlet.

Radiowave-based local networking systems such as wireless-LANs and Bluetooth seem likely candidates for solving the last 1 meter problem. However, radiowaves often scatter beyond the intended space and interfere with other devices. Therefore, the communication bandwidth allocated to one user will be

M. Beigl et al. (Eds.): UbiComp 2005, LNCS 3660, pp. 1–18, 2005.

extremely small when many people and objects occupy a small area such as a crowded station or event space. In this case, it is effective to lay many access points which have a small service area (called micro-cell) for assuring bandwidth per user. However, it is impossible to create tiny cells (of less than a few meters) with no dead space between them, even if transmission power control and directional antennas are used. Optical communication is another candidate since it minimizes interference with surrounding devices. Unfortunately, it is also difficult to ensure many peer-to-peer communications with many randomly moving users.

Another unresolved requirement for realizing the ubiquitous world is highly accurate indoor positioning. GPS provides meter-level accuracy on a global basis, but it cannot be used indoors. Wireless-LAN based systems are commonly used, but their positioning accuracy is on the order of 10 meters, when only one access point is used as positioning. Some systems use the strength of radiowaves from multiple access points for increasing accuracy[1]. It is somewhat unstable in operation, however, because of interference with household furniture and the human body. There are highly accurate pointing systems that use ultrasonic sound or infrared rays. Ultrasonic-based systems[2] provide centimeter-level accuracy, though the service area is relatively narrow and they are weak against obstacles. Infrared-based systems[3] can provide both positioning and high-speed data links, but the service area is very narrow and thus it is only being used at information posts or kiosks. As a result, there is no known effective method for realizing both indoor high-speed networks and accurate positioning systems, which is needed for realizing the ubiquitous world.

This paper describes a new method that uses the floor and human body as transmission media (called CarpetLAN) that resolves the above issues. Wearable devices are connected to a tile-carpet style network via the floor's surface and the human body, so that wireless "-like" communication is realized. Objects such as computers and home appliances can also be connected to the network just by "putting" them on the floor. CarpetLAN is a contact-based communication system that uses weak electric fields so that interference caused by signal leakage into adjoining cells is greatly suppressed. Micro-cells of 1 meter size are easily realized by shrinking the tile-carpet size, and sufficient communication bandwidth can be assured even when many users occupy the same room. In addition, a positioning function of about 1 meter accuracy indoors is also realized using CarpetLAN's micro-cell capability. Therefore, CarpetLAN can solve both issues of the last 1 meter and indoor positioning.

Section 2 describes the communication method of CarpetLAN. Extended communication distances and high-speed data links are enabled using high-sensitivity Electro-Optic (EO) sensors. The electric field distributions of some communication situations are shown in simulations. A prototype is shown to offer 10Mbps communication speed and 1-meter level micro-cell capability.

Section 3 introduces the networking and positioning method of CarpetLAN. Simply laying the carpet-units contiguously forms a self-organized network. Each carpet-unit operates as a small gateway, so the positions of mobile devices can be acquired and appropriate packet routing provided. Effective traffic control that matches the user's movements is also established by predicting the user's position based on prior movements.

Finally, an example of the CarpetLAN prototype in operation and remaining issues are shown.

1.1   Related Works

Some surface-based sensing and networking systems have been proposed. *SmartSkin*[4] and *DiamondTouch*[5] detect touching position (and area) with a finger, hand, or arm using an electric field or capacitive sensing system. *WeightTable*[6] and *Active Floor*[7] detect positions of objects on the table and humans on the floor using signal computation of multiple load-cells embedded under the table and floor. *MagicCarpet*[8] uses a PVDF wire matrix to detect human foot positions. Though these systems can detect position(s) on the floor and table, sensors and connecting wires are not modularized, making it difficult to fit real rooms which have various sizes and shapes.

A brick- or tile-based modular system has scalability and easy-installation capability. It also provides an understanding of the entire room shape by gathering connection information of each module. *Z-Tile*[9] enables the detection of pressure and location information by covering the floor with networked sensor units. *Triangles*[10] also detects the connection topology of multiple tiles. However, ordinary systems just detect sensor data and connection information, and do not provide any data transmission between the floor and objects or humans.

Some communication and power supply systems use magnetic coupling between the floor surface and objects. *Magic-Surfaces*[11] provides not only position and orientation detection but also bidirectional communication with floor-mounted objects. It is difficult, however, to communicate with hand-held or head-mounted objects, since the human body cannot be utilized as the transmission route of magnetic fields.

2   System Structure

This section details the communication method of CarpetLAN. **Figure 1** illustrates the basic principle of the communication.

There are two types of transceivers: one is a mobile device such as wearables, PDAs, and appliances; the other is a floor-device mounted in the floor carpet-units. A pair of electrodes is placed on the body-contact side (WB) and the opposite (untouched) side (WG) of a mobile transceiver. Another pair of electrodes is placed on the foot-contact side of the carpet-unit (FB) and the surrounding (untouched) part (FG) of the carpet-unit[3]. Every carpet-unit is a network-node, and all nodes are connected to each other, while groups of carpets are connected to outside networks via one or more room gateways.

---

[3] 'W'earable-device, 'F'loor-device, 'B'ody-side-electrode, 'G'round(return)-side

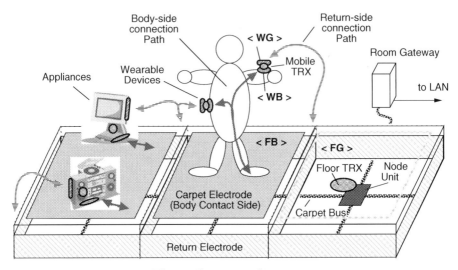

Fig. 1. System architecture.
Each carpet-unit works as a network cell.

To transmit a signal from a mobile device to the floor device, a high-speed switching voltage signal is applied across the mobile transceiver's electrodes (WB–WG). The current system uses a 10Mbps baseband signal, the same as Ethernet (10Base-T); signal voltage is 25V. The electric field surrounding the mobile transceiver is changed by the signal. The human body offers good conductivity for high-frequency (over 10kHz) electric signals, and so it acts as an electric wire. Thus, part of the electric field from the WB is conveyed through the body to the floor electrode FB. At the same time, the electric field from WG leaks into the surrounding space and reaches the floor electrode FG via air. Therefore, the transmitted signal can be decoded from the electric field that appears between the floor electrodes (FB–FG). When a signal is transmitted from the floor-side, the reverse process occurs.

However, most of the generated electric field is closed between the transmitter's electrodes (WB–WG). Thus a high-sensitivity electric field sensor is needed to realize this communication method.

2.1   Intrabody Communication

Electric field based communication methods are usually called "Intrabody Communication". Most systems use FET (Field Effect Transistor) -based devices as the electric field sensor. Since the sensitivity of FETs is not so high, operation constraints are usually severe such as demanding the use of shoe-insert transceivers[12] or short transmission distances[13][14][15]. Another problem with FET devices is the reduction in operation bandwidth seen when the earth ground floats. The maximum communication speed of an ordinary FET-based system is about 40kbps[16].

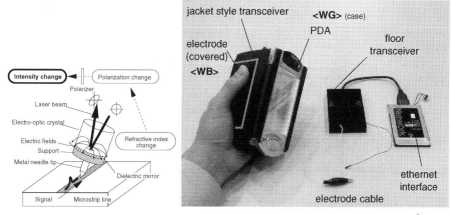

Fig. 2. EO Sensor
Laser-beam is used for sensing.

Fig. 3. Transceivers
(L) Handy trx (in PDA's jacket) / (R) Floor trx

CarpetLAN can overcome these problems using an Electro-Optic (EO) device as the electric field sensor. The EO device detects electric field as the polarization change of a laser beam, and it has high sensitivity and high-speed operation capability[17][18] (**Figure 2**). PDA-style and floor-mounted transceivers are shown in **Figure 3**. All transceivers are 10Base-T (half-duplex) Ethernet compatible.

All electrodes are covered by an insulator, and no metal parts contact the human body directly. In addition, induction current generated by the transceiver is very weak and less than that occurring in everyday life.

2.2   Simulations of Electric Field(EF) Distribution

Simulations were conducted to determine the electric field distribution in the space surrounding the floor and human body when a mobile device and floor device are communicating. Some electric field simulations of intrabody networking have been published[19]. Unfortunately, they considered only the small area between the human arm and hand, and no simulations examined the large area containing the whole human body and the floor.

Cell Separation: Figure 4-(a1) shows the basic structure of the carpet-units considered in our simulations. Each carpet-unit is 100 x 100 cm. The floor-side electrode FB (approximated as Cu ($\rho = 5.8\text{x}10^7\text{S/m}$)) is rather small (95cm x 95cm) to avoid shorting against the neighboring carpet-unit, and is 10cm above the earth ground. FB is covered with 10mm thick (smallest mesh size) of insulated material (approximated as natural rubber ($\varepsilon_r = 2.4$, $\rho = 0.067\text{S/m}$)). The earth ground is approximated as a 500 x 500 cm copper film, it also works as a return-side electrode FG. The nine carpet-units are aligned in a 3 x 3 pattern and are simulated by electromagnetic field analyzing software[4]. Analysis mesh

---

[4] Micro-Stripes

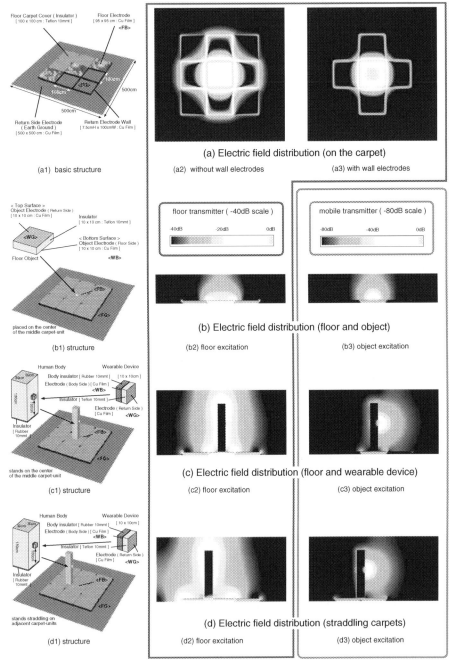

Fig. 4. Electric Field Simulations of CarpetLAN
Electric field generated by the floor-tx is about 30dB greater than by the mobile-tx.

size is 25mm for most of the volume, and 10mm in the vicinity of the electrode and insulators.

Figure 4-(a2) shows the electric field distribution when applying 3V voltage between floor-side electrode FB and earth ground (= return-side electrode) FG of the middle carpet-unit. This figure shows the horizontal distribution on the upper surface of the insulator (height =11cm). The magnitude of the electric field is normalized to give 30V/m (applied voltage) = 0dB, full scale is −40dB. Analysis frequency is 10MHz, a typical frequency of the 10Base-T baseband signal. In this figure, an electric field of −3.5dB(20V/m) is generated at the edges of the middle carpet-unit, and −14dB(6V/m) seen at the center of the carpet. However, the electric field is not efficiently isolated, since an electric field of −17dB(4V/m) appears at the outside edge of the adjacent carpet-units.

Figure 4-(a3) shows the electric field distribution when adding a return-side electrode with double-cross shape (length=100cm, height=75mm; see also Figure 4-(a1)) on the borders of each carpet-unit. With this arrangement, the electric field leakage to the outside edge of the adjacent carpet-unit is reduced to −26dB(1.4V/m). In addition, leakage to the center position of the adjacent carpet-unit is reduced to under −40dB(450mV/m).

Thus, we can achieve a cell isolation of about 20dB between adjacent carpet-units using a wall-shaped return-side electrode. The remaining analyses assume the use of this return-side electrode.

Communication with Floor Object: We next simulated communication with a mobile device placed on the surface of the carpet. The mobile device's electrodes (WB and WG) were modeled as a pair of 10cm square copper film separated by a 10mm thick insulator (approximated as teflon $\varepsilon_r = 2.16$, $\rho = 0S/m$) placed at the center of the middle carpet-unit as the transceiver of an appliance-style mobile device (see also **Figure 4**-(b1)).

Figure 4-(b2) shows the electric field distribution when applying 3V between FB and FG of the middle carpet-unit. This figure shows the vertical distribution at the cutting plane of the mobile device's electrodes (WB and WG). The other conditions are the same as in the previous simulation (30V/m = 0dB, full scale is -40dB). In this figure, an electric field of −25dB(1.6V/m) appears between two electrodes of the mobile device. It means a voltage of roughly 16mV was generated between the 10mm separated receiver electrodes (WB–WG), and it follows that an electric field sensor with a sensitivity of a few mV could detect the carpet-unit's signal. Note that the electric field generated by the floor carpet-unit rises to about 100cm above the carpet's surface.

Figure 4-(b3) indicates communication from the mobile device to the carpet-unit, and 3V is applied between WB and WG. Though normalization was performed as in the previous simulation (30V/m = 0dB), full scale is expanded to −80dB, because only small signals appear in the field. In this figure, the electric field created by the mobile device is only −59dB(35mV/m) at the center position under the middle carpet-unit, and the corresponding voltage generated between FB and FG is just 3.5mV. This result is at least 30dB smaller than the value seen in the opposite situation (from the carpet-unit to the mobile device), so the carpet-side receiver must offer higher sensitivity for realizing bi-directional communication. In addition, electric field leakage to the adjacent carpet-unit's receiver is under -80dB, thus over 20dB separation can be ensured. This means that the position of the mobile device can be detected with 1 meter accuracy.

Figure 4-(b2) also shows that a signal transmitted from the middle carpet-unit interferes with the adjacent carpet-unit's receiver. The leakage is about -31dB(850mV/m), a value that is about 30dB higher than the signal from the mobile device at the center of its own carpet-unit. This interference cannot be eliminated using a signal level filter. It can be eliminated, however, by the network node module installed in each carpet-unit through the use of techniques such as MAC address filtering. In addition, CarpetLAN automatically duplicates data packets from the carpet-unit to the mobile device for tracking human movement speed (described later), so this interference has no adverse effect.

Communication with Wearable Device: The next simulation examined communication with a wearable device. The human body was assumed to be a rectangular solid 180cm(H) x 30cm(W) x 30cm(D), and its material was approximated as human muscle ($\varepsilon_r = 81$, $\rho = 0.62$S/m)[19]. The wearable device was attached to the waist of the human body (100cm above the foot) and matches the mobile device of the above simulations (10cm square electrodes, 10mm thick insulator). Another insulator (10mm thick natural rubber) was installed under the human body's foot representing the shoe's insole. The same rubber was also placed between the human body and the wearable device, so no electrode contacted the human body directly (**Figure 4**-(c1)).

Figure 4-(c2) shows the electric field distribution when applying 3V to FB and FG of the middle carpet-unit. This figure shows the vertical distribution at the cutting plane of the wearable device's electrode. The other conditions are the same as in **Figure 4**-(b2) (full scale is -40dB). In this figure, the electric field lies around the human body, and about -19dB(3.5V/m) appears between WB and WG. Although the wearable device is some distance above the floor, the received signal is roughly twice that captured by the floor-mounted device (1.6V/m). This indicates that the human body works well as a signal transmission route.

Figure 4-(c3) indicates communication from the wearable device to the carpet-unit, and 3V is applied between WB and WG (full scale is -80dB). The electric field created by the wearable device is -58dB(39mV/m) at the middle carpet-unit. As with the floor-mounted mobile device, the received signal is very weak so that the carpet-side receiver must have high sensitivity.

Carpet Straddling: The final simulation examined the case of the human body straddling two carpet-units (**Figure 4**-(d1)). The other conditions are the same as in the previous simulation.

Figure 4-(d2) shows the electric field distribution when applying 3V to FB and FG of the middle carpet-unit (full scale is -40dB). This figure indicates that the electric field surrounding the human body is reduced slightly, but it is

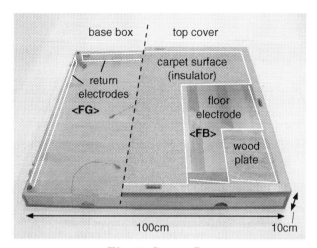

Fig. 5. Carpet Box
(left) Return electrode strips / (right) Floor top electrode (covered)

sufficient for communication. However, interference to the left carpet unit has occurred via the human body. It is difficult to reduce interference in the physical layer; some network-level protection such as packet filtering is needed.

Figure 4-(d3) indicates communication from the wearable device to the carpet-units, and 3V is applied between WB and WG (full scale is −80dB). The electric field of −64dB(18mV/m) appears at the two carpet-units and is about half the single carpet condition. If the floor-side receiver has sufficient sensitivity, the "straddling" condition can be detected while two carpet nodes receive the same signal. It can be utilized for more accurate positioning of mobile and wearable devices.

2.3   Prototype Carpet Unit

Prototype carpet-units were made based on the above simulation results. **Figure 5** shows one carpet-unit. The carpet box is made of wood, and its dimensions are 100cm square and 10cm thick. The floor-side electrode (FB) is a copper sheet (90cm square, 0.3mm thick), and is covered by an insulator (vinyl flooring: 90cm square, 2.3mm thick[5]). Four return-side electrodes (FG) are metal plates (90cm long, 5cm high, 0.3mm thick) that are installed along the inner lateral sides of the box.

The nine carpet-units were aligned in a 3 x 3 grid following the simulations, and a 10MHz sine wave was transmitted from the middle carpet-unit. **Figure 6** shows the measured signal strength[6] at the center of each carpet-unit(a) and the waist position (height=100cm) of a standing human body(b). This figure

---

[5] Insulator is thinner than simulation, so the generated electric field may be much larger.

[6] Maximum value is normalized to 0dB.

-26.5	-27.5	-27.0
-28.3	**-5.2**	-28.3
-26.8	-28.0	-26.7

dB

(a) At the floor-surface

-26.5	-26.9	-26.0
-26.5	**0**	-27.6
-26.7	-26.3	-26.7

dB

(b) At the human-waist

Fig. 6. Electric field strength
About 20dB separation is achieved.

Type	Object (floor surface)		Wearable (waist)	
Direction	floor → object	object → floor	floor → wearable	wearable → floor
Error rate	4%	23%	3%	12%

Fig. 7. Packet error rate
Measured using 100 UDP packets

indicates that a cell isolation of about 20dB can be achieved between neighboring carpet-units. It also follows the simulation results in that the signal strength at the human waist is greater than at the floor's surface.

Figure 7 shows the packet error rate when a PDA-style transceiver (shown in Figure 3) was placed on the center of the floor's surface(left) and at the waist position of the standing human body(right). 100 UDP packets (64bytes length) were transmitted from the PDA and from the carpet-side in turn, and the error rate was measured. The results show that most packets to the PDA were received, while 10% to 20% of the packets to the carpet were lost. It is noted that the signal level at the carpet-side receiver is about 30dB smaller than that at the PDA-side receiver, as shown by the measured and simulation results. Packet loss can be reduced by improving the carpet-unit's receiver sensitivity[7].

3   Networking and Positioning System

CarpetLAN can provide a "network reachable" environment across entire indoor spaces such as rooms and buildings by covering the floors with these carpet-units. This section describes suitable approaches to carpet-networking and positioning system realization. Ordinary unit-based floor network systems use common shaped cells and a bucket-brigade style packet forwarding method[9][10]. However, some issues appear when realizing a practical network system in real rooms and passages.

– Forwarding delay:
  Forwarding delay becomes serious when a large-scale network is built using single-layer bucket brigade forwarding. Assuming that 1 hop forwarding time is 1msec, a communication delay of about 200msec will occur between the opposing corners of a 100m square room paved with 1m square cells. This means that realtime communication services such as IP phones or TV phones are problematic.
– Shape flexibility:
  There are various room shapes. It is difficult to cover the entire space using just one standard cell such as a rectangle or hexagon. Decreasing the cell size offers more flexibility, but forwarding delay is increased.

---

[7] The measured error rate is much higher than is expected in a regular wireless LAN system. The main reason is that the baseband modulation used by the current prototype transceiver is susceptible to interference by surrounding noise. Packet loss can be greatly reduced using a more robust modulation method.

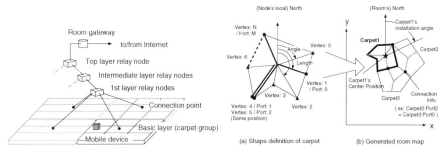

Fig. 8. Structure of CarpetLAN Network
Grouped carpet and layered relay nodes.

Fig. 9. Shape definition of carpet
Room map is generated by connections.

Table 1. Group and layer size and communication delay (65,536 carpets).
Carpet grouping and multi-layer network enables short communication delay.

Group size	256x256	128x128	64 x 64	32 x 32	16 x 16	8 x 8	4 x 4	2 x 2	1 x 1
Layer	1	2	3	4	5	**6**	**7**	8	9
Relay nodes	0	1	5	21	85	**341**	1365	5461	21845
Delay (ms)	512	258	132	70	40	**26**	**20**	18	16

3.1   Hierarchical Network Structure

As mentioned above, the single-layer bucket brigade network cannot minimize the forwarding delay if network scale is increased. CarpetLAN, however, suppresses the forwarding delay by combining the bucket brigade forwarding and a hierarchical network.

The basic network structure of CarpetLAN is shown in **Figure 8**. The carpet-units are connected to each other and constitute a mesh-style network (called the basic-layer). Connection points to the upper-layer network are placed at intervals on the basic-layer. Upper-layer relay nodes constitute a tree-structure network with multiple branches. The top-layer relay node is connected to the outside network via the room gateway, typically one per room.

Table 1 shows the maximum delay and required relay node numbers when 256 x 256 (total: 65,536) carpet-units are connected. In this table, it is assumed that each carpet-unit is square in shape, and all nodes have four connection ports for the mesh network. Network delay is calculated between opposing corners of the network area, as 1msec per 1 hop. This table indicates that forwarding delay can be suppressed to under 30msec even for a network at a scale of 65,000 units, when carpet-units are grouped into 8 x 8 units and a 6-layer relay node network is used. Thus, a CarpetLAN network can support 256m x 256m spaces such as large offices, warehouses, and stadiums when using 1m-square carpet-units.

3.2   Automatic Configuration with Free-Shaped Carpet-Units

It is difficult to cover all rooms using carpet-units of the same shape, since real rooms and buildings have various configurations. In CarpetLAN, each carpet-unit knows "its own shape", and shape information is reported to the upper-layer with connection information of surrounding carpet-units when laid. **Figure 9** shows the shape definition of one carpet-unit(a) and an example of the map information generated from connections between 3 carpet-units(b). The room gateway can understand the room's whole shape and network structure by gathering each carpet's shape and connecting information between carpet-units.

3.3 Routing Control

After all connection information is determined, the room gateway calculates routing information and downloads to each carpet-unit. At first, carpet groups of the basic-layer are configured. For each carpet-unit, the closest connection point to the upper-layer is found[8]. Then, carpet-units that have the same connection point are grouped. Upper-layer relay nodes constitute a tree-structure network.

Forwarding procedure is quite simple. Each carpet-unit and relay node forwards the incoming packets to "the output port that has the shortest route to the destination mobile device". As a result, packets are forwarded to the target device with minimum hop count. If the target device is not present in the room, the packet is delivered to the top node and forwarded to the outside network (other rooms or the Internet) via the room gateway.

3.4 Positioning

The room gateway knows the position information of each carpet-unit and all mobile devices in the room. Therefore, indoor positioning of humans and objects with 1m (cell-size) accuracy can be easily realized without additional devices. Even more accurate positioning is possible if the user straddles two or more carpet-units.

3.5 Routing with Position Estimation

CarpetLAN is a kind of mobile communication system because the users can communicate while moving around on the carpet-units. A mobile communication system must change the destination cell (called a handover) according to the movements of the target device. Handover is not so difficult in regular radiowave-based systems, since user movement speed is relatively low compared to cell size, and the boundary area between adjacent cells is overlapping. However, it is difficult for a CarpetLAN system that has large cell separation to deliver packets reliably to the fast moving target[9].

One solution is to deliver duplicated packets to the cells that the moving target is predicted to enter in the future. In this case, delivery mistakes can

---

[8] Hop count is used as the distance; the shortest route is identified using Dijkstra's method.

[9] For example, about 10 handovers are needed per second when a human runs across 1-meter carpet-units.

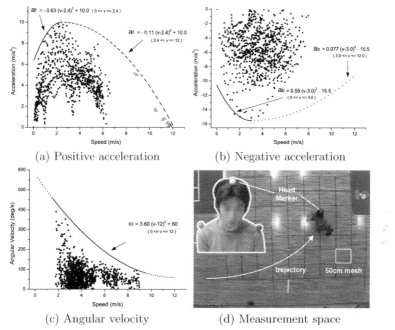

(a) Positive acceleration   (b) Negative acceleration

(c) Angular velocity   (d) Measurement space

Fig. 10. Performance limits of humans (acceleration and angular velocity)

easily be reduced by increasing the number of duplicated cells, though network load is also increased. Since the CarpetLAN system targets use by humans, estimation can be enhanced by understanding the typical movement patterns and limits of human beings.

Movement Limits of Humans: We conducted an experiment to determine the limits of human movements in which the positive and negative acceleration and sharp turns of humans were measured. A 6m x 4m measurement space overlaid by a 50cm mesh and a 10m long runway were set up (**Figure 10-(d)**). The subject wore a head marker ($3.5cm\phi$) that was captured by a DV camera mounted at the center of the measurement space (height=6m). The marker position was recorded at 30 times per second. The subjects were 12 adult males.

First, rapid acceleration patterns were gathered for determining positive acceleration limits. The subject moved from stationary to full speed and marker position was recorded; the subjects performed a total of 21 movements. Instantaneous speed vs. instantaneous positive acceleration was calculated at 1/30 second intervals[10]. Measurement results are shown in **Figure 10-(a)**. Another acceleration data captured from split times of a 100m course run by an athlete[20] are also shown in the figure (marked with $\triangle$).

---

[10] Moving averages using a 9-point window were calculated to suppress measurement noise such as head shaking.

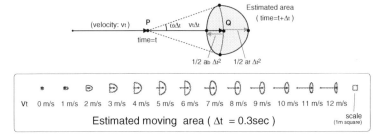

Fig. 11. Estimated area
Estimated area is changed by moving speed.

Next, rapid braking patterns were gathered to determine negative acceleration limits. The subject entered the measurement space at various speeds (from
8m/s to 2m/s) and tried to stop as quickly as possible; the subjects performed
a total of 59 movements. Instantaneous speed vs. instantaneous negative acceleration was calculated at 1/30 second intervals. Measurement results are shown
in **Figure 10**-(b).

Finally, rapid turn patterns were gathered to determine turn limits. The subject entered the measurement space at various speeds (from 9m/s to 2m/s) and
made the tightest possible turn; the subjects performed a total of 50 movements.
Instantaneous speed vs. instantaneous angular velocity was calculated at 1/30
second intervals. Measurement results are shown in **Figure 10**-(c).

Estimation of Moving Area: From measured data, the maximum values (human limit) of positive and negative acceleration, and angular velocity
were determined, when human moves at specified instantaneous speed. The
approximations[11] are also shown in **Figure 10**-(a,b,c). The human, whose movement vector is v_t, is expected to occupy the after-time period Δt as shown in
Figure 11. This figure also shows the estimated moving areas of 0.3sec ahead
for each speed.

4   Implementation and Discussion

4.1   CarpetLAN Node

Figure 12 shows prototype node units placed in each carpet-unit. Each node
unit has a total 6 network ports: 4 ports for the mesh network, 1 port for connecting to the upper-layer, and 1 PCMCIA port for the electric field transceiver;
all ports are Ethernet compatible. The node unit has an RISC CPU(VR5500),
16MB Flash-ROM, and 64MB SDRAM, and runs on the Linux-VR operating
system. The same hardware and software is used for the carpet-units and relay
nodes. Each node unit decides its operation mode according to the connections
made to surrounding node units when starting up. In addition, one Linux PC is
used as the room gateway.

---

[11] Quadratic approximations were used.

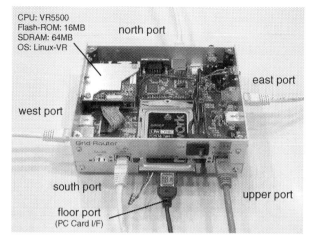

Fig. 12. CarpetLAN Node
Linux-based six-port node unit

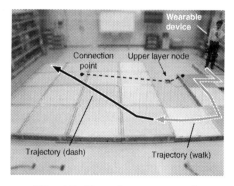

Fig. 13. Experiment network
Moving with hand-held PDA.

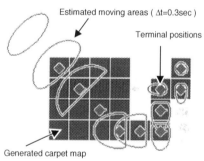

Fig. 14. Estimated areas
Each area shows estimated position
0.3sec ahead.

4.2   Experimental Network

Experimental network consists of 22 square cells (**Figure 13**). All adjacent cells are connected in a mesh network, and one relay node is used.

Automatic Network Configuration: It takes less than 1 minute after power-on to all node units to gather the connection structure and download the routing information to each carpet-unit[12]. We also confirmed that routing information is correctly updated when some node units are disconnected or new units are added.

---

[12] Most of this time is occupied by operating system booting; only a few seconds is needed for the shortest route calculation and downloading.

Network Access: Concurrent network access from multiple mobile devices was confirmed with experimental network. Three people holding PDA-style transceivers accessed the outside network (web browsing and TV-phone application) while roaming around on the carpet-units. Access with stand-straddling carpet-units and multiple-user access on one carpet unit was also confirmed. In this experimental network, each node can relay packets within 1msec, and network delay is under 10msec (10 hop count).

Estimation of Movement Area: The trajectory of an actual user holding a PDA-style transceiver and roaming around on the carpet is shown in **Figure 14**. Estimated movement areas (predicted ahead by 0.3 sec) are also shown. In this example, the user walks at the beginning but then starts to run. The results confirm that the estimated area changes with the user's speed.

4.3   Discussion

Here we present the remaining issues of the current prototype system and some possible solutions.

Interference with Adjacent Human Body: CarpetLAN may experience interference if several people stand close to each other. Especially, when people's bodies are directly touching each other in a crowded space, interference may reach beyond a few people. If people whose shoulder width is 50cm are crammed in 1m square cells, signals may reach two cells ahead. This means that cell size is expanded about 5m in diameter, and throughput and positioning accuracy may deteriorate. Throughput can be maintained using code or frequency interleaved modulation which is commonly used in radiowave-based wireless access. However, the structure of the transceiver and handover process become more complex.

Scalability: Networking delay does not increase using a hierarchical network structure, even if tens of thousands of carpets are used. However, packets for object tracking may increase when thousands of objects are moving on the carpets frequently. In the current system, all routing and location information packets are aggregated to the room server at any time when the mobile object moves to another carpet. The traffic of routing packets can be excessively reduced using the hierarchical routing information delivery method in which routing information packets are sent to the upper-layer only when a large movement to exceed the boundary of the local layer has occurred.

Energy Consumption and Cost: The current prototype node-unit is rather large (1000cc) and requires much power (8W). Its cost is also high, as it uses ordinary devices. However, the electric field communication method has low-power operation capability compared with other radiowave-based communication, since in principle very little current is needed for transmission. The size, cost, and power consumption of network processing parts can also be reduced by making a special LSI chip. It is not difficult to miniaturize the node unit into a card size that consumes only a few watts of power. However, this must be achieved under a few dollars and 100mW per node-unit to compete with wireless LAN systems that require hundreds of dollars and about 10W per room[13].

In addition, distribution of the electric field may vary when carpet size and thickness are changed. Additional simulation is needed to obtain appropriate electrode alignment of "tile-carpet" compatible units.

Timing Synchronization: In the current implementation, "packet sending time" is used for estimating the mobile device's speed. This is not perfect, as the carpet-units are not completely synchronized. NTP (Network Time Protocol) can synchronize many nodes, however, it is not precise, since dozens of milliseconds may be needed to distribute timing information to tens of thousands of carpet-units. One solution may be to superimpose a carpet-wide master clock on the power lines.

Easy Installation: Since the current prototype uses ordinary network connectors (RJ-45) and power-lines, installation is troublesome. The carpet-units should employ an easy "snap-in" style connection mechanism with one connector for all signals and power-lines. Non-contact connectors that use light or electromagnetic coupling are suggested for avoiding short-circuits due to spilled water.

Speed Up: The current backbone network between nodes use 10/100Base-T Ethernet, and the speedup is easy. However, it is hard to increase the connection speed of electric field communication above 10Mbps, since impedance control of the human body and large carpet electrodes is difficult.

5   Conclusion

This paper introduced a new indoor wireless(-like) networking system that uses the human body and floor surfaces as transmission media. Mobile devices can be accessed while either being worn on the body or put on the floor. Furthermore, the positions of people and objects can be detected with 1-meter accuracy, the current size of the carpet-units. CarpetLAN is effective for realizing a ubiquitous environment in homes, offices, transportation systems (installed on the floor of buses and trains), and event spaces. We are planning to downsize each component and create effective CarpetLAN applications. It is our goal that node-units are embedded in all "tatami" (Japanese straw mat) and tile-carpets, and all floors of the world are connected to the network.

---

[13] It is assumed that one room is 10m square and covered with 1m square carpet-units.

References

1. P.Bahl and V.N.Padmanabhan, "RADAR: An In-building RF-based User Location and Tracking System", Proc. of IEEE Infocom2000, Vol. 2, pp. 775-784, 2000.
2. A.Harter, A.Hopper, P.Steggles, A.Ward, and P.Webster, "The Anatomy of a Context-Aware Application", Proc. of the ACM MOBICOM'99, pp. 59-68, 1999.
3. R.Want, A.Hopper, V.Falcao, and J.Gibbons, "The Active Badge Location System", ACM Trans. on Information Systems, Vol. 10, pp. 91-102, 1992.
4. J.Rekimoto, "SmartSkin: An Infrastructure for Freehand Manipulation on Interactive Surfaces", Proc. of ACM CHI2002, pp. 113-120, 2002.
5. P.Dietz and D.Leigh, "DiamondTouch: A Multi-user Touch Technology", Proc. of ACM UIST2001, pp. 219-226, 2001.
6. A.Schmidt, M.Strohbach, K.V.Laerhoven, A.Friday, and H.W.Gellersen, "Context Acquisition based on Load Sensing", Proc. of Ubicomp2002, pp. 333-351, 2002.
7. M.D.Addlesee, A.Jones, F.Livesey, and F.Samaria, "ORL Active Floor", IEEE Personal Communications, Vol.4, No.5, pp. 35-41, 1997.
8. J.Paradiso, C.Abler, K.Hsiao, and M.Reynolds, "The Magic Carpet: Physical Sensing for Immersive Environments.", In Late-Breaking/Short Demonstrations of CHI'97, pp. 277-278, 1997.
9. L.McElligott, M.Dillon, K.Leydon, B.Richardson, M.Fernstrom, and J.Paradiso. "'ForSe FIElds' - Force Sensors for Interactive Environments", Proc. of Ubi-Comp2002, pp. 168-175, 2002.
10. M.G.Gorbet, M.Orth, and H.Ishii, "Triangles: Tangible Interface for Manipulation and Exploration of Digital Information Topography", Proc. of ACM CHI '98, pp. 49-56, 1998.
11. M.Minami, Y.Nishizawa, K.Hirasawa, H.Morikawa, and T.Aoyama, "MAGIC-Surfaces: Magnetically Interfaced Surfaces for Smart Space Applications", Adjunct Proc. of Pervasive2005, pp.59-64, 2005.
12. T.G.Zimmerman, "Personal Area Networks: Near-field Intrabody Communication", IBM Systems Journal, Vol. 35, Nos. 3&4, pp. 609-617, 1996.
13. M.Fukumoto and Y.Tonomura, "Body Coupled FingeRing: Wireless Wearable Keyboard", Proc. of ACM CHI'97, pp. 147-154, 1997.
14. N.Matsushita, S.Tajima, Y.Ayatsuka, and J.Rekimoto, "Wearable Key: Device for Personalizing Nearby Environment", Proc. of IEEE ISWC'00, pp. 119-126, 2000.
15. K.Doi, M.Koyama, Y.Suzuki, and T.Nishimura, "Development of the communication module used human body as the transmission line", Proc. of Human Interface Symposium 2001, pp. 389-392, 2001 (in Japanese).
16. K.Partridge, B.Dahlquist, A.Veiseh, A.Cain, A.Foreman, and J.Goldberg, "Empirical Measurements of Intrabody Communication Performance under Varied Physical Configurations", Proc. of ACM UIST 2001, pp. 183-190, 2001.
17. M.Shinagawa, M.Fukumoto, K.Ochiai, and H.Kyuragi, "A Near-Field-Sensing Transceiver for Intrabody Communication Based on the Electrooptic Effect", Trans. on IEEE Inst. and Meas., Vol. 53, No. 6, pp. 1533-1538, 2004.
18. M.Fukumoto, M.Shinagawa, K.Ochiai, and T.Sugimura, "ElectAura-Net", Emerging Technologies, ACM Siggraph 2003.
19. K.Fujii, K.Ito, and S.Tajima, "A study on the receiving signal level in relation with the location of electrodes for wearable devices using human body as a transmission channel", Proc. of IEEE Antennas and Propagation Society Int'l Sympo. 2003, Vol. 3, pp. 1071-1074, 2003.
20. J.R.Mureika, "Donovan Bailey's Split Time at 1997 World Championships, Athens GRE", http://myweb.lmu.edu/jmureika/track/splits/splits.html#87wc.

u-Texture: Self-Organizable Universal Panels for Creating Smart Surroundings

Naohiko Kohtake, Ryo Ohsawa, Takuro Yonezawa, Yuki Matsukura,
Masayuki Iwai, Kazunori Takashio, and Hideyuki Tokuda

Graduate School of Media and Governance, Keio University,
Delta S213, Endo 5322, Fujisawa, Kanagawa 2528520, Japan
{nao,ryo,takuro,matsu,tailor,kaz,hxt}@ht.sfc.keio.ac.jp
http://www.ht.sfc.keio.ac.jp/~nao/

Abstract. This paper introduces a novel way to allow non-expert users
to create smart surroundings. Non-smart everyday objects such as furniture and appliances found in homes and offices can be converted to smart
ones by attaching computers, sensors, and devices. In this way, non-smart
components that form non-smart objects are made smart in advance. For
our first prototype, we have developed u-Texture, a self-organizable universal panel that works as a building block. The u-Texture can change
its own behavior autonomously through recognition of its location, its
inclination, and surrounding environment by assembling these factors
physically. We have demonstrated several applications to confirm that
u-Textures can create smart surroundings easily without expert users.

1 Introduction

Owing to recent improvements in computer, sensor, and network technology,
many non-smart objects are converted into smart objects by various approaches.
These environmental smart objects such as smart furniture [1], smart rooms [2],
smart homes [3], and smart buildings [4] are defined as "smart surroundings"
and support human activities. However, it is difficult for users who are unfamiliar with computing technology to select and prepare the essential devices, to set
them at appropriate positions, and to create and maintain smart surroundings
without expert help. Our goal, therefore, is to develop technology that enables
non-expert users to create smart surroundings easily. With this technology, anyone would be able to create smart surroundings anytime anywhere and to obtain
a context-aware application.

This research focuses on block materials that have uniform shapes to allow
users to create various objects such as furniture, floors in homes, sidewalks outdoors, homes, or buildings by connecting or assembling them. There are many
kinds of block materials such as bricks, panels, and tiles in our surroundings.
As our approaches in developing the technology for non-expert users, we have
been developing smart objects' block materials in advance, not by converting
existing non-smart objects to smart objects. Required operations for users are
just to assemble the block materials in shapes suitable for what users wish to do.

M. Beigl et al. (Eds.): UbiComp 2005, LNCS 3660, pp. 19–36, 2005.

The advantage of this system is that customization or calibration, which require computing skills, are unnecessary. Table 1 shows the examples of objects with block materials. Users can create various kinds of objects with each material. If each material becomes a smart one, such objects can provide context-aware applications corresponding to their shape. For example, if a ceiling or a floor is created with smart tiles, by recognizing users and their positions on the smart floor or by the smart ceiling, it will be possible to control appliances such as an air conditioner and lighting appropriately.

Table 1. Examples of objects with block materials

Block Material			
	Brick	Panel	Tile
Object with Materials	Building Fence	Table Shelf	Floor Ceiling
Application of Smart Object	- monitoring structural health - pushing message to users	- enhancing collaboration - recognizing real objects	- maintaining home security - sensing users' position

Until now, researches that aim to create smart surroundings without experts and researches that apply building block interfaces for creating context-aware applications have been investigated. The former researches [5, 6, 7] are mainly aimed at realizing each particular smart surroundings defined beforehand and enable users to create it with their physical interactions without expert help. In addition, the latter researches [8, 9, 10] recognize 3D structures of assembled blocks and enable users to create 3D modeling or tangible programming.

This paper proposes u-Texture, a self-organizable universal panel created beforehand as a smart building block material. Assembled u-Textures create smart surroundings that have shapes such as shelves, tables, and walls, which correspond to assembled shapes. Figure 1 shows example of u-Textures and how to create smart surroundings and context-aware applications by assembling them. In this case, u-Textures are used as several smart surroundings for discussing and creating a logo design for our project. First, each u-Texture is used as a drawing tool individually. Afterwards, users can connect their u-Textures each other horizontally and exchange and merge their drawing data among connected u-Textures by drag-and-drop operations. Finally, when the u-Textures are assembled horizontally and set in vertical, users can look four candidates of drawing data on each u-Texture at the same time and expand one of them on four u-Textures. Once assembled in shapes, u-Textures can autonomously provide suitable actions to the shapes by recognizing the shapes through exchanges of information on their connections and inclinations among each u-Texture. Without knowing anything about electrical connections, users can assemble u-Textures into smart objects practically and operate them to correspond to their assembled shapes. Table 2 shows a comparison of procedures for making smart surroundings with the typical electrical devices such as computers, sensors, and instruments, and with u-Textures.

Fig. 1. Example of u-Textures and the assembly of smart surroundings

Table 2. Comparison of procedures for making smart surroundings with the typical electrical devices and u-Textures

	Using Various Devices		Using u-Textures	
Step	**Who**	**Actions**	**Who**	**Actions**
Step 1	Users	select and arrange devices such as computers, sensors and instruments.	Users	prepare u-Textures which include computers, sensors and instruments.
Step 2	Users	set the devices at appropriate positions.	Users	assemble u-Textures into shape appropriate for using.
Step 3	Users	connect the devices electrically.	u-Textures	recognize the assemble shape.
Step 4	Users	install software in computers and calibrate the devices.	u-Textures	extract candidate applications corresponding to the shape.
Step 5	Users	select and use context-aware applications	Users	select and use context-aware applications.

The sections of this paper are structured to make each point independently. After outlining u-Textures in Section 2, this paper continues with describing the system design in Section 3 and the system architecture in Section 4, covers potential applications in Section 5, explains the user experience in Section 6, and finally discusses the advantages of using u-Textures in Section 7. Section 8 describes past work related to u-Texture and Section 9 concludes our current work and outlines future work.

2   u-Texture

2.1   Concept

To explain our purpose in this research, the main concepts of the u-Texture are considered as follows:

Easy Assembling A user can assemble u-Textures easily without knowing the configuration with computers, sensors, and networks inside each u-Texture. No specific tools are necessary for assembling u-Textures.

Self-Recognition As a user assembles u-Textures, the assembled u-Textures exchange information such as whether connected or not, connection directions, IDs of adjoining u-Textures, and the u-Textures' inclination. With that information, each u-Texture recognizes its assembled shape as well as its location and inclination in the assembled shape.

Behaviors to the Shape Available applications corresponding to the shape of the assembled u-Textures will be extracted automatically among multiple applications pre-installed in each u-Texture. When there are several candidate applications to the shape, with minimum selection of the user, each u-Texture behaves autonomously and runs the same application together.

2.2   Assembling u-Textures

Figure 2 shows a user assembling u-Textures and establishing a shelf-shaped smart object: from top; A user assembles u-Textures. The u-Textures indicate application candidates corresponding to the assembled shapes. A user selects a desired application. The u-Textures cooperate and run the selected application.

3   System Design

Figure 3 shows an appearance of a u-Texture (right). The prototype of u-Texture is 320 mm square, 48 mm thick, and weights 4300 g. Every u-Texture is designed to the same specification to enable users to assemble smart objects with any u-Textures. It costs more to equip full functions in all the u-Textures than to install them with limited functions according to assembled systems. Since one of our purposes for developing this prototype is to confirm various potential advantages that u-Textures can provide, we designed sensors and networks redundantly. The u-Texture should have a structural function possible to be assembled and an electrical function possible to be connected electrically. In the current version, a blockable prop, u-Joint (Figure 3, left), supports to assemble u-Textures.

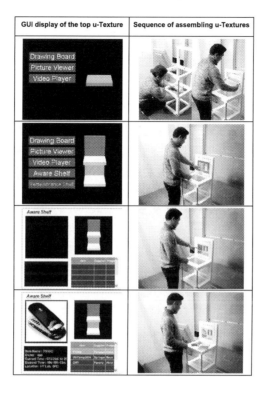

Fig. 2. Sequence in creation of a shelf-shaped smart object

3.1 Structures to Be Assembled

The u-Texture is designed with a reasonable size and strength to be able to create furniture like tables and shelves; the u-Texture is also designed for easy assembly in various forms as furniture as a square-shaped plate, which is a basic component shape. A connecting structure is required to assemble one u-Texture and another one, and the connections can be implemented both horizontally and vertically. To create an easy-to-assemble system for every user, the u-Texture and the u-Joint are designed to have a simple structure for connections.

3.2 Interactions with Other u-Textures and Users

We consider it is appropriate that each u-Texture has its own computer and battery to be able to work autonomously. It is necessary to assign connection sensors on each of the four sides of u-Texture, so that the u-Texture can determine whether it is connected to another u-Textures or not and its direction if connected, as well as obtain the IDs of the connected u-Textures. It is essential to include electrical connectors in the structural connectors which support u-Textures to create electrical connections physically connecting. An inclination

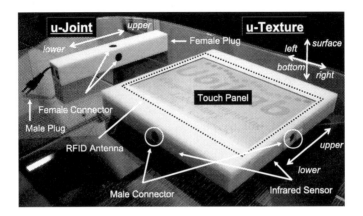

Fig. 3. A u-Texture (right) and a u-Joint (left)

sensor is required for the u-Texture to recognize itself. The connection sensor data and the inclination sensor data are essential that a u-Texture recognizes its assembled shape, and location and inclination in the assembled shape. It is necessary that the both data is shared together. The two kinds of sensor data are categorized into the **"global sensor data"**.

Proximity sensors will be assigned on its four sides in order to recognize neighboring u-Texture's IDs and their directions. Sensors such as RFID tag readers that can discriminate between u-Textures, objects and users are useful. Interactive touch panels and mikes are also effective because users can interact with u-Textures without input devices. These sensor data which are used in each u-Texture inside are categorized into the **"local sensor data"**. In this proto-type, two kinds of networks are used individually to avoid network congestion. A wired network exchanges data among the assembled u-Textures internally, and a wireless network exchanges data among other smart objects.

3.3   State Transition

Figure 4 shows a state transition diagram of u-Texture. The state sequentially moves through five layers of states: *Initialized, Recognized, Application Wait, Application Ready*, and *Application Running*. When a u-Texture detects a change in global or local sensor data, the state will be moved to the *Ready to Detect* state. Then, when the u-Texture receives the shutdown command from a user, the state will be moved to the *Ready to Shutdown* state at all time. Each state in the state transition diagram is described as follows:

Initialized: u-Texture initializes all systems.

Recognized: u-Texture recognizes the assembled shape with the other u-Tex-tures and each location and inclination of the assembled u-Textures.

Application Wait: u-Texture extracts the available applications corresponding to the shape of the assembled u-Textures.

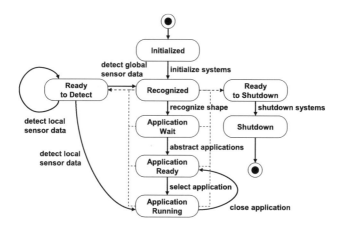

Fig. 4. State transition diagram

Application Ready: u-Texture is ready to run the available applications and indicates a list of them to users.

Application Running: u-Texture runs the application selected by a user.

Ready to Detect: u-Texture is ready to detect global or local sensor data. In case of global sensor data, both changes that occur internally or externally are sent to the *Recognized* state. In this case, internal data refers to the change within the system and external data refers to the change of assembled u-Textures. On the other hand, when local sensor data of internal sensors is detected, it is sent to the *Application Running* state.

Ready to Shutdown: u-Texture prepares to shutdown all systems.

Shutdown: u-Texture shuts all systems down.

4   System Architecture

4.1   Hardware

Sensing Capability Figure 5 shows a block diagram of the u-Texture and the u-Joint. Each side of the u-Texture and the u-Joint is equipped with an RS-232C interface as a connection sensor examines whether the u-Texture is connected to other u-Textures or not, and its direction if it is connected. The 3D sensor is used to obtain inclination data. The sensor is created with two dual axis accelerometers (ADXL202, Analog Devices). Infrared sensors are located on each side of the u-Texture as a proximity sensor, and are used to detect nearby or incoming remote u-Textures. All sensors outputs mentioned above are processed by a microcontroller (H8/3664F 16MHx, Hitachi). The microcontroller dispatches the network ID of the u-Texture and the network IDs of the connected u-Textures located on its sides. The microcontroller can also simultaneously receive the same data from connected u-Textures, and then send the data to the main computer to have the data processed.

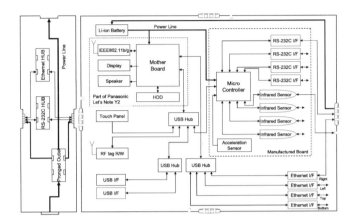

Fig. 5. Block diagram of the u-Texture (right) and the u-Joint (left)

Computing and Networking Capability The main computer consists of the Mobile Pentium processor, a speaker, an IEEE 802.11b wireless network and display (SXGA 14.1type). All are parts adapted from a laptop computer (CF-Y2DM1AXR, Panasonic). A tough panel (AST-140, DMC) enables direct inputs. An RFID tag reader/writer (13.56MHz, Sofel) is embedded and antennas are built-in around the display. Ethernet interfaces are also implemented on each side of u-Texture. The basic idea behind a wired network for exchanging data among the assembled u-Textures internally is to create an extemporaneous bridge network with broadcast support and loop back prevention. This is accomplished by binding each Ethernet interface into one pseudo network device, and binding an active network ID to the device. With additional help from a loop back prevention protocol, the packet storming within the network can be reduced. The detailed design is described in our other paper [11].

u-Joint The u-Joint provides power to connected u-Textures. The RS-232C and Ethernet interfaces are built into the u-Joint to transmit and receive data between u-Textures.

Structural Interface The u-Texture is defined with directions of up and down, and left and right physically as shown in Figure 3. u-Joint is also defined up and down. To simplify the automatic structure recognition by the software, there are three assembly regulations as follows. (1) u-Texture should be assembled to others horizontally or vertically via u-Joints. (2) The surfaces of the u-Textures should be connected with the same directions when assembling them horizontally. (3) The top of the u-Texture should be connected to the bottom of the other u-Texture and the right side to the left side. The structure of the u-Texture has an original connecting mechanism to make users unconsciously adhere to the regulations.

4.2   Software

A block diagram of software module is shown in Figure 6. The software module consists of three modules pre-installed in each u-Texture: the *Event Sharing Module*, the *Structure Recognition Module*, and the *Application Launcher Module*. The *Application Module* is created and installed by developers, and runs one application. Each *Application Module* has the *Application Description Data* (hereinafter "*AD Data*") which describes the minimum structure data that the application can be executed.

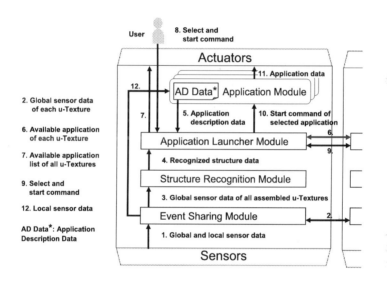

Fig. 6. Block diagram of software modules

Recognition Phase The *Event Sharing Module* obtains global and local sensor data from all sensors (Figure 6, No.1), exchange the global sensor data with all assembled u-Textures (Figure 6, No.2) and sends all the global data to the *Structure Recognition Module* (Figure 6, No.3). The *Structure Recognition Module* recognizes the structure of u-Textures with the exclusive coordinates for u-Textures. The global sensor data consists of the connected or disconnected status of four sides, each ID of the connected u-Textures, and inclination data. Figure 7 shows an example of global sensor data which describes that the lower edge of u-Texture A is connected with u-Texture B and u-Texture C. The part A of Figure 7 describes that the ID of u-Texture A is 192.168.1.7, which is its own IP address. The u-Texture A is connecting with others on the lower edge, and the inclination of the u-Texture A is vertical. The part B of Figure 7 describes the IP address, the connected edge, and the inclination of the u-Textures connected with the lower edge of u-Texture A.

The coordinates definition on assembled shape, location, and inclination of u-Textures is shown in Figure 8 (left). Each corner of u-Texture has a number

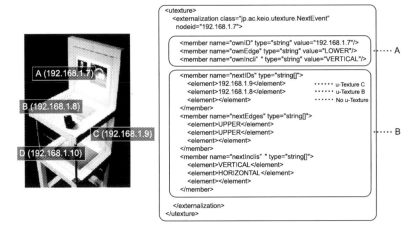

Fig. 7. Example of global sensor data

of coodinates. Figure 9 shows an example of re-calculation of the u-Texture C. When the u-Texture C does not connect to other u-Textures, the number coordinate at the bottom left corner is always (0, 0, 0) (Figure 9, left). When a u-Texture assembles with other u-Textures, all assembled u-Textures re-calculate its own coordinates and the assembled shape individually. A position and inclination of each u-Texture is described as {(bottom left corner's coordinate), quadrant}. Before connection, the bottom left corner of each u-Texture is (0, 0, 0). Primarily, if there are some u-Textures which stand horizontally in the assembled u-Textures, the bottom left one is determined as {(0. 0. 0), QuadXY}(Figure 9, left). Secondarily, if there are no horizontal u-Textures, the bottom left u-Texture which stand vertically is determined as {(0, 0, 0), QuadXZ}. The u-Texture C is {(0, 0, 0), QuadXZ} and the u-Texture D is {(0, 0, 0), QuadXY} before connection (Figure 9, left). After connection, the u-Texture C starts re-calculating with considering the bottom left corner as the starting point (Figure 9, center). Finally, if there are minuses in the coordinates of the assembled u-Textures, all coordinate is shifted to change the minuses to pluses or zero (Figure 9, right). After re-calculation, the u-Texture C results the coordinates of the assembled u-Textures as unique coordinates and recognizes their structures of them.

Adaptation Phase When the *Application Launcher Module* receives the recognized structure data (Figure 6, No.4), it acquires the *AD Data* from each *Application Module* (Figure 6, No.5). Afterwards, the *Application Launcher Module* extracts available applications by comparing the *AD Data* with the recognized structure data. If the recognized structure includes a minimum structure described in an *AD Data*, the application will be considered an available application. Figure 10 shows a DTD of the *AD Data* in XML format. The ⟨**available-condition**⟩ shows the minimum data structure and has three attributes. ⟨**number**⟩ shows the total number of the minimum structure, ⟨**form**⟩

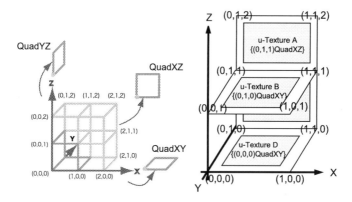

Fig. 8. Coordinates definition(left) and coordinates of shelf-shaped object(right)

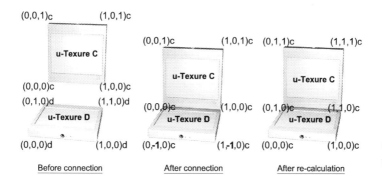

Fig. 9. Example of re-calculation of u-Texture C

shows the assembled form, and ⟨**inclination**⟩ shows the inclination that at least one u-Texture is set. ⟨**form**⟩ has three definitions of the assembled form. "sequential" means the minimum number of u-Textures are on the same plane and have a sequential connecting part, "cross" means they have a rectangular connecting part, and "square" means they are on the same plane and set squarely. Figure 11 shows an example of an application description data. In this case, if the assembled u-Textures have a rectangular connecting part and one of them is set on the QuadXY, the *Application Launcher Module* will extract this application as an available application. When the assembled u-Textures are in complicated forms, various available applications will be indicated to users in this case. In this prototype, we take priority not to indicate unavailable applications to users without fail because we consider that the desired application is different depending on users even though they assemble the same structure with u-Textures. After extracting available applications, the *Application Launcher Module* exchanges the list of them with all other assembled u-Textures (Figure 6, No.6) and merges the lists into the one list. Finally, the list is indicated to users (Figure 6, No.7).

```
<!ELEMENT application (path, executable-condition)>
<!ATTLIST application name CDATA #REQUIRED>
<!ATTLIST application id CDATA #REQUIRED>

<!ELEMENT path (#PCDATA)>
<!ELEMENT executable-condition(number, form?, inclination?)>

<!ELEMENT number (#PCDATA)>
<!ELEMENT form (square | cross | sequential)>
<!ELEMENT inclination (QuadXY | QuadXZ | QuadYZ)>
```

```
<?xml version="1.0" encoding="UTF-8" ?>
<!DOCTYPE application SYSTEM "structure.dtd">

<application name="AwareShelf" id="012876">
    <path>jp.ac.keio.utexture.AwareShelf</path>
    <executable-condition>
        <number>2</number>
        <form>cross</form>
        <inclination>QuadXY</inclination>
    </executable-condition>
</application>
```

Fig. 10. DTD of AD Data   **Fig. 11.** AD Data Example

Cooperation Phase When the *Application Launcher Module* receives a selection command and a start command of the available applications from a user (Figure 6, No.8), the module broadcasts the commands to the same modules of other u-Textures (Figure 6, No.9). Afterwards, the *Application Launcher Module* sends a start command to the *Application Module* of a selected application (Figure 6, No.10). *Application Modules* of u-Textures run the selected application and cooperates together gradually (Figure 6, No.11). Each *Application Module* receives local sensor data periodically (Figure 6, No.12) and changes the u-Texture's behavior corresponding to the data. The functionality of the main body of the *Application Module* is described in pseudo code in Figure 12. The invocation received by **getEvent** is processed according to the type of the sensor event. **Structure_Event** monitors the structural data of the assembled u-Textures, **Connection_Event** and **Inlination_Event** monitor the events of each global sensor data of the all assembled u-Textures, and **RFIDtag_Event** and **IRsensor_Event** monitor the events of each local sensor data of the u-Texture. Each application is described in appropriate parts in each *Application Module*. To develop a new application, it is necessary to make both a new *Application Module* and a new AD Data.

5   u-Texture Based Smart Surroundings

We have implemented eleven context-aware applications to confirm the effectiveness of u-Texture. Some of the applications are described in the following subsections.

5.1   AwareShelf

The "AwareShelf" can be created on a shelf-shaped u-Textures as shown in Figure 2. When a user puts a real object such as a camera, a book, or a key on a u-Texture, it enables to browse information of the real object on the display on another u-Texture. The u-Textures have to be connected vertically to the

```
// Main Body of Application Module
while (1) {
  struct SensorEvent event;
  // checking the sensor data changes or not.
  switch(getEvent (component, &event)){
  // events from global sensors
  case Structure_Event:
    //application code space for using structure data
    break;
  case Connection_Event:
    //application code space for using connection data
    break;
  case Inclination_Event:
    //application code space for using inclination data
    break;
  // events from local sensors
  case RFtag_Event:
    //application code space for using RFIDtag data
    break;
  case IRsensor_Event:
    //application code space for using IRsensor data
    break;
  }
}
```

Fig. 12. Main body of Application Module

u-Texture on that a thing is placed. For example, a user can check an electrical manual of a camera, or duration of times that a key was put on the AwareShelf before. In this application, real objects are attached unique RFID tags and u-Texture recognizes the tag IDs. When the AwareShelf connects to an external network, a user can look for real objects. Currently, the advanced application has been implemented so that a user can find the AwareShelf on which the real object was placed by using a mobile phone. In this application, the AwareShelf is used as a system for storing and recognizing objects (Figure 13).

Fig. 13. AwareShelf

5.2   CollaborationTable

The "Collaboration Table" is a system that supports cooperative work with several participants by connecting u-Textures horizontally as shown in Figure 14. Users can exchange and merge drawing data among connected u-Textures by drag-and-drop operations. One advantage of this application is that it is possible to expand users' creative ideas and collaborations in cooperative works. Another advantage is that it is possible to use a u-Texture both privately and publicly by connecting a u-Texture or setting it closer to another u-Texture.

Fig. 14. CollaborationTable

5.3 ProjectionWall

The "ProjectionWall" magnifies a connected u-Texture's small display onto a big one as shown in Figure 15. It is effective for displaying a large picture that is too small to be shown on only one u-Texture. Data can be handled interactively by users with touch panels. Although the similar interactive large display can be created with projectors, users have to establish or attach computers, sensors connected to the projector and to calibrate them. Converting coordinates for magnifying data is implemented by automatic cooperation among u-Textures, which can be one of the advantages for application developers and non-expert users in the respect that it is not necessary to be aware of changing coordinates.

Fig. 15. ProjectionWall

6 User Experience

Before implementing the current version of u-Texture, we have developed two earlier prototypes and conducted preliminary investigations. In this version, we have implemented sixteen u-Textures and eleven applications. The u-Textures have been placed in a demonstration room of our university and exhibited at several conferences and symposiums. Many people have tried assembling and dismantling u-Textures in practice. During the experience, interesting user reactions were observed and many opinions and comments were received.

6.1   Advantages of u-Texture

Several applications can share data externally in the current version. Some people tried a task such as making design drawings with multiple applications using the same u-Textures as shown in Figure1. As the progress of the task, users could modify their smart surroundings by changing the assembled shape of u-Textures. Most users who had experiences of such usage liked this advantage. Without u-Textures, the data exchange among several smart surroundings is also possible via a network. However, some users, especially for non-experts, commented that changing smart surroundings by physical interactions was intuitive and acceptable. Availability of multiple smart surroundings with the same u-Textures was also welcomed.

6.2   Features in Assembling

The idea that the shape of u-Textures is recognized automatically by physical assembling them was accepted favorably. Many users commented that it was not necessary to be aware of electrical connections to assemble u-Textures. However, since both physical and electrical connections require u-Joints, users found it troublesome to assemble u-Textures. We had an opinion that the prop of u-Texture is too thick, which would reduce the advantages of u-Textures for using some applications such as the ProjectionWall. Now, we are modifying structures for assembling in the next version of u-Texture. In this version, u-Joint will be not necessary for assembling 2D objects such as a board and a wall.

6.3   Indication of Available Applications Corresponding to the Shape

The approach to indicate available applications according to the shapes of u-Textures was well received by users. There was sometimes a comment that indicating list of application candidates corresponding to the shapes of u-Textures was both enjoyable and stressful. It also seems suitable for users to indicate candidates of the final shape by users selecting applications in advance.

7   Discussions

This research is still in an early phase, and we are considering several research issues and possible future directions.

7.1   Application Domain

One promising area of the u-Texture is to be used at homes, in offices, and at schools. In the case of using u-Textures in classrooms, there will be many collaborative works or presentations among students. In fact, we have tried some collaborative tasks and confirmed the potential advantages. We also see a future of our system in home usage, because of the increase in assemblable modular furniture which allows free adjustment of its size. Business shows and conferences are also one of our targets. Users can assemble various interactive booths as smart surroundings easily and quickly.

7.2   Other Types of Smart Block Material

The shapes and sizes of smart block materials are not limited to panels. Users can create many kinds of smart objects with various materials as shown in Table 1. The objects can provide applications corresponding to the features of the material. When designing any smart block material, it is essential for non-expert users to include electrical interfaces in the structural interfaces of the block materials. The design for maintaining and debugging corresponding to each material is also considered.

7.3   Extraction of Available Application

In this current prototype, each application defines executable shapes with only several primitive shapes based on three parameters. The available applications are extracted if the assembled u-Texture includes the executable shapes the applications defined. The selection mechanism was appropriate for assembling sixteen u-Textures and using about eleven applications. However, when users assemble many u-Textures and use a number of applications, the finer, more flexible and exhaustive definition toward all possible structures will be necessary. The definition should be elegant for application developers and we are investigating the novel definition now.

7.4   Re-design for Practical Use

To apply u-Textures for practical use as well as normal panels, several re-designs are desired. First, electrical system should be sophisticated and the next version will have the minimum configuration which can keep the advantage of u-Texture. For instance, network capability creates internal and external communications with only a wireless network. Second, a spacer module which has the same structural capability as a normal u-Texture is effective for huge assembled surroundings. The module has only a network capability as a connecter among u-Textures. Structural strength and error indication and handling for software are also necessary for various uses and considered for the next version. Colors, exteriors, and balance with surroundings are important points for users to select objects such as furniture and appliances, and we are also investigating this matter.

8   Related Work

Our inspiration for using building block materials as furniture came from the square paper tubes and panels of MUJI [12] which can form various furniture such as racks, tables, and stools.

Researches that enable users to create smart surroundings easily have been already pursued. Most of them create it with physical interaction of the system, such as connecting, bumping, and setting without experts. ConnecTable [5] is a table that has a display embedded in its surface. ConnecTable can be used a personal display and a part of public display by attaching physically two tables. Ken Hinckley's multiple tablet computer system [6] can also form dedicated connections by physically bumping together displays with their distributed sensors. Impromptu [7] is a concept that allows users to create smart surrounding without set-ups, maintaining or administering. It enables to build such environments rapidly with autonomous cooperation of consumer appliances. Compared to the above systems, the advantage of u-Texture is that it can recognize assembled shapes and autonomously extract appropriate context-aware applications corresponding to the shape.

Researches on building blocks with embedded computations have been carried out until now. However, their target users and applications are different from our research and most of them enable the recognition of 2D structure only. Algo-Block [8] is an educational system of cubical aluminum blocks for programming by docking each other on a table. Triangle [9] is a tangible programming system of a triangular shaped block. The three sides are connected with a joint with an electrical joint, and can recognize the entire shape. Both of above systems show the entire shape on a display of a remote computer and enable users to control the data with physical operation of the building blocks. Computational Building Block [13] is also an input device for structuring information. The target application of the system is 3D geometric modeling with 3D structure recognition. DataTiles [10] is a system which changes its function by re-arranging tiles with built-in RFID tags with displays with build-in computers. As sample applications, sending email, editing pictures, and operating home appliances are created corresponding to the combination of the DataTiles on the plat-panel display with RFID tag readers. Mostly, these systems are made to have fixed executable applications beforehand. In case of u-Texture, it collaborates with other ones by autonomous according to the 3D structure of u-Textures.

9   Conclusions and Future Work

This paper has contributed a smart building block as a self-organizable universal panel that allows non-expert users to create smart surroundings. The assembled u-Textures create smart surroundings that have shapes of every day objects such as shelves, tables, and walls without experts. Then, the smart surroundings are utilized as systems for supporting various activities of each user or for cooperative works among multiple users. The effectiveness has been confirmed by introducing several applications using the u-Texture and conducting user experiments.

We are also interested in implementing smaller and bigger versions of smart building blocks with other types of material. Users can assemble other smart building blocks and create many context-aware applications in various situations. We believe the smart building blocks will be one of the standard ways for creating smart surroundings.

10   Acknowledgements

This research has been conducted as part of Ubila Project supported by Ministry of Internal Affairs and Communications, Japan. We would like to express our appreciation to Keio Ubila team and Uchida Yoko Co.,Ltd. for supporting this research. And thanks to the reviewers for helpful suggestions and comments.

References

[1] Tokuda, H., Takashio, K., Nakazawa, J., Matsumiya, K., Ito, M., Saito, M.: Sf2: Smart furniture for creating ubiquitous applications. In: International Workshop on Cyberspace Technologies and Societies (IWCTS2004). (2004) 423–429

[2] Streitz, N., Tandler, P., Muller-Tomfelde, C., Konomi, S.: Roomware: Towards the next generation of human-computer interaction based on an integrated design of real and virtual worlds. In: HCI in the New Millenium. (2001) 553–578

[3] Kidd, C.D., Orr, R., Abowd, G.D., Atkeson, C.G., Essa, I.A., MacIntyre, B., Mynatt, E.D., Starner, T., Newstetter, W.: The awarehome: A living laboratory for ubiquitous computing research. In: Cooperative Buildings. (1999) 191–198

[4] Snoonian, D.: Smart buildings. IEEE Spectrum 40 (2003) 18–23

[5] Tandler, P., Prante, T., Muller-Tomfelde, C., Streitz, N.A., Steinmetz, R.: Connectables: Dynamic coupling of displays for the flexible creation of shared workspaces. In: Annual ACM Symposium on User Interface Software and Technology (UIST'01). (2001) 11–20

[6] Hinckley, K.: Distributed and local sensing techniques for face-to-face collaboration. In: Fifth international conference on Multimodal interfaces (ICMI'03). Volume 36.7. (2003) 81–84

[7] Beigl, M., Zimmer, T., Krohn, A., Decker, C., Robinson, P.: Creating ad-hoc pervasive computing environments. In: Pervasive 2004 Advances in Pervasive Computing. (2004) 377–381

[8] Suzuki, H., Kato, H.: Interaction-level support for collaborative learning: Algoblock an open programming language. In: The first international conference on Computer support for collaborative learning (CSCL'95). (1995) 349–355

[9] Gorbet, M.G., Orth, M., Ishii, H.: Triangles: Tangible interface for manipulation and exploration of digital information topography. In: The SIGCHI conference on Human Factors in Computing Systems (CHI'98). (1998) 49–56

[10] Rekimoto, J., Ullmer, B., Oba, H.: Datatiles: a modular platform for mixed physical and graphical interactions. In: The SIGCHI Conference on Human Factors in Computing Systems (CHI'01). (2001) 269–276

[11] Yanagihara, T., Sakakibara, H., Ohsawa, R., Ideuchi, M., Kohtake, N., Iwai, M., Takashio, K., Tokuda, H.: A self configurable topology-aware network for smart materials. In: Fifth IEEE International Workshop on Smart Appliances and Wearable Computing (IWSAWC2005). (2005) 469–474

[12] MUJI: (http://www.muji.net/eng/)

[13] Anderson, D., Frankel, J.L., Marks, J., Agarwala, A., Beardsley, P., Hodgins, J., Leigh, D., Ryall, K., Sullivan, E., Yedidia, J.S.: Tangible interaction + graphical interpretation: a new approach to 3d modeling. In: 27th annual conference on Computer graphics and interactive techniques (SIGGRAPH'00). (2000) 393–402

Fast and Robust Interface Generation for Ubiquitous Applications

Krzysztof Gajos, David Christianson, Raphael Hoffmann, Tal Shaked,
Kiera Henning, Jing Jing Long, and Daniel S. Weld

University of Washington
Seattle, WA, USA
{kgajos,dbc1,raphelh,tshaked,kierah,jingjing,weld}@cs.washington.edu
http://www.cs.washington.edu/ai/supple/

Abstract. We present SUPPLE, a novel toolkit which automatically generates interfaces for ubiquitous applications. Designers need only specify declarative models of the interface and desired hardware device and SUPPLE uses decision-theoretic optimization to automatically generate a concrete rendering for that device. This paper provides an overview of our system and describes key extensions that barred the previous version (reported in [3]) from practical application. Specifically, we describe a functional modeling language capable of representing complex applications. We propose a new adaptation strategy, *split interfaces*, which speeds access to common interface features without disorienting the user. We present a *customization facility* that allows designers and end users to override SUPPLE's automatic rendering decisions. We describe a distributed architecture which enables computationally-impoverished devices to benefit from SUPPLE interfaces. Finally, we present experiments and a preliminary user-study that demonstrate the practicality of our approach.

1 Introduction

The growth of mobile and ubiquitous computing has caused increased dependance on digitally encoded information and has increased users' expectations of being able to access, create and manipulate digital content in a variety of situations. As a result users frequently rely on devices other than desktop computers for their digital needs. These devices include mobile phones, PDAs, tablet computers, touch panels, and increasingly wall-sized displays operated by finger or laser pointing. These devices not only differ in their screen size and resolution; they also support very diverse kinds of input devices and modes of interaction.

These trends put an enormous pressure on software developers to make their products available for a large number of platforms. While the logic of the application may often transfer easily across different platforms, the user interfaces typically have to be designed and implemented from scratch. Of course, interface design is always time-consuming, but there are several aspects of ubiquitous

M. Beigl et al. (Eds.): UbiComp 2005, LNCS 3660, pp. 37–55, 2005.

applications that are especially challenging: 1) New kinds of devices enter the market at a rapid pace. 2) Since ubiquitous computing is a young field, there is a smaller track record of successful interface designs and increased need for iterative prototyping. 3) In ubiquitous computing new functionality often emerges from interactions of spontaneously aggregated devices and services [10].

This paper describes SUPPLE, a fast and efficient UI toolkit for ubiquitous applications which addresses these issues by automatically generating a personalized interface for a wide range of hardware platforms. We argue that such a toolkit should satisfy the five requirements listed below.

- **Easy:** The toolkit should support rapid prototyping and be easy for application developers to use. Section 2 explains how SUPPLE's high-level interface representation speeds development, and Table 2 in Section 6 details the code complexity of the examples in this paper.
- **Capable:** The toolkit should handle complex interfaces and rich data types. Section 2 describes our expanded modeling language, and Table 3 demonstrates that SUPPLE can render reasonably complex interfaces very quickly.
- **Adaptive:** Generated interfaces should possess adaptation and customization features to make convenient operation by users with widely varying activities, styles and preferences. However, automated changes to an interface must minimize the chance of user disorientation. Section 3 introduces a novel interface-adaptation mechanism called *split interfaces* and describes a preliminary user study suggesting user acceptance. Section 4 presents a complementary customization capability, which allows users to tailor any SUPPLE interface to their desires as well as to undo unwanted adaptations.
- **Portable:** A single interface specification should enable rendering that interface on every supported hardware platform, including devices which are computationally impoverished and which may not have network connectivity. Section 2 explains how SUPPLE takes a device description as input and uses a decision-theoretic optimization algorithm to render an interface specifically tailored to the capabilities and constraints of that hardware platform. Section 5 describes our distributed architecture and caching infrastructure, which supports remote rendering and wireless operation. Section 6 provides preliminary performance data for our system.
- **Extensible:** It should be easy to extend the set of hardware devices supported by the toolkit. The most difficult aspect of getting SUPPLE to generate interfaces for a new hardware platform is specifying the cost model [3] for that device's interaction modes. In the past, this was indeed a laborious process, but we have recently developed a preference-elicitation methodology and machine-learning algorithm which quickly generates these cost models. Space precludes a description of our technique, but see [4] for details and experiments showing its efficacy.

The next section summarizes SUPPLE's rendering algorithm and describes its extended modeling language which now supports more complex applications and data types required by ubiquitous applications. Section 3 explains SUPPLE's

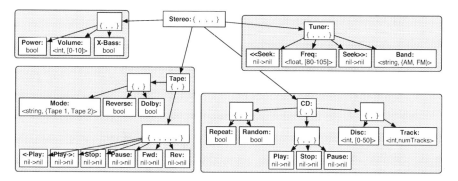

Fig. 1. Graphical representation of the functional specification for a stereo controller. For clarity, different parts of the specification are grouped with gray shading.

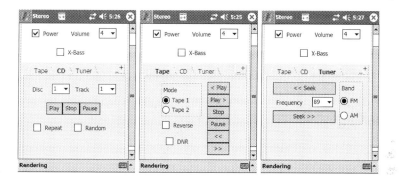

Fig. 2. Three tab views of the stereo specification, rendered for a PDA.

novel method of supporting dynamic improvements to the UI in a manner which doesn't disorient the user; a preliminary user-study validates the approach. Section 4 presents a mechanism to allow a designer to override decisions made by the automatic rendering engine. Section 5 describes the distributed architecture, which enables SUPPLE to run on computationally impoverished platforms such as PDAs. Section 6 presents experimental results, which confirm SUPPLE's fitness as a toolkit for ubiquitous applications. We end the paper with a discussion of related and future research.

2   Overview of Supple

SUPPLE takes three inputs: a *functional specification* of the interface, a *device model* and a *user model*. The functional specification defines the *types* of data that need to be exchanged between the user and the application (*e.g.* Figure 1). The device model describes which widgets are available on the device and provides a *cost function*, which estimates the user effort required to manipulate

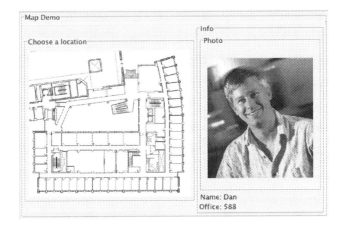

Fig. 3. An interface utilizing images and clickable maps.

these widgets with the interaction methods supported by the device. Finally, a user's typical activities are modeled with a device- and rendering-independent *user trace*. SUPPLE's rendering algorithm combines constraint propagation with branch-and-bound search, guided by an admissible heuristic.

In this section, we describe SUPPLE's functional specification language, briefly discuss its optimization-based rendering algorithm and provide an overview of its implementation, focusing on aspects not elucidated in [3].

2.1   Functional Specification Language for Interface Modeling

The interface elements included in the functional specification correspond to units of information that need to be conveyed via the interface between the user and the controlled appliance or application. Each element is defined in terms of its type. There are several classes of types:

Primitive types include the common basic data types such as integers, floats, strings and booleans. As an example, the power switch for the stereo system is represented as a Boolean in the specification of Figure 1. The primitive types also include several more specialized constructs that often benefit from special handling by user interfaces such as dates, times, images and clickable maps. These last two types are illustrated in a concrete interface shown in Figure 3, where a user can point at different offices on a building map, causing the occupant's image to be displayed.

Container types, formally represented as $\{\tau_1, \tau_2, \ldots, \tau_n\}$, are used to create groups (or records) of simpler elements. For example, all of the interior nodes (*e.g.*, Tuner, Tape, CD, Stereo or the unnamed intermediate nodes) in the specification tree in Figure 1 are instances of the container type.

Constrained types: $\langle \tau, \mathcal{C}_\tau \rangle$ denotes a constrained type, where τ is any primitive or container type and $\mathcal{C}_\tau$ is a set of constraints over the values of this type. In the stereo example, the volume is defined as an integer type whose values

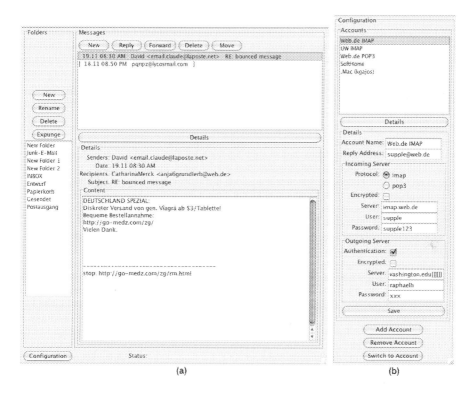

Fig. 4. An email client that uses SUPPLE to render its user interface. (a) The main view. (b) The configuration pane.

are constrained to lie between 0 and 10. In the email client shown in Figure 4(a) the list of email folders shown on the left is represented as a String whose values are constrained to be the names of the folders in the currently selected email account (note here that the constraints on the legal values of an element can change dynamically at run time *e.g.*, when new folders are created). In most cases elements of the constrained type are rendered as a discrete selection widget (list, combo box, etc) except for number ranges where continuous selectors such as sliders may be used.

Constraints can also be specified for container types. For example, consider the list of available email accounts in the email example of Figure 4(b). Each account is modeled as an instance of the container type. Yet the user wants not only to see the settings of a single account, but she also wants to select different accounts to view. Thus, we model the interface element representing the current account as a container object whose domain of values is restricted to all registered email accounts for that user. When SUPPLE renders this container, it allows the user to select which account to view, and also displays that account's settings. When enough screen space is available, SUPPLE will render both the selection mechanism and the details of the content side-by-side, as in Figure 4(b). When

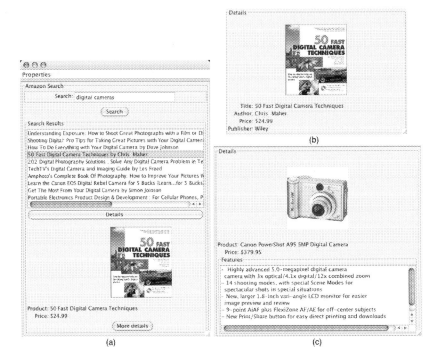

Fig. 5. A simple client for Amazon Web Services. (a) Search results with a pane showing properties of a selected object — only those properties which are common to all items are shown there, but the "More Details" button brings up a more specialized view for each item. (b) Detailed view for a book. (c) Detailed view for a digital camera.

space is scarce, SUPPLE will show just the list of available accounts; in order to view their contents, the user must double-click on an element in the list, or click the explicit "Details" button.

While this approach makes modeling easy, it assumes that all the objects in a container's domain are of exactly the same type. In practice, this is not always the case. For example, consider Figure 5's interface to Amazon Web Services. Items returned by search may come from any of several categories, each of which can have different attributes. Books, for example, have titles and authors while many other items do not. To alleviate this problem, SUPPLE allows the elements of a container of type τ to be a subtype τ' of τ.[1] In such situations, if space permits, SUPPLE renders all the attributes of the common ancestor type τ statically, next to the choice element (Figure 5(a)). Any time a specialized object is selected by the user, another button is highlighted, alerting the user

---

[1] A subtype of a container type is created by adding zero or more new elements; the subtype cannot rename, remove or change type of the elements defined in its parent type.

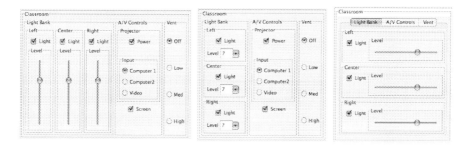

Fig. 6. SUPPLE optimally uses the available space and robustly degrades the quality of the rendered interface if presented with a device with a smaller screen size. This figure shows three renderings of a classroom controller on three devices with progressively narrower screens.

that more detailed information is available, which can be displayed in a separate window as in Figures 5(b) and (c).

Vectors: elements of type $vector(\langle \tau, \mathcal{C}_\tau \rangle)$ are used to support multiple selection; they denote an ordered sequence of zero or more values of type τ. The constraints $\mathcal{C}_\tau$ define the set of values of type τ that can be selected from. For example, the list of emails in the email client (Figure 4(a)) is represented as a vector of Message elements, whose values are constrained to the messages in the currently selected folder; this allows the user to select and move or delete several messages at once.

Actions are denoted as $\tau_1 \mapsto \tau_2$, where τ_1 stands for the type of the object containing parameters of the action, while τ_2 describes the return type *i.e.,* the interface component that is to be displayed after the typical execution of the action. Unlike the other types which are used to represent the application's *state*, the action type is used to invoke the *methods*. The "Reply" button in the rendering of the email client interface in Figure 4(a) is represented as an action with a null parameter type (since it operates on the current message) and Message as the return type. The Search in the Amazon browser example in Figure 5(a) is an action with String as a parameter type and a null return type.

2.2   Algorithm

Unlike previous model-based rendering systems (*e.g.* the Personal Universal Controller [6]), which use templates or rule-based approaches to generating user interfaces, SUPPLE uses decision-theoretic, combinatorial optimization. Conceptually, SUPPLE enumerates all possible ways of laying out the interface and chooses the one which minimizes the user's expected cost of interaction. Efficiency is obtained by using branch and bound search and a novel, admissible heuristic to explore the space of candidate renderings; full constraint propagation is used to maximize the pruning effect of violated constraints. Several variations on the algorithm are empirically evaluated in [3].

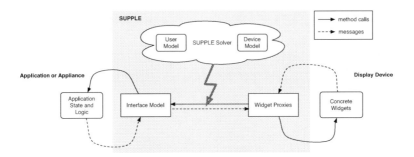

Fig. 7. SUPPLE's implementation: The interface model exposes the state variables and methods that should become accessible through the interface. The widget proxies generated by the device model are assigned to interface model elements by SUPPLE's optimization algorithm.

SUPPLE's use of a cost function to guide the choice of rendering has several advantages. Unlike a rule set that needs to be created by hand, the cost function can be quickly constructed automatically from designer's responses to examples of concrete renderings of different interfaces [4]. Furthermore, optimization is relatively robust, flexibly handling tradeoffs and interactions between choices in different parts of the interface. In contrast, rule-based systems are fragile because small changes to device constraints (e.g., display size) may require a major change to the rendering. A rule derivation which works well on one PDA might fail when used with a slightly smaller screen, since the candidate interface might no longer fit. Conversely, a rule-based system will likely fail to exploit an increase in screen size (or decrease in interface complexity) by using more convenient but larger widgets. In contrast, SUPPLE's search algorithm always selects an interface that is optimal (with respect to the cost function) for a given interface and device specification. Figure 6 illustrates how SUPPLE robustly degrades the quality of the generated user interfaces as it is presented with devices with progressively narrower screens.

2.3 Implementation

SUPPLE is written in Java and is designed to integrate easily with existing application code — especially with applications whose state is maintained in beans — in such cases SUPPLE automatically maintains two-way consistency between the interface and application states. Communication between SUPPLE's implementation components is illustrated in Figure 7. User interfaces are specified by creating UI objects for each property or method to be exposed through the interface. When asked to generate a concrete user interface, SUPPLE proceeds in the following way:

1. The device model is engaged to generate a set of candidate widget *proxies*, serializable objects that are capable of generating a concrete widget, for each element of the interface model.
2. Using combinatorial search, SUPPLE generates the best assignment of widget proxies to interface model elements and establishes the connections between them. If necessary, the proxies may now be serialized for caching or transport to computationally-impoverished devices.
3. The widget proxies are triggered to generate a concrete user interface on the final display device.

For most applications, new windows or dialog boxes (or equivalent elements on other platforms) need to be displayed at run-time. SUPPLE renders them dynamically as needed.

3   Automatic Adaptation Without Disorientation

Automatically generating interfaces on the fly opens up the possibility of incorporating knowledge about the user and his tasks into the design of the concrete interface. Our initial paper on SUPPLE explained how analysis of a user trace enabled the system to automatically adapt an interface to a given user's work habits by fully replacing one rendering with another [3]. This approach, however, could result in dramatic changes to the interface and consequently disorient the user. In this section, we compare alternative designs for adaptive interfaces in an exploratory user study; we then describe our implementation of *split interfaces*, a technique which reconciles adaptivity with predictability.

3.1   Exploratory User Study

For our study, we compared four interfaces: two traditional and two adaptive siblings. One of the traditional interfaces organized operations hierarchically, and the other used a "flat" structure, in which operations are always visible. Because these structures have different strengths and weaknesses, we considered different adaptation methods in each case.

A hierarchical interface offers clear organization, but makes certain operations harder to access, so we employ adaptation in an effort to speed access to commonly used functionality. Following [13,16,2] we advocate a generalization of *split menus* which we call *split interfaces* (Figure 8(b)). We partition an interface into *static* and *dynamic* sections. The static portion always maintains the same organization, while the dynamic portion displays speedy ways to invoke commonly used functions that might be otherwise hard to access. Note that in contrast to Sears and Shneiderman [13], who removed recently used items from their original locations when ordering them near the head, we propose *duplicating* functionality when placing it in the dynamic portion of the interface.

A flat interface organization makes every operation ready-at-hand, but may promote so many operations, that the result confuses the user. Thus, we use

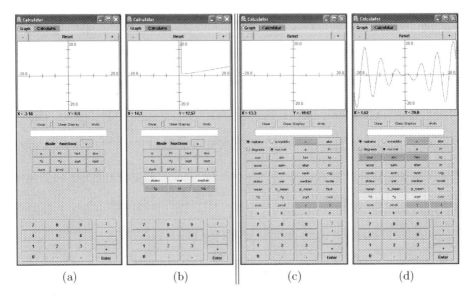

(a)   (b)   (c)   (d)

Fig. 8. The (handcrafted) interfaces used in our preliminary user study: (a) a
static interface that requires users to use hierarchical pull-down menus to access
advanced functions, (b) *split interface* — an adaptive version of the hierarchical
interface in which families of the most frequently accessed functions are added to
the (previously empty) "dynamic" area in the middle of the interface, (c) a static,
flat interface with every button present at all times (d) *altered prominence* —
an adaptive version of the flat interface, which highlights the two most recently
used families of buttons. (The parenthesis and the x variable are highlighted at
all times.)

adaptation in an effort to facilitate navigation, directing the user to commonly
used options. Specifically, we develop the notion of *altered prominence*, dynamically highlighting commonly used keys (Figure 8(d)).

Our hypothesis was that the split interface would be more universally accepted, because the original (static) portion of the interface is never changed,
maintaining a sense of user control. We expected altered prominence to be more
controversial, because adaption modifies the interface in ways that users can't
ignore.

For our experimental domain, we chose a graphing calculator application,
because most tasks require numerous interactions with clickable UI elements.
This provides a copious stream of user-activity data, allowing for relatively fast
adaptation. We enrolled 16 users from a population of graduate students and
staff in the Department of Computer Science & Engineering at the University of
Washington. Half the users were assigned to the hierarchical/split interface and
half to flat/altered prominence. We asked each user to complete two sets of 18
formula entry tasks. Users entered one set of formulae in an adaptive interface
and the other in a static UI. To neutralize learning effects, half the users started

with the adaptive interface, while the other half first used the static UI. Users reported their subjective experience on two questionnaires.

Due to the moderate sample size, most of our results were not statistically significant. On average, the subjects completed the tasks faster using the adaptive interfaces. The speedup was very small for the split interface, but noticeable for the interface with altered prominence. Furthermore, when compared to the corresponding static interface, the error rate increased for the split interface, but decreased slightly for altered prominence.

The subjective comments were more surprising. Users considered altered prominence to be intuitive, but deemed the split interface to be slightly less intuitive than its static alternative. Interestingly, however, users expressed a strong and nearly-universal preference for the split interface when compared with its static version (this result was statistically significant with $p < 0.02$). In contrast, there was no statistically significant preference for altered prominence in the flat interface; in fact, some users expressed a strong dislike for that method of adaptation claiming that it caused them to get disoriented every time the highlighting changed.

In both cases, the interface adapted at a rapid pace: several times during the course of a 10–15 minute-long session. We believe that both adaptation strategies would have had more impact if they were performed at a slower pace, giving the user a chance to notice and take full advantage of them. In addition, the prominence might better have been altered more gradually, so that the changes were imperceptible and hence not a distraction.

3.2   Adaptation in SUPPLE

Since our study indicated that users strongly favored split interfaces, we adopted this method in SUPPLE. Figure 9 shows an example where, in response to a particular user trace that repeatedly used "Landscape" printing, SUPPLE has automatically populated the "Common Activities" area of the top-level print dialog box with a one-click shortcut to this orientation. SUPPLE's split interfaces generally work well on interfaces that involve navigating among different windows or tab panes (or cards/pages on cell phones and pages on the Web).

Rendering a split interface is computationally harder than rendering an interface where each piece of functionality exists in exactly one place. In addition to finding the best assignment of widgets to interface elements, SUPPLE now must also decide what amount of space to set aside for the dynamic content, what functionality to represent in the dynamic area, and how to render it (duplicated functionality need not be rendered exactly as it was in the interface's static part).

Ideally, SUPPLE should duplicate functionality with the highest expected *utility* (*i.e.*, favoring the product of access likelihood and the difficulty of navigation with the static interface). Note, however, that the presence of a dynamic shortcut for an element E will likely reduce the chance that a user will navigate to E through the static interface. This in turn may cause a different rendering to be preferable for the static part. Thus the choice of static and dynamic aspects

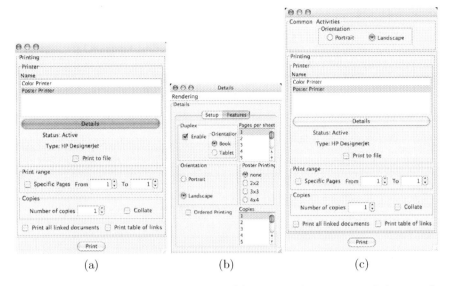

(a)   (b)   (c)

Fig. 9. In the original print dialog box (a) it takes four mouse clicks to select landscape printing: details button, features tab (b), landscape value and then a click to dismiss the pop-up window. (c) shows the interface after automatically adaptation by SUPPLE given frequent user manipulation of document orientation; the adapted interface is identical to the one in (a) except for the Common Activities section that is used to render alternative means of accessing frequently used but hard to access functionality from the original interface.

interact, and choosing the optimal static interface requires considering the *distribution* over possible dynamic content. Since this computation is intractable, we use a simple approximation — first choosing a static rendering in isolation, then greedily adding the best dynamic shortcuts in turn. We define the utility of a particular set of *duplicatedFunctionality* for a particular *concreteInterface* and a usage *trace* as:

`utility`(*duplicatedFunctionality | concreteInterface, trace*) =
    `expectedEffort`(*concreteInterface | trace*)
    − `expectedEffort`(*concreteInterface+duplicatedFunctionality | trace*)

To compute `expectedEffort`, SUPPLE simulates use of the interface by replaying the trace of past interactions through a hypothesized interface and estimating the total "effort" required. The usage traces are recorded in terms of the functionality accessed and are stored in a rendering-independent manner. For desktop interfaces, the number of mouse clicks (for changing tabs, opening new windows, dismissing them, etc) is used as the approximation of the total effort. On WAP cell phones, the number of button presses is used as the metric. In cases where the functionality that the user wants to access has been duplicated in several parts of the interface, SUPPLE assumes that the user will use the most convenient copy of the functionality. While this model of expected effort is imperfect, our initial experience suggests that it is a good approximation for evaluating the potential utility of duplicated functionality.

In theory, a system might calculate the optimal percentage of space to allocate to the dynamic and static parts of an interface, respectively. Unfortunately, a principled approach to this optimization is computationally prohibitive. As a result, SUPPLE ignores this decision and only includes area for dynamic content if a user explicitly requests it or if the best available rendering does not fill all available space. Table 1 summarizes the algorithm that SUPPLE uses for selecting which interface elements to display in the "Common Activities" area of each interface view:[2]

selectCommonActivities(*interfaceModel, concreteInterface, trace*)
1. **initialize** *duplicatedFunctionality*
2. **while** there is still a *view* with space for duplicated functionality
3.   *currentBestUtility* ← 0
4.   *currentBestCandidate* ← null
5.   **foreach** *view* in *concreteInterface* that has space for duplicated functionality
6.   **foreach** *element* in *interfaceModel*
7.   *temp* ← *duplicatedFunctionality* + duplicate *element* into *view*
8.   **if utility**(*temp* | *concreteInterface, trace*) > *currentBestUtility*
9.   **then** *currentBestCandidate* ← duplicate *element* into *view*
10. **if** (*currentBestCandidate* != null)
11.   **then** *duplicatedFunctionality* ← *duplicatedFunctionality* + *currentBestCandidate*
12.   **else return** *duplicatedFunctionality*
13. **return** *duplicatedFunctionality*

Table 1. SUPPLE's algorithm for selecting elements to be displayed in the "Common Activities" area of each interface view.

4   Overriding Automated Rendering Decisions

SUPPLE's committment to completely-autonomous rendering hinders acceptance with users as it originally provided no means for either designers or the end users to control the presentation or organization of the final concrete interfaces. In order to encourage adoption (and satisfy requirements of ease and adaptivity), we devised a convenient way to override optimization-based choices. SUPPLE includes a comprehensive *customization* facility that allows a designer or end user to make explicit changes to an interface: rearranging elements, duplicating functionality, removing elements, and constraining the choice of widgets used to render any part of the functional specification. Operation is simple on a windows

---

[2] A *view* is a unit of a user interface such as a window on a desktop computer or a card in a WML document.

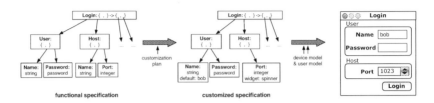

Fig. 10. SUPPLE's customization architecture. The user's customization actions are recorded in a *customization plan*. The next time the interface is rendered (possibly in a differently sized window or on a different device) the plan is used to transform the functional specification into a *customized specification* which is then rendered using decision-theoretic optimization as before. The interface shown in this figure is for a small FTP client.

and mouse platform — one simply right-clicks the interface element (primitive widget or container) and options are revealed. Duplication and rearrangement are specified with drag and drop.

Combining explicit customization with optimization-based rendering requires a major change to the original SUPPLE architecture (Figure 10). SUPPLE records a complete history of the user's customization operations in a *customization plan*. Rendering an interface proceeds in two phases. First, SUPPLE applies the plan to the functional specification in order to create a graph called a *customized specification*. In the second phase, SUPPLE applies decision-theoretic optimization (described in Section 2) to the device model, user model, and customized specification to render the interface.

The functional and customized specifications may have very different structures, *e.g.*, the customization specification may omit, duplicate or move functionality; it may also contain constraints on the set of widgets which may be used to render certain elements.

Note that the customization plan can be applied to *any* functional specification, including ones that the user (and SUPPLE) have not yet seen; it also may be applied when rendering an interface on a novel device (however, constraints requiring specific widgets may not be satisfiable). Explicitly representing the customization plan also allows SUPPLE to support a flexible undo system which encourages users to experiment with alternative interfaces.

5   Handling Computationally-Impoverished Devices

As required by the portability and extensibility requirements, SUPPLE supports the major modes of operation required by ubiquitous computing. In some situations, users will want to access applications on their desktop computers (PCs). It is also likely that users will want to use their desktop computers to access applications running on a remote server or appliance. Finally, mobile users may want to access either local or remote applications using computationally-impoverished

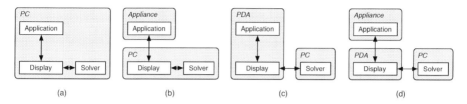

Fig. 11. SUPPLE allows the application, solver server, and interface to run on different devices; the following modes of operation are common: (a) An application running on a PC is displayed on the same machine — the user interface is rendered locally. (b) A remote application is displayed on a PC — the user interface is rendered on the PC. (c) An application running on a PDA is displayed on that same PDA — a remote server may be used for faster rendering of an interface which is then cached. (d) A remote application is displayed on a PDA — again a remote server may be used to quickly fill the cache with the required interfaces.

devices such as PDAs and cellphones. These scenarios require that SUPPLE be able to present interfaces on devices other than those executing application logic.

Furthermore, our measurements show that SUPPLE optimization-based rendering can take up to 40 seconds to render an interface on a PDA such as a Dell Axim v50x. Thus we require that SUPPLE be able to utilize a remote rendering service (we refer to it as the *solver server*) to accelerate the rendering process, whenever network connectivity is available. Figure 11 illustrates different modes of operation supported by SUPPLE. In order to enable disconnected operation and to save power, aggressive caching of rendering results is also supported. In the remainder of this section we summarize SUPPLE's distributed architecture.

Being able to render interfaces for remote application is a common feature of today's interface generation systems, like the previously mentioned Personal Universal Controller [5] and the Ubiquitous Interactor [7]. However, the computational complexity of our decision-theoretic rendering algorithm create unique challenges for the distribution of our system.

SUPPLE naturally supports distribution of the application and the interface, when its XML-based syntax is used to describe the functional specification. We have also implemented a distributed framework, based on Java RMI, that achieves the same result when the programatic interface is used. SUPPLE automatically choses local or remote bindings depending on the configuration, and the application programmer need not be aware that distributed operation is involved.

Currently the remote solver server can only be invoked using Java RMI, because our device model is not fully declarative.[3] In the future, however, we plan to implement the solver server as a web service.

---

[3] Both the factors comprising cost functions and the elements of the widget factory are described procedurally. As a result, appropriate class definitions may need to be submitted together with a rendering request.

As a bootstrapping measure, we have implemented a local discovery mechanism based on Multicast DNS (base protocol for Apple's Bonjour) so that display devices can easily detect available applications and solver servers in their
environments. Developers are free to replace it with whatever local or global
discovery mechanism is most appropriate for their deployment environment.

6   Quantitative Evaluation

In this Section, we evaluate SUPPLE's versatility, quantify the complexity of
interface specifications, report on the rendering time for different devices, and
measure the size of messages transmited during distributed operation. Additionally, Section 3.1 described our user study which evaluated the split interface and
altered prominence adaptation methods.

We demonstrate SUPPLE's versatility by exhibiting the wide range of different types of interfaces it has generated. Earlier in the paper, we presented
a stereo controller (Figure 2), a fully functional email client (Figure 4), an interface to Amazon web services (Figure 5), a map-based interface (Figure 3),
a controller for classroom equipement (Figure 6), and an adaptive print dialog
box (Figure 9). The wide diversity of these applications demonstrates SUPPLE is
capable of handling complex interfaces and rich data types (*i.e.*, the capability
requirement).

Comparisons of the code quantity or complexity among different approaches
are often controversial. Yet, we feel it is useful to report on the amount of code[4]
devoted to the description and management of the user interface for all the
examples reported in this paper (*e.g.*, as a proxy for easy of use requirement).
These numbers are reported in Table 2 and are for the programmatic (as opposed
to the XML-based) encoding of the interfaces.

In service of the extensibility requirement, Table 3 reports the rendering
times for different interfaces and different platforms. For interfaces running on a
desktop computer, the generation times support fully interactive operation. PDA
users can also experience fast interface generation times if they have network
access to a remote solver. Even disconnected PDA users are not prevented from
using SUPPLE but they may have to endure a substantial wait (*e.g.*, up to 40s) the
first time any given interface is rendered. Future renderings are instantaneous,
because of the caching mechanism.

We have also measured the sizes of the messages that need to be exchanged
in order to invoke a remote solver. The functional specification sizes vary from
4.8kB to 11.5kB while the rendered solutions are all smaller than 3.6kB. These
sizes make a solver server an option, not only on WiFi networks, but also on
slower Bluetooth or 3G cellphone connections.

---

[4] Numbers were calculated using the Metrics plugin for Eclipse available at
`metrics.sourceforge.net`.

	Print Dialog	Map	Amazon	Email	Stereo	Classroom
Lines of code	117	47	59	475	133	73

Table 2. Lines of code used to construct and manage the user interfaces for the applications presented throughout this paper and for the Classroom controller from [3].

	Print Dialog	Map	Amazon	Email	Stereo	Classroom
PC	0.31s	0.25s	1.2s	0.21s	1.5s	0.55s
PDA (local)	—	—	—	—	40s	29s
PDA (remote)	—	—	—	—	3.1s	2.5s

Table 3. Time required to render user interfaces on different platforms. The three conditions include interfaces being rendered locally on a desktop computer (PC) and interfaces rendered on a PDA either locally or on a remote solver server running on a desktop computer. In the last case the times include the communication overhead.

7   Related Work

Researchers have investigated model-based user interface systems including automatic interface generation for many years, yielding impressive systems [15]. Unfortunately, none of the prior work meets our five requirements. Projects like the UIML [1], XIML [11] or the Ubiquitous Interactor [7] provide a device-independent way of representing various aspects of the user interface but ultimately all require that the application designer specify how abstract elements be mapped to concrete widgets on various target platforms.

The Personal Universal Controller (PUC) [5] comes closer to meeting our requirements as it provides a domain-independent language for abstractly describing user interfaces in terms of their functionality and it provides a set of rendering algorithms for a small number of different platforms. This system, however, is intended mainly for rendering interfaces for appliances as a replacement for traditional remote controls. Its rule-based rendering algorithms relies on specific domain knowledge and makes it inflexible even to the changes in the screen size of the device it runs on. XWeb [8], is even further limited by the fact that leaf widgets are pre-specified and only their layout is chosen dynamically.

Adaptive interfaces were also pursued in the context of web sites [9] and mobile portals [14] but in the desktop context, most work was limited to menus and list selections like the Split Menus research [13].

8   Conclusions

This paper presents SUPPLE — an automatic user interface generation toolkit that supports rapid prototyping and deployment of ubiquitous applications across different platforms. We make the following contributions that turned a research prototype into a practical and powerful tool:

- We provide a detailed description of the functional specification language for modeling user interfaces and we extend it with three new classes of features: explicit support for subtyping; new types for representing images, map locations and vectors; and the *alternatives* specification elements that give the designers greater control over different subsets of functionality to be presented on different classes of devices.
- We describe a new adaptation strategy, termed *split interfaces* that provides the benefits of allowing users fast access to frequently used functionality without needlessly disorienting them. This change required a fundamental extension to our rendering algorithm, enabling it to handle functional specifications which are directed acyclic graphs not trees.
- We support explicit customization actions, which allows both users and the designers to change the structure of the interface or to override SUPPLE's automatic rendering choices.
- We use a distributed architecture, that enables user interfaces to be presented on remote device; it also allows impoverished devices with network connectivity to use remote interface solver servers for faster rendering of the interfaces. Our architecture also supports caching of the previously rendered interfaces for faster presentation and disconnected operation.
- Our evaluation demonstrates the feasibility of the practical deployment of SUPPLE. Our user study (Section 3.1) supports the *split interfaces* as an effective and non-distracting method to adapt interfaces to user's tasks.

SUPPLE satisfies the five desiderata listed in Section 1 and is a promising platform for ubiquitous interfaces. In order to fully evaluate SUPPLE's impact, we are releasing it as an open source toolkit for public use.

In the future we plan to extend the specification language to allow drag and drop operations on platforms that provide that capability and to support more complex map-based interactions where additional interactive objects can be overlaid over the map. Finally, following [12], we plan to extend SUPPLE to work with multiple modalities, including speech.

Acknowledgments We thank Don Patterson, Michael Cafarella and the anonymous reviewers for comments on the earlier versions of the manuscript. This research is supported by NSF grant IIS-0307906, ONR grant N00014-02-1-0932 and by DARPA project CALO through SRI grant number 03-000225.

References

1. M. Abrams, C. Phanouriou, A. L. Batongbacal, S. M. Williams, and J. E. Shuster. UIML: An appliance-independent xml user interface language. *WWW8 / Computer Networks*, 31(11-16):1695–1708, 1999.
2. L. Findlater and J. McGrenere. A comparison of static, adaptive, and adaptable menus. In *Proceedings of ACM CHI 2004*, pages 89–96, 2004.

3. K. Gajos and D. S. Weld. Supple: automatically generating user interfaces. In *IUI'04*, Funchal, Madeira, Portugal, 2004. ACM Press.
4. K. Gajos and D. S. Weld. Preference elicitation for interface optimization. In *Proceedings of UIST 2005*, Seattle, WA, USA, 2005.
5. J. Nichols, B. Myers, M. Higgins, J. Hughes, T. Harris, R. Rosenfeld, and M. Pignol. Generating remote control interfaces for complex appliances. In *Proceedings of UIST'02*, Paris, France, 2002.
6. J. Nichols, B. A. Myers, M. Higgins, J. Hughes, T. K. Harris, R. Rosenfeld, and M. Pignol. Generating remote control interfaces for complex appliances. In *UIST'02*, Paris, France, 2002.
7. S. Nylander, M. Bylund, and A. Waern. The ubiquitous interactor - device independent access to mobile services. In *CADUI'2004*, Funchal, Portugal, 2004.
8. D. R. Olsen, S. Jefferies, T. Nielsen, W. Moyes, and P. Fredrickson. Cross-modal interaction using XWeb. In *UIST'00*, pages 191–200, San Diego, California, United States, 2000. ACM Press.
9. M. Perkowitz and O. Etzioni. Towards adaptive web sites: Conceptual framework and case study. *Artificial Intelligence*, 118:245–276, 2000.
10. S. Ponnekanti, B. Lee, A. Fox, P. Hanrahan, and T. Winograd. ICrafter: A service framework for ubiquitous computing environments. In *Proceedings of Ubicomp 2001*, pages 56–75, 2001.
11. A. Puerta and J. Eisenstein. XIML: A universal language for user interfaces, 2002. unpublished paper available at http://www.ximl.org/.
12. D. Reitter, E. Panttaja, and F. Cummins. UI on the fly: Generating a multimodal user interface. In *HLT/NAACL-04*, 2004.
13. A. Sears and B. Shneiderman. Split menus: effectively using selection frequency to organize menus. *ACM Trans. Comput.-Hum. Interact.*, 1(1):27–51, 1994.
14. B. Smyth and P. Cotter. Personalized adaptive navigation for mobile portals. In *Proceedings of ECAI/PAIS'02*, Lyons, France, 2002.
15. P. Szekely. Retrospective and challenges for model-based interface development. In F. Bodart and J. Vanderdonckt, editors, *Design, Specification and Verification of Interactive Systems '96*, pages 1–27, Wien, 1996. Springer-Verlag.
16. D. S. Weld, C. Anderson, P. Domingos, O. Etzioni, K. Gajos, T. Lau, and S. Wolfman. Automatically personalizing user interfaces. In *IJCAI03*, Acapulco, Mexico, August 2003.

Analysis of Chewing Sounds
for Dietary Monitoring

Oliver Amft[1], Mathias Stäger[1], Paul Lukowicz[2], and Gerhard Tröster[1]

[1] Wearable Computing Lab.,
Swiss Federal Institute of Technology (ETH) Zürich, Switzerland,
www.wearable.ethz.ch
{amft,staeger,troester}@ife.ee.ethz.ch
[2] Institute for Computer Systems and Networks, University for Health Sciences,
Medical Informatics and Technology (UMIT), Hall in Tirol, Austria,
http://csn.umit.at
paul.lukowicz@umit.at

Abstract. The paper reports the results of the first stage of our work on an automatic dietary monitoring system. The work is part of a large European project on using ubiquitous systems to support healthy lifestyle and cardiovascular disease prevention. We demonstrate that sound from the user's mouth can be used to detect that he/she is eating. The paper also shows how different kinds of food can be recognized by analyzing chewing sounds. The sounds are acquired with a microphone located inside the ear canal. This is an unobtrusive location widely accepted in other applications (hearing aids, headsets). To validate our method we present experimental results containing 3500 seconds of chewing data from four subjects on four different food types typically found in a meal. Up to 99% accuracy is achieved on eating recognition and between 80% to 100% on food type classification.

1 Introduction

Healthy lifestyle and disease prevention are a major concern for large portions of the population. Considering the worrying trend of sky-rocketing health care costs and the ageing population, these are not just personal but also important socio-economic issues. As a consequence all concerned parties: individuals, health insurance and governments are willing to spend considerable resources on tools that help people develop and maintain healthy habits. In Europe a considerable portion of research funding in this area is directed at mobile and ubiquitous computing technology. Within this program our group is involved in the 34 Million Euro MyHeart project that includes 35 medical, design, textile and electronics related research institutions and companies.

The aim of the consortium is to develop schemes that combine long term physiological monitoring and behavioral analysis with a personalized direct or professional-observed feedback to help users reduce their risk of cardiovascular disease. As is well known, the three main aspects that need to be addressed are

M. Beigl et al. (Eds.): UbiComp 2005, LNCS 3660, pp. 56–72, 2005.

stress, exercise and diet. In the project our group focuses on the later. Our aim is to develop wearable sensing technology to aid the user in monitoring his eating habits. In this paper we report on results of the first stage of this work: using wearable microphones to detect and classify chewing sounds (called mastication sounds) from the user's mouth.

1.1 Dietary Monitoring

Dietary monitoring includes a variety of factors starting from the diet composition to frequency, duration and speed of eating, all of which can be relevant health issues. Today such monitoring is almost entirely done 'manually' by user questionnaires. Electronic devices are at best used as intelligent log books that can derive long term trends, calculate calories from entered data and give simple user recommendations. The collection and entry of the data has to be done by the user which involves considerable effort. As a consequence, as anyone who has ever attempted a diet knows, compliance tends to be very poor.

Since prevention involves the adaptation of a healthier lifestyle, long term, quasi permanent monitoring (months or years) is needed to really make an impact on the risk of cardiovascular diseases. Thus any, even very rudimentary, tool that reduce the effort and interaction involved in data collection and entry could make a big difference.

1.2 Automating Dietary Monitoring

The ultimate goal of a system that precisely and 100% reliably determines the type and amount of all and any food that the user has consumed is certainly more of a dream then a realistic concept. However, we believe that with a combination of wearable sensors and a degree of environmental augmentation useful assistive systems are conceivable. On one hand, such systems could provide a rough estimate on the food consumption much like many today's physical activity monitoring devices provide only a rough guess of the caloric expenditure. On the other hand, it could be used as an entry assistant that, at the end of the day, would present the user with its best guess of when, how much, and what he has eaten and ask him to correct the errors and fill the gaps.

Overall we imagine such a non-invasive dietary monitoring support system to rely on the following three components:

1. Monitoring of food intake through appropriate wearable sensors. The main possibilities are
   (a) detecting and analyzing chewing sounds,
   (b) using electrodes mounted on the base of the neck (e.g in a collar) to detect and analyze bolus swallowing,
   (c) using motion sensors on hands to detect food intake related motions.
2. Monitoring food preparation/purchase through appropriate environmental augmentation. Here, approaches such as using RFID-tags to recognize food components or communicating with the restaurant computer to get a description and nutrition facts of the order are conceivable.

3. Including user habits and high level context detection as additional information sources. Here, one could accentuate the fact that eating habits tend to be associated with locations, times and other activities. Thus information on location (e.g in the dining room sitting at the table), time of day, other activity (unlikely to eat while jogging) etc. provide useful hints.

1.3   Paper Contributions

In the paper we concentrate on the first component of the envisioned system: food intake detection. Specifically, we consider the detection and classification of chewing sounds. To this end the paper presents the following results:

1. We show that good quality chewing sound signal can be obtained from a microphone placed in the ear canal. Since much of the acoustic signal generated by mechanical interaction of teeth and food during occlusion is transmitted by bone conduction, these sounds are actually much stronger than the speech signal. At the same time the location is unobtrusive and proven acceptable in applications such as hearing aids or recent high end mobile phone headsets.
2. We show that chewing sequences can be discriminated from a signal containing a mixture of speech, silence and chewing.
3. We present a method that detects the beginning of single chews in a chewing sequence.
4. We show that chewing sound based discrimination between different kinds of food is possible with a high accuracy.

For the above methods we present an experimental evaluation with a set of four different food products selected to represent different categories of food that might be present in a meal. The experiments consists of a total of 650 chewing sequences, from 4 subjects that amount to a total of 3500 seconds of labeled data. We show that recognition rates of up to 99% can be achieved for the chewing segment identification and of between 80 and 100% for the food recognition.

Overall, while much still remains to be done, our work proves the feasibility of using chewing sound analysis as an important component in a diet monitoring system. An important aspect of our contribution is the fact that the type of information derived by our system (what has actually been eaten) is very difficult to derive using other means.

1.4   Related Work

Activities of daily living are of central interest for high-level context-aware computing. Information acquisition can be realized by distributing sensors in the environment and on the human body. Realization of intelligent environments have been studied, e.g. in the context of smart homes [1] and mobile devices [2]. These works are generally focused on enhancing the quality of life, e.g. for independent living [3,4]. Smart identification systems have also been developed [5] which may provide information associated to nutrition phases, e.g. smart cups [6].

The interaction of chewing, acoustic sensation and perception of textures in food has been studied intensively in food science. Work in this area has been dedicated mainly to the relation of chewing sounds on the sensation of crispness and crunchiness. This was done by investigating air-conducted noises produced during chewing [7, 8] or by instrumental monitoring of the deformation under force [9,10,11,12] and studying correlation with sensory perception [13,14]. The loudness of a foodstuff during deformation depends mainly on the inner structure, i.e. cell arrangement, impurities and existing cracks [15]. Wet cellular materials, e.g. apples and lettuce, are termed wet crisp since the cell structures contain fluids whereas dry crisp products, e.g. potato chips have air inclusions [16]. A general force deflection model has been proposed [17] interpreting the acoustic emissions as micro-events of fracture in brittle materials under compression.

Initially Drake [9] studied the chewing sound signal in humans when chewing crisp and hard food products. It was found that a normal chewing cycle after bringing the food piece to the mouth cavity can be partitioned into two adjacent phases: Gross cutting the ingested material and conversion in fine grained particles. This process is understood as a gradually decomposition of the material structure during chewing and is audible as a decline of the sound level [9]. A swallowable bolus is formed after a certain level of lubrication and particle size has been reached. A first attempt was made by DeBelie [18] to discriminate two classes of crispness in apples by analyzing principal components in the sound spectrum of the initial bite.

Originating from the pioneering work on the auscultation of the masticatory system (system related to chewing) done by Brenman [19] and Watt [20] the stability of occlusion and has been assessed in the field of oral rehabilitation by analyzing teeth contact sounds (gnathosonic analysis) [21]. Similarly the sounds produced by the temporomandibular joints during jaw opening and closing movements have been studied regarding joint dysfunction [22]. It is not expected that these sound sources provide a audible contribution to chewing of food materials in healthy subjects. However, these studies provide information regarding sound transducer types and mounting position that may be usable also for the analysis of chewing sounds. Recent investigations [23, 21] evaluated measurement methodology, applicable transducers types and positions.

2   Methodology

This section will give an overview of our approach. It is important to note that, as described in the introduction, we consider the sound analysis to be just one part of a larger dietary monitoring system. This means that sound analysis is not meant to solve the entire dietary monitoring problem by itself. Instead the goal of our work is to demonstrate that a significant amount of useful information *that is difficult to obtain through other means* can be extracted from chewing sound analysis. Furthermore, the question how it can be expected to interact with other context information is an important research question pursued by our group (although it is not the focus of this paper).

2.1   Approach

Nutrition intake can be coarsely divided into three phases: fracturing (tearing) the food mainly with the incisors, chewing of the pieces and swallowing of the bolus. Ultimately, all three phases should be analyzed since the bolus formation process differs for characteristic food materials [24], e.g. a dry potato chip differs in structure, fluid compartments and chewing from cooked pasta. Initial bites may have more distinctive properties [18], but occur less often and are not available for all food types. A combination of fracture sound and bolus production process features may permit the acoustic detection of food products.

In this paper, we concentrate on the longest phase. Therefore we have chosen to analyze the sound of normal chewing cycles, i.e. beginning after intake of the food piece up to and excluding swallowing of the bolus. We stopped with analyzing the sound when the amplitude level decayed to approximately 5dB above the noise level.

Fig. 1 illustrates the overall structure of our approach. It consists of three main steps: signal acquisition, chewing segment identification and food type classification.

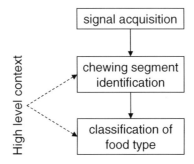

Fig. 1. Approach to the analysis of chewing sounds

The challenge of signal acquisition is to identify a microphone position that combines good amplitude levels for the chewing sounds, with good suppression of other sounds at a location that is comfortable and socially acceptable to the user.

For chewing segment identification this paper considers only sound-related means. In particular, we investigate a classifier that can distinguish between a broad range of chewing sound and various speech/conversation sounds. In a wearable computing environment, other means are possible. E.g., food intake is usually accompanied by moving the arm up and bringing the hand close to the users mouth. The lower arm is then pointing away from the earths center of gravity; something which can easily detected by an accelerometer mounted on the users wrist. However, the user can perform similar movements for other activities (e.g. scratching his chin) so other information from sensors in the environment might be needed (e.g. location information that the user is in the kitchen or the dining room).

Once a segment is classified as being a chewing sound, the type of food needs to be identified. Again, we focus on the audio analysis of the chewing sound. In doing so, we do not aim to be able to pick any of the thousands of possible food types. This would clearly be unrealistic. Instead we assume (1) that we have a certain prior knowledge about the type of foods that are relevant to the particular situation and (2) that often it is sufficient to just be able to identify a general type of food or be able to say "could have been XY". The first assumption is not as far fetched as it might sound. The intelligent refrigerator/cardboard that knows what food is inside and what has been taken out (e.g. through RFID) is the prototypical ubiquitous application. In a restaurant credit card information or an electronic menu could be used to constrain the number of possibilities. Additionally, people have certain fairly predictable eating habits. The second point relates to the type of application that is required. As stated in the introduction, the system does not need be fully automated to be useful and to be an improvement over current 'manual' monitoring. Thus it is perfectly sufficient if at the end of the day the system can remind the user that for example "at lunch you had something wet and crisp (could have been salad) and some soft texture stuff (spaghetti or potatoes)" and asks him to fill in the details. From the above considerations we concentrate our initial work on being able to distinguish between a small set of predefined foods and on the distinction between certain food classes.

2.2   Experiments

The evaluation of all methods described in the remainder of the paper has been performed using the following experimental setup.

Test subjects: Four subjects (2 female, 2 male, mean age 29 years) were instructed to eat different food products normally, with the mouth closed during chewing. In this way the chewing phase of the nutrition cycle is covered: Beginning after intake of the food piece up to swallowing of the bolus (see Sec. 2.1).

By restricting our experiments to the chewing phase, we ensure that the recognition works solely on chewing. Specifically, we exclude swallowing and tearing sounds since these phases have different acoustic characteristics. Fracturing (tearing) and swallowing sounds are regarded as additional source of information and may be analyzed independently. Since these events are not occurring at the same high frequency than chewing, they are considered less relevant.

The subjects had no denture, no acute teeth or facial pain and no known history of occlusion or temporomandibular joint dysfunction. Furthermore none of the subjects expressed a strong dislike of any food product in this study.

Test objects: The food products shown in Table 1 have been selected since they imitate typical components in a meal or daily nutrition. The food groups reflect the acoustic behavior during chewing and not their nutrition value. They can be

simply reproduced with a high fidelity. Furthermore some of the crisp-classified
products have been referenced in texture studies before: Potato chips [17] and
apples [18]. Beside the dry-crisp and wet-crisp categories, a third acoustic group
of "soft texture" foods have been included: Cooked pasta and cooked rice.

Table 1. Details for the food products and categorization

Food product	Food group	Product/Ingredients/Preparation
Potato chips	dry-crisp	Zweifel, potato chips (approx. 3cm in diameter)
Apple	wet-crisp	type "Jonagold" and "Gala" washed, cut in pieces, with skin
Mixed lettuce	wet-crisp	endive, sugar loaf, frisée, raddichio, chicory, arugula
Pasta	"soft texture"	spaghetti (al dente)
Rice	"soft texture"	rice without skin

Initial evaluation of the sound data showed that the rice recordings were
smallest in amplitude of all recorded foods. The potato chips produced the highest amplitude for all subjects. Fig. 5 illustrates a typical waveforms recorded for
apples.

Table 2 depicts the inspected sound durations for the food products from all
subjects. The number of single chews is the number given by the single chew
detection algorithm explained in Sec. 5.1. The single chews per chewing sequence
reflects the authors' experience that usually potato chips are destruced with only
a few chews, whereas pasta or lettuce require several chews to masticate properly.

Table 2. Statistics of the acquired and inspected sound database for all food
products

Food product	Time recorded and inspected	No. of chewing sequences	Detected No. of single chews	Single chews per chewing sequence
Potato chips	677 sec	179	979	5.5
Apple	1226 sec	245	1538	6.3
Mixed lettuce	1054 sec	152	1691	11.1
Pasta	630 sec	74	1290	17.4
Rice[a]	240 sec	-	-	-
Total	3827 sec	650	5498	

[a] omitted because of small amplitude, see Sec. 4

Test procedure: A electret condenser microphone (Type Sony ECM-C115) was
placed in the ear canal as described in Sec. 3. After positioning, the microphone

fixation was checked to avoid interference between movements of the jaw and the microphone in the ear canal. A second microphone of the same type was used at collar level, at the side of the instrumented ear, as reference to detect possible environmental sounds during inspection. The waveforms were recorded at a sampling frequency of 44.1 kHz, 16 bit resolution.

All products were served on a plate. Cutlery was used for the mixed lettuce, pasta and rice. Subjects were instructed to take pieces, small enough to be ingested and chewed at once, as described above. The temperature of pasta and rice was cold enough to allow normal chewing.

3   Positioning of the Microphone

Sound produced during the masticatory process can be detected by air- and bone-conduction. Frequency analysis of air-conduced sounds from chewed potato chips showed spectral energy between zero and 10 kHz [10] although the frequency range with highest amplitude for various crisp products are in the range of 1 kHz−2 kHz [25]. Bone-conducted sounds are transmitted through the mandibular bones to the inner ear. The soft tissue of mouth and jaw damp high frequencies and amplify at the resonance frequency of the mandible (160 Hz) when chewed with closed mouth [11].

Condenser or dynamic microphone transducers have been used in texture studies literature at various places with the goal to detect and reproduce human perception. Mainly the following positions were evaluated: In front of the mouth [9,10], at the outer ear above the ear canal [13], a few centimeters in front of the ear canal opening [12], pressed against the cheek [9,12] or placed over the ear canal opening [9,18]. Gnathosonic studies used a stereo-stethoscope technique [20] and microphones [11] at the forehead or over the zygoma [26]. More recently a method using head-phones with the microphones positioned over the ear canal opening has been proposed [21].

Table 3. Evaluated microphone positions

Microphone	Position
1	Inner ear, directed towards eardrum (Hearing aid position)
2	2cm in front of mouth (Headset microphone position)
3	At cheek (Headset position)
4	5cm in front of ear canal opening (Reference position for audible chewing sounds)
5	Collar (Collar microphone position)
6	Behind outer ear (Hidden by the outer ear, used by older hearing aid models)

Several positions for the microphone have been evaluated for this study as indicated in Table 3. This list includes some of the positions used in previous work. The evaluation of ubiquitous positions, not hindering the user's perception was emphasized. To this end, positions 1, 5 and 6 are favorable because their implementation can be hidden in human anatomy or in cloths.

Potential artifacts introduced by daily use could interfere significantly with the microphone function. This may affect position 5 since it has the disadvantage of being hidden under cloths or disturbed by cloth sounds. Position 1 has the advantage of being less affected by loud environmental noises since it is embedded directly into the ear canal: With a directional microphone oriented towards the eardrum, the intensity of any noise from the environment is reduced.

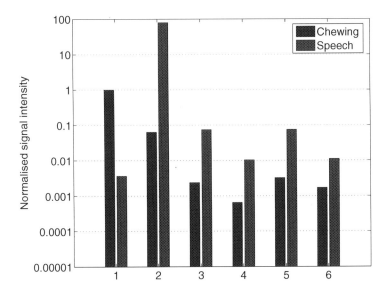

Fig. 2. Signal intensity of different microphone positions (see Table 3)

The position of the microphone was evaluated while a subject was chewing potato chips and while the subject was speaking. The mean amplitude perceived at position 1 was used as reference for normalization. Fig. 2 depicts the relation of the signal amplitude intensity shown on a logarithmic scale. It can be seen clearly that position 1 not only has the highest intensity for chewing sounds but it is also the only position with chewing sound intensity higher than speech intensity. Therefore for all further measurements position 1 was used.

A microphone at position 1 does not need to hinder the person, as modern hearing aids prove. Applicable microphones could be very small and combined with an earphone be used for other applications, e.g. mobile phones. For example, modern hearing aids already operate with a combined microphone/earphone.

4 Chewing Segment Identification

The identification of chewing segments in a continuous sound signal can be regarded as a base functionality and hence is of high importance for the detailed analysis of the masticated food type. We see mainly two different methods based on audio signal processing.

A: Intensity of Audio Signal: In an environment, like a living room, with background music playing or in a quiet restaurant, the chewing sound picked up in the inner ear is much louder than a normal conversation or background music. This is indicated in the sample recording shown in Fig. 3.

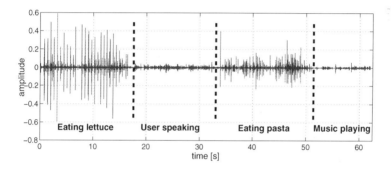

Fig. 3. Chewing sound and speech recording in a room with background music

B: Chewing Sound – Speech Classifier: Despite the general suppression of the speech signal, loud speech can at times develop amplitude peaks similar to chewing signals. Therefore it is necessary to be able to separate these two classes. This is achieved by calculating audio features from a short signal segment of length t_w, averaging the features over N_{avg} segments and then finally classifying them with a previously trained classifier [27].

Features: We used features that are popular in the area of speech, audio and auditory scene recognition [28,29,30]. In the temporal domain, those were zero-crossing rate and fluctuation of amplitude. Frequency domain features were evaluated based on a 512-point Fast Fourier Transformation (FFT) using a Hanning window. Here, the features included: frequency centroid, spectral roll-off point with the threshold of 0.93, fluctuation of spectrum and band energy ratio in 4 logarithmically divided sub-bands. Additionally 6 cepstral coefficients (CEP) were evaluated. Both time and frequency domain features were evaluated on a window of $t_w = 11.6$ ms. No overlap between the windows was used.

The features were averaged over N_{avg} windows to improve the recognition results. This method helped to bridge pause gaps between the chewing sounds. These gaps vary between 100 ms and 600 ms depending on the chewed material and the progression of decomposition (see Fig. 5). Longer pauses may be observed at the beginning of a chewing sequence for larger food pieces as well as before and after partial bolus swallowing.

Classifiers: A C4.5 decision tree classifier from the Weka Toolkit [31] was trained with the aforementioned features. The classifier was 10-fold cross-validated on a two class data set. The first class contained all food products as specified in Table 2 except cooked rice. Rice was excluded since individual classification of food products against speech signals showed weak results for rice. This was expected from the low signal-noise ratio of the rice sounds. The second class included various speech signal segments from several speakers as well as conversation of test subjects and the authors.

Since the accuracy of a classifier depends on the class distribution, the ROC curve (Receiver Operating Characteristic) is presented instead (see Fig. 4). ROC curves help to visualize classifier performance over the whole range of frequency of occurrence [32]; the best classifier is the one to the top-left corner. This is useful in our case since the number of occurrences of speech and chewing sounds may vary and may not be known beforehand. Clearly, the classifier that uses the CEP features dominates. This was expected since the CEP features help to pick out speech sequences. Furthermore, the number N_{avg} of averaging frames was varied. We found that the highest recognition rates can be achieved if N_{avg} is chosen so that the features are at least averaged over one single chew which takes about one second. In our case this occurs if $N_{avg} > 1 \text{ sec}/t_w = 86.2$.

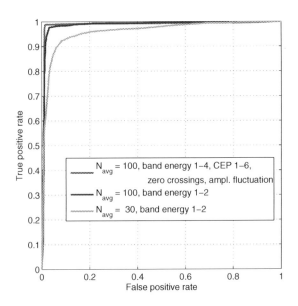

Fig. 4. ROC curve for chewing sounds (positives) and speech sounds (negatives)

5   Discrimination of Foods Products

5.1   Isolation of Single Chews

First trials in separating different food products with the same methods as in the previous section (i.e. calculating features over a large window) produced recognition rates around 60%. The reason for this is mainly due to the rather long pause between single chews, which produces the same audio signature for all food items.

To overcome this problem we have looked in more detail at the temporal structure of a typical chewing sequence (see Fig. 5). It can be seen that the audio signal of one chew is mainly composed of four phases: The closing of the mandible to crush the material, a small pause, the opening of the mandible in which material that stick to the upper and lower teeth is uncompressed, and again a pause. The timing between those phases is given mainly by the mechanical properties of the food and the physical limitations of the mandible. All test subject showed almost the same timing for the same food, with the exception of a longer or shorter pause in phase 4 (fast/slow eater). The four phases are very well distinguishable in crispy food, in softer food like pasta the phases tend to merge. Still, the pause in phase 4 and the increase in amplitude at the beginning of phase 1 remain.

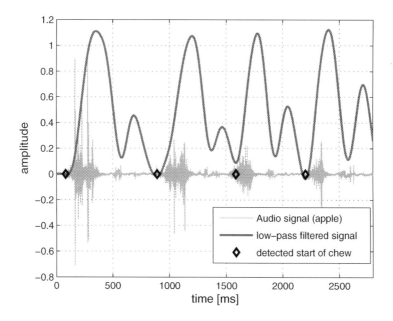

Fig. 5. Sample sound signal observed for chewing an apple

A relatively simple algorithms helps us the detect the beginning of each chew. The short-time signal energy in a 20 ms window is compared to a energy threshold and the resulting signal is set to 1 if the short-time signal energy is larger than the threshold and to 0 otherwise. The resulting signal is low-pass filtered with a 4th order butterworth filter. We found that a filter with a 3dB cut-off frequency of 4 to 5 Hz reliably responds to the pause in phase 4 while filtering out the shorter pause in phase 2. With help of the hill climbing algorithm the beginning of each chew is detected as shown in Fig. 5. We found that this algorithm can detect the start point of about 90% of all chews while producing only very little insertions.

5.2   Classification

Once the audio signal is segmented into single chews, the segments are classified using the same procedure as in Sec. 4. Several features were applied to a short window that was consecutively shifted. We found that a 11.6 ms window with a shift of 8.7 ms works best for our sound classes. The most promising features were: zero crossing rate, band energy ratios, fluctuation of amplitude, fluctuation of spectrum and bandwidth. The features were further averaged over the length of a single chew. The length of a single chew was used as an additional feature and helped to improve the recognition rate of especially the pasta, since soft-texture foods have shorter durations of chews. The features were then 10-fold cross-validated with a C4.5 decision tree classifier. Recognition rates range around 66% to 86% and the corresponding confusion matrix is listed in Table 4.

Table 4. Confusion matrix for single chews

a	b	c	d	← classified as	Accuracy
669	170	25	115	a = Chips	68.34%
183	1024	41	290	b = Apple	66.58%
25	39	1112	114	c = Pasta	86.20%
125	293	95	1178	d = Lettuce	69.66%

Since the material inside the mouth can not change between single chews, a majority decision over a whole chewing cycle was performed. This measure resulted in an increase of recognition rate of 15 to 20% as shown in Table 5. It can be seen that there is some confusion between apple and lettuce which can

Table 5. Confusion matrix for chewing cycles

a	b	c	d	← classified as	Accuracy
156	12	1	10	a = Chips	87.15%
24	198	1	22	b = Apple	80.82%
0	0	74	0	c = Pasta	100.00%
4	21	0	127	d = Lettuce	83.55%

be explained by them belonging into the same food category (see Table 1) and therefore having similar mechanical properties.

6   Conclusion and Future Work

6.1   Conclusion

The work presented in this paper has proven that chewing sound analysis is a valuable component for automated dietary monitoring systems. Specifically we have shown that:

1. A microphone location inside the ear can acquire good quality chewing sounds while suppressing many other sounds originating inside the oral cavity such as speech. At the same time it is a location that has been proven to be acceptable to users in other applications (e.g. hearing aids, headsets). Applicable microphones could be very small, not hindering the normal perception. Moreover, a combination of microphone and earphone for shared use with other applications, e.g. a mobile phone, could be employed.
2. Chewing sounds can be reliably separated from the main sound source inside the mouth cavity: speech.
3. Individual chews can be isolated and partitioned into phases with a simple low pass filter based algorithm
4. Audio analysis can be used to distinguish between a small predefined set of different food types as for example found in a single meal.

The food groups introduced in the experiments reflect the acoustic behavior during chewing and not their nutrition value. The results show, that our approach is not limited to a specific group of foods. Moreover, it is possible to discriminate foods from the same group. The actual nutrition value can be derived either precisely from other monitoring components, e.g. RFID tags of packages, or as an estimate from a generic food database.

An important aspect of our work is the fact that information about the specific type of food which is being chewed is very difficult to derive using other sensor modalities. The only alternative we could think of is video analysis of the items inserted into the mouth. While theoretically feasible it has many problems of its own, in particular sensitivity to light conditions and background clutter as well as large computational complexity.

Overall the results presented in this paper provide crucial groundwork for further development that, we believe, will lead to complete automated dietary monitoring systems. Within the scope of the EU funded MyHeart project we aim to have first versions of such a system within the next two to three years. Additionally, points 1 and 2 have implications beyond dietary monitoring as they allow a fairly accurate recognition of the fact that the user is eating. This in itself is an important context information.

6.2   Future Work

On the sound analysis the next steps that we will undertake are:

1. Modeling temporal evolution of the signal from individual chews with hidden Markov models to further increase the recognition rates and allow similar food types to be distinguished.
2. Modeling the temporal evolution of the individual chewing signals over an entire chewing cycle to extract food type specific parameters. This shall include the number of individual chews needed, their length and the evolution of the sound intensity.
3. Performing studies about the robustness of the system by adding controlled levels of noise.
4. Performing more studies with more, different food types.
5. Performing studies to determine how the recognition performance degrades with increasing number of food types that need to be differentiated.
6. Using a hierarchical approach with an initial classification of the category (dry crisp, wet crisp etc.) and then a category specific algorithm for further recognition, to overcome the above limitation.

Furthermore, other components of a dietary monitoring system will also be investigated. In particular, we will look at the detection of swallowing motion with collar electrodes, analyze the hand motions related to food intake and integrate high level context information relevant to eating habits into the system.

References

[1] Mynatt, E., Melenhorst, A.S., Fisk, A.D., Rogers, W.: Aware technologies for aging in place: understanding user needs and attitudes. In: IEEE Pervasive Computing. Volume 3. (2004) 36–41
[2] Gellersen, H.W., Schmidt, A., Beigl, M.: Multi-sensor context-awareness in mobile devices and smart artifacts. Mobile Networks and Applications 7 (2002) 341–351
[3] Philipose, M., Fishkin, K., Perkowitz, M., Patterson, D., Fox, D., Kautz, H., Hahnel, D.: Inferring activities from interactions with objects. IEEE Pervasive Computing 3 (2004) 50–57
[4] Mihailidis, A., Carmichael, B., Boger, J.: The use of computer vision in an intelligent environment to support aging-in-place, safety, and independence in the home. IEEE Transactions on Information Technology in Biomedicine 8 (2004) 238–247
[5] Römer, K., Schoch, T., Mattern, F., Dübendorfer, T.: Smart identification frameworks for ubiquitous computing applications. In: PerCom 2003: Proc. of the First IEEE Int'l Conference Pervasive Computing and Communications. (2003)
[6] Beigl, M., Gellersen, H.W., Schmidt, A.: MediaCups: Experience with design and use of computer-augmented everyday artefacts. Computer Networks, Special Issue on Pervasive Computing 35 (2001) 401–409
[7] Vickers, Z., Christensen, C.: Relationships between sensory crispness and other sensory and instrumental parameters. Journal of Texture Studies (1980) 291–307
[8] Vickers, Z.: Relationships of chewing sounds to judgements of crispness crunchiness and hardness. Journal of Texture Studies (1981) 121–124

[9] Drake, B.: Food crushing sounds. an introductory study. Journal of Food Science (1963) 233–241

[10] Lee, W., Schweitzer, G., Morgan, G., Shepherd, D.: Analysis of food crushing sounds during mastication: Total sound level studies. Journal of Texture Studies (1990) 156–178

[11] Kapur, K.: Frequency spectrographic analysis of bone conducted chewing sounds in persons with natural and artifcial dentitions. Journal of Texture Studies (1971) 50–61

[12] Dacremont, C., Colas, B., Sauvageot, F.: Contribution of air- and bone-conduction to the creation of sounds perceived during sensory evaluation of foods. Journal of Texture Studies (1991) 443–456

[13] Vickers, Z.: Sensory acoustical and force? Deformation measurements of potato chip crispness. Journal of Texture Studies (1987) 138–140

[14] Szczesniak, A.: Texture: Is it still an overlooked food attribute? Food Technology (1990) 86–95

[15] AlChakra, W., Allaf, K., Jemai, A.: Characterization of brittle food products: Application of the acoustical emission method. Journal of Texture Studies (1996) 327–348

[16] Edmister, J., Vickers, Z.: Instrumental acoustical measures of crispness in foods. Journal of Texture Studies (1985) 153–167

[17] Vincent, J.F.V.: The quantification of crispness. Journal of Science in Food Argiculture (1998) 162–168

[18] DeBelie, N., De Smedt, V., J., D.B.: Principal component analysis of chewing sounds to detect differences in apple crispness. Journal of Postharvest Biology and Technology (2000) 109–119

[19] Brenman, H., Weiss, R., Black, M.: Sound as a diagnostic aid in the detection of occlusion discrepancies. Penn Dental Journal (1966)

[20] Watt, D.: Gnathosonics - a study of sound produced by the masticatory mechanism. Journal of Prosthetic Dentistry (1966)

[21] Prinz, J.: Computer aided gnathosonic analysis: distinguishing between single and multiple tooth impact sounds. Journal of Oral Rehabilitation (2000) 682–689

[22] Widmalm, S., Williams, W., Zengh, C.: Time frequency distribution of tmj sounds. Journal of Oral Rehabilitation (1991)

[23] Tyson, K.: Monitoring the state of occlusion - gnathosonics can be reliable. Journal of Oral Rehabilitation (1998) 395–402

[24] Hutchings, J., Lillford, D.: The perception of food texture - the philosophy of the breakdown path. Journal of Texture Studies (1988) 103–115

[25] Brochetti, D., Penfield, M., Burchfield, S.: Speech analysis techniques: A potential model for the study of mastication sounds. Journal of Texture Studies (1992) 111–138

[26] Watt, D.: Gnathosonics and Occlusal Dynamics. Praeger New York (1981)

[27] Stäger, M., Lukowicz, P., Perera, N., von Büren, T., Tröster, G., Starner, T.: SoundButton: Design of a Low Power Wearable Audio Classification System. In: ISWC 2003: Proc. of the 7th IEEE Int'l Symposium on Wearable Computers. (2003) 12–17

[28] Li, S.Z.: Content-based audio classification and retrieval using the nearest feature line method. IEEE Transactions on Speech and Audio Processing 8 (2000) 619–625

[29] Li, D., Sethi, I., Dimitrova, N., McGee, T.: Classification of general audio data for content-based retrieval. Pattern Recognition Letters 22 (2001) 533–544

[30] Peltonen, V., Tuomi, J., Klapuri, A., Huopaniemi, J., Sorsa, T.: Computational auditory scene recognition. In: IEEE Int'l Conf. on Acoustics, Speech, and Signal Processing. Volume 2. (2002) 1941–1944

[31] Witten, I.H., Frank, E.: Data Mining: Practical Machine Learning Tools and Techniques with Java Implementations. Morgan Kaufmann (1999)

[32] Provost, F., Fawcett, T.: Analysis and visualization of classifier performance: Comparison under imprecise class and cost distributions. In: KDD '97: Proc. of the 3rd Int'l Conference on Knowledge Discovery and Data Mining. (1997) 43–48

Preventing Camera Recording by Designing a Capture-Resistant Environment

Khai N. Truong, Shwetak N. Patel, Jay W. Summet, and Gregory D. Abowd

College of Computing & GVU Center
Georgia Institute of Technology
Atlanta, GA 30324-0280 USA
{khai, shwetak, summetj, abowd}@cc.gatech.edu

Abstract. With the ubiquity of camera phones, it is now possible to capture digital still and moving images anywhere, raising a legitimate concern for many organizations and individuals. Although legal and social boundaries can curb the capture of sensitive information, it sometimes is neither practical nor desirable to follow the option of confiscating the capture device from an individual. We present the design and proof of concept implementation of a capture-resistant environment that prevents the recording of still and moving images without requiring any cooperation on the part of the capturing device or its operator. Our solution involves a tracking system that uses computer vision for locating any number of retro-reflective CCD or CMOS camera sensors in a protected area. A pulsing light is then directed at the lens, distorting any imagery the camera records. Although the directed light interferes with the camera's operation, it can be designed to minimally impact the sight of other humans in the environment.

1 Introduction and Motivation

By the last quarter of 2004, approximately 75% percent of mobile phones in Japan were camera phones; it is expected this number will saturate at 75%-85% in 2005.[1] By 2006, more than 80 percent of mobile phones shipped in the United States and Western Europe will have cameras.[2] Camera phones, and related consumer technologies, make it easy to capture still and moving images anywhere, creating a legitimate concern among those who wish to retain some level of privacy or secrecy. Companies concerned that camera phones compromise the security of their intellectual property often ban such devices from their facilities. These confiscation practices, however, are not always desirable or practical. Although some legal controls and social boundaries may curb inappropriate capture behaviors [2, 3, 8], we believe technological solutions can safeguard against undesired recording without requiring confiscation by an authority or cooperation by the public at large.

---

[1] Source: Eurotechnology, Japan K.K., Camera phones: disruptive innovation for imaging, Market and trend report, 5th Version of October 11, 2004

[2] Source: Gartner Inc. http://www3.gartner.com/press_releases/pr3mar2004a.html

M. Beigl et al. (Eds.): UbiComp 2005, LNCS 3660, pp. 73-86, 2005.
© Springer-Verlag Berlin Heidelberg 2005

Previous work addresses this challenge by disabling recording features in the cameras [5, 6, 9]. In this paper, we present an alternative that requires neither instrumentation nor control of the recording device. Instead, we present a technique for safeguarding the environment itself against recording, creating a so-called "capture-resistant" environment.   Our system detects camera phones in the environment and emits a strong localized light beam at each device to neutralize it from capturing. Although our approach does have limitations, its main strength is that it requires no cooperation on the part of the camera or its owner and it minimally disturbs the natural viewing experience by the human eye.

2   Related Work

Technical solutions have been proposed to prevent or to react to undesired camera capture. Most of these solutions require some sort of instrumentation of a capture device. For example, solutions, such as Safe Haven, leverage the short-range wireless capability available on camera phones (such as Bluetooth or WiFi) to allow the environment to notify the device that the space does not allow photography or other forms of recording [5, 6, 9]. There are many drawbacks to this solution. First, it assumes that the user of the camera would install and use special software on the device and that she would abide by the environmental constraints. Hewlett-Packard has proposed a *paparazzi-proof* camera [7] that automatically modifies images when it receives commands from a remote device. This camera includes a facial recognition feature that selectively blurs certain parts of an image. Other approaches also require different forms of cooperation on the part of the camera or its operator. The Cloak system addresses privacy concerns with surveillance cameras by having users carry a "privacy enabling device" (PED) [1]. This device informs the environment that any footage of the carrier of this device must be sanitized at a later time. A solution called "Eagle Eye" couples a light sensor to a flash unit [4]. When a flash of light is detected, this small wearable device instantaneously flashes back. This technique obscures a portion of the photographic image, similar to the approach described in this paper. However, Eagle Eye only works against still, flash photography.

We take a significantly different approach from these previous solutions in the design of our capture-resistant environment. First, rather than requiring users to trust cameras to sanitize images after the recording has occurred, we actively impede recording at the point of capture, as with Eagle Eye. Second, unlike many previous solutions, our system does not rely on any cooperation or instrumentation on the part of the capture devices or the people operating them. Finally, our solution addresses video capture in addition to still imagery.

We initially focused on protecting stationary regions of an environment, such as a wall. Surfaces in an environment can be covered to prevent capture, but then the surfaces would not be visible. There are numerous commercially-available retro-reflective sprays and shields that can also be placed over a surface to reflect light and flashes in a manner that prevents recording; for example, these products are intended to prevent traffic cameras from capturing the license plate of a car running a red light. These solutions create glares that impact visibility from the human eye as well as the camera sensor. Our solution minimally impacts what an observer in the environment sees while still preventing a camera from being able to record.

3   Design Goals for a Capture-Resistant Environment

Our primary goal in addressing this problem was to design an environment that prevents certain portions of that space from being captured by mobile phones that include a CCD or CMOS camera.[3] This motivation, and review of past related work, highlights the major design goals for building a capture-resistant environment. These are:

- elimination of the need for cooperation or control of the recording devices before, during or after capture;
- prevention of the capture of both still images and video; and
- minimal impact to the view of the environment by the naked human eye.

In addition, this approach should allow for two interesting improvements:

- the ability to allow authorized cameras to record; and
- the possibility of making mobile entities (*e.g.,* people) similarly capture-resistant.

Our design uses a combination of computer vision and projection, described in the next section, to actively search for cameras and systematically block them from recording clear pictures, as opposed to relying on removal or alteration of content later. We envision uses of our system for situations like conferences, tradeshows and museums. For example, some artists want to prevent people taking pictures of their artwork. Similarly, companies may want to limit capture of early prototypes and designs on display in research laboratories or exhibits at tradeshows.

4   A Capture-Resistant Environment

In this section, we present our capture-resistant environment, which consists of two components. First, a camera detector actively tracks CCD sensors in the environment. When the system detects a camera's CCD sensor, the second system component, the camera neutralizer, directs a localized beam of light at each camera's lens to obstruct its view of the scene. For each component, we describe the theory of operation and our proof of concept implementation. We then critically evaluate the limitations of this prototype, distinguishing the theoretical limits from the current engineering limitations of our specific implementation and discuss how we can extend our system.

---

[3] CCD and CMOS cameras both use semi-conductor based sensors. Our approach works against both types. We will refer to this category of cameras as "CCD cameras" throughout the rest of the paper.

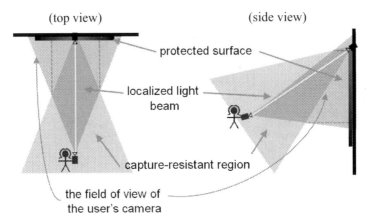

Figure 1. System diagram. When a user introduces a camera into the capture-resistant environment, a camera detector component locates the device within its field of view and the camera neutralizer component emits a localized light beam (yellow) at the camera to block the camera's view of a portion of the surface the system attempts to guard from capture. The red bar indicates the protected surface. The blue indicates the field of view of the user's camera. The pink indicates the camera neutralizer's field of influence. Dashed lines indicate the portion of the protected surface that is affected by the neutralizer's light beam.

4.1 Detecting Cameras in the Environment

CCD cameras have an optical property that produces well-defined light reflections. By tracking these reflections, we can effectively locate and track cameras.

4.1.1 Theory of Operation

Our camera detector leverages the retro-reflective property of the CCD sensor found on most consumer-level digital cameras. Retro-reflection causes light to reflect directly back to its source, independent of its incident angle. This effect is often noticed on photographs when the camera flash can make a subject's eyes appear to glow red, caused by the retro-reflective property of the retina at the back of the eye. Commercial applications of retro-reflection include traffic signs and reflective clothes commonly worn by road construction workers.

CCD sensors are mounted at the focal plane of the camera's optical lens, making them very effective retro-reflectors. Although many objects in the environment exhibit this property, they are typically imperfect retro-reflectors and can be distinguished from CCD cameras as we demonstrate in Section 5. By tracking these retro-reflections we can detect and track cameras pointed at a given area.

4.1.2 Implementation

To detect cameras in the environment, we used a Sony Digital HandyCam video camera placed in *NightShot* mode. IR transmitters surround the lens and a narrow bandpass IR filter covers the detector's lens (Figure 3a). This instrumentation, referred to as the *detector*, projects an IR light beam outwards from the camera and detects any retro-reflective surfaces within the field of view. The specific placement of the IR illuminator around the perimeter of the detector's lens ensures a bright retro-reflection from cameras within the field of view of the detector. The detected CCD cameras can be pointed directly at it or tilted away at slight angles (which we computed to be up to roughly $\pm20°$). This retro-reflection appears as a bright white circular speckle through the IR filtered camera (Figure 2).

We detect reflections by simply locating bright regions in the camera view above a certain luminance threshold (Figure 2). By using a thresholding technique, there is no limit to the number of the cameras that can be detected within the cross-section of the camera detector. In the next section, we discuss the handling of both false positives and false negatives.

Our system effectively tracks cameras at a rate of 15 Hz. A more powerful computer could track at 30 Hz, however 15 Hz is sufficient because a user must hold the average camera still for at least this period of time to avoid motion blur in her picture.

The camera detector has approximately a 45° field of view. Reflections from cameras of varying shapes and sizes can be detected up to 10 meters away. In our proof of concept, at 5 meters away, the cross-section of the detector camera's field of view is roughly a 4m width x 3m height area. Although a zoom lens can be added to a camera, we estimate that 5 meters is roughly the length of a reasonably-sized room. Room sizes and walls naturally prevent people from recording our capture-resistant environment from afar. Our current proof of concept only involves a single detector unit. To ensure that we can detect cameras from all angles, we can measure the angle at which users can approach the surface. Accordingly, we can determine how many detector units we must use to cover that range. We can add additional detectors throughout the environment to find cameras from farther away if needed.

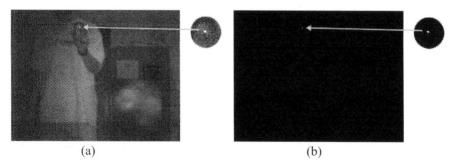

(a)   (b)

Figure 2. On the left is an unprocessed IR view captured by our camera detector with plenty of ambient light in the room. A person holds a camera phone pointed at a region in the environment we want to protect from capture. On the right is the processed view. The camera is detected by locating a bright white circular speckle.

(a)   (b)

Figure 3. The left picture shows our camera detector unit. We outfitted a Sony HandyCam, placed in *NightShot* mode, with a collection of IR transmitters and covered the lens with a narrow bandpass IR filter. The right picture shows our camera detector coupled with a projector to neutralize cameras in the environment.

4.2   Neutralizing Cameras

Once the system detects cameras in the environment, the camera neutralizer component emits localized light beams at each camera lens, resulting in a strong reduction in quality of the taken image for several reasons. First, this effect is similar to taking pictures *contre le soleil*, in which the concentrated light source overwhelms the picture taken (Figure 4a). Secondly, the system emits light beams in a pattern that prevents the CCD cameras from adjusting to the light and prevents the camera from taking a good picture (Figure 4b).

4.2.1   Theory of Operation

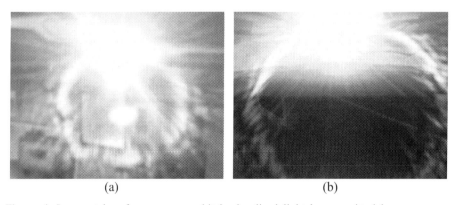

(a)   (b)

Figure 4. Images taken from a camera hit by localized light beam emitted by our camera neutralizer. The picture on the left shows a localized light beam generated using a single color. The picture on the right shows a localized light beam generated using color patterns that do not allow the cameras to adjust to the light source (notice the scan line).

The camera neutralizer leverages the inherently imperfect sensing capabilities of CCD cameras that result in three specific effects, over-exposure, blooming and lens flare. Over-exposure results in an image that is saturated with light obscuring detail. Blooming occurs when a portion of the camera's sensor is exposed to excessive luminosity, resulting in leakage to neighboring regions. For example, a candle in an otherwise dark setting may cause blobs or comet tails around the flame. Although some cameras are capable of compensating for these effects, they typically only handle moderate amounts of light. Lens flare is caused by unwanted light bouncing around the glass and metal inside the camera. The size of the lens flare depends on the brightness of the entering light. High-end cameras with well-designed and coated optics can minimize, but not completely eliminate, lens flare. By shinning a beam of light at the camera lens, such as that emitted by a projector, blooming and lens flare can block significantly any CCD camera from capturing the intended image. Digital cameras employ automatic exposure control algorithms, which reduce blooming and flare. However, there is typically a delay before the sensor stabilizes. Thus a flashing light prevents the camera from stabilizing to the light source.

4.2.2   Implementation

To emit a strong localized light beam at cameras, we pair a projector of 1500 lumens with our camera detector. The projector emits localized light beams of an area slightly larger than the size of the reflection. Pixels in the projected image change between white, red, blue, and green. This approach prevents cameras from adjusting to the light source and forces the cameras to take pictures flooded with light (Figures 4 and 5). In addition, interleaving various projection rates neutralizes a larger variety of cameras. The camera neutralizer continuously emits this light beam until the camera

Figure 5. Left is a camera phone being neutralized by our system (notice the neutralizing light beam over the lens). Top right is the camera view neutralized by the system and bottom right is the camera view when the camera is permitted to capture.

lens is no longer detected. Therefore, this approach works against both still image and video cameras.

We found that the projector can still generate an effective localized light beam when we focus it for up to 5 meters away. Although light from a projector can travel much farther, its luminance decreases with distance. Using the estimate of 5 meters as the length of most rooms, the projector can generate an effective localized light beam in a room. At 5 meters, projected localized light beams within a pyramidal region that has a base of 6 m width x 4.5 m height. To ensure neutralization of cameras from all angles, we can measure the angles from which users can approach the surface and accordingly, determine the number of projectors required to cover that range. We can add additional projectors mounted away from the surface to neutralize cameras from farther away if necessary.

5   Assessing the Design Challenges and Limitations

At this time, we have not measured the performance of the system. We are still experimenting with our proof-of-concept implementation to determine situations in which it breaks down or cases that would cause the system to falsely detect cameras in the environment. This experimentation will result in a list of the necessary conditions against which we will test the system in the future.

In this section, we present how we addressed our original design goals and the challenges and limitations faced in the design of our system. We also describe how our approach addresses the potential attacks or workarounds people may use to circumvent the capture-resistant environment. Finally, we discuss the known theoretical limitations and the engineering deficiencies in our initial prototype.

5.1 Design Goals

The goals of our capture-resistant environment were:
- to remove the need for cooperation or control of the recording devices before, during or after capture;
- to prevent both still images and video from being captured; and
- to minimally impact the view of the environment by the naked human eye.

Our implementation requires neither cooperation from nor control of the recording cameras. Instead, the environment takes sole responsibility for blocking capture of certain parts of an environment. The capture-resistant environment actively tracks CCD cameras present in the space and blocks them with a localized beam of light directed at the camera's lens. The system works with both still and video cameras on all camera phones that use CCD sensors. Our system has little impact on the human eye, only a slight glow that a person may see (caused by the projector). Future implementations of the camera neutralizer will not use projectors and thus would not produce a glow.

In addition, we wanted our solution to allow for two interesting extensions:
- the ability to allow authorized cameras to record; and
- the possibility of making mobile entities (*e.g.,* people) similarly capture-resistant.

In the current implementation we can authorize users to take pictures by turning off the system, but this solution does not allow selected cameras to take pictures while blocking other cameras. A simple enhancement to our system would be to use 2D retro-reflective glyphs (Figure 6) to permit certain cameras to capture while blocking others. The 2D glyph encodes a unique identifier that allows the system to recognize the camera. The owner of the physical space gives out a tag when she wants to allow a specific camera to capture within that space. The glyph must be physically attached near the lens of that camera and would be detected by the camera detector. The system then allows the camera to take pictures in the environment by simply not directing localized light beams at the permitted devices.

Figure 6. A 5 cm x 5 cm retro-reflective glyph pattern is temporarily attached near a camera phone's lens.

Although we do not implement the ability to make moving objects, such as humans similarly resistant, we imagine building a wearable version of our camera detector and neutralizer to prevent records of individuals in public spaces. We discuss in the Section 5.3 how a much more lightweight version of the neutralizer component might be constructed.

5.2   Challenges

Implementation of a capture resistant environment faces two major challenges. First, the system must handle errors involved in detecting cameras. Second, the system must address potential attacks or "workarounds" for circumventing the environment.

82   Khai N. Truong et al.

5.2.1 Errors in Detecting Cameras

A false negative occurs when the camera detector fails to identify a camera. A false positive occurs when the camera detection system mistakenly detects a camera in the environment where one is not actually present.

Handling false negatives
False negatives are detrimental to the security of the space. One solution is to take a naïve approach that assumes that any reflection is a potential camera. This may be appropriate when security is of utmost importance. However, this approach does not work when the CCD camera does not produce a reflection. Occlusion of the CCD from the camera detector would remove the reflection but typically also physically blocks capture. The camera can be angled sufficiently enough away that the incident light fails to reach the detector camera. In this case, the camera is already turned far enough away such that the capture-resistant space does not appear in its field of view. Thus, if there is no light reflection from the CCD then that CCD camera cannot see the region around the detector. We can place multiple pairs of camera detector and neutralizer units around a space for added security

Handling false positives
False positives can be the result of the detection system interpreting reflections from metallic or mirrored surfaces present in the space. Because these surfaces potentially produce the same reflective speckle as a CCD sensor, the system would target a non-existent camera.

False positives are not detrimental to the operation of the system. However, when the system reacts to these false positives, the superfluous projector light produced by the false positive may be distracting or even bothersome for people in the environment. We can address these problems by further analyzing the potential camera speckles. In the case of a reflection caused by metallic or other lens-like surfaces we can determine a false positive by inspecting the suspected reflection from multiple vantage points. The reflection off the surface of a CCD camera is always consistent. If the reflection moves in different vantage point views, then it is not a CCD camera reflection, because these other surfaces are imperfect reflectors, usually due to surface curvature, such as is present with eyeglasses or imperfect finishes like brushed metal. Two camera detectors spaced apart and pointed at the same region can reduce the number of false positives.

The worst false positive situation occurs when the system incorrectly identifies a region near a person's face as a potential camera, irritating or even harming the person's vision. As previously mentioned, the retina in the eye is also retro-reflective to visible light (*e.g.,* from a camera flash), but in our experiments eyes did not reflect enough IR light to become false positives. In our current proof-of-concept implementation, we also do not react to infrared reflections above a certain height, a simplified solution to prevent incorrect identification of human eyes as cameras. In addition, we can enhance the implementation with software that detects facial features in a field of view [7] to address this problem more completely.

5.2.2 Attacks and Workarounds

Aside from physical vandalism to the capture resistant environment, we identify some "workarounds" users may employ with their CCD cameras. We discuss how our system design handles some of these attacks; in many cases, we point out the unobvious ways that our solution inherently addresses the problem. Where appropriate, we provide some theoretical justification for the solutions proposed.

Masks and filters

An attacker may try to mask the camera lens with surfaces like those used in typical sunglasses. These surfaces, however, do not block IR light; thus, our system would still detect the CCD sensors. Mirrored and even polarized sunglasses also fail to prevent the camera detector from finding the CCD. However, sunglasses are effective at mitigating the effects of the neutralizer on the camera. Sunglasses drastically reduce the intensity of the projected light. Despite this reduction, the light pattern and intensity used in this implementation is still effective at neutralizing cameras from capture. A neutralizing beam, such as from a laser, could also solve this problem.

IR filters pose the greatest problems for this particular implementation. The current solution uses pure IR light (880 nm) for CCD sensor detection. An 880 nm notch IR filter could be placed in front of a camera, preventing IR light from reaching the CCD sensor while still allowing other visible light to pass. We can mitigate this attack with a design that also detects IR filters in the environment and treats them as suspected cameras. An IR filter reflection looks very similar to CCD sensor reflection to our camera detector (the only difference is a larger speckle size), thus it is a straightforward task to detect IR filters and treat them as cameras. However, this solution will result in more false positives. Since IR filters allow visible light to penetrate, the camera neutralizer is not affected by this attack.

Mirrors

A user can avoid pointing a camera at the capture-resistant region by using a mirror and taking a picture of the reflection on the mirror. However, our experience indicates that the camera detector can still clearly spot the CCD sensor in the mirror and the camera can be effectively neutralized by aiming back at the mirror.

An attacker could hide a camera behind a one-way mirror to prevent it from being detected. Similar to the sunglass situation, IR light can still be detected appearing behind a one-way mirror, making it an ineffective attack. In addition, images taken from behind a one-way mirror tend to produce low quality images in the first place.

Modifying Camera Sample Rate

The camera could be pre-programmed to sample at the rate of the neutralizer pattern. This problem can be addressed by interleaving random frequencies for each pixel in the neutralizing projection pattern. In this case, CCD cameras would not be able to synchronize to the projected pattern and frequency because of its inability to sample each pixel at different rates. This is a fairly straightforward extension to our system, which we have tested independent of our proof of concept implementation.

The camera could also move faster than the detector tracks, but there is a limit to how fast the camera can be moved without producing motion blur. The 15 Hz tracking rate of our implementation is sufficient for all camera phones and most digital cameras. As previously mentioned, a more powerful computer could track at 30 Hz. Blocking of cameras with extremely fast shutter speeds requires faster tracking. Increasing the area covered by the neutralizing beam could also address this problem because of the larger movement needed to move outside the beam of the light.

5.3 Limitations

The current implementation is limited to indoor environments, although we have found that cameras can be successfully blocked near widows and areas where there is significant amount of natural light. However, for venues like an outdoor concert, this system would need to be modified extensively to accommodate for such a large setting.

We have found that the current implementation is well suited to blocking camera phones and most consumer-level digital cameras, including pinhole cameras. In the future, we will test the system against different camera types to determine its success against the variety of capture technology that currently exist. For example, the system may have problems with high-end cameras that have very fast shutter speeds, fast frame rates, and retracting shutters that cover their CCD sensors, such as SLR cameras. SLR cameras are still very hard to produce cheaply and we do not expect to see such high-end components integrated into a mobile phone anytime soon. Although the quality and resolutions of camera phones will increase, they do not have a direct impact on the effectiveness of this system (e.g., our system performs just as well on a 4 megapixel CCD digital camera). Capture technologies that do not employ CCD sensors, such as ordinary film cameras, cannot be detected nor neutralized by our system.

Most camera systems employ some type of optical system; by instrumenting the environment to locate any reflection from optical devices, it is possible to detect any camera, including SLRs and ordinary film cameras. However, this approach would increase the false positive rate.

The current implementation requires manual calibration between the camera detector and the neutralizer (the projector) to a planar surface. Although the detector camera and projector are physically near one another, parallax still poses a problem when cameras are too far in front or behind the calibrated plane. There are two ways to address this problem. The first is to use a stereoscopic vision system that tracks in 3D space. The second is to make the projector coaxial with the view of the detector with a beam splitter. The first approach provides flexibility in placement of the neutralizer and the camera detectors, but it requires two cameras. The latter approach requires the neutralizer and camera detector to be collocated but only requires one camera.

The conical region of the camera detector poses a problem with "dead zones" close to the detector/neutralizer system. A "dead zone" exists a short distance in front of the protected surface, directly underneath the detector unit, and on the azimuth

(Figure 7a). A person standing in this dead zone will be able to take a picture, although the resulting image will be very warped. Placement of a physical barrier could limit proximity of users to the protected region and the "dead zone" (Figure 7b). Installation of another neutralizer at a lower level or different angle could cover the "dead zones" inherent to elevation and azimuth concerns.

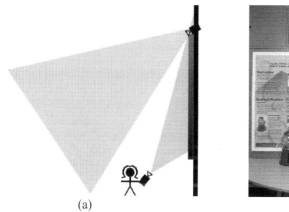

(a)   (b)

Figure 7. (a) A dead zone exists a short distance in front of the protected surface, directly underneath the detector unit. A user standing in this dead zone will be able to take a picture, although the resulting photo will be very warped. (b) We place a table in front of the surface to obstruct users from entering this dead zone. The right picture shows a sample setup of our system that prevents people from taking pictures of posters in our lab. In this example, the posters and prototypes can be viewed by the human eye, but they can not be captured by cameras within a 45° sweep in the azimuth in front of the table.

The prototype implementation consists of three significant elements: a camera, a DLP projector, and a PC, costing approximately $2500 USD. However, a commercial product implementation would be significantly cheaper. Video cameras are decreasing in price significantly with time. The PC is easily replaced with a very inexpensive microcontroller. The projector is the most expensive of the three elements. We used a projector because of the ease in projecting concentrated light at very specific regions. Typical projectors are designed to produce high quality images at high resolutions, have tuner components, and incorporate sophisticated optical components. The required projection region, however, is very small and does not require the level of optical precision and resolution available in typical projectors. We can imagine a projector designed specifically for this application could be significantly cheaper. Furthermore, the projector could be replaced with a scanning laser (similar to those used in laser light shows). By spinning a mirror and pulsing different tri-colored lasers, we could produce the same effect as the projector. This is not only a much less expensive solution, but also a more effective solution than a diffuse projector beam, thereby allowing for the practical placement of many of these systems throughout a space for increased coverage.

6   Conclusions

The increasing ubiquity of mobile phones that include cheap CCD cameras raises legitimate concerns around awareness and prevention of capture. In this paper, we present a proof of concept implementation of a capture-resistant environment that prevents the recording of still images and movies of regions within that physical space. The system actively seeks cameras on mobile phones in the environment and emits a strong localized light beam at each device to neutralize it from capturing. Although the directed light interferes with the camera's operation, it minimally impacts a human's vision in the environment. This approach also requires no cooperation on the part of the camera nor its owner. Additionally, we discuss how this work can be extended to permit certain cameras to take pictures in the environment while preventing others. Although the proof of concept implementation effectively blocks cameras within its 45° field of view up to 5-10m away, we can easily add additional detector and neutralizer units to prevent capture within a larger sweep. This implementation provided a platform for investigation of the challenges inherent to producing a capture resistant environment. We explain how our approach resolves many of these challenges and describe potential extensions to this work to address others. This work presents a proof-of-concept implementation that can be engineered in the future to detect and to neutralize camera recording for a wider variety of situations including large environments and mobile entities, such as people.

References

1.   Brassil, J. Using Mobile Communications to Assert Privacy from Video Surveillance. To appear at *1st International Workshop on Security in Systems and Networks 2005*. April 2005.
2.   Art. 29 Data Protection Working Party. Opinion 4/2004 on the Processing of Personal Data by means of Video Surveillance. Document 11750/02/EN WP89, European Commission (2004). http://europa.eu.int/comm.
3.   Chung, J. Threat Of Subway Photo Ban Riseth Again," Gothamist, 2004 November 30.
4.   Eagle Eye. Bulletin of the Connecticut Academy of Science and Engineering. Vol. 12, No. 2, 1997.
5.   Halderman, J.A, Waters, B., and Felten E.W. Privacy Management for Portable Recording Devices. *In The 3rd Workshop on Privacy in Electronic Society (WPES 2004)*. Washington, DC. October 2004.
6.   Iceberg's Safe Haven. http://www.iceberg-ip.com/index.htm.
7.   Perry, S. HP Blur Photos with Camera Privacy Patent. http://www.digital-lifestyles.info/display_page.asp?section=business&id=1888. January 2005.
8.   Video Voyeurism Prevention Act of 2004. 18 USC 1801. December 2004.
9.   Wagstaff, J. Using Bluetooth To Disable Camera Phones. http://loosewire.typepad.com/blog/2004/09/using_bluetooth.html. September 2004.

Self-Mapping in 802.11 Location Systems

Anthony LaMarca, Jeff Hightower, Ian Smith, Sunny Consolvo

Intel Research Seattle

Abstract Location systems that are based on scanning for nearby radio sources can estimate the position of a mobile device with reasonable accuracy and high coverage. These systems require a calibration step in which a map is built from radio-readings taken on a location-aware device. War driving, for example, calibrates the positions of WiFi access points using a GPS-equipped laptop. In this paper we introduce an algorithm for *self-mapping* that minimizes or even eliminates explicit calibration by allowing the location system to build this radio map as the system is used. Using nearly 100 days of trace data, we evaluate self-mapping's accuracy when the map is seeded by three realistic data sources: public war-driving databases, WiFi hotspot finders, and sporadic GPS connectivity. On average, accuracy and coverage are shown to be comparable to those achieved with an explicit war-driven radio map.

1 Introduction

Location has long been established as a key element of a mobile device's context [13]. One class of location systems, which we refer to as *beacon-based* location systems, estimates the position of a device by referencing nearby radio sources. Beacon-based systems have been shown to provide both good accuracy and high coverage in a variety of settings [7, 10]. Creating the necessary map of the radio sources, however, can be a costly and time-consuming process. In this paper, we introduce and evaluate an algorithm for *self-mapping* that enables beacon-based systems to build a radio map on-the-fly, while the system is in use.

Beacon-based systems typically use signals from 802.11 access points (APs) [1, 4], but Bluetooth devices, GSM cell towers, FM radio transmitters and combinations of these have also been used [7, 10]. Beacon-based systems have two advantages over other types of location systems. First, the huge number of fixed radio sources in the environment provides high coverage [10]. Second, because beacon-based systems use standard radios built into the user's device, there is no need for special hardware.

A drawback of beacon-based systems that estimate a device's absolute location is that they require a map of nearby radio sources to interpret the radio-scan results. For systems like Active Campus [4] that employ a predictive radio model, the map takes the form of the latitude and longitude of each 802.11 access point. In the case of "fingerprinting" systems like RADAR [1], this map is composed of a collection of radio-scan results and the locations in which those scans were taken. In all cases, these systems depend on this data and cannot translate radio observations into location estimates without it.

Typically, the radio map is manually built for the areas of interest, loaded onto the appropriate clients or servers, and then deployed to users. Re-mapping may be

M. Beigl et al. (Eds.): UbiComp 2005, LNCS 3660, pp. 87–104, 2005.

88   Anthony LaMarca et al.

performed occasionally to take into account new radio beacons that have been deployed or old ones that have been moved or decommissioned. Both the initial mapping and subsequent re-mappings are time consuming and represent the biggest cost in deploying and maintaining the system. In this paper, we propose a *self-mapping* algorithm that can reduce or even eliminate the overhead of mapping.

With self mapping, only a small amount of initial map data, what we call *seed data*, is needed to deploy the system. As the location system runs, radio scans are used to "grow" the seed data into a full radio map, as well as estimate the device's location. An immediate benefit of this approach is the time and energy saved by system managers, as they do not need to collect a full set of map data to deploy their system. Another advantage is that the system managers need not predict exactly which geographic areas must be mapped for the system to be useful, as the map will be refined in the most heavily used areas. Self-mapping also obviates the need to manually refresh the radio map. New radio sources will automatically and incrementally be incorporated as the system is used. The challenge in building a self-mapping system is that with a small set of mapping data, the radio scans are of limited use in meaningfully extending the map.

We present a graph-based algorithm for mapping radio beacons given a small set of seed data:

- Nodes in the graph represent radio beacons, and weighted edges represent the nearness of the two beacons.
- Edge weights are determined by using the radio scans to infer which beacons are near which other beacons.
- By anchoring the beacons in the seed set at their known locations, we can treat the graph as a constraint problem and compute likely locations for the unknown beacons by minimizing constraint violations.

To test our self-mapping algorithm, we gathered radio trace data from three volunteers over an eight-week period, totaling nearly 100 days worth of traces containing over 20 million radio readings. Using this data, we evaluated how well the maps produced by our algorithm compared both in accuracy and coverage to a traditional radio map when used by a location system. For the location system, we used the 802.11 scanner and the centroid tracker from the Place Lab toolkit [10]. We tested our algorithm with seed data from a variety of real-world sources, including public war-driving databases, WiFi hotspot finders, and sporadic GPS connectivity.

Our results show that self-mapping works well in practice and is a viable alternative to explicit mapping. Due to the large amount of structure that can be extracted from radio traces, self-mapping with a seed set containing as little as 10% of the radio sources can build a radio map that provides almost 90% coverage. Self-mapping with a seed set drawn from a public war-driving database provided median accuracy of 80 meters with 96% coverage while a seed set built from the user's own sporadic GPS coverage (so-called "opportunistic war driving") provided median accuracy of 56 meters with 84% coverage.

Our results also show that for an up-to-date radio map, self-mapping can add new beacons with nearly the same accuracy as war-driving. We show that our self-mapping algorithm's beacon location estimates were within 31m of an AP's true location on average, 5m worse than a war-driving estimate.

This paper is presented in three parts. First we outline how radio maps are currently built and describe our self-mapping technique. Then, we explain our data-collection strategy and sources of seed data. Finally, we present our results and conclusions.

2 Related Work

In this section, we describe how radio maps are built for two types of beacon-based location systems: those using predictive radio models and those using radio fingerprinting. We also discuss how self-mapping has been applied in symbolic location systems as well as sensor networks and robotics.

Estimating Location with a Predictive Radio Model

Both Active Campus and Place Lab are beacon-based systems that use a predictive radio model to estimate location [4, 10]. Radio models range from simple heuristics (*e.g,.* 802.11 can be heard for 100 meters in all directions from the access point) to complex ones that consider antenna types and the attenuation of various building materials [12]. The radio map in these systems contains an estimated position of each known radio beacon as well as other possibly useful characteristics (*e.g.,* antenna height or transmit-strength). This data can be directly measured, as was done in the Active Campus deployment during which the locations of approximately 200 802.11 APs were manually determined.

Less accurate, but faster and not requiring physical access, beacon locations can be inferred by measuring where they can be observed. This technique is often performed by the "war driving" community to find the location of 802.11 APs. War driving requires a laptop or PDA with 802.11, GPS, and one of many publicly-available war-driving programs (netstumbler.com, kismetwireless.net). These programs log the APs that they hear, and estimate the beacons' locations using a predictive model. Our results in Section 6.3 show that for a small sample of APs, war-driving estimates are within 26m of the true location on average. War driving data has been shown to be an effective source of radio map data, allowing a user to be located using 802.11 with 15-20m accuracy in areas with high AP density [10].

The simple nature of the mapping data used by predictive systems like Active Campus makes them good candidates for self-mapping. In addition, 802.11 AP locations can be downloaded from public sources like WiFi clubs and war-driving databases. For these reasons, we chose to develop our initial self-mapping algorithm for a predictive beacon-based location system.

Estimating Location with Radio Fingerprints

Fingerprinting-based location systems are powerful and simple. In a fingerprinting system, the radio map takes the form of radio-scans tagged with the location where the scans were performed. When a device wants to estimate its location, it performs a scan, finds the radio scan in the map that it most closely matches, and estimates the device to be located where that matching scan was taken. To reduce errors, these systems generally average the location of the closest k scans where k is a small number, often 4.

A benefit of the fingerprinting approach is that there is no need to model radio propagation; it simply remembers what should be seen and where. RADAR [1] and Ekahau (ekahau.com) are fingerprinting systems that are accurate to 1-3m. Unfortunately, to perform this well, these systems require a highly-detailed and densely populated radio map compared to predictive systems. For example, the RADAR experiments employed a radio map with approximately one scan every square meter.

The match between fingerprinting and self-mapping is not as clear as for predictive systems. While high coverage can likely be obtained, accuracy may degrade, undermining the key advantage of fingerprinting. Second, all of the public radio-beacon databases we have found exported only summaries and none provided the raw radio scans that would be needed to seed a fingerprint radio map. Thus, finding a workable seed set for self-mapping with fingerprinting presents a challenge.

Self-Mapping in Sensor Networks

A variety of self-mapping algorithms have been developed for sensor networks. Some assume that a small percentage of sensor nodes know their own location and the algorithms estimate every sensor node's absolute location. Other algorithms assume no information and estimate only the relative location of sensor nodes. Some sensor network self-mapping algorithms use only the knowledge of which other nodes are in range [6], while others utilize observed signal strength [2], or acoustic ranging [3]. The graph structure used by many of these algorithms is similar to what we present in Section 3. The key difference is that in the case of sensor networks, the sensor nodes are trying to locate themselves, and can directly measure which other nodes are in range. In our case, we observe radio beacons from an independent vantage point and from these observations, must indirectly infer the relationship between beacons.

Priyantha et al. expand on the algorithms used in fixed sensor networks to show how mobile devices can aid non-mobile devices in estimating their location [11]. They show that with assistance from mobile device, fixed devices can locate themselves more efficiently and can also disambiguate so called "non-rigid" configurations. This work is similar to ours in that a mobile device aids in the location estimation of a collection of non-mobile devices. In their work, location is computed using a mix of readings from mobile and fixed devices, while ours is more extreme and only employs measurements taken by mobile devices. Priyantha et al. employ a polynomial-time closed-form solution to find the optimal assignment of locations, an acceptable approach for the small 16-256 node networks they consider. Given that hundreds of thousands of radio beacons may be in a metropolitan area, we employ a less accurate, but faster iterative approach, to approximate the optimal location assignments given the readings.

Other Approaches

Of all the 802.11-based location systems, NearMe comes the closest to performing self-mapping [8]. NearMe is a service designed to determine when two devices are in proximity. As an extension, NearMe allows 802.11 APs to be associated with physical places (*e.g.,* '2nd floor copy room') or resources (*e.g.,* 'duplex printer'). NearMe uses radio traces to build a neighborhood graph of which APs are near each another out to eight hops. Although NearMe does not estimate absolute locations, it does estimate ranges between APs based on the traces and the neighborhood graph.

Laasonen et al. [9] built a cell-phone application that constructs a graph of a user's "places" based on the cell towers he visits with his phone. To overcome the limitation of knowing only the single cell tower the phone is currently associated with, the graph is built by observing transitions between cells.

Self-Mapping in Robotics

Robots can construct accurate maps of their environment during normal operation using a technique known as Simultaneous Localization and Mapping (SLAM). SLAM is similar to the work in this paper, however much of the research in SLAM focuses on solving the data-association problem. Data association is the challenge of matching environmental features that the robot observes (typically using a camera or laser range-finders) with the contours or features in the partial map [5]. Our self-mapping task has no data association problem because access points and other beacons all have unique IDs. When a device sees an ID in a scan there is no ambiguity about which beacon it is. Robots also typically make heavy use of odometry or inertial sensors which are uncommon on mobile and handheld devices.

3 A Graph Algorithm for Self-Mapping

In this section we introduce our algorithm for self-mapping the locations of radio beacons. For clarity, we describe our algorithm in the context of 802.11. The same algorithm should work with other radio technologies, provided the ID and observed signal strength are available from the radio scans. For simplicity, we present examples using a two-dimensional representation of location, but this algorithm also works in three dimensions.

3.1 Inputs

We assume that there are two sets of data available: The *seed set* and the *radio traces*. The seed set contains the unique identifier *(id)* and location *(latitude, longitude)* of a set of beacons with known location.

$$SeedSet = \{(id_1, lat_1, lon_1)\,,\,(id_2, lat_2, lon_2)\,,\,\ldots\,,\,(id_n, lat_n, lon_n)\}$$

The radio traces are made up of a collection of time-stamped radio scans. Each radio scan contains a timestamp *(ts)*, zero or more beacon identifiers *(id)*, and the observed signal strength *(ss)*.

$$RadioTraces = \{RadioScan_1, RadioScan_2,\,\ldots\,,\,RadioScan_m\}$$

$$RadioScan = (ts, \{(id_1, ss_1)\,,\,(id_2, ss_2)\,,\,\ldots\,,\,(id_o, ss_o)\})$$

3.2 Exploiting Signal Strength

If a radio scan sees more than one beacon, we know that since both beacons were observed from one location, they must be within twice the maximum transmit radius of each other. In the case of 802.11, this means that the two APs are likely within 400-500m of each other. We can often tighten this rough constraint by using the signal strength with which each beacon was observed. Since the falloff in signal strength is weakly correlated with an increase in distance [12], we can use it as a hint that the user was either close or far from each of the beacons. Signal strength does not tell us the angle between the beacons, but it still helps constrain the maximum distance. Consider the scans depicted in Figure 1. In the first scan, beacons b_1 and b_2 are both observed with weak signal strengths, establishing a distant proximity. The second scan shows a stronger reading (*-60dBm*) for b_1. This provides new information: since b_1 was heard strongly, the user was probably close to b_1, and since b_2 was also heard from the same location, b_1 and b_2 are probably closer than twice their maximum range. The third reading makes the likely separation between b_1 and b_2 smaller still, as both are observed with a reasonably strong signal.

To quantify this distance, we use Seidel's model for propagation of signals in the wireless networking band [12]. According to the model, expected signal strength (*ss*) at distance *d* is:

$$ss = ss_0 - 10 \cdot n \cdot log_{10}(d/d_0)$$

where ss_0 is the signal strength that would be observed in free space at reference distance d_0 from the transmitter. The constant *n* is based on characteristics of the particular radio and the physical environment (density of obstacles, etc), with *n* typically varying between 2 and 5. At 1m, 802.11 APs do not typically return signal strength greater than -32dBm, so we use $d_0 = 1$ and $ss_0 = -32dBm$. Since we operated in a city with primarily wood and glass structures, and since we can assume nothing about the radios being modeled, we chose *n* to be on the low side: $n = 2.5$. Solving for *d* with these values, we get:

$$ss = -32 - 10 \cdot 2.5 \cdot log_{10}(d/1)$$

$$d = 10^{(-32-ss)/25}$$

This establishes an estimated distance between the user and the observed beacons.

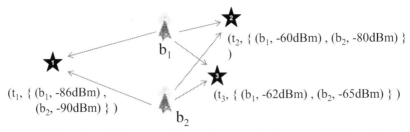

Fig. 1. An illustration of three scans that see the same two beacons. Starting with scan 1 on the left and proceeding clockwise, each scan reveals the two beacons to be closer together as their combined signal strengths grow larger

Given a pair of observations for two different beacons, we can establish the following constraint on the two beacons.

$$\textit{The distance between } b_1 \textit{ and } b_2 \leq 10^{(-32-ss1)/25} + 10^{(-32-ss2)/25} \quad (1)$$

In the example depicted in Figure 1, we only compared beacons that were observed in the same scan. In reality, because scans are taken at a rate of 1-4Hz, the user is unlikely to move far during a scan. Thus it is reasonable to compare across a few scans taken in rapid succession. If beacon b_i is observed in one scan, and beacon b_j is observed in a successive scan 500ms later, it is fairly safe to assume that the scans were taken "in the same place" and to infer a proximity relationship between b_i and b_j based on these scans. Varying the acceptable time threshold trades off the accuracy of the constraints against the connectivity of the graph: increasing the threshold allows more edges to be added to the graph, but also increases the error introduced by the user's motion[1]. To balance these factors, we ran our experiments using a time threshold of 1 second.

3.3 Graph Construction

The graph contains one node for every beacon that appears in either the seed set or in a scan from the radio traces. The radio traces are then traversed in time order and a fixed sliding-window's worth of scans are considered. (We used a one second window in our experiments). For each window, we select the strongest observation of each beacon seen in the window, and then consider all pairings of these beacons. For each of these pairs of beacons b_i and b_j, we estimate the maximum distance d_{max} between b_i and b_j using Equation 1 and the strongest signal strengths ss_i and ss_j. If no edge exists in the graph between the node for b_i and b_j, one is added with weight d_{max}. If there is an existing edge with a higher weight, it is replaced with an edge with weight d_{max}.

When all of the radio traces have been considered, the locations of the beacons in the seed-set are assigned to their nodes. Since these nodes already have a known location, we call them *anchor nodes*. The remaining task is to assign locations to the non-anchor nodes while trying to minimize violations of the constraint that for all nodes *i* and *j* that are connected by an edge, the distance between them should be less than the weight of that edge.

3.4 Finding a Solution

We assign locations to nodes using the following iterative approach. First, we assign all non-anchor nodes the location of the nearest anchor node in the graph. (If no path exists between a node and an anchor node, the node will not be assigned a location.) This location assignment will almost certainly violate a large number of edge constraints which we correct by iteratively reducing the error in the graph.

---

[1] An improvement to a simple time threshold would be to allow edges to be added for beacons seen many seconds apart, factoring the likely distance moved into the edge weight

The error of an edge is defined to be the proportion by which the edge's nodes are violating their shared constraint. If two nodes are 80m apart and share an edge of weight 100, the edge has zero error. If two nodes are 250m apart and share an edge of weight 100, the edge has an error of (250/100 – 1.0) or 1.5. The error for a node is defined to be the sum of the error of all of its edges. The error of the graph is defined to be the sum of the error of all nodes.

Error is reduced by repeatedly choosing a random non-anchor node and trying to reduce its error. We attempt to reduce a node's error by considering random Gaussian-distributed alternate locations for this node and measuring how they would affect the node's error. If a reduction in error can be achieved, the node is moved and the errors for that node and its neighbors are updated. This continues until either error for the graph is reduced to zero (meaning a solution satisfying all constraints has been found) or improvements have reduced to an unproductive level. When the algorithm completes, the locations of the anchor and non-anchor nodes are exported as a new radio map.

4 Test Data

Because self-mapping occurs as users go about their daily lives (*i.e.,* the areas in which trace data is collected is unpredictable), it would be unrealistic to test our algorithm using war driving radio traces that make systematic, serpentine traversals of a collection of streets. Therefore, we collected radio-traces from three volunteers from Intel Research Seattle as they went about their daily lives. Volunteer 1 (V1) lived 1.5 miles east of our lab and commuted to and from work by walking, Volunteer 2 (V2) lived 1 mile west and commuted by a mix of walking and driving, and Volunteer 3 (V3) lived 3 miles south and commuted by bus.

To collect the trace data, the volunteers carried laptops outfitted with hardware and software to continuously collect 802.11 and GPS traces; external batteries were provided so that the volunteers would not need to recharge the laptops throughout the day. Except for having to carry the laptop at all times, volunteers were asked to behave as they normally would. The one exception to this request was that we asked the volunteers to place their laptop near a window when they were in a vehicle to maximize the chance of obtaining a GPS lock.

The trace data was collected over a period spanning the end of 2004 and the beginning of 2005 (each volunteer collected data for four to eight weeks). During this period, we collected a total of 98 days worth of radio traces, consisting of 13.3 million 802.11 readings and 7 million GPS readings. A total of 9450 unique 802.11 APs were seen in the logs. Overall, there was a GPS lock 20.5% of the time and at least one 802.11 AP was seen in 90.2% of the scans.

Using these logs and a variety of self-mapping scenarios described in the next section, we tested both the coverage and accuracy offered by the radio maps generated by our self-mapping algorithm.

5 Self-Mapping Scenarios

One of our goals was to investigate the effectiveness of self-mapping in real-world scenarios. Accordingly, we identified three real-world sources of seed data to bootstrap self-mapping. This section describes each of these sources, as well as the war-driving scenario we use as the control in our experiments.

5.1 Self-Mapping with Sporadic GPS Coverage

As GPS chipsets become smaller and cheaper, more mobile devices will include integrated GPS. Since GPS usually requires a clear view of the sky, it seldom works indoors and does not provide sufficient coverage to be used as the sole source of location information. It can, however, be used as a source of seed data for self mapping. In this scenario, the device starts out with an empty seed-set. At the end of each day, that day's traces are mined for any trace fragments in which the user had a GPS lock. These log fragments are treated as a set of short war drives; a standard war-driving algorithm is applied to these fragments to estimate the locations of any beacons that were observed. These beacons are then added to the seed-set and are used to bootstrap the self-mapping for future days.

5.2 Self-Mapping with Public Beacon Data

Another source of seed data is the internet, namely public databases that share the location of 802.11 APs. This is probably the most compelling scenario, as no mapping effort is required by the user and his device does not require GPS. In this scenario, the user downloads public beacon information to his device. Each day the device is used, self-mapping is applied to the traces it has collected, using the public beacon information as a seed-set. We identified and evaluated two public sources of beacon location information: *war-driving databases* and *hotspot finders*, both of which are discussed below.

War Driving Databases

Sharing the discovered APs with the rest of the community is part of the war-driving culture. Many war-driving repositories exist, but the largest to date is http://wigle.net/ with over 2 million known AP locations as of February 2005. The data from wigle.net is publicly available and contains both the BSSID and location for the APs.

Of the 9450 unique 802.11 APs observed in our test traces, wigle.net contained 4000, or 43%. This is a significant portion of the observed APs which suggests that this data should work well with self-mapping. One issue, however, is that the wigle.net APs are primarily located near main roads and downtown/commercial areas, with little coverage in residential neighborhoods. As we will see in Section 6, this distribution has an impact on the accuracy of the self-mapping.

Hotspot Finders

A service commonly advertised to mobile workers is the *hotspot finder*: websites that list where both free and for-pay wireless networking can be obtained in a neighborhood. Hotspot finders are offered by web portals like Yahoo! (mobile.yahoo.com/wifi) and specialty companies like Jiwire (jiwire.com), and are all potential sources of seed data.

These hotspot finders list hotspot locations using street addresses rather than geo-coordinates. This issue can be managed by using an address translation service like MapPoint.net. A bigger issue is that these services list networks by the human-readable SSID (*e.g.* 'Northwest Coffee'), rather then the unique BSSID (*e.g.* 0F:34:9A:29:00:67). SSIDs are not guaranteed to be unique and it is common for franchised hotspots to assign all of their APs the same SSID. This creates a problem, as our algorithm must know the *unique* key that identifies an AP. One possible technical solution is to disambiguate APs with the same SSID using the structure in the self-mapping graph. This problem may also solve itself if providers begin exporting BSSIDs. For the purpose of these experiments, we assume that this problem will be solved, and we constructed a public hotspot data set using the following heuristic: from the complete set of APs observed in the test traces, we extracted those with SSIDs clearly indicating public access -- known large service providers like TMobile and Wayport, known local coffee shops and stores with public hotspots, and networks with suggestive SSIDs like 'guest' and 'public'. This yielded a seed-set of 750 APs, less than 8% of the 9450 observed in the traces. Even more so than the wigle.net data, these APs were heavily concentrated in commercial areas. This can be seen in Figure 2, which shows the position of seed set beacons (squares) and the self-mapped beacons (circles) for one of our test neighborhoods.

5.3 Self-Mapping with an Existing Radio Map

One final source of possible seed data for self-mapping is an existing radio map. Corporate IT departments generally have maps of their AP locations, as do many universities. The key characteristic of an existing radio map is its age. Since APs exhibit a fair rate of turnover, a radio map's quality will decay over time and can

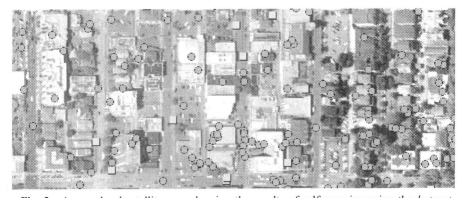

Fig. 2. An overhead satellite map showing the results of self-mapping using the *hotspot finder* seed set. The squares mark the locations of the beacons in the seed set, while the circles denote the beacons placed by the self-mapping algorithm

substantially degrade in six months to a year. In this final scenario, we consider how well our self-mapping algorithm works with existing radio maps of different ages.

To simulate an existing radio map, we begin with the "control" radio map described in the next subsection, then artificially age this map by randomly dropping 50%, 75% and 90% of the known beacons to form different seed sets. This essentially models the uniform addition of new beacons over time. It does not model the movement or decommissioning of beacons. Since this random thinning is artificially uniform, we believe this measures the best-case performance of our algorithm.

5.4 A Control: War-Driving Radio Map

To separate the performance of beacon-based location from the performance of self-mapping for beacon-based location, we introduce a control scenario that uses war-driving results as the radio map used by the system. To construct a war driving radio map, we extracted the GPS-locked segments the traces from the all three volunteers (this amounted to over 300 hours of data). These trace segments were then fed through a war-driving program that estimated the position of each beacon by averaging the locations in which it was observed. Due to incomplete GPS coverage, this data set contained the locations for 6200 of the 9450 beacons that were observed during the eight weeks. Ideally, we would be able to do an explicit war drive of the test area to build a more complete control data set. This was not feasible however, as our volunteers covered substantial parts of the city as well as each taking at least one trip out of state during the test period. Despite its limitations, our war-driving map provides excellent coverage, containing a known beacon location for over 99% of the scans that contain at least one beacon.

6 Results

All self-mapping scenarios were tested in the following way: each volunteer's traces were divided by calendar days 1..n based on the days the traces were recorded. For each day i, the trace was run through a location tracker that used that volunteer's radio map for day i. A volunteer's radio map for day i was constructed by running the self-mapping algorithm using the appropriate seed-set and the volunteer's traces from days 1..(i-1). This models the situation that each night, the volunteer's device performs self-mapping with what it already knew, plus the new trace from that day.

- *Coverage* was measured by counting what percentage of non-empty radio scans contained at least one beacon that was in the radio map for day i.
- *Accuracy* was measured by comparing the GPS-locked portions of the trace from day i to the beacon-based location estimates produces by Place Lab's centroid tracker for the same time period.
- *Error* for a given radio scan is the distance between the location estimate given by the beacon-based location system and the location in the corresponding GPS readings. Error for a given day is the median error for all of that day's radio scans. The error for the entire test period is the mean of the daily median errors.

This approach to testing has a few shortcomings. First, it uses GPS as ground truth. Standard (non-differential) GPS has a median error of 8m, bounding the accuracy of our error estimates. Second, this approach can only estimate accuracy when the volunteer had a GPS lock. As most people spend a large portion of their days at either home or work, we made a special allowance for those places. Since the set of beacons seen in the same place is very consistent over time, we measured the geo-coordinates and set of beacons for each volunteer's home and workplace. This way, we knew the volunteer's location when he was at work or home, even if he did not have a GPS lock, thereby increasing the percentage of the time we could perform accuracy comparisons.

One final distinction remains to be introduced. Like most people, our volunteers spent a significant portion of their time in a few key places, most notably home and work. This made the performance of a particular scenario for a given volunteer heavily dependent on how it performs in those few places. In one respect, this is absolutely correct, since accuracy over a user's day is a very appropriate interpretation of 'accuracy'. Such a definition of accuracy could be said to be temporal, as it computes average accuracy over the time period of a day.   Another reasonable approach, however, is to measure the accuracy over all the places a user goes, independent of how long he spends at each place.

To addresses these two notions of accuracy, we present two sets of numbers for each scenario: performance for the full traces that contain all of the data (including long periods of inactivity such as when the volunteers slept at night) and a set of *transit* traces. The transit traces are the full traces with sections removed in which the set of beacons seen by a volunteer was stable for more than two minutes. (Manual validation showed that this simple heuristic was highly effective at identified times when a volunteer stayed in one place). These transit traces represent the times that a volunteer spent walking around, commuting, shopping, etc.; arguably some of the most important times for a location system to perform well.

6.1 Accuracy and Coverage

Table 1 shows the accuracy and coverage for each volunteer in each scenario for full and transit logs. Accuracy is the average of the daily median accuracies; coverage is the percentage of the time the self-mapping radio map contained a location estimate for at least one beacon. We normalize the coverage numbers to the 90.2% average coverage that a complete beacon map could provide to show the coverage of the self-mapping radio map, not 802.11-based location estimation.

All three reality-inspired scenarios average between 84% and 96% coverage. This shows that there is sufficient connectivity in the self-mapping graph to estimate the position of a large fraction of the observed beacons. This is even true in the *hotspot finder* scenario in which the seed-set started off with less than 8% of the observed beacons.

Of the three scenarios, the best accuracy is provided by the *sporadic GPS* scenario. This is not surprising, as the occasional GPS readings cause the seed-set to grow over time, providing more information in the long run than the other scenarios. For V1 and V2, the accuracy of *sporadic GPS* is only 15% worse than the *war-driving* control scenario on average. This is not the case for V3 who saw better accuracy with the *wigle.net* and *hotspot finder* seed-set than with *sporadic GPS*. This is due to the difference in GPS coverage between volunteers: V1 and V2 reported walking to work, and this is reflected in GPS coverage of 43% and 54% respectively in their transit traces. In contrast, V3 had only 24% GPS coverage in his transit logs. This does not mean that *sporadic GPS* is not a viable bootstrapping scenario for people like V3; it just means that it will take longer for their radio maps to reach war-driven accuracy.

Of the two public database scenarios, *wigle.net* performed better than *hotspot finder* in nearly every scenario. This was expected, as the *wigle.net* data set was bigger and largely a superset of the *hotspot finder* data. (Of the 750 APs in the *hotspot*

Table 1. This table summarizes the accuracy and coverage of self mapping for the test data. Each scenario from Section 5 is represented. This table also includes the accuracy and coverage of a war-driving map

	Transit Logs		Full Logs	
Scenario/User	Accuracy	Coverage	Accuracy	Coverage
Explicit mapping via war driving				
V1	21 m	-	9 m	-
V2	34 m	-	82 m	-
V3	33 m	-	79 m	-
Average	*30 m*	-	*57 m*	-
Self mapping with sporadic GPS				
V1	25 m	88%	10 m	88%
V2	47 m	84%	95 m	85%
V3	94 m	80%	124 m	79%
Average	*56 m*	*84%*	*76 m*	*84%*
Self mapping with wigle.net data				
V1	80 m	93%	829 m	89%
V2	72 m	97%	88 m	98%
V3	88 m	99%	110 m	98%
Average	*80 m*	*96%*	*342 m*	*95%*
Self mapping with hotspot finder data				
V1	174 m	94%	1450 m	88%
V2	106 m	90%	144 m	81%
V3	69 m	97%	54 m	96%
Average	*117 m*	*94%*	*550 m*	*88%*
Self mapping with random 10% of beacons				
V1	83 m	94%	600 m	90%
V2	124 m	94%	129 m	89%
V3	58 m	92%	57 m	87%
Average	*88 m*	*94%*	*262 m*	*89%*
Self mapping with random 25% of beacons				
V1	45 m	96%	32 m	92%
V2	49 m	98%	53 m	96%
V3	51 m	99%	117 m	98%
Average	*48 m*	*97%*	*67 m*	*95%*
Self mapping with random 50% of beacons				
V1	30 m	96%	25 m	93%
V2	33 m	88%	28 m	97%
V3	39 m	99%	93 m	99%
Average	*34 m*	*97%*	*49 m*	*96%*

finder data set, 510, or 68%, were also in the *wigle.net* data set.) These scenarios showed good coverage and accuracy of around 100m in the transit case. Recall that self-mapping only requires an 802.11 radio and involves no pre-mapping. Given the effort required of the user, these scenarios offer considerable potential.

Probably the starkest contrast is the difference in consistency of performance between the transit and full traces. In the transit cases, accuracy was typically within 50% across users, with a worst case of a factor of 2.5. In the full traces, nearly every scenario, including the war-driving control map, had more than a factor of 10 variation between some volunteers. This illustrates the critical effect that the placement of the dozen or so beacons situated around the volunteer's home and work have on overall accuracy. Part of this can be explained by where the volunteers lived. V3 lives in a downtown hi-rise building, and is in range of many more APs than V1 and V2 when at home. Accordingly, V3 had the best performance for full logs with the small *hotspot finder* seed set. Conversely, V1 lived in a residential neighborhood and was more than 500m from any of the APs in the *wigle.net* and *hotspot finder* seed sets, making his performance poor for the full traces. But the differences seen in the *war-driving* control scenario can only be explained by chance. All three volunteers had multiple beacons visible at home, and the war-driving placement was coincidentally very accurate for V1 and less so for V2 and V3.

This last observation highlights the effectiveness of the selective refinement technique used by Active Campus [4]. Active Campus allows users to override the radio model and click on a map to, in effect, say "Right now, I am here". This correction is stored in the radio map and supersedes the radio model in the future. Since the correction is based on a fingerprint, accuracy for these corrections should be 2-3m. Since our volunteers spent two thirds of their time at either work or home, correcting only these two places would have a drastic impact on average accuracy.

We now discuss the results for the last three scenarios in which a random 10%, 25% and 50% of the war driving radio map are used as a seed set for self-mapping. As expected, accuracy grows better as the size of the seed set is increased. Self mapping with the 10% seed set provides accuracy three times worse than war-driving in the transit case, while the 50% seed set is nearly as good. This shows that existing out-of-date radio maps can make excellent seed sets for self-mapping.

By dropping random beacons from the war-driving data set, we have created a uniform, random distribution. This provides an interesting opportunity to compare the non-uniform *wigle.net* and *hotspot finder* seed sets to these uniform seed sets. Despite the fact that the *wigle.net* seed set contained over 40% of the observed APs, its performance was closest to the 10% random seed set. Similarly, despite the fact that the *hotspot finder* seed set contained close to 10% of the observed beacons, its accuracy was considerably worse than the 10% random seed set. Intuitively, adding a new beacon in an area with no other known beacons should add more value than adding one in an area already populated with known beacons. This data illustrates that the even distribution of a seed set is as important as its size.

Finally, Figure 3 shows the effect that the number of neighbors that a node has in the graph has on the accuracy of beacon placement. These graphs show aggregate results from all three volunteers in all scenarios. The y axis on both graphs shows the distance between the war-driven position of a beacon and its placement by the self-mapping algorithm. Assuming the war-driving estimate is accurate (we validate this assumption in Section 6.3), this is a measure of the self-mapping algorithm's accuracy at placing beacons. On the graph on the left, the x axis shows the number of neighbors, or edges that a beacon's node has in the self-mapping algorithm. As the number of neighbors grows, the location estimates grow more accurate. This fits the intuition that more constraints yield more accurate solutions. The graph on the right of Figure 3 shows how the accuracy of beacon placement varies with the number of *anchored* neighbors. This graph shows a pronounced improvement in accuracy when going from 0 to 1 anchored neighbor, meaning that inferring a beacon's location from observations containing known beacons yields much better results than doing a chained inference through other non-anchored beacons. Beyond the first three anchored neighbors, little to no extra accuracy is gained. This further reinforces our claim that seed sets with clusters of beacons within range of each other will not yield as accurate a radio map as a similar sized seed set with a more uniform distribution of beacons.

6.2 Performance over Time

To show how self-mapping works over time we present a set of time-series graphs in Figure 4. These graphs show results for three scenarios (*sporadic GPS*, *wigle.net* and *random 25%*) for the transit traces for V2. Every graph is a time series over the 31 days of V2's traces. Each scenario is shown as two stacked graphs. The top graph in each case shows the coverage offered by the self-mapping radio map that day and the cumulative percentage of beacons that were mapped to that point. The bottom graph for each scenario shows the median accuracy for that day and includes the median accuracy for the war-driving control data set to serve as a comparison.

Since the *sporadic GPS* scenario starts out with an empty seed set, its coverage and percentage of beacons mapped start at zero and ramp up more steeply than the other scenarios. The most drastic feature of the coverage graphs is the large drop that occurs during days 6-8. This dip corresponds to a trip that V2 took out of state. The dip is most pronounced in the *sporadic GPS* scenario as V2 had no mapped beacons on arrival. During these three days, the coverage increases each day as the self-mapping algorithm places beacons in this new locale. Upon returning home, the coverage resumed more or less where it had been before V2 left town. A similar, but less

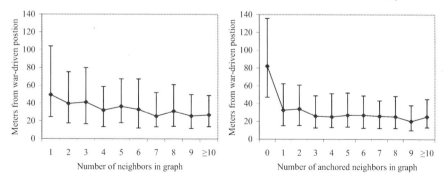

Fig. 3. These plots show how the structure of the self-mapping graph affects the accuracy of beacon placement. The left plot shows how accuracy varies with the number of neighbors. The right plot shows how the accuracy varies with the number of anchored neighbors

pronounced dip can be seen on days 23-25 when V2 spent portions of his day visiting places that were not yet mapped. Note that for each of these periods of low coverage, there is a corresponding bump in the percentage of beacons mapped; visiting new places results in periods of poor coverage, accompanied by an increase in the size of the radio map.

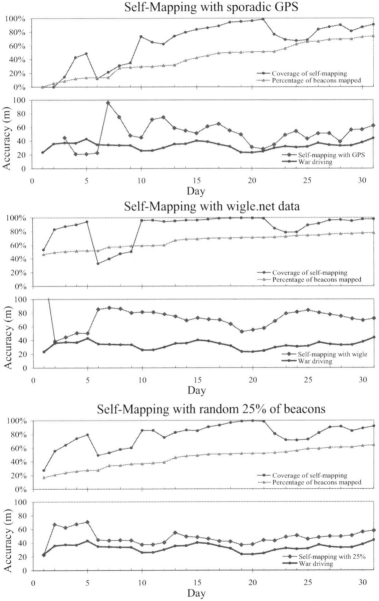

Fig. 4. Timelines comparing the coverage and accuracy of three self-mapping scenarios for V2's transit data. For each scenario, the upper graph shows coverage provided that day and percentage of total beacons mapped. The lower graph compares the median accuracy provided by the self-mapped radio map with the war-driven map

Table 2. A comparison of the accuracy of self-mapping and war driving beacon placement

Error in AP Placement (Meters)		
Access Point	Self-Mapping	War Driving
00:09:d7:c4:3c:81	35	27
00:09:5b:99:a9:c0	54	37
00:04:5a:0e:6e:fc	24	32
00:02:3a:9e:a3:d7	11	14
00:0f:3d:4f:84:a0	31	18
Average	**31**	**26**

We were pleased by how quickly the accuracy stabilized. Our self mapping algorithm reaches its peak accuracy after only a visit or two, causing accuracy to stabilize in days rather than weeks. This suggests that in real use, users would start to see improvements in accuracy and coverage quickly.

6.3 Keeping a Radio Map Fresh

Since a key benefit of self-mapping is the incorporation of new beacons, we wanted to quantify the accuracy of the location estimates of new beacons. To simulate newly deployed beacons, we chose five beacons from the war-driving radio map described in Section 5.4 and manually surveyed their locations. (One beacon was in the home of an acquaintance, while the others were in publicly accessible businesses.) The comparison of the manual survey and the self-mapping are shown in Table 2. For each beacon, we removed it from the radio map and ran the self-mapping algorithm using V1's traces. We then measured the error in the location predicted by the self-mapping algorithm. For comparison, we also calculated the error in the original war-driving placement that was used as ground truth in Section 6.1.

Table 2 shows that given an up-to-date radio map, the self-mapping placements are almost as accurate as war-driving. For these APs, the self-mapping placement was less than twice the error of the war-driving placement and was within 5m on average. Thus with reasonable beacon density and an up-to-date radio map, self-mapping can add new beacons with nearly the same accuracy as war-driving.

7 Conclusions

We have presented a graph-based, algorithm that allows a small set of known beacon locations, or *seed data*, to be expanded as users naturally use the system. We believe self-mapping is a key to enabling radio-beacon based location become a widely used high-coverage, indoor/outdoor location technology. We have presented three realistic scenarios for seeding our algorithm, each of which we tested with nearly 100 days worth of traces containing over 20 million readings. Our results have shown that:

1. Due to the structure present in radio scans, even small seed sets can be used to bootstrap a self-mapped set of radio locations that provides high coverage.

2. The accuracy of self-mapping is highly dependent on the distribution of the beacons in the seed set. Our results showed that a uniformly distributed seed set performed as well as a clustered seed set four times as large.
3. Both public access point databases and sporadic GPS coverage are viable, real-world sources of seed data. Neither requires users to explicitly perform mapping, and both showed the ability to ramp up to reasonable coverage within a few days of normal use.
4. With as little as 50% of the beacon locations, self-mapping can produce a radio map that estimates a user's location as well as a war driving database. Further, we showed that when new beacons are introduced, self-mapping estimates their positions nearly as accurately as war driving.

8 References

1. BAHL, P. & PADMANABHAN, V. RADAR: An In-Building RF-Based User Location and Tracking System *Proceedings of IEEE INFOCOM*, pp. 775-784 (2000)
2. DOHERTY, L., PISTER, K. S. J. & GHAOUI, L. E. Convex Optimization Methods for Sensor Node Position Estimation, *INFOCOM 2001.*(2001)
3. GIROD, L., BYCHKOVSKIY, V., ELSON, J. & ESTRIN, D. Locating Tiny Sensors in Time and Space: A Case Study, *ICCD 2002.*(2002)
4. GRISWOLD, W. G., SHANAHAN, P., BROWN, S. W., BOYER, R., RATTO, M., SHAPIRO, R. B. & TRUONG, T. M. ActiveCampus - Experiments in Community-Oriented Ubiquitous Computing, *To Appear: IEEE Computer.*
5. HAEHNEL, D., BURGARD, W., FOX, D. & THRUN, S. An Efficient FastSLAM Algorithm for Generating Maps of Large-scale Cyclic Environments From Raw Laser Range Measurements *IROS 2003* (IEEE/RSJ).(2003)
6. HE, T., HUANG, C., BLUM, B. M., STANKOVIC, J. A. & ABDELZAHER, T. F. Range-free localization schemes for large scale sensor networks, *MOBICOM 2003.*(2003)
7. KRUMM, J., CERMAK, G. & HORVITZ, E. RightSPOT: A Novel Sense of Location for a Smart Personal Object, *UbiComp 2003.*(2003)
8. KRUMM, J. & HINCKLEY, K. The NearMe Wireless Proximity Server, *UbiComp 2004.*(2004)
9. LAASONEN, K., RAENTO, M. & TOIVONEN, H. Adaptive On-Device Location Recognition, *Pervasive Computing 2004.*(2004)
10. LAMARCA, A., CHAWATHE, Y., CONSOLVO, S., HIGHTOWER, J., SMITH, I., SCOTT, J., SOHN, T., HOWARD, J., HUGHES, J., POTTER, F., TABERT, J., POWLEDGE, P., BORRIELLO, G. & SCHILIT, B. Place Lab: Device Positioning Using Radio Beacons in the Wild, *Pervasive 2005*, Munich, 2005.(2005)
11. PRIYANTHA, N. B., BALAKRISHNAN, H., DEMAINE, E. & TELLER, S. Mobile-Assisted Localization in Wireless Sensor Networks, *IEEE INFOCOM*, March.(2005)
12. SEIDEL, S. Y. & RAPPORT, T. S. 914 Mhz Path Loss Prediction Model for Indoor Wireless Communications in Multifloored Buildings, *IEEE Transactions on Antennas and Propagation*, 40, 207-217. (1992)
13. WANT, R., SCHILIT, B., ADAMS, N., GOLD, R., PETERSEN, K., GOLDBERG, D., ELLIS, J. & WEISER, M. The ParcTab Ubiquitous Computing Experiment, *Mobile Computing*, pp. 45-101.(1997)

A Study of Bluetooth Propagation Using Accurate Indoor Location Mapping

Anil Madhavapeddy and Alastair Tse

University of Cambridge Computer Laboratory, Cambridge, CB3 0FD, UK
avsm2@cl.cam.ac.uk, acnt2@cl.cam.ac.uk

Abstract. The ubiquitous computing community has widely researched the use of 802.11 for the purpose of location inference. Meanwhile, Bluetooth is increasingly widely deployed due to its low power consumption and cost. This paper describes a study of Bluetooth radio propagation using an accurate indoor location system to conduct fine-grained signal strength surveys. We discuss practical problems and requirements encountered setting up the infrastructure using the ultrasonic Active Bat indoor location system, and limitations of the commodity Bluetooth devices used. We conclude that Bluetooth is poorly suited to the purpose of fine-grained, low latency location inference due to specification and hardware limitations, and note that the movement speed of mobile devices is an important factor in calculating available bandwidth. We publish our data sets of signal strength samples for the community to freely use in future research.

1   Introduction

A number of recent projects have sought to use wireless protocols as accurate location estimators for mobile users. WiFi has proven to be an especially popular candidate for this purpose, as research projects such as RADAR [2] showed its viability, and commercial implementations of the technology have begun to appear in the marketplace. Place Lab [19] has even more ambitious goals by seeking to create a comprehensive location database which uses fixed commodity WiFi, GSM and Bluetooth devices as global beacons.

In this paper, we describe a systematic methodology for the evaluation of wireless signal-strength propagation. We use the accurate Active Bat indoor location system as a "location oracle" which allows us to: (*i*) perform sweeping surveys to measure signal strengths across a building-wide area; (*ii*) algorithms to correct errors from the location system present in those traces; and (*iii*) visualize and analyze the data to deduce location estimation properties of the wireless protocol. This paper also contributes guidelines which apply to other ultrasound- or radio-based location systems being used as survey tools (e.g. Cricket [18]).

In particular, we focus on the indoor location properties of the Bluetooth wireless protocol. Bluetooth has steadily gained popularity in many Ubicomp projects due to its emphasis on short-range, low-power, and ease of integration

M. Beigl et al. (Eds.): UbiComp 2005, LNCS 3660, pp. 105–122, 2005.

into devices. It is most commonly used as a "cable replacement protocol" to perform connection establishment between devices without requiring physical contact between them. In the wireless location estimation space, Bluetooth is especially important due to its ubiquitous and "always-on" presence in commodity everyday devices such as mobile phones and PDAs. This is in contrast to the more power-hungry WiFi, which is generally only switched on in stationary devices (e.g. a laptop is rarely used when a person is walking around).

Although some Ubicomp projects such as Place Lab have begun to use Bluetooth as a coarse-grained "on or off" indicator in their location databases, we contribute the first systematic and detailed analysis of more accurate Bluetooth location sensing by using our survey technique. In addition to sharing our analysis, we announce the availability of our data-sets of signal-strength/location samples [14] which will be of use to future projects seeking to exploit Bluetooth location information.

Previous attempts to accurately measure location with commodity Bluetooth hardware have been difficult because: (*i*) unlike WiFi, measuring Bluetooth signal strength requires the establishment of an active Bluetooth connection; (*ii*) many common Bluetooth chipsets, especially those found in mobile phones, only support a single Bluetooth connection at a time which makes triangulation difficult; and (*iii*) Bluetooth devices use frequency hopping algorithms which make location inference more difficult (see Section 4.3).

The rest of the paper is structured as follows. Section 2 begins by introducing the basics of the Bluetooth protocol and the Active Bat indoor location system. Section 3 describes our experimental setup and methodology, and Section 4 presents our results and discussion. Finally, we cover related work in Section 5 and conclude in Section 6.

2   Background

Section 2.1 introduces some of the concepts and background for the Bluetooth wireless protocol. Section 2.2 then describes the Active Bat ultrasonic indoor location system which provided the accurate location information needed for the experiments we conducted.

2.1   Bluetooth

Bluetooth is a short-range, wireless, cable-replacement protocol operating in the license-free 2.4GHz spectrum. Unlike WiFi, which offers higher transfer rates and distance, Bluetooth is characterised by its low power requirements and low-cost transceiver chips. Over 69 million Bluetooth ICs shipped in 2003 [12] in mobile devices such as cellphones, PDAs and laptop computers, providing a ubiquitous mechanism for wireless transfer of relatively small amounts of data.

In order to ensure robustness in noisy environments, Bluetooth divides the band into 79 channels and frequency hops across them up to 1600 times per second. A connection between two devices is time-division multiplexed with $625\mu s$

time slots, coordinated by one device designated as the "master". A hopping code is used to frequency hop between the channels for each time slot. The Bluetooth baseband defines two types of links: (i) the Asynchronous Connection-Less (ACL) link; and (ii) the Synchronous Connection-Oriented (SCO) link. The SCO link offers isochronous communication via reserved time slots and is primarily used by voice traffic. ACL links offer reliable communication via packet retransmission, and are used to build the control and data transfer protocols.

Although the Bluetooth protocol allows a master to support up to 3 simultaneous SCO links and 7 simultaneous ACL links, typical consumer hardware only supports a single SCO link and 3 ACL links. Very lightweight devices such as the current generation of Bluetooth-enabled mobile phones only support a single SCO and ACL link at a time (which is sufficient to drive a wireless headset).

2.2 Active Bat System

The Active Bat system [21,10] is a sophisticated indoor location system in which small active devices ("Bats") periodically emit narrowband ultrasound pulses. This ultrasound is detected by multiple sensors in the ceiling which use the time-of-flight information to multi-laterate the position of the Bats—a process which is accurate to 3 cm 95% of the time.

The Bat ultrasonic pulses are scheduled via a radio channel, and can trigger up to 50 location updates per second per radio zone; there are two such radio zones in the current installation. The system adaptively schedules Bat updates and offers highly-mobile Bats increased priority by scheduling them more often. Applications can request a higher update rate from the scheduler for a set of Bats for limited periods of time.

The Active Bat system is designed to locate tags inside a room to a high degree of accuracy, but is susceptible to multipath effects and reflections arriving at the receivers. The receivers are carefully surveyed and know their positions in the building to sub-centimetre accuracy. The system processes the raw Bat updates and rejects incorrect ultrasound responses by using a multi-lateration algorithm which requires at least three receivers to agree on a triangulation.

The SPIRIT spatial indexing middleware [1] provides applications with an easy CORBA interface to get notifications when location events occur, such as a person entering or leaving a room. SPIRIT provides feeds of various granularities; for the purposes of our measurements, we use the raw location feed which eliminates readings that fail to pass the multi-lateration algorithm. In addition to location events, SPIRIT also has a record of the *world model* of the building and categorises them by type (such as desks, walls, windows, and partitions).

The Active Bat system provides higher update rates, lower latency and greater levels of accuracy than are likely to be found in any deployed commercial indoor location system in the near future. It provides an excellent research platform for conducting fine-grained measurement surveys to better understand the problem of real-world wireless radio propagation.

3 Methodology

We aim to characterise the properties of Bluetooth by gathering a large number of signal strength measurements across a typical office environment. An Active Bat is attached to a Bluetooth device enabling us to gather: (*i*) the link quality readings from the device; (*ii*) the device's precise location from the Bat; and (*iii*) the time of measurement. This data collection method allowed us to cover nearly all 2D positions in every room except for those with obvious obstructions.

The experiments described analyse the signal strengths in a typical office building which consists of locations that are both obstructed from the transmitter and in line-of-sight. By varying the speed of movement during collection, we also gain insight into the link quality under dynamic conditions.

Section 3.1 defines our use of the term *signal strength*. We then detail our experimental setup in Section 3.2, and describe the post-processing performed on the measurements in Section 3.3.

3.1 Bluetooth Link Quality

The term *signal strength* is somewhat ambiguous in the Bluetooth specification. The Bluetooth Core Specification [3] mandates that vendors provide access to the link quality of established connections through the Host Controller Interface (HCI). The HCI interfaces provides access to two values: (*i*) the Link Quality (LQ); and (*ii*) the Received Signal Strength Indication (RSSI). Additionally, if a Bluetooth link is established, the remote device's perceived RSSI can also be obtained via the "AT+CSQ" command [17] through the Serial Port Profile.

An LQ query returns an 8-bit unsigned integer that quantifies the perceived link quality at the receiver, but the exact coding of that integer is allowed to be device specific. For most Bluetooth chipsets, this number is a proportion of the Bit Error Rate (BER) recorded by the hardware. The reported RSSI value is the difference between the real RSSI in dB and the optimal receive power range, also known as Golden Receive Power Range. RSSI values reported through the HCI are also device dependent, but generally of considerably lower resolution and accuracy than the LQ.

The reported RSSI accuracy level in the Bluetooth specifications only requires a device to report the correct sign of the difference against the Golden Receive Power Range. Cambridge Silicon Radio (CSR) [4] chipsets make no guarantees about the accuracy of the magnitude. Therefore the only source of signal strength information we can rely on for Bluetooth devices is the link quality.

For our experiments we chose to use the popular USB Bluetooth adaptors from CSR as our base stations. The choice of vendor was an important one, as the resolution of link quality data available from the chip varies significantly across different manufacturers. For example, the Broadcom Bluetooth adaptors only offered updated measurements every 5 seconds, with little variation in the actual values reported. The LQ value (Q_l) ranges from $0 \leq Q_l \leq 255$ and is updated once per second by the CSR chipset. Equation 1 describes how to convert Q_l to a percentage BER β.

$$\beta = \begin{cases} 0, & Q_l = 255 \\ (255 - Q_l) \times 0.0025, & 255 < Q_l \le 215 \\ 0.1 + (215 - Q_l) \times 0.08, & 215 < Q_l \le 90 \\ 10.1 + (90 - Q_l) \times 0.64, & 90 < Q_l < 0 \\ 67.7, & Q_l = 0 \end{cases} \qquad (1)$$

CSR chipsets report Link Quality values with lower resolution as BER increases. Figure 1 illustrates three separate resolutions for the range of reported BER values. The BER is a reported average of errors encountered over the connection over a period of approximately 10 seconds. This smoothing property restricts us to a slow survey to ensure the average has an opportunity to settle closer to a representative average at that point (discussed further in Section 4.1).

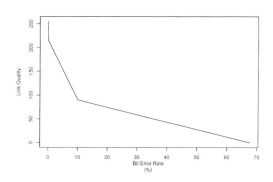

Fig. 1. Link Quality to BER relation for CSR Chipsets

Another factor in measuring link quality is the adaptive properties of Bluetooth transmission. The Bluetooth specification recommends a number of interference reduction techniques to boost reliability in crowded environments. These include power control, Channel Quality Driven Data Rate (CQDDR) and Adaptive Frequency Hopping [11]. The support for these optional enhancements are communicated when a Bluetooth link is established. Users may also explicitly query a remote device for supported features.

Bluetooth power control is an optional feature for the receiver to ask the transmitter to increase or decrease the power output according to its perceived RSSI in relation to the Golden Receiver Power Range. Power control should only be used if both parties in the connection support the feature. Class 1 devices must support this feature whereas lower powered Class 2 and Class 3 devices optionally support it. We found that both CSR and Broadcom chipsets support power control, but the Nokia Bluetooth chipsets found in their mobile phones do not advertise support for it. Using a hardware Bluetooth protocol analyser [16], we were able to verify during our measurements that no power control signalling occurred and thus was not a factor in the results presented here.

CQDDR is an adaptive scheme to select different Bluetooth packet sizes and types depending on the link quality. A receiver may signal the transmitter to use different packet types in order to compensate for bit errors on received packets. Bluetooth allows for 3 packet sizes (1-slot, 3-slot and 5-slot) corresponding to the number of time slots the packet consumes. In addition to that, each packet size can contain no forward error correction (FEC) or 2/3 FEC coding. In the presence of increased BER, a receiver may wish to sacrifice transmission speed with more robust encoding to prevent retransmission. Again, the Nokia chipset did not support this feature whereas both Broadcom and CSR did support it.

Adaptive Frequency Hopping [11] was introduced in the Bluetooth 1.2 specification in order for Bluetooth to avoid using channels which have high levels of interference. It requires that the master device detects which channels produce high BER or low RSSI, and instruct the slave device to avoid those channels. By querying the device and analysing the packets exchanged, we found that none of the Bluetooth hardware we used supported this feature. However, we anticipate that this will be an important factor to consider when performing link quality measurements for future Bluetooth devices.

3.2   Experimental Setup

Fig. 2. An Active Bat attached to a Bluetooth capable mobile phone used to correlate signal strength readings with their locations

Our experiments were conducted in a typical office-like environment where the Active Bat system is installed. For the portable client, we utilised a standard Nokia 6600 mobile phone with Bluetooth capabilities. An Active Bat was physically attached to the back side of the phone to facilitate retrieving the position of the phone in 3D space (see Figure 2). Throughout the experiment, a Bluetooth RFCOMM connection was established to the phone from a notebook PC running Linux 2.6.7 (using the Bluez Bluetooth stack) with a D-Link DBT120 Class 2 Bluetooth USB Adaptor (using a CSR Bluetooth chipset). A USB extension cable was used to place the adaptor in an open area 1 m above the floor.

The link quality of the established RFCOMM connection was queried every time a Bat sighting occurred, which is about 20-30 times per second. The RFCOMM link was used to transmit a remote RSSI query command defined in the AT specification [17]. Position information for the attached Bat was retrieved from the Active Bat system and recorded along with the most recent link quality status of the open RFCOMM connection, remote perceived RSSI and time-stamp.

The low latency and accuracy of the Active Bat system is crucial for data collection since it allows a device's current location to be correlated with the signal strength readings. The Active Bat system is traditionally used to locate tags worn by humans in the building. Context-aware applications access location information via the SPIRIT middleware, which performs aggregation and filtering of readings to cull outliers and artifacts introduced by multi-path reflections and other ultrasonic noise sources.

Using a positioning system in a surveying mode allows us freedom to perform post-processing filtering off-line rather than incur a delay for the system to perform real-time filtering. We opted to obtain the raw positioning information before any filtering had occurred other than the basic multi-lateration outlier rejections.

Link quality observed from the CSR Bluetooth adaptor is a result of a running average over previous values recorded by the chipset. We performed the experiments in a slow sweep of the area, to both ensure stability of the positioning results and also to allow time for the running average to converge closer to a stable value at that position.

Surveys were conducted during after hours in the building to minimise the impact of human interference to propagation. We took care to ensure that the surveyor did not obscure the path between the Bluetooth device and access point to ensure consistency of measurements.

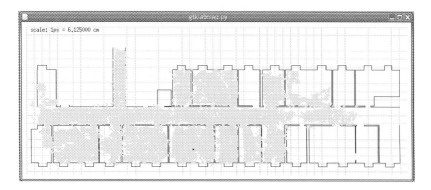

Fig. 3. A GTK application which plots the progress of a survey in real-time, ensuring good coverage of the target area by the surveyor.

We placed the Bluetooth adaptor at different places in the building. All were placed roughly 1 m from the ground at least 50 cm away from any other electronic devices. A real-time graphical map of results was produced from the collection program to ensure we covered the all the available positions in the survey area (see Figure 3).

3.3   Post Processing

Before performing analysis of the recorded measurements, the data was post-processed to remove outliers and inaccurate sightings. These errors consisted of: (i) the surveyor moving faster than the desired speed for the experiment and skewing the recorded Link Quality; and (ii) errors in the locations reported by the Bat system itself (recall that the Bat system has a reported accuracy of 3cm, 95% of the time).

Since the Active Bat system uses the time-of-flight information from ultrasonic pulses to determine the location of a Bat, it is vulnerable to indoor multipath and reflection effects from walls and other obstacles. The Bat system has a degree of built-in robustness to mitigate these effects; at least three Bat receivers must agree on a location using their multi-lateration algorithms before a sighting is considered valid. While this system works very well in the middle of rooms, it breaks down slightly when a Bat is placed very close to a large obstacle such as a wall. This is because the Bat system has limited knowledge of the world model (i.e. the presence of the wall), and thus occasionally extrapolates a reflected signal as originating from beyond the wall. Harle et al. implemented automated mechanisms for the Bat system to infer this information [9,8]; however, these algorithms work at a higher level than the raw data feed we used. The "teleportation effect" is characterised in location traces by a few sightings moving to the other side of a wall before snapping back to the correct location.

Spurious ultrasound emissions in the environment may also cause the Active Bat system to report a single sighting seemingly from a far away room. The effect can be attributed to ultrasonic noise detected by the ceiling receivers just between the time the surveying Bat is polled for an update and when the pulse from the Bat reaches the receivers.

Algorithm 1 describes the "teleportation filter" for detecting incorrect sightings that jump across walls. Given the set of sightings S of size N, we require a look-ahead window of L future sightings and the function $CheckWalls(P_1, P_2)$ to detect wall intersections (described later by Algorithm 2). The algorithm iterates over all the sightings and checks for intersections between the last known good sighting and the current sighting. If an intersection is detected (i.e., a potential teleportation), the next L sightings are also tested for interference against both the last good sighting and the current candidate. The current sighting is erroneous if it exhibits a larger number of future wall intersections than the last good sighting does (remember that a user walking near a wall will trigger the occasional teleport, but the bulk of future sightings will still be along the wall). Experimentally, using a look-ahead of $L = 50$ worked effectively to remove teleportation effects from our data.

Algorithm 1 Teleportation filtering algorithm

Require: $L \geq 0$ and $N > 2$
1: $LastValid \leftarrow S_1$
2: **for** $i = 2$ to N **do**
3:    **if** $CheckWalls(LastValid, S_i) > 0$ **then**
4:       $last \leftarrow \sum_{i+L}^{x=i} CheckWalls(S_x, LastValid)$
5:       $cur \leftarrow \sum_{i+L}^{x=i} CheckWalls(S_x, S_i)$
6:       **if** $last > cur$ **then**
7:          $LastValid \leftarrow S_i$
8:          $Valid(S_i)$
9:       **else**
10:         $Invalid(S_i)$
11:       **end if**
12:    **else**
13:       $Valid(S_i)$
14:    **end if**
15: **end for**

The speed of sightings was also clamped to a maximum value in order to account for the occasional incorrect distant sighting and the surveyor walking too fast. This was done by deriving the velocity v from the time-stamps and distances of subsequent sightings, and eliminating any above v_{max} (which varied depending on the target movement speed for that particular survey).

Algorithm 2 Intersection test for two line segments

1: $q \leftarrow (y_1 - y_3)(x_4 - x_3) - (x_1 - x_3)(y_4 - y_3)$
2: $d \leftarrow (x_2 - x_1)(y_4 - y_3) - (y_2 - y_1)(x_4 - x_3)$
3: **if** $d = 0$ **then**
4:   $false$ {lines are parallel}
5: **else**
6:   $s \leftarrow (y_1 - y_3)(x_2 - x_1) - (x_1 - x_3)(y_2 - y_1)$
7:   **if** $d < q < 0 \parallel d < s < 0$ **then**
8:     $false$ {not on line segment}
9:   **else**
10:     $x_{intersect} \leftarrow x_1 + \frac{r(x_2 - x_1)}{d}$
11:     $y_{intersect} \leftarrow y_1 + \frac{r(y_2 - y_1)}{d}$
12:   **end if**
13: **end if**

---

4 Survey Results

In this section, we present the results of the measurements described earlier. Section 4.1 details the tests which determined an optimal movement speed for conducting the rest of the surveys. Section 4.2 then describes the results from our main surveys of the building with transmitters placed at different points.

4.1   Movement Speed

The purpose of the first experiment conducted was to determine the best movement pace at which to take the subsequent measurements. This was done by selecting a long corridor with no obstructions such that free-space path loss could be expected. A transmitter was placed in the middle of the corridor, and the surveyor repeatedly walked up and down at a constant pace while holding the receiver (a Nokia 6600 Bluetooth mobile phone) towards the transmitter at all times. The results were then filtered to remove outliers and portions where the surveyor walked too fast or too slowly (see Section 3.3 for more details on the filtering algorithms used).

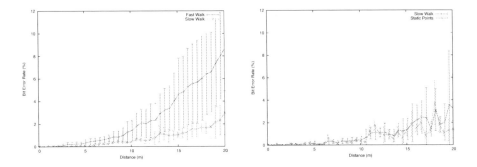

Fig. 4. On the left graph, the BER is plotted for a "fast walk" ($v_{max} = 2\ m/s$) and a "slow walk" ($v_{max} = 0.22\ m/s$), showing how unreliable signal strength readings for a fasting moving user are. The right graph illustrates very little BER variation between a slow walk ($v_{max} = 0.22\ m/s$) and stationary measurements (where the receiver has been idle for over 10 seconds).

Figure 4 *(left)* shows a graph of the measured BER against the distance between the receiver and transmitter. We observe that the BER (both average and standard deviation) of an observer moving at a fast walking pace was far higher than that of a slower walk. With this in mind, all the future surveys were done at a slower pace in order to give the BER adequate time to settle.

Interestingly, an experiment to measure the BER of a completely static receiver and transmitter pair failed to achieve a better result than the slow walk. This experiment was conducted by mounting the mobile phone and Bat on a wooden stand, placing it at the desired location, and leaving it to settle for 10 seconds. After this time, BER reading were taken for another 10 seconds to measure the receiver in its "steady-state".

Figure 4 *(right)* shows very similar measurements of the BER between a slowly moving receiver and a static receiver. A common source of problems in indoor environments is multi-path reflections, which can cause a loss of signal strength by out-of-phase signals causing destructive interference. In order to mitigate this effect, Bluetooth uses pseudo-random frequency hopping algorithms which shift frequencies between 2.4-2.4835GHz. This change of frequency (and thus, change of phase of incoming signals) causes a Bluetooth receiver to effectively "jitter" as if it were constantly in a small amount of motion in its environment. The jitter is useful to push the receiver in and out of zones of destructive interference even if the receiver is static, and accounts for the lack of differences between a slowly moving and a static receiver.

4.2   Signal Strength

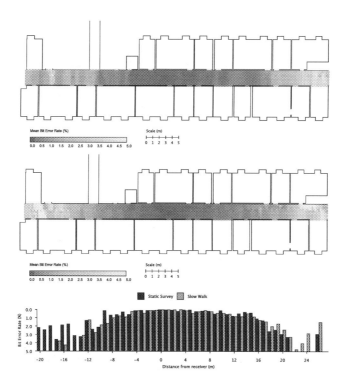

Fig. 5. Measurements of signal strength from a fixed points along the corridor *(middle)* with receiver stationary for more than 10 seconds and signal strength measured from a slow walk *(top)*. A graph of BER versus distance from receiver *(bottom)* shows little difference between the two surveys until the signal degrades significantly at over 12m.

To verify our experimental setup, we first conducted an experiment with a known result. Figure 5 *(middle)* illustrates the free space path loss of a signal in a long corridor in the building. A Bluetooth transmitter was placed in the middle of the corridor, and a mobile phone was placed at points along the corridor and left for 10 seconds. This allowed the running average BER value to settle down to a stable value. We recorded 26938 raw points, out of which 26690 (99.0%) were valid samples after post-processing. This survey confirms that our location measurements were accurate, as we expected to see the standard free-space path loss shown in the figure. The slight disruption in path loss to the right of the figure is due to large metal cupboards at that location which were difficult to move. Figure 5 *(top)* plots the free-space path loss with the surveyor moving at a slow walk surveying the same area. Figure 5 *(bottom)* confirms the observation from Section 4.1 that there is little difference between a survey with a static receiver and one moving slowly until the signal degrades significantly after separation exceeds 12m.

Figure 6 *(top)* shows the results of a conducted by placing a Bluetooth transmitter towards the west end of the building, and performing a slow survey with a Nokia 6600 mobile phone. This survey consisted of 79742 raw samples, of which 66815 (83.7%) were valid samples which passed the post-processing error filters. Each grid location represents the average value of all the signal strengths located inside it. The survey shows that the Bluetooth transmitter has a practical range of around 2 rooms, after which the BER exceeds 2% and the bandwidth on the connection drops below useful levels.

Figure 6 *(bottom)* plots the standard deviation of the values for each grid location. The standard deviation gives an indication of the stability of the connection, and a stable value is very useful for determining the location of the user with respect to the transmitter. The standard deviation is low when the user is close to the transmitter, as the signal strength remains consistently high. As the user moves away, the chipset reports inconsistent signal strength values (cycling between low and high values). This can be partially attributed to the frequency hopping that Bluetooth uses; as the distance from the transmitter increases, the effect of reflected waves introducing constructive or destructive interference for a particular frequency increases. Bluetooth encounters both types of interference as it hops through the 2.4GHz frequency range, accounting for the inconsistent link quality values. Adaptive Frequency Hopping has been proposed as a solution to this problem in future Bluetooth devices, but it is currently not implemented on any consumer Bluetooth chipsets such as CSR, Nokia or Broadcom, so it is irrelevant for the current generation of widely deployed hardware.

A second survey, shown in Figure 7, picked a more central area to help confirm this observation. This survey covered a wider area and consisted of 113686 samples, 91428 (80.4%) of which were valid samples after post-processing. The Nokia 6600 mobile phone could maintain a Bluetooth base-band connection without terminating it even in areas of 5% BER. However, no payload data could be transmitted over the connection during this time; the phone buffered the data until the surveyor moved closer to the fixed Bluetooth transceiver and the BER decreased.

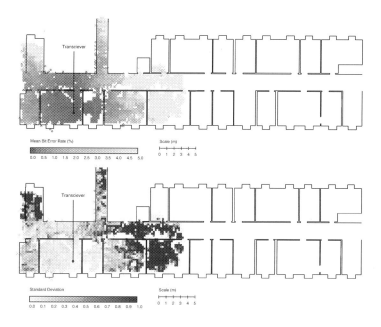

Fig. 6. Measurement of signal strengths *(top)* and the standard deviation *(bottom)* from the west end of the building.

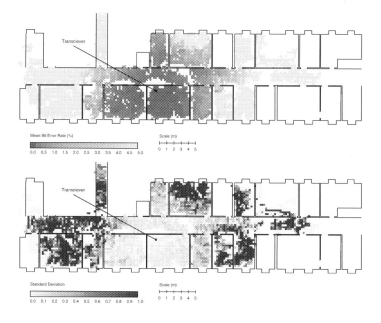

Fig. 7. Measurement of signal strengths *(top)* and the standard deviation *(bottom)* from the centre of the building

4.3   Discussion

Recall from Figure 4 that at a regular walking speed, the average link quality behaves as expected, and BER increases as the distance between transceivers increases. However, the variance of the BER values is much greater at high speeds than when compared to slow movement or stationary readings. This suggests that users walking around a building at normal walking pace would have an adverse impact on their link quality and available bandwidth. This is of concern to location-based services deployed in public buildings such as shopping malls— in order to push high-bandwidth content reliably, the user would have to be relatively stationary rather than walking through the Bluetooth zone.

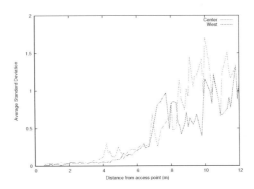

Fig. 8. Distance between the receiver and transmitter versus the average standard deviation of the BERs observed at those points. This was plotted for the data-sets shown in Figures 6 and 7 to show that they both show the trend of increased standard deviation as distance increases.

Figure 8 plots the distance between the receiver and transmitter versus the standard deviation of the BERs observed at all the points of the Bluetooth surveys shown in Figure 6 and Figure 7. Standard deviation for BER values exhibit a slow gradual increase in standard deviation between 0 to 6.5 m followed by a steep increase. At distances further than 6.5 m, BER values are unstable and thus using BER at such distances would produce unreliable distance predictions. For distances under 4 m from the transceiver, there is only a small magnitude of variance when moving at slow speeds. A low standard deviation of BER values is important for low-latency location-sensing, as it allows for a stable and accurate distance prediction of the user from the transmitter.

We observe several factors that lead us to conclude that Bluetooth is a poor choice for the use of signal strength for low-latency location sensing: (*i*) all the hardware we surveyed only exposes a running average of the BER which is updated at different intervals depending on the hardware (1s for CSR and 5s for the Broadcom dongles); (*ii*) measured BER had a high variance as the distance increased beyond about 6m; (*iii*) none of the mobile phones supported more than a single Bluetooth connection, making triangulation difficult; and (*iv*) the reported RSSI values was of little or no use due to the lack of resolution and slow update rate. One must also take into account possible adaptive features available in future revisions of the mobile phone chipsets, which further blur location inferencing.

Although the actual propagation distance achieved is dependent on hardware (e.g. antenna type and construction), we believe our results would apply to different omnidirectional Class 2 Bluetooth devices because of the restriction in power output of the device. Limitations in consumer hardware prevented us from obtaining higher resolution data from the Bluetooth hardware itself. Compared to WiFi, none of the reported link quality values give high enough accuracy and dependability to enable location-sensing based on signal strength alone.

The Bluetooth specification could improve support for location inferencing if changes were introduced requiring devices to: (*i*) expose a fine-grained RSSI dBm value via HCI (similarly to 802.11); (*ii*) accept multiple simultaneous Bluetooth connections in order to assist triangulation; and (*iii*) update RSSI values per-packet without a significant time lag.

However, Figure 8 indicates show a positive trend of standard deviation as the distance to the transmitter varies. This implies that if a Bluetooth location system is willing to increase the latency of reported results, it could estimate the distance of a slow moving user based on the combination of standard deviation and average values of measured signal strength over a period of time. For tracking stationary objects, it may also be feasible to overcome the restriction of one Bluetooth connection at a time by polling the device from multiple co-operating base stations.

Our use of the Active Bat system as a positioning system proved valuable to understanding the useful characteristics of using indoor location systems for this purpose: (*i*) systematic stable latency between the real position and reported sightings enables easy correlation of external signal strength readings with their associated positions; (*ii*) high rate of readings allowed us to understand the dynamic behaviour of signal strength on moving devices; and (*iii*) reported location sightings must be stable before signal strength readings are taken; Bluetooth Class 2 devices have a useful range of 10 m, for which the BER varies between 0-2%, with around 50 possible link quality steps reported by the CSR chipset. If these readings were spread out linearly, it would require 0.2 m intervals to record them all distinctly. The Active Bat system offered much higher precision than is needed for a survey of a Bluetooth Class 2 device.

As reported in the literature, inaccurate world models have a significant negative impact on context-aware applications and services [8]. For our purpose, surveying and propagation measurements required more detailed world model information that would not be useful to existing context-aware applications (e.g. wall and object material composition). Other objects such as switching cabinets and server room equipment were not in the world-model, but are still variables which affect indoor radio propagation.

5   Related Work

Wireless LAN technology (WLAN) has been a popular candidate for indoor location estimation based on signal strength. Most of these methods rely on a surveying phase where checkpoints in the environment are statically surveyed to obtain calibration data. The position of a device is determined by correlating the signal strength measurements at different access points using Bayesian analysis [20] or simple triangulation [2]. Our Bluetooth survey attempt to map all physical space covered by the location system and also allows us to map the signal strength rate of change for moving targets.

The advantage of WLAN positioning is that signal strength information can be obtained at a per packet level and signal strength can be sampled from a number of access points simultaneously. Under Bluetooth, signal strength information is only obtained indirectly through the BER value (a running average over a 10 s interval). Furthermore, many mobile Bluetooth devices cannot accept more than one connection at a time, which is needed to calculate signal strength between two end points. Bluetooth devices are more attractive because of their low power usage and proliferation in current consumer devices; e.g. in previous work, we used a preliminary version of our survey technique to integrate Bluetooth mobile phones into a fast-paced location-aware game [15].

Projects such as Place Lab [19] and the Location Stack [6] have used the coarse-grained metric of Bluetooth device sightings along with other sources such as WiFi or GPS to infer user location. Our work complements this by performing more fine-grained analysis on Bluetooth indoor propagation using the Active Bat system and making these data sets freely available to other researchers interested in Bluetooth [14].

Gwon et al also propose a mechanism of location estimation for mobile and stationary users based on signal strength measurements [7]. They report their Region of Confidence (RoC) algorithm performs better using Bluetooth than WiFi, but this is a result of using a denser collection of Bluetooth nodes for the same area. Simulations of Bluetooth channel capacity [13] and its efficient coexistence with other protocols in the same frequency range (such as WiFi) have been extensively studied [5]. In this paper, we isolate Bluetooth and consider its propagation through comprehensive measurements.

6   Conclusions and Future Work

The extensive signal strength surveys using the Active Bat system have made a wealth of data available for future analysis [14]. In order to minimise the number of variables in our study, we chose to restrict the surveys in this paper to a single Bluetooth transmitter and receiver. There has been extensive simulation work into how effectively multiple Bluetooth devices can co-exist [13] with each other, or with other protocols in the 2.4GHz range (e.g. WiFi). We intend to extend our measurements to investigate the actual impact of these interactions on moving devices such as PDAs and mobile phones. Although the current generation of mobile phones do not yet support them, future versions of Bluetooth will support Adaptive Frequency Hopping [11] and Channel Quality Driven Data Rate (CQDDR) that will have a negative impact on location inferencing based on signal strength. The survey methodology described in this paper allows researchers to easily perform an analysis of the real-world impact of these features with mobile devices of varying speeds.

In this paper, we have presented a measurement-based approach to help evaluate and visualize the accuracy of wireless signal propagation. The Active Bat ultrasonic indoor location system was used to gather a large number of samples of Bluetooth signal strengths from transceivers placed around a building. The samples exhibited a number of artifacts which are to be expected from a high-resolution, raw location feed from a multi-lateration-based location system, and we presented algorithms which filtered out bad samples to a high degree of accuracy. These samples were then analyzed for receivers moving at different speeds to simulate the movements of real users (running, walking or staying stationary). We observed a significant increase in BER variance for users moving at walking speeds or faster, implying that location-based "push services" operating over Bluetooth will have less bandwidth available to transmit multimedia content in busy public areas where consumers are not standing still.

We conclude from our measurements that Bluetooth is ill-suited for the purpose of accurate, low-latency location sensing due to: (i) common chipsets only exposing a running average of signal strengths and updating it infrequently; (ii) the high variance in signal strengths for longer distances; and (iii) the inability for consumer mobile phones to maintain multiple Bluetooth connections simultaneously for triangulation purposes. Finally, we have made our data-sets available on-line [14] for other researchers to benefit from the large number of samples gathered during this research.

7   Acknowledgments

Thanks to David McCall from Cambridge Silicon Radio for prompt and accurate replies to our queries about the BlueCore Bluetooth chipset. We are grateful to Andrew Rice, Kieran Mansley, Alastair Beresford, Ford Long Wong, Robert Harle, Ian Wassell and our shepherd Anthony LaMarca for their valuable discussions and contributions to this work, and to the members of the Digital Technology Group who tolerated strange people repeatedly sweeping through their offices armed with mobile phones and Bats. This work was partly funded by Intel Research Cambridge.

References

1. M. Addlesee, R. Curwen, S. Hodges, J. Newman, P. Steggles, A. Ward, and A. Hopper. Implementing a sentient computing system. *IEEE Computer*, 34(8):50–56, August 2001.
2. P. Bahl and V. N. Padmanabhan. RADAR: An in-building RF-based user location and tracking system. In *IEEE Infocom*, March 2000.

3. Bluetooth Special Interest Group. Bluetooth core specification 1.1. https://www.bluetooth.org/spec/.
4. Cambridge Silicon Radio. BlueCore Bluetooth chipset. Online at http://www.csr.com/products/bc-family.htm.
5. N. Golmie, R. E. V. Dyck, A. Soltanian, A. Tonnerre, and O. Rebala. Interference evaluation of Bluetooth and IEEE 802.11b systems. *Wireless Networks*, 9(3):201–211, 2003.
6. D. Graumann, J. Hightower, W. Lara, and G. Borriello. Real-world implementation of the Location Stack: The Universal Location Framework. In *Fifth IEEE Workshop on Mobile Computing Systems and Applications*, October 2003.
7. Y. Gwon, R. Jain, and T. Kawahara. Robust indoor location estimation of stationary and mobile users. In *IEEE Infocom*, March 2004.
8. R. K. Harle. *Maintaining World Models in Context-Aware Environments*. PhD thesis, University of Cambridge, 2004.
9. R. K. Harle, A. Ward, and A. Hopper. Single Reflection Spatial Voting: A novel method for discovering reflective surfaces using indoor positioning systems. In *First International Conference on Mobile Systems, Applications and Services*, pages 1–14, May 2003.
10. A. Harter, A. Hopper, P. Steggles, A. Ward, and P. Webster. The anatomy of a context-aware application. In *5th Annual ACM/IEEE International Conference on Mobile Computing and Networking*, 1999.
11. C. Hodgdon. Adaptive frequency hopping for reduced interference between Bluetooth and wireless LAN, May 2003. Ericsson Technology Licensing.
12. In-Stat/MDR. Bluetooth-enabled products poised to swim in the mainstream, April 2004. Order Code R97-1590.
13. A. Kumar and R. Gupta. Capacity evaluation of frequency hopping based ad-hoc systems. In *Proceedings of the 2001 ACM SIGMETRICS international conference on Measurement and modeling of computer systems*, pages 133–142. ACM Press, 2001.
14. A. Madhavapeddy and A. Tse. Bluetooth propagation datasets. Available online at http://www.cl.cam.ac.uk/Research/DTG/research/bluetoothsurvey/.
15. K. Mansley, D. Scott, A. Tse, and A. Madhavapeddy. Feedback, latency, accuracy: exploring tradeoffs in location-aware gaming. In *SIGCOMM 2004 Workshops: Proceedings of ACM SIGCOMM 2004 workshops on NetGames '04*, pages 93–97, New York, NY, USA, 2004. ACM Press.
16. Mobiwave. Bluetooth protocol analyser BPA-D10. http://www.mobiwave.com/bpa.htm.
17. Nokia Mobile Phones. AT command set for Nokia GSM products. Online at http://www.forum.nokia.com/.
18. N. B. Priyantha, A. Chakraborty, and H. Balakrishnan. The Cricket Location-Support System. In *6th ACM MOBICOM*, Boston, MA, August 2000.
19. B. Schilit, A. LaMarca, G. Borriello, D. M. William Griswold, E. Lazowska, A. Balachandran, and J. H. V. Iverson. Challenge: Ubiquitous location-aware computing and the Place Lab initiative. In *First ACM International Workshop of Wireless Mobile Applications and Services on WLAN*, September 2003.
20. P. Tao, A. Rudys, A. M. Ladd, and D. S. Wallach. Wireless LAN location-sensing for security applications. In *Proceedings of the Second ACM Workshop on Wireless Security (WiSe)*, San Diego, CA, Sept. 2003.
21. A. Ward. *Sensor-driven Computing*. PhD thesis, University of Cambridge, 1998.

A New Method for Auto-calibrated Object Tracking*

Paul Duff[1], Michael McCarthy[1], Angus Clark[1], Henk Muller[1], Cliff Randell[1], Shahram Izadi[2], Andy Boucher[3], Andy Law[3], Sarah Pennington[3], and Richard Swinford[3]

[1] Department of Computer Science, University of Bristol, U.K.
duff@cs.bris.ac.uk
[2] Microsoft Research, Cambridge, U.K.
[3] Royal College of Art, U.K.

Abstract. Ubiquitous computing technologies which are cheap and easy to use are more likely to be adopted by users beyond the ubiquitous computing community. We present an ultrasonic-only tracking system that is cheap to build, self-calibrating and self-orientating, and has a convenient form factor. The system tracks low-power tags in three dimensions. The tags are smaller than AAA batteries and last up to several years on their power source. The system can be configured to track either multiple near-stationary objects or a single fast moving object. Full test results are provided and use of the system within a home application is discussed.

1 Introduction

Position sensing is an important aspect of pervasive computing. As a form of context input, it provides context-aware applications with the ability to model relationships between users and their environment. With this information, applications can provide a number of useful interactions in scenarios ranging from an audio tour-guide to an augmented reality application.

Narrowband ultrasonic positioning is an attractive form of positioning because it is low cost. Transducers are cheap and readily available, and expensive, high-precision oscillators are unnecessary because ultrasonic signals travel relatively slowly when compared to other signals such as RF. There are a number of narrowband ultrasound systems described in the literature that compute positions using a variety of different techniques. Some, such as the Active Bat [1], perform position *tracking* where a single governing application tracks multiple objects within a framework. Others perform *positioning*, where each object calculates its own private position, such as the systems developed at the University of Bristol [2, 3].

The issue of cost addressed by these applications, however, does not consider the expense of setting up and configuring the infrastructure supporting them.

* Funding for this work is received from the U.K. Engineering and Physical Sciences Research Council as part of the Equator IRC, GR-N-15986.

M. Beigl et al. (Eds.): UbiComp 2005, LNCS 3660, pp. 123–140, 2005.

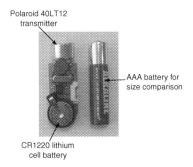

Polaroid 40LT12
transmitter

AAA battery for
size comparison

CR1220 lithium
cell battery

Fig. 1. Ultrasonic Tag

The uptake of positioning technologies by users outside of the ubiquitous computing community relies on us making them *accessible*. This term refers to all costs surrounding the technology:

- component cost;
- configuration expense;
- power consumption;
- form factor.

We have developed an object tracker that addresses each of these issues. Unlike most systems that utilise RF and ultrasound, including the Active Bat and Cricket [4], our system uses only ultrasonic signals. The absence of RF circuitry improves the power consumption, component cost, and form factor of tags tracked by the application. Our prototype tags are smaller than AAA batteries, run on 3V CR1220 cell batteries (see Fig. 1), and weigh 8 grammes (including CR1220 battery). We have also developed auto-calibration and self-orientation applications that greatly reduce the time and expertise needed to set-up the infrastructure, making it easier for artists and non-experts to use. Furthermore, the system can be configured to track either multiple near-stationary objects or a single fast moving object. The total component cost for the system, including the infrastructure and one tag, is around $100.

We explore the use of the ultrasonic system for tracking objects as they move around the home. In this test, non-technical researchers installed and used the system without any 'expert' help. A discussion of the use of the tracker as a part of this project is presented at the end of the paper.

2   System Description

The tracking system consists of a set of fixed receivers and one or more transmitting tags. The tags are each powered by a 3V coin cell battery. A PIC microcontroller on each tag controls the periodic activation of a 40kHz narrowband ultrasonic transducer. In the case of a single object tracking system, the tag

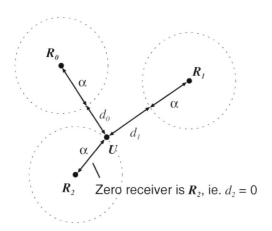

Fig. 2. Ultrasonic tracking. U is the position of the transmitter tag, R_0, R_1, R_2 are three receiver positions

chirps regularly with an operational life of several months. In the case of multiple objects that are to be tracked individually, each tag chirps with a specific signature (described in detail in Sect. 5.1). The operational life increases to several years because chirping is less frequent.

The receivers are connected to a controller which determines the relative timing of the input signals. The controller sends the recorded timing information over a serial cable to a PC running the tracking software. The system requires at least four receivers in order to locate objects (discussed in Sect. 3). We use six for the system described here in order to provide some redundancy and increase accuracy. The maximum range of the tags is around 8m; this is sufficient to provide coverage for a room of 6×6m, for example.

When a signal emitted by a tag is detected by the nearest receiver, it is assigned a relative distance of zero metres. As the chirp travels outward from its source, the other receivers detect it after an additional delay. By factoring with the speed of sound, these delays can be converted into relative distances. Hence for a system using m receivers, the distances can be expressed as follows:

$$d_i + \alpha = |R_i - U| \qquad (0 \leq i < m) \tag{1}$$

Here d_i is a relative distance measured using receiver position R_i, U is the origin of the chirp, and α is an unknown offset. Note that the nearest receiver R_z will always give a relative distance $d_z = 0$. We refer to receiver R_z as the *zero receiver*. Figure 2 shows a 2D example of this arrangement.

The constant offset α can be eliminated by observing that for the zero receiver R_z:

$$\alpha = |R_z - U| \tag{2}$$

Hence we are left with a system of equations in terms of fixed receiver positions R_i, the chirp origin U, and measured relative distances d_i. We assume a fixed speed of sound, though it is possible to estimate this at the cost of an additional receiver [5]. Note that this is only feasible once the system is calibrated.

$$d_i = |\boldsymbol{R}_i - \boldsymbol{U}| - |\boldsymbol{R}_z - \boldsymbol{U}| \qquad (0 \le i < m, i \neq z) \tag{3}$$

In the next section we describe how we determine the positions of the tracking system's fixed receivers $\boldsymbol{R}_i$ by auto-calibration, using an approach similar to calibrating a positioning system [9]. In Sect. 4 we describe the auto-orientation algorithm, while in Sect. 5 we examine two alternative methods for determining the chirp origin $\boldsymbol{U}$.

3   Auto-calibration

Tracking is only possible once the positions of the receivers $\boldsymbol{R}_i$ are known. As we do not want to rely on people surveying the space by hand, our aim is to determine the positions of $\boldsymbol{R}_i$ algorithmically. To accomplish this, we take a single transmitting tag and move it around the room, taking care to collect distance readings from all parts of the room. This stage takes around 30 seconds, in contrast to taking measurements manually which can take 20 minutes or more, especially when receivers are mounted out of reach. In our experience, manual measurements require the work of two people, and often involve reaching awkwardly and noting down large numbers of distances and offsets. Auto-calibration obviates the need for this inconvenient process.

Once we have a representative set of distance measurements, we aim to solve (4), where m receivers and c tag positions are used, and only distances d_{ij} are known. There are thus m receiver positions $\boldsymbol{R}_i$, c zero receivers $\boldsymbol{R}_{z_j}$, and c tag positions $\boldsymbol{U}_j$ to be determined.

$$d_{ij} = |\boldsymbol{R}_i - \boldsymbol{U}_j| - |\boldsymbol{R}_{z_j} - \boldsymbol{U}_j| \qquad (0 \le i < m, i \neq z_j, 0 \le j < c) \tag{4}$$

A solution can only be found if there is more information known about the system than is unknown and to be computed—the system must be *over-specified*. Each unknown receiver position has three degrees of freedom in 3D space that must be found. Additionally, each new tag position contributes a further three unknowns. This is balanced by $m - 1$ relative positions and one zero receiver index gained with each new chirp transmission.

Six degrees of freedom can also be eliminated by describing the planar relationship between the first receiver and two others. By fixing the co-ordinates of one receiver, we set an origin for the 3D space in which solutions will be computed. The remaining three co-ordinates set the axes for the 3D co-ordinate system. In this way we avoid a situation where the same solution could be rotated or translated to produce an infinite number of solutions. Setting the axes leads to an arbitrarily rotated solution, a problem that is solved in Sect. 4.

The approximate constraint generalised to a system of m receivers and c chirp transmission positions is:

$$3(c + m) - 6 < (c - 1)m \tag{5}$$

The constraint is an under-bound; in reality an excess of known data is needed for good results. Readings from the same location are redundant as they will not contribute any additional information to the system. The algorithm must also be able to handle noisy measurements from the ultrasonic sensors.

It is clear from (5) that we must use a minimum of four receivers in order to over-specify the system. In the case of our six receiver example, this constraint suggests that at least six sets of relative distance data are needed, though more are desirable.

Given perfect data, it would be possible to find perfect solutions for the receiver and tag positions, balancing (4). In practice this is not possible, since distance readings have a limited granularity and are subject to noise and distortions. We can only hope to minimise the overall error and find a *best fit* for the unknown values.

Taking a least squares approach to error minimisation, we express the problem in terms of a minimisation function F, as shown in (6).

$$F = \sum_{i=0, \; i\neq z_j}^{m-1} \sum_{j=0}^{c-1} \left(d_{ij} - |\boldsymbol{R}_i - \boldsymbol{U}_j| + |\boldsymbol{R}_{z_j} - \boldsymbol{U}_j|\right)^2 \tag{6}$$

We use the Levenberg-Marquardt nonlinear least squares fitting algorithm [6], as it is reasonably suited to problems of high dimensionality. Attempts using other techniques such as Simulated Annealing [7] revealed that they converge less reliably on good solutions. We use an implementation provided within the GNU Scientific Library (GSL) [8], and refer to this central part of the algorithm as the *solver*.

As a randomised search process, the solver is not guaranteed to produce a good solution on any one occasion. We therefore execute the solver multiple times, using different seed values and input data to increase the probability of finding receiver positions accurately. The most promising solutions can then be selected according to quality heuristics. This process is repeated in several rounds, where each round applies more demanding criteria for convergence than the previous one.

At the end of a round, we select the most promising 10% of the candidate solutions [9]. The best solutions are taken forward to the next round, and the process repeated until there is a final set of candidate solutions remaining. In this way we survey the search space broadly without a prohibitive computation cost.

The remaining candidate solutions are then each represented in terms of the distance between respective pairs of receivers. This representation is independent of the origin and rotation of the solution, and hence can be used to compare different solutions. We can expect that two geometrically similar solutions will share similar distances between corresponding receiver pairs, even if one solution is rotated with respect to the other. There are 15 distances between the six receivers, hence we describe the solution as a point in a 15-dimensional space. We found that good solutions cluster around one point in this 15-dimensional space, while poor solutions are scattered at lower density in other arrangements.

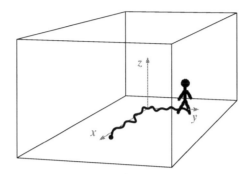

Fig. 3. The user walks along an L-shaped path, defining the x and y axis of the co-ordinate system.

By performing a greedy clustering algorithm on these distances we identify where the correct solution lies.

4   Orientating an Auto-calibrated Solution

Once the system has selected a best solution for the positions of the receivers, we find that the axes of the solution are placed arbitrarily. This is inherent to the problem, as we do not constrain the use of a particular origin or orientation. Specifically, the solver is allowed to invent any co-ordinate system it sees fit, provided it is orthogonal. As such, these axes may appear to bear little resemblance to the layout of the room. In order to place the receivers within a pre-defined co-ordinate system—for example one where the axes align conveniently with the walls and floor—we allow the user to specify the co-ordinate frame that they would like to use through an auto-orientation stage.

In keeping with the principle of ease of deployment, the method automates much of the process and requires no technical knowledge on the part of the user. All the user must do is take a single transmitting tag in hand and walk along an L-shaped path which defines the axes that they would like the system to use, as shown in Fig. 3.

The system collects tag positions as the user walks along the path. This set of position data defines the L-shape path in terms of the internal co-ordinate frame used by the system, as shown in Fig. 4(a). A two stage search process is then applied to the position data, in order to determine the transformation that aligns the L-shape path to the axes of the internal co-ordinate frame. Splitting the search into two stages greatly simplifies the process and improves the reliability of the system.

The first stage borrows techniques from Principal Components Analysis [10] and attempts to find the best fitting plane through the set of training points. Let $X = \{X_1, X_2, ..., X_n\}$ be the set of tag positions. We first calculate the

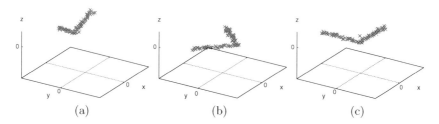

Fig. 4. The L-shaped path defined by user. (a) shown in the internal co-ordinate system, (b) transformed onto the XY-plane, (c) aligned with the axes.

mean, $\bar{X}$, and covariance matrix Σ of the data set X. The eigenvectors, e_1, e_2, e_3 of the covariance matrix define an alternative orthogonal basis. If we order the eigenvectors by their corresponding eigenvalues, each axis accounts for a diminishing proportion of the variance present in the data. In our system the first two eigenvectors will lie on the plane defined by the L-shaped path (ie. the XY-plane), while the third eigenvector accounts for any variations in height along the path (ie. the z-axis).

Converting the points to this new co-ordinate system, we get:

$$X'_i = [\hat{e}_1, \hat{e}_2, \hat{e}_3]^T (X_i - \bar{X}) \tag{7}$$

where $\hat{e}$ denotes the normalised vector e.

We have now arrived at a co-ordinate system where the L-shape lies on the XY-plane, and with height represented by the z-axis, as shown in Fig. 4(b). The next stage is to find the translation $T = [t_x, t_y, 0]^T$, and the rotation around the z-axis, $R_z(r_z)$, that will align the L-shape path with the x and y-axis, and with the corner located at the origin.

In order to achieve this, we first project the set of points X' onto the XY-plane, thereby removing any height variations present along the L-shaped path. Next we apply an adaptive simulated annealing algorithm [7, 11] that minimises the following energy function.

$$E(t_x, t_y, r_z) = \sum_{i=1}^{n} e_{xi}^2 \times e_{yi}^2 \tag{8}$$

where

$$\begin{bmatrix} e_{xi} \\ e_{yi} \\ 0 \end{bmatrix} = R_z(X'_i - T) \tag{9}$$

The energy function captures the notion that the L-shape should be aligned to the axes. However, the system has no knowledge as to which section of the L-shape should be located on the x-axis, and which should be located on the y-axis. We therefore examine the start and end points of the L-shape to ensure that they lie on the positive x-axis and positive y-axis respectively, updating the rotation $\boldsymbol{R}_z$ as required ($+90^o$, $+180^o$ or $+270^o$).

The transformations derived above can be combined to give a single homogeneous transformation. The result yields a transformation that converts points from the internal co-ordinate frame used by the system to the co-ordinate frame defined by the user, as shown in Fig. 4(c). This transformation is applied to all subsequent points thereby providing position information in the co-ordinate frame specified by the user.

The current implementation assumes the L-path specified by the user lies on the XY-plane. The system could easily be extended to allow the user to specify which co-ordinate plane (XY, XZ or YZ) the L-shape should reside. However, this introduces further complexity for the user and in most cases will be unnecessary.

5   Tracking Objects

Our system can be used to track multiple objects with a low resolution in time, or a single object with a high time resolution (33Hz).

5.1   Multiple Objects

A fully calibrated system can be used to track one or more ultrasonic transmitters. It is often desirable to track multiple objects, each with a transmitting tag attached. In order to track individual objects reliably, each tag needs to transmit a signature that uniquely identifies the source, separating it from background noise and signals from other tags.

Estimator In order to determine the position U of a tag, we solve the system of equations described in (10).

$$d_i = |\boldsymbol{R}_i - \boldsymbol{U}| - |\boldsymbol{R}_z - \boldsymbol{U}| \qquad (0 \le i < m, i \ne z) \tag{10}$$

The receiver positions $\boldsymbol{R}_i$ are known from the auto-calibration stage, and relative distances d_i are measured by the system when the tag transmits. The zero receiver $\boldsymbol{R}_z$ is determined trivially by checking the relative distances recorded by each receiver. To solve the system of equations for U, we use a least-squares minimisation process very similar to that described in Sect. 3. However, since there is much more known information in the system, we only need to run the Levenberg-Marquardt algorithm once to find a solution.

As we have opted to use cheap ultrasonic transmitters with a narrow transmission frequency range, it is not feasible to encode the signature by altering the frequency of the transmitted ultrasound wave. Instead, the tags are configured to transmit three short pulses in quick succession. The time between transmission of each of the pulses is selected from a set of six discrete durations, varying from 30-40ms. These durations are permuted so that each tag has a unique timing signature, as illustrated in Fig. 5.

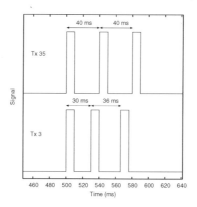

Fig. 5. Example signal timing for two tags

We expect that the computed positions of a tag will be virtually the same for each of the three pulses, as the tag cannot move very far between pulses. This allows us to remove noisy transmissions more reliably, as we can discount any ultrasound transmission that does not fall within the limits of the expected timing pattern. It also allows for a small amount of error correction; if the timing is correct but positioning is poor for one of the three pulses, then we can remove the outlier.

Tag ID	Period multiplier	$T_1 - T_0$ (ms)	$T_2 - T_1$ (ms)
0	947	30	30
1	953	30	32
2	967	30	34
⋮	⋮	⋮	⋮
35	1193	40	40

Table 1. Tag timing signatures

A further consideration with multiple tags is the use of the shared 40kHz audio channel. In order to reliably identify an individual tag, the tag must have exclusive use of channel for the duration of its three pulses, and for a brief time before and after transmission. It must then remain silent while other tags are active. With this constraint, there is a trade-off between the number of objects that can be tracked and the frequency with which their position can be updated. Thus the object tracker is best suited to applications where a large number of objects are tracked several times per minute, or where one or two objects are to be tracked several times per second.

132   Paul Duff et al.

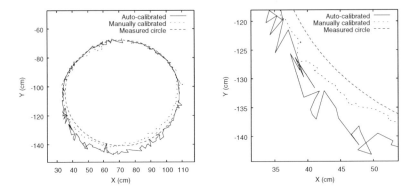

Fig. 6. Moving transmitter track (left) and close-up (right)

As the tags are independent of one another, is is not possible to co-ordinate them to transmit consistently in a particular order. However, we reduce the likelihood of a collision between one or more tags by configuring each tag to pause for a different length of time after transmitting a set of pulses. By carefully choosing these times to be a constant multiple of the set of prime numbers, we can avoid aliasing, where two tags collide regularly. Table 1 shows possible signal timing patterns for a set of transmitting tags. Note that the prime period multipliers are approximate, since each tag has its own clock which will drift with respect to other tag clocks.

Performance The auto-calibration algorithm was executed using a set of recorded distances as described in Sect. 3. Execution time for calibration was approximately 5 minutes on a 1GHz Pentium processor. The best solution was then used to track a transmitting tag. The computed track was compared with a manually measured ground truth, plus a track computed using manually calibrated receivers. Figure 6 shows an aerial view of these three tracks, overlaid to give an indication of the scale of their accuracies. The close-up view shows the region of greatest difference between the tracks. The slightly lower accuracy of the auto-calibrated result is clear, with computed positions jumping around more erratically than in the manually calibrated track.

We observe a systematic scaling error, resulting in an error of 5-7 cm in the bottom part of the track. This may have been caused by a consistent offset in the distance data recorded. It is important to note that the systematic errors will drop out of the system if it is trained with information about the positions of objects in a room. Often we are only interested in knowing that we are next to some object, rather than precise co-ordinates for measuring distances.

The reproducibility of results using the auto-calibrated system was analysed using sets of over 1000 readings taken at stationary transmission positions. Running this data through both a manually calibrated and an auto-calibrated tracker revealed some variability in the placing of points even after systematic

	SEP 50%	SEP 95%	RMS
Manually calibrated system	1.28	2.71	1.70
Auto-calibrated system	1.87	4.02	2.29
Ratio manual/auto	0.68	0.68	0.74

Table 2. 50% and 95% SEPs and RMS errors given in centimetres

errors were taken into account. These radial errors give a better indication of how reproducible results are using the tracking system. Table 2 shows accuracies of the system in terms of 50% and 95% spherical error probability (SEP) and root mean square error (RMS).

The SEP and RMS values all show that on average the manually calibrated system performs a little better than the auto-calibrated one, though not significantly so. The errors for the auto-calibrated system are still well within the limits of many applications that currently use manually calibrated systems, and the ratios indicate that the distributions of errors are similar in both cases. RMS values give a more representative indication of the system's consistency at producing results.

5.2 Single Object

The system can also change modes to track a single object to a high degree of accuracy. By giving one mobile device a monopoly on the 40kHz audio channel we are able to increase the ultrasound transmission rate to frequencies up to 33Hz. This gives our system a shorter response time and allows us to track objects moving at higher velocities and accelerations. When we receive regular readings from one object, we can use a more effective method to calculate this object's position.

Estimator The estimator we use for this mode of operation is the Kalman filter [12]. Although it is not well suited for the large transmission periods of the multiple object tracker, the Kalman filter does fit well with the new tracking conditions. Specifically, it is more efficient and predictable than Levenberg-Marquardt, it uses knowledge of the previous system state, and it provides a method for modelling the dynamics of the system. In our filter, we employ a position-velocity model that assumes the velocity of the tracked object is constant and subject to acceleration 'noise'. In the following process equations, U and V are the position and velocity of the tag, P is the transmission period and E is the transmission time.

$$U_k = U_{k-1} + P_{k-1} \cdot V_{k-1}$$
$$V_k = V_{k-1}$$
$$E_k = E_{k-1} + P_{k-1}$$
$$P_k = P_{k-1}$$

The state vector falls from these equations as $[\, U \ V \ E \ P \,]^T$.

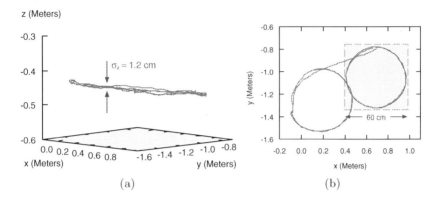

Fig. 7. Path of single tag operating at 33Hz, (a) 3D view showing position along z-axis, (b) 2D view showing position along x and y axes.

For each receiver i, we have one measurement equation that relates the state, the known position of the receiver, $\boldsymbol{R}_i$ (from auto-calibration), and the speed of sound, v, to the reception time of the signal, T_i.

$$T_i = E + \frac{|\boldsymbol{U} - \boldsymbol{R}_i|}{v} \tag{11}$$

Although the reception times recorded by each receiver are obtained almost instantaneously, we integrate the measurements with the filter in a serial fashion. This method, known as single-constraint-at-a-time (SCAAT) Kalman filtering [13], provides advantages in terms of efficiency and outlier detection.

Performance Figure 7 shows the path of a tag mounted on the back of an office chair. The chair was spun on its base, rolled, and spun again to create the two circles illustrated. The height of the tag was kept constant throughout as is reflected by the accuracy of the filter along the z-axis. In terms of standard deviation from the mean position, this value is 1.2cm. To gauge the dynamic accuracy in the x-y plane, we compare the diameter of the circles in Fig. 7 to the true 60cm swivel diameter of the chair. The circles are approximately 6% smaller than the diameter created by the chair. We attribute the discrepancy to errors in the value used for the speed of sound, a non-ideal arrangement of the receivers having a high dilution of precision, varying transmitter-receiver incident angles, and errors in the positions of the receivers from auto-calibration. The stationary 3D accuracy of the system, in terms of spherical error probability over a 40 second time frame, is 5mm for 95% of the readings and 6mm for 99%.

With these accuracies, the single object tracking system could be used with applications such as home gaming systems (Xbox, PlayStation, etc.) and motion tracking for animation. Fused with inertial sensors, the system also has the potential to be used with augmented or virtual reality applications. A combined

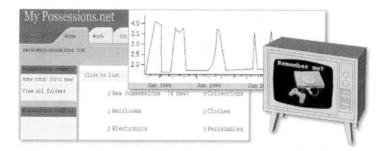

Fig. 8. Initial design sketches for an application that tracks possessions, shows usage over time and re-advertises "ignored" objects using channels in the home.

ultrasonics-inertial-sensor approach has been used successfully by InterSense Inc. in a number of their high performance products [14, 15, 16].

6 Explorations of Ultrasonic Tracking Within the Home Environment

We have been developing a series of interactive scenarios based around tracking objects within the home. The scenarios follow earlier studies involving domestic probes and experiments within the home [17, 18]. In this environment we want to experiment with designs without having to repeatedly calibrate a tracking system by hand. This is very much work in progress, but our initial experiments offer interesting insights into the use of such a system, and its practical impact and value for Ubicomp applications.

Below we use the term *engineer* to denote a person who designs ultrasonic systems, and the term *designer* to denote a person who designs ubicomp experiences. A *user* is someone who interacts with the final experience.

6.1 A Motivating Scenario

Our aim is to track a series of objects within the home, in order to indicate current object positions and patterns of usage. Small objects are tagged and registered with an application running on a computer connected to the ultrasonic controller. The application shows a list of registered possessions and allows new items to be added. The designer can specify a name, description and photo to map onto an underlying tag ID. During tracking, 3D co-ordinates of the tags are time-stamped and added to a database.

The database is used to provide a map view of the current position of each object, and a graph (called the "affection radar") that plots the distance each object has moved over time. Whilst many objects achieve high initial attention, the novelty often quickly fades. The affection radar allows the user to reflect on an object's changing patterns of usage. The data can also be used by applications.

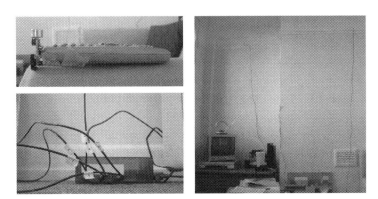

Fig. 9. An initial deployment of the ultrasonic tracker within the home. Tag attached to a remote control (top left). Ultrasonic controller (bottom left) and receivers attached to walls (right).

For example, objects that have become old, ignored or unused could re-advertise themselves to the user through output channels in the home in the form of an occasionally appearing photo. An initial set of design sketches for the application, including the affection radar and re-advertising objects, is shown in Fig. 8.

6.2   Experiments with Ultrasonic Tracking in the Home

In order to realise the scenario described previously, we conducted various trials of the ultrasonic tracker within domestic environments. Key technical questions were: How easy is it to set up? How fine-grained is the tracking in practice? We also need to consider key design questions, such as whether movement is a good metric for determining usage, and how often different types of object move.

Figure 9 shows an installation of the system within the home of a designer. The receivers were fixed to the walls of the space to provide coverage over the living room. Tags were attached to various objects in the home to show movement around the space. These included a chair, remote control, camera, and books. Tag data captured by the receivers were relayed onto a connected laptop, where absolute 3D coordinates were calculated and logged. Initially this recorded data was processed using visualisation software back in the design studio, and only console output was available to verify readings in real-time. After refinement, the visualisation software was also deployed in the home to provide real-time graphical feedback to users.

The system was installed manually at first, and later using auto-calibration to compare experiences. Manual installation involved a designer measuring the co-ordinates of the receivers relative to a point of origin in the middle of the room. Measurements were entered manually into an application running on a laptop. The space contained large household objects (tables, chairs and so on), some of which had to be cleared so that distances could be calculated between

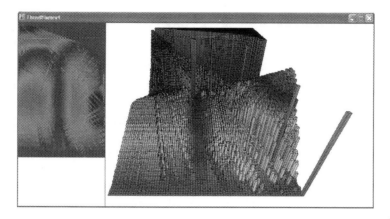

Fig. 10. One example of ultrasonic data visualisations.

the point of origin and the receivers. This added to the initial disruption caused by the placement of receivers.

During tracking, readings for each tag were displayed in the console. The designer used a simple test to verify these readings: manually measure the X, Y and Z distances between corners of a chest of drawers and compare these with distances calculated with a tag. This simple test revealed poor tracking accuracy due to human errors introduced during receiver measurement, and poor coverage of the room. Manual calibration was repeated several times until coverage and accuracy were deemed acceptable. This involved repositioning and recalculation of receiver coordinates, with an engineer to help take measurements. This added considerably to the time taken to calibrate the system.

In contrast, the auto-calibration process took considerably less effort and time. To accomplish this, the designer ran software on the laptop, which captured data from a single tag. The designer moved the tag around the room, taking care to collect distance readings from all parts of the room. After approximately one minute, the designer stopped data capture on the laptop and ran the auto-calibration software. Within approximately 5 minutes a solution had been found, and transmitting tags were tracked in absolute 3D co-ordinates. Various activities were performed to test the tracking capabilities of the system. For example, moving slowly around a dining table or moving from one corner of the room to the centre, and viewing whether the visualisations plotted a similar path. The designer also used a tape measure to manually resolve the 3D coordinates of a tag, testing these against the data generated on the laptop. These tests showed promising results, indicating reliable tracking accuracy of 7cm. After some minor tweaking of receiver positions, rerunning of auto-calibration software, and retesting (using methods described previously), the designer achieved a tracking accuracy of 3cm.

Spatial information captured from the tracking system was interfaced with a design tool called Processing [19]—a popular high-level programming language used to rapidly prototype graphical applications. Visualisations were generated based on this data, including maps highlighting an object's trajectory through a space, activity maps indicating areas in which objects predominately resided, and maps showing areas in which line of sight to one or more receivers was occluded. For example, the occlusion map in Fig. 10 shows a view of the home where line of sight was occluded by large objects such as a dining table or a sofa (shown in light grey). They also illustrated whether objects did indeed move frequently, and where in the space they were most often used.

6.3   Initial Reflections

Initial trials of the ultrasonic system within a number of domestic settings showed promising results and allowed us to refine our application designs further. During our trials, we found several advantages to using auto-calibration over a manual approach:

- *The ability to quickly reposition receivers and retest in order to maximise coverage and tracking accuracy within the space.* The accuracy and coverage of ultrasonic trackers is clearly heavily dependent on the placement of receivers. We found a need to reconfigure receiver positions several times in order to improve tracking and coverage. This process is greatly simplified if the designer can avoid re-measuring receiver distances each time manually.
- *The ability to minimise human errors being introduced by manually measuring receiver coordinates.* We also found that errors crept in during manual calibration, requiring designers to re-measure receiver positions, a process that would often become frustrating.
- *The ability for a single non-technical designer to setup the tracker.* In our experience, manual measurements require the work of two people, and often involve reaching awkwardly and noting down large numbers of distances and offsets, and carrying out calculations. Non-technical designers can find this process daunting. Auto-calibration obviates the need for this inconvenient process.

During these initial tests, we found that the auto-calibration algorithm works well for most arrangements of receivers. Tracking was most accurate when the receivers were set up on the ceiling and walls to avoid reduced precision in the Z-axis. Care was also taken to point the receivers toward the centre of the tracking area, to maximise the chance of receivers detecting tag transmissions.

Our visualisations indicated that smaller objects such as books, electronic items and toys move much more than larger objects such furniture, as expected. Often patterns arise over a period when viewing the paths of objects through a space—for example, in our deployment the remote control often followed a set path from the shelf by the CD player to the coffee table and back. Therefore one must be careful in using movement as a metric for determining usage, as this only applies to certain objects which are small enough to be mobile and their everyday interaction relies on movement (such as a camera).

Initially, when the system was deployed it was passively capturing data to be processed asynchronously back in the design studio. At this early stage, participants felt that these tests were a little intrusive, voicing concerns about privacy and the ways that data would be used. This level of intrusiveness began to fade once the users were provided with more feedback and control over the data capture. For example, in the second series of tests visualisation software ran on the home desktop, and could be stopped and restarted by the user at any point. Participants felt much more comfortable living with the system when they could see the information captured in real-time, and could choose when it was appropriate for the system to begin capture.

These initial experiments also showed that during everyday use, certain objects would move in and out of a room frequently. As an extension to the scenario one could imagine a setup that incorporated several ultrasonic systems, one in each room—this, however, raises issues about setup time and data management across multiple receiver boxes. Designers also suggested whether more coarse grained tracking technologies could be used to compliment the ultrasonics system, particularly for objects that only move short distances.

Our experiments have shown the viability of using an ultrasonic tracking system as a low cost, fine grained mechanism for tracking objects. We are now moving to realise the interactive applications described earlier.

7   Conclusions and Future Work

We have presented an ultrasonic-only tracking system aimed at users beyond the ubiquitous computing community. The system uses algorithms to self-calibrate and self-orient, so that little technical knowledge is required for setup. It gives the user an easy way to calibrate the system and for aligning the system with the user's origin and principal axes (by walking along an imaginary L).

Tracking is performed in one of two alternative modes, providing a choice between tracking multiple near-stationary objects, or one object at a high frequency. The mode can be changed without a need to re-calibrate the receiver infrastructure. Where multiple objects are tracked, each object is preprogrammed with a unique pulse timing signature.

The results show that tracking multiple objects using an auto-calibrated system can be performed to an RMS accuracy of approximately 2.3cm, which is sufficient for our target applications. Single object tracking achieves accuracies of around 3cm in the dynamic case.

We have deployed our system in the home and allowed designers to create an installation. This has provided experience using the system in a more typical setting than the laboratory, and we have described some initial reflections that may be of use to other researchers wishing to implement a tracking system. Future work is planned to further the accessibility of the system to designers, including the use of toolkits that provide a more meaningful interface to the system's outputs.

References

[1] A. Ward, A. Jones, and A. Hopper. A New Location Technique for the Active Office. In *IEEE Personnel Communications, volume 4 no.5*, pages 42–47, October 1997.

[2] C. Randell and H. Muller. Low Cost Indoor Positioning System. In Gregory D. Abowd, editor, *Ubicomp 2001: Ubiquitous Computing*, pages 42–48. Springer-Verlag, Sept 2001.

[3] Michael McCarthy and Henk L. Muller. RF Free Ultrasonic Positioning. In *Seventh International Symposium on Wearable Computers*. IEEE Computer Society, October 2003.

[4] Nissanka B. Priyantha, Anit Chakraborty, and Hari Balakrishnan. The Cricket Location-Support System. In *Mobile Computing and Networking*, pages 32–43, August 2000.

[5] Ajay Mahajan and Maurice Walworth. 3-D Position Sensing Using the Differences in the Time-of-Flights from a Wave Source to Various Receivers. In *IEEE Transactions on Robotics and Automation*, pages 91–94. IEEE, 2001.

[6] J. J. Moré. The Levenberg-Marquardt Algorithm: Implementation and Theory. In G. Watson, editor, *Lecture Notes in Mathematics, v630*, pages 105–116. Springer Verlag, 1978.

[7] Lester Ingber. Very Fast Simulated Re-annealing. In *Mathematical Computing Modelling*, pages 967–973, 1989.

[8] Brian Gough. *GNU Scientific Library - Nonlinear Least Squares Fitting*, chapter 36. Network Theory Ltd, 2001.

[9] Paul Duff and Henk Muller. Autocalibration Algorithm for Ultrasonic Location Systems. In *Proceedings of the Seventh IEEE International Symposium on Wearable Computers*, pages 62–68. IEEE Computer Society, October 2003.

[10] I.T. Jolliffe. *Principal Component Analysis*. Springer-Verlag, New York, 1986.

[11] L. Ingber. Adaptive Simulated Annealing (ASA). http://www.ingber.com/.

[12] R. E. Kalman. A New Approach to Linear Filtering and Prediction. In *Journal of Basic Engineering (ASME)*, pages 82(D):35–45, March 1960.

[13] Greg Welch and Gary Bishop. SCAAT: Incremental Tracking with Incomplete Information. In *SIGGRAPH 97 Conference Proceedings, Annual Conference Series*, August 1997.

[14] Eric Foxlin, Michael Harrington, and George Pfeifer. Constellation: a wide-range wireless motion-tracking system for augmented reality and virtual set applications. In *Proceedings of the 25th annual conference on Computer graphics and interactive techniques*, pages 371–378. ACM Press, 1998.

[15] Eric Foxlin, Michael Harrington, and Yury Altshuler. Miniature 6-DOF Inertial System for Tracking HMDs. In *Aerosense 98, Orlando*, April 1998.

[16] Intersense Inc. Website. http://www.isense.com/, 2003.

[17] W. Gaver, A. Boucher, S. Pennington, and B. Walker. Subjective Approaches to Design for Everyday Life. In *CHI Tutorial, Ft. Lauderdale*. ACM Press, 2003.

[18] W. Gaver, A. Dunne, and E. Pacenti. Cultural Probes. In *Interactions Magazine*, volume VI(1), pages 21–29, 1999.

[19] Processing. Website. http://www.processing.org/.

Accurate GSM Indoor Localization

Veljo Otsason[1], Alex Varshavsky[2], Anthony LaMarca[3], and Eyal de Lara[2]

[1] Tartu University, `veljo.otsason@utoronto.ca`
[2] University of Toronto, `walex,delara@cs.toronto.edu`
[3] Intel Research Seattle, `anthony.lamarca@intel.com`

Abstract. Accurate indoor localization has long been an objective of the ubiquitous computing research community, and numerous indoor localization solutions based on 802.11, Bluetooth, ultrasound and infrared technologies have been proposed. This paper presents the first accurate GSM indoor localization system that achieves median accuracy of 5 meters in large multi-floor buildings. The key idea that makes accurate GSM-based indoor localization possible is the use of *wide* signal-strength fingerprints. In addition to the 6-strongest cells traditionally used in the GSM standard, the wide fingerprint includes readings from additional cells that are strong enough to be detected, but too weak to be used for efficient communication. Experiments conducted on three multi-floor buildings show that our system achieves accuracy comparable to an 802.11-based implementation, and can accurately differentiate between floors in both wooden and steel-reinforced concrete structures.

1 Introduction

The accurate localization of objects and people in indoor environments has long been considered an important building block for ubiquitous computing applications [7,8]. Most research on indoor localization systems has been based on the use of short-range signals, such as WiFi [3,5,11], Bluetooth [1], ultra sound [15], or infrared [16]. This paper shows that contrary to popular belief an indoor localization system based on wide-area GSM fingerprints can achieve high accuracy, and is in fact comparable to an 802.11-based implementation.

GSM-based indoor localization has several benefits: (i) GSM coverage is all but pervasive, far outreaching the coverage of 802.11 networks; (ii) the wide acceptance of cellular phones makes them ideal conduits for the delivery of ubiquitous computing applications. A localization system based on cellular signals, such as GSM, leverages the phone's existing hardware and removes the need for additional radio interfaces; (iii) because cellular towers are dispersed across the covered area, a cellular-based localization system would still work in situations where a building's electrical infrastructure has failed. Moreover, cellular systems are designed to tolerate power failures. For example, the cellular network kept working during the massive power outage that left most of the Northeastern United States and Canada in the dark in the Summer of 2003; (iv) GSM, unlike 802.11 networks, operates in a licensed band, and therefore does not suffer

M. Beigl et al. (Eds.): UbiComp 2005, LNCS 3660, pp. 141–158, 2005.

from interference from nearby devices transmitting on the same frequency (e.g., microwaves, cordless phones); and (v) the significant expense and complexity of cellular base stations[4] results in a network that evolves slowly and is only reconfigured infrequently. While this lack of flexibility (and high configuration cost) is certainly a drawback for the cellular system operator, it results in a stable environment that allows the localization system to operate for a long period before having to be recalibrated.

This paper presents the first accurate GSM-based indoor localization system. The key idea that makes accurate GSM-based indoor localization possible is the use of *wide* signal-strength fingerprints. The wide fingerprint includes the 6-strongest GSM cells and readings of up to 29 additional GSM channels, most of which are strong enough to be detected, but too weak to be used for efficient communication. The higher dimensionality introduced by the additional channel dramatically increases localization accuracy.

We present results for experiments conducted on signal-strength fingerprints collected from three multi-floor buildings located in Toronto and Seattle. These structures span a wide spectrum of urban densities, ranging from a busy downtown core to a quiet residential neighborhood. The results show that our GSM-based indoor localization system can effectively differentiate between floors and achieves median within-floor accuracy as low as 2.5 meters.

We make the following contributions: (i) we present the first accurate GSM-based indoor localization system and show that it achieves accuracy comparable to an 802.11-based implementation; (ii) we show that a GSM-based localization system can effectively differentiate between floors for both wooden and steal-reinforced concrete structures; (iii) we show that there is significant signal diversity across metropolitan environments [5] and that this diversity enables the GSM-based system to achieve high localization accuracy; and (iv) we show that the availability of signal strength readings from cells other than the 6-strongest cells traditionally used in GSM increases localization accuracy by up to 50%.

The rest of this paper is organized as follows. Section 2 describes related work. Section 3 describes our methodology, and Section 4 presents results for our experimental evaluation. Finally, Section 5 concludes the paper and discusses directions for future work.

2   Related Work

This paper examines the effectiveness of GSM fingerprinting as an indoor localization technique. While this combination is new, indoor localization, radio fingerprinting and use of GSM for localization have all been explored before. We describe these efforts and key distinctions between these efforts and ours.

---

[4] A macro-cell costs $500,000 to $1 million. Micro-cells cost about a third as much, but a larger number is needed to cover the same area [14].

[5] In all three indoor environments (including the private residence) we were able to detect at least 24 different GSM signals.

2.1 Indoor Localization

While outdoor localization is almost exclusively performed using the Global Positioning System (GPS), indoor location systems have successfully employed a variety of technologies. The original Active Badge system [7] and follow on commercial systems like Versus [20] use infrared emitters and detectors to achieve 5-10m accuracy. Both the Cricket [15] and the Bat [16] systems use ultrasonic ranging to estimate location. Depending on the density of infrastructure and degree of calibration, ultrasonic systems have accuracies between a few meters and a few centimeters. Most recently, ultra-wideband emitters and receivers have been used to achieve highly accurate indoor localization [19]. The common drawback of all of these systems is that they require custom infrastructure for every area in which localization is to be performed. As a result, these systems have not seen significant deployment outside of high-value applications like hospital process management. In contrast, GSM fingerprinting makes use of the existing GSM infrastructure, obviating the need for infrastructure investment and greatly increasing the possible area in which the system will work. This increases the likelihood of GSM fingerprinting achieving popular adoption.

2.2 Indoor Localization Using 802.11 Fingerprinting

Bahl *et al.* observed that the strength of the signal from an 802.11 access point does not vary significantly in a given location. They used this observation to build RADAR [3], a system that performed localization based on which access points would be heard where, and how strongly. This was the first *fingerprinting* system that showed that it is possible to localize a laptop in the hallways of a small office building within 2-3 meters of its true location, using fingerprints from four 802.11 access points. There have been improvements to RADAR's fingerprint matching algorithm that have improved accuracy [2,11,17] and differentiated floors of a building with a high degree of precision [6]. In addition, commercial localization products have been built using 802.11 fingerprinting [18]. The differences between our work and 802.11 fingerprinting systems are primarily due to the differences between 802.11 and GSM that were outlined in Section 1: Due to higher coverage, GSM fingerprinting works in more places than 802.11 fingerprinting. Due to more stable infrastructure, 802.11 radio maps will degrade more quickly than GSM radio maps. Due to the larger range of GSM cells, 802.11 fingerprinting will be more accurate than GSM fingerprinting given the same number of radio sources.

2.3 Localizing Using GSM

A number of systems have used GSM to estimate the location of mobile clients. The Place Lab system employed a map built using war-driving software and a simple radio model to estimate a cell phone's location with 100-150 meter accuracy in a city environment [13]. The goal of Place Lab was to provide coarse-grained accuracy with minimal mapping effort. This is different, and complementary to our goal of doing accurate indoor localization given a detailed radio survey. Another distinction is that Place Lab used a cell phone platform that only programmatically exported the single associated cell tower.

Laitinen *et al.* [12] used GSM-based fingerprinting for outdoor localization. They have collected sparse fingerprints from the 6-strongest cells, achieving 67th percentile accuracy of $44m$. Finally, Laasonen *et al.* used the transition between GSM cell towers to build a graph representing the places a user goes [10]. Like Place Lab, Laasonen's system used cell phones that only exported the single cell-tower the phone was associated with. In contract to the other systems we have mentioned, Laasonen's system did not attempt to estimate absolute location, but rather assigned locations symbolic names like *Home* and *Grocery Store*.

These previous efforts to use GSM for localization differ from the work reported in this paper in that they are based on sparse fingerprints collected tens to hundreds of meters apart from each other. Moreover, these efforts used *narrow* fingerprints obtained from commercial GSM phones that report the signal strength for the current cell [10,13] or the 6-strongest cells [12]. In contrast, we collected GSM fingerprints in a dense grid with 1.5 meters granularity. Moreover, we collected *wide* fingerprints that include up to 29 different GSM channels in addition to the 6-strongest GSM cells.

3   Methodology

This section first gives an overview of GSM and wireless signal fingerprinting. We then describe our data collection process and the localization algorithms that we use in our evaluation.

3.1   GSM Primer

GSM is the most widespread cellular telephony standard in the world, with deployments in more than 100 countries by over 220 network operators [4]. In North-America, GSM operates on the 850 MHz and 1900 MHz frequency bands. Each band is subdivided into 200 KHz wide physical channels using Frequency Division Multiple Access (FDMA). Each physical channel is then subdivided into 8 logical channels based on Time Division Multiple Access (TDMA). There are 299 non-interfering physical channels available in the 1900 MHz band, and 124 in the 850 MHz band, totaling 423 physical channels in North-America.

A GSM *base station* is typically equipped with a number of directional antennas that define sectors of coverage or *cells*. Each cell is allocated a number of physical channels based on the expected traffic load and the operator's requirements. Typically, the channels are allocated in a way that both increases coverage and reduces interference between cells. Thus, for example, two neighboring cells will never be assigned the same channel. Channels are, however, reused across cells that are far-enough away from each other so that inter-cell interference is minimized while channel reuse is maximized. The channel to cell allocation is a complex and costly process that requires careful planning and typically involves field measurements and extensive computer-based simulations of radio signal propagation. Therefore, once the mapping between cells and frequencies has been established, it rarely changes.

Every GSM cell has a special broadcast control channel (BCCH) used to transmit, among other things, the identities of neighboring cells to be monitored by mobile stations for handover purposes. While GSM employs transmission power control both at the base station and the mobile device, the data on the BCCH is transmitted at a full constant power. This allows mobile stations to compare signal strength of neighboring cells in a meaningful manner and choose the best one for further communication. It is these BCCH channels that we use for localization. In the rest of this paper, we refer to the BCCH channels simply as *channels*.

3.2   Fingerprinting

Two factors lead to the good performance of radio fingerprinting in the wireless band used by GSM and 802.11 networks. The first is that the signal strengths observed by mobile devices exhibit considerable spatial variability at the 1-10M level. That is to say, a given radio source may be heard stronger or not at all a few meters away. The second factor is that these same signal strengths are consistent in time; the signal strength from a given source at a given location is likely to be similar tomorrow and next week. In combination, this means that there is a radio profile that is feature-rich in space and reasonably consistent in time. Fingerprinting-based location techniques take advantage of this by capturing this radio profile for later reference.

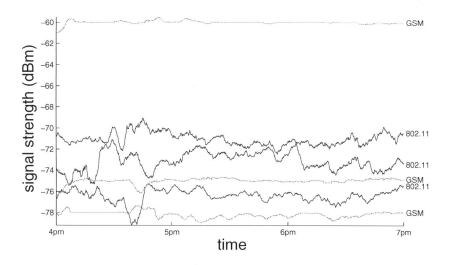

Fig. 1. 802.11 and GSM signal stability over time.

To compare the stability of GSM and 802.11 signals, we recorded the signal strength of nearby 802.11 access points (AP) and 6-strongest GSM cells at several locations in one of the buildings that houses the Department of Computer Science at the University of Toronto. Figure 1 shows a 3-hour segment of the signal strength measurements at a location on the fifth floor of the building during a workday afternoon. The plot shows the three-strongest GSM cells and the three-strongest 802.11 APs. GSM signals appear to be more stable than 802.11 signals. We believe that this is because 802.11 uses unlicensed overcrowded 2.4 GHz band, and therefore suffers from interference from nearby appliances such as microwaves and cordless phones. An analysis of GSM signal stability under different weather conditions (e.g., rain, snow, fog) is left for future work.

Fingerprinting relies on a "training phase" in which a mobile device moves through the environment recording the strength of signals emanating from a group of radio sources (e.g., 802.11 access points, GSM base stations, FM radio [9] or TV stations). We refer to the physical position where the measurement is performed as a *location*, to the radio scan as a *measurement* and to the recording of the signal strength of a single source as a *reading*. That is, to build a radio map of the building, a mobile device takes a series of measurements in multiple locations of the building. Each measurement is composed of several readings; one for each radio source in range. The set of data recorded in a single location is also referred to as a *training point*. Since fingerprinting systems do not model radio propagation, a fairly dense collection of radio scans needs to be collected to achieve good accuracy. The original RADAR experiments, for example, collected measurements every square meter on average[3]. To achieve their advertised accuracy, the commercial 802.11 fingerprinting product from Ekahau [18] recommends a similar density.

Once the training phase is complete, a client can estimate its location by performing a radio scan (or equivalently collecting a *testing point*) and feeding it to a *localization algorithm*, which estimates the client's location based on the similarity of the signal strength signatures between the testing and the training points. The similarity of signatures can be computed in a variety of ways, but it typically involves finding measurements in the training points that have the same radio sources with similar signal strengths. The easiest technique for estimating location is to choose the location of the training point with the closest Euclidean distance in a signal space. Better accuracy can be achieved by averaging the location of the K closest neighbors (or training points) in the radio map, where K is some small constant. It is also beneficial to use weighted averaging, so that neighbors closer in signal space are given higher weights.

In this paper, we compare the accuracy of localization based on 802.11 and GSM fingerprinting using the popular weighted K nearest neighbors algorithm. Investigating the applicability of other localization algorithms to GSM fingerprinting is a topic for future work.

3.3   Data Collection

We collected multi-floor measurements in two office buildings and one private detached house. The office buildings are the home to the Intel Research Seattle Lab and part of the Department of Computer Science of the University of

Toronto. In the rest of this paper, we refer to these buildings as: University, Research Lab, and House. University is located in Toronto's busy downtown core, and Research Lab and House are located in Seattle's commercial midtown and a quiet residential neighborhood, respectively.

University is a large ($88m$x$113m$) 8-storey building with lecture rooms, offices and research labs. Since we had no access to the offices, we collected training points in the hallways of the 5th and 7th floors of the building [6]. Research Lab is a medium size ($30m$x$30m$) 6-storey building. Space inside the building is partitioned with semi-permanent cubicles. Due to access restrictions, we collected readings from the whole 6th floor, but only a half of the 5th floor. House is a 3-storey wooden structure ($18m$x$6m$) that includes a basement and two floors above ground. We collected measurements on all 3 floors. The distance between floors is about 6 meters for University and Research Lab, and about 3 meters for House.

We collected 802.11 and GSM fingerprints using a laptop running Windows XP. To collect 802.11 fingerprints, we used an Orinoco Gold wireless card configured in active scanning mode, where the laptop periodically transmits probe requests and listens to probe responses from nearby 802.11 APs.

We collected GSM fingerprints using a Sony/Ericsson GM28 GSM modem, which operates as an ordinary GSM cell phone, but exports a richer programing interface. The GSM modem provides two interfaces for accessing signal strength information: *cellsAPI* and *channelsAPI*. The *cellsAPI* interface reports the cell ID, signal strength, and associated channel for the n strongest cells. While the modem's specifications does not set a hard bound on the value of n, in practice in the 3 environments we measured n was equal to 6. The *channelsAPI* interface simultaneously provides the signal strength for up to 35 channels, 13 of which can be specified by the programmer, with up to 22 additional channels picked by the modem itself. In practice, 6 of the 35 channels typically corresponds to the 6-strongest cells. Unfortunately, *channelsAPI* reports signal strength but does not report cell IDs. We speculate that the cell ID information for other than the 6-strongest cells cannot be determined because the signals of those cells are strong enough to be detected, but too weak to be used for efficient communication.

	University (downtown)	Research Lab (midtown)	House (residential)
Cells	−87.69	−76.74	−88.35
Channels	−96.41	−102.19	−105.27

Table 1. Average signal strength (dBm) for cells and channels.

Table 1 shows the average signal strength returned by the *cellsAPI* and *channelsAPI* interfaces. As expected, the average signal strength reported by *cellsAPI*

---

[6] We did not take measurements on the 6th floor because at the time of this study it was under going extensive renovations.

is significantly higher than the average reported by *channelsAPI*. Note that the average signal strength reported by the *channelsAPI* interface is close to modem's stated receiver sensitivity[7] of -102 dBm. Efficient GSM communication requires an SNR higher than -90 dB.

The lack of cell ID information for some channels raises the possibility of *aliasing*, i.e., a situation when two or more cells transmitting simultaneously on the same channel appear to be a single radio source and therefore cannot be differentiated. In the extreme case, a fingerprinting system that relies exclusively on channel-based data may suffer from worldwide aliasing. Because channels are reused throughout the world, fingerprints taken in two far-away locations may produce similar fingerprints. To alleviate the aliasing problem, we combine the information returned by the *cellsAPI* and *channelsAPI* interfaces into a single fingerprint. We then restrict the set of fingerprints to which we compare a *testing point* to fingerprints that have at least one cell ID in common with the *testing point*. This practice effectively differentiates between fingerprints from our three indoor environments.

As we show in Section 4, even with the potential for aliasing, our localization system based on wide GSM fingerprinting significantly outperforms GSM fingerprinting based on the 6-strongest cells, and is comparable to 802.11 based fingerprinting. This is because our fingerprints are wide (have many readings), and therefore, in order for the aliasing to reduce accuracy, many readings in the fingerprints of distant locations need to match, which is highly unlikely in practice.

Fig. 2. Experimental setup

Fig. 3. Measuring signal strength and identifying location by clicking on the map

---

[7] In practice, the modem reports signal strength as low as -115 dBm.

	University (downtown)		Research Lab (midtown)		House (residential)		
	5th	7th	5th	6th	basement	1st	2nd
per floor	130	154	53	181	17	44	50
per building		284		234		111	

Table 2. Training points collected on each floor for the three buildings.

We developed a simple Java-based application to assist us in the process of gathering fingerprints. To record a fingerprint, we first identify the current position by clicking on a map of the building. The application then records the signal strengths reported by the 802.11 card and the *cellsAPI* and *channelsAPI* interfaces of the GSM modem. To collect the measurements, we placed the laptop on an office chair and moved the chair around the building. While primitive, this setup assures measurements collected at a constant height. Figures 2 and 3 show our experimental setup and a screen shot of the Java-based application, whereas Table 2 summarizes the number of training points collected on each of the floors of the three buildings. In all three indoor environments, we collected 802.11 and GSM fingerprints for points located 1 to 1.5 meters apart. We collected 2 measurements per location, waiting 5 seconds between the scans (the default value according to the modem specification).

Practical Considerations We collected our wide fingerprints using a programmable Sony/Ericsson GSM modem, which operates as an ordinary GSM cell phone, but exports a richer programing interface that provides access to readings from up to 35 GSM channels. In contrast, commercial phones limit access to signal strength information to the 6-strongest cells or even just the current cell. However, we speculate that the software on commercial phones could be easily enhanced to provide signal strength measurements for a richer set of channels. Once extended, those phones could take advantage of the wide-fingerprinting technique introduced in this paper. We base this speculation on the observation that the Sony/Ericsson GSM modem is implemented using standard GSM electronics, and that the GSM standard requires phones to be able to scan all channels in the GSM band.

3.4   Localization Algorithms

We implemented four localization algorithms which differ in the structure of their fingerprints: (i) *802.11*, uses only readings from 802.11 access points; (ii) *onecell*, uses the reading of the single strongest GSM cell; (iii) *cell*, uses readings of the 6-strongest GSM cells; and (iv) *chann*, uses readings from up to 35 GSM channels.

All our localization algorithms use the K-nearest neighbors algorithm described in Section 3.2. For each algorithm, we varied the number of nearest neighbors to average over, and selected the value of K that gave the best results.

In most cases, the best K was a small constant (2 or 4). We also experimented
with assigning higher weights to neighbors that appear closer in the signal space.
The weight is the reciprocal of the distance in signal strength space between the
testing point and the specific nearest neighbor.

An initial evaluation of chann uncovered cases in which the algorithm selected points that are neighbors in the signal space, but are actually located
far away from the true location of the testing point in the physical space. To
ameliorate the effect of these false positives, we applied the K-mean clustering
algorithm to split the set of nearest neighbors into two geographical clusters[8].
We then removed the points that belong to the smaller cluster from the final
location calculation. In the rest of this paper, we refer to the version of chann
that uses geographical clustering as $chann_{cl}$.

4 Evaluation

In this section, we first analyze the collected data and then evaluate localization
accuracy obtained by 802.11 and GSM fingerprinting.

4.1 Data Analysis

Table 3 shows the total number of 802.11 APs, GSM cells, and GSM channels
recorded during the data collection phase for each of the 3 buildings. The University building has a much denser 802.11 deployment than the Research Lab
building both because the University building is much larger and because while
the APs at the Research Lab building are maintained by IT personnel, numerous APs at the University building are owned and maintained by independent
research groups.

The total number of GSM cells seen at the University building is larger than
in other buildings because of the higher coverage and the larger building size.
The lower number of cells seen at the Research Lab is the consequence of both
the much smaller building size and the much stronger signal received from nearby
cells. Because of the proximity of a few base stations, the strongest cells reported
by the modem in the Research Lab benefit from less variations than in other
buildings (i.e., the same group of cells appears in most of the cell measurements).
The total number of channels seen in the residential area is somewhat lower than
in other areas due to lower coverage.

Figure 4 plots the cumulative distribution function (CDF) of the number
of transmitters per location detected at the University building. Shown are fingerprints based on 802.11 AP, GSM cells, and GSM channels. The figures for
the Research Lab and the House show similar patterns and are therefore not
included. The median width of 802.11 AP and GSM cells fingerprints is 5 and
6, respectively. In contrast, the median width of GSM channel fingerprints is 25.
We will show in the next section that the larger fingerprint has a dramatic effect
on localization performance.

---

[8] We experimented with different numbers of clusters, but 2 clusters produced the
best results.

	University (downtown)	Research Lab (midtown)	House (residential)
802.11 APs	44	10	5
Cells	58	14	18
Channels	34	33	24

Table 3. Total number of 802.11 APs, GSM cells and GSM channels recorded.

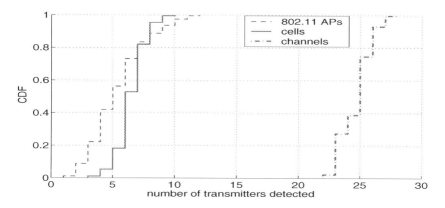

Fig. 4. Cumulative distribution of the number of transmitters per location detected at the University building. Shown are fingerprints based on 802.11 AP, GSM cells, and GSM channels.

4.2   Performance

The results reported in this section were obtained by taking one point at a time out of the training set and using it as the testing point. This technique is similar to that used by Bahl [3], and is a somewhat pessimistic approach since it makes sure that there is no training point in the radio map that has exactly the same fingerprint as the testing point. On the other hand, all our measurements were performed with a single modem in a course of two days. In the future, we plan to investigate the effects of using different hardware for training and testing, as well as the effect of separating the training and testing of the system by larger time intervals.

Floor Classification Table 4 summarizes the effectiveness with which the localization algorithms introduced in Section 3.4 differentiate between floors in the three indoor environments. All algorithms predict the current floor as the one where most of the K-nearest neighbors are located. $chann_{cl}$ achieves similar performance to chann and is therefore not shown.

As expected, 802.11 does an excellent job differentiating between floors in the University and Research Lab buildings. The reinforced concrete floors in these structures effectively block the propagation of 802.11 signals between floors,

	University (downtown)	Research Lab (midtown)	House (residential)
`802.11`	100	100	62.16
`chann`	89.08	97.01	93.69
`cell`	89.08	81.2	51.35
`onecell`	74.65	77.35	57.66

Table 4. % of succesful floor classifications.

significantly simplifying the task of floor prediction. These results are consistent with previous findings [6].

In the house environment, however, 802.11 achieves low classification accuracy as the house's wood structure presents little obstacle to radio propagation, making it harder to differentiate between signal fingerprints on different floors. Not surprisingly, all but 3 of the 42 misclassifications happen at locations on the first and second floors of the house. In the house scenario, 4 out of 5 of the available 802.11 signals emanate from neighboring residences. These signals propagate easily through the wooden frame of the first and second floors, but suffer significant attenuation propagating through dirt and the house's foundations to reach the basement. The low power at which neighboring access points are heard (if at all) in the basement helps to identify basement locations. On the other hand, the 802.11 signals from neighboring households contribute little to improving the accuracy of predictions for the above-ground floors.

In contrast, the GSM-based chann algorithm shows strong performance across all three buildings, and significantly outperforms 802.11 for the House environment. Overall, chann achieves up to 42% better accuracy than cell and onecell. This is strong evidence that extending fingerprints to include signal strength information from channels other than the 6-strongest cells, even when the identity of the transmitter cannot be determined, can dramatically increase localization accuracy.

Within-Floor Localization Error Table 5 summarizes the localization errors within specific floors for the 5 algorithms introduced in Section 3.4 for the three indoor environments. For each floor, the table shows the 50-percentile localization error, calculated as the Euclidean distance between the *actual* and *predicted* location of the point within the specific floor. All calculations assume a training set restricted to include only points that are on the same floor as the point whose position is being determined.

Table 5 also presents results for random, an algorithm that determines localization by picking an arbitrary position in the building. Therefore, random provides a lower bound on the performance of localization systems for a given floor and building. The localization error in random depends on the size of the floor, which accounts for difference in its localization error across floor and building.

	University (downtown)		Research Lab (midtown)		House (residential)		
	5th	7th	5th	6th	basement	1st	2nd
802.11	4.22	4.78	2.20	2.59	3.49	3.43	3.87
chann$_{cl}$	5.44	3.98	2.48	4.77	3.28	2.95	3.96
chann	6.47	4.07	3.40	4.82	3.28	3.36	4.55
cell	11.06	8.02	4.82	6.99	3.41	3.40	5.27
onecell	15.05	14.64	8.39	7.93	3.42	4.85	6.13
random	33.87	30.43	10.40	13.35	4.68	6.21	7.07

Table 5. Single-floor median localization error (meters).

Across the three buildings, 802.11 achieves median accuracy between 2.2 and 4.8 meters. These results are consistent with results previously reported in the literature. Differences in accuracy between building reflect discrepancies in the granularity of the measurement grid which varied between 1 and 1.5 meters.

There are large differences in the performance of the various GSM-based algorithms. chann and chann$_{cl}$ outperform cell and onecell in all cases. Moreover, chann$_{cl}$ achieves between 25% to 50% better performance than cell for at least one floor in each of the three buildings. Across the three buildings, chann$_{cl}$ achieves median accuracy between 2.5 and 5.4 meters, and in 3 out of the 7 floors, chann$_{cl}$ even achieves better accuracy than 802.11 (e.g., 7th floor of University building).

The strong performance of chann$_{cl}$ demonstrates the advantage of wide fingerprints including measurements from a large number of channels rather than just the 6-strongest cells. Moreover, the significant accuracy improvement of chann$_{cl}$ over chann shows that geographical clustering manages to reduce the effect of false-positives introduced by channel aliasing. Geographical clustering, on the other hand, did not have a significant effect on the performance of 802.11 as channel aliasing does not occur in this case.

Figure 5 shows the cumulative distribution (CDF) of the localization error of all algorithms for the 7th floor of the University building. Most remarkable is the closeness with which chann$_{cl}$ approximates 802.11, and the large difference in performance between chann$_{cl}$ and cell.

Effects of Multi-floor Fingerprints   In the previous section, we evaluated within-floor localization accuracy assuming that the training set was limited to fingerprints in the same floor, i.e., we predicted the floor first, and then predicted position within that floor. In contrast, in this section, we evaluate the effects on within-floor localization accuracy of including in the training set fingerprints taken on different floors. For this purpose, we project the training points collected on different floors of a building onto a single X, Y plane, therefore removing all floor information. We then ran the K-nearest neighbors on the extended training set. Table 6 shows the results of this experiment.

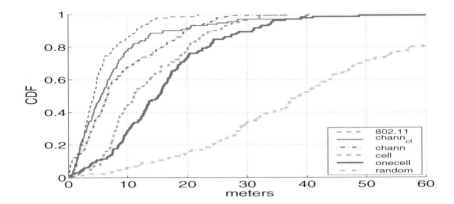

Fig. 5. CDF of the localization error for 7th floor of the University building.

	University (downtown)		Research Lab (midtown)		House (residential)	
	50%-ile	90%-ile	50%-ile	90%-ile	50%-ile	90%-ile
802.11	4.40	10.27	2.49	4.94	3.11	5.80
chann$_{cl}$	4.98	18.74	4.41	9.43	3.66	7.02
chann	5.76	21.75	4.72	9.44	4.10	7.18
cell	9.86	22.31	6.41	11.64	4.35	8.05
onecell	14.92	29.80	8.55	14.31	4.67	8.95
random	35.61	59.36	13.85	21.33	6.46	15.18

Table 6. Localization error with multi-floor fingerprints (meters).

Projecting the points collected on different floors onto a single plane has several effects. On the one hand, this practice may reduce the localization accuracy as the training points of other floors add "noise" (e.g., potential aliasing), which may result in larger localization errors. On the other hand, if the training points at a specific $< X, Y >$ location on all floors have similar signal strength signatures, combining the training data from multiple floors will increase the density of the measurement's grid, which may result in higher accuracy.

The multi-floor performance of 802.11 in the House is better than in any of the single-floor experiments. We found that the signal strength from the APs outside the building varies more with distance within a floor than within similar position on different floor. As a result, the training data from multiple floors overlaps, tightening the grid and increasing localization accuracy. The performance of 802.11 in a multi-floor setting in the University and Research Lab buildings is close to the average of the single-floor experiments, which is further indication that 802.11 can effectively differentiate between floors in office buildings with heavy concrete and steel frames.

The multi-floor localization error for GSM-based algorithms is also close to the average of the single-floor experiments. Therefore, for most cases, first identifying the floor and then performing localization using single-floor training data results in higher accuracy than performing the localization using multi-floor data. However, when the number of readings per location is low or differences in signal strength across floors are small, combining the training sets of multiple floors may produce higher localization accuracy.

4.3 Sensitivity Analysis

In this section, we analyze the best GSM performer, $chann_{cl}$, in more detail. Specifically, we test the localization accuracy of $chann_{cl}$ as a function of the number of channels used, the number of measurements collected per location and the training grid size.

Number of Channels Figure 6 plots the median localization error for the multi-floor experiment as a function of the number of channels used. Increasing the number of channels results in a larger fingerprint, which allows a better comparison between neighboring points and therefore for increased localization accuracy. The channels picked are sorted by popularity (i.e., the number of fingerprints on which a specific channel appears). For example, the median localization error for 6 channels, corresponds to an algorithm where the 6 (fixed) most popular channels are picked from the training set. Notice that the accuracy of the algorithm that picks the 6 most popular channels is lower than of the cell algorithm. This is because the cell algorithm picks the 6 strongest cells for each measurement, which may result in much larger fingerprint vector (e.g., completely different 6 cells may be picked in two distant locations, increasing the fingerprint vector to 12 entries).

Figure 7 plots the percentage of incorrect floor classifications as a function of the number of channels. As expected, picking more channels decreases classification error. Interestingly, in all cases, picking about 20 channels is sufficient for achieving good localization accuracy.

Number of Measurements Per Location Although all the results reported so far were based on the average of 2 measurements per location, we actually obtained 10 measurements per location for the University building dataset. However, experiments varying the number of measurements per location between 2 and 10 showed virtually no difference in the accuracy of the algorithms. This is because our readings are stable and therefore adding more measurements per location does not improve localization accuracy.

Data Collection Grid Size Figure 8 and Figure 9 show the effects of reducing measurement grid size on the median multi-floor localization error and the floor classification error, respectively. We simulate the effect of increasing the measurement grid size by uniformly removing points from the training set. In most cases, reducing the measurement grid size results in lower localization accuracy, but occasionally we do see anomalies. As it turns out, decreasing the size of the

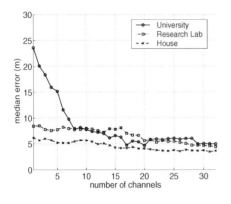

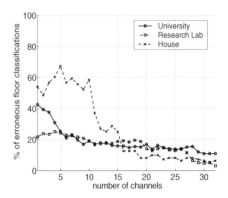

Fig. 6. Localization error as a function of fingerprint size.

Fig. 7. % of erroneous floor classifications as a function of fingerprint size.

grid may eliminate (in some cases) "problematic" or "aliased" points, which in turn increases localization accuracy.

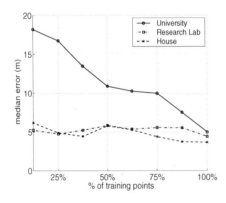

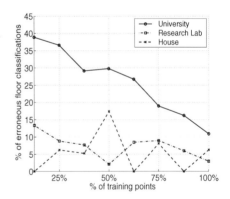

Fig. 8. Localization error as a function of the measurement grid size.

Fig. 9. % of erroneous floor classifications as a function of the measurement grid size.

4.4   Combined 802.11 and GSM Localization

In this section, we present an initial attempt to combine 802.11 and GSM fingerprinting. Since we collected both 802.11 and GSM channels information simultaneously, we have been able to combine the readings of both into one large fingerprint. The results are summarized in Table 7. The combined algorithm achieves moderately better accuracy in the University building, underperforms 802.11 in the Research Lab, and achieves similar performance in the House. An explanation for the lackluster performance of the combined algorithm may be found in the way in which we combine the fingerprint data. By simply concatenating fingerprint vectors we implicitly give more weight to the more numerous and less accurate GSM readings. In the future, we plan to investigate better ways of combining the two fingerprints (e.g., give higher weight to 802.11 readings).

	University (downtown)		Research Lab (midtown)		House (residential)	
	50%-ile	90%-ile	50%-ile	90%-ile	50%-ile	90%-ile
802.11+chann$_{cl}$	4.03	8.65	3.35	6.39	3.24	4.29
802.11	4.40	10.27	2.49	4.94	3.11	5.80
chann$_{cl}$	4.98	18.74	4.41	9.43	3.66	7.02

Table 7. Multi-floor localization error (meters).

5 Conclusions and Future Work

We presented the first GSM-based indoor localization system that achieves median accuracy comparable to an 802.11-based implementation. We showed that accurate indoor GSM-based localization is possible thanks to the use of *wide* signal-strength fingerprints that include readings of up to 29 GSM channels in addition to the 6-strongest cells.

While the lack of cell ID information for some channels raises the possibility of *world wide aliasing*, we showed that filtering fingerprints based on the subsets of the cell IDs of the 6-strongest cells is sufficient for differentiating between locations in our three indoor environments.

We presented evaluation results of our system in three multi-floor buildings located in the Toronto and Seattle metropolitan areas, covering a wide range of urban densities. Our GSM-based indoor localization system achieves a median accuracy ranging from $2.48m$ to $5.44m$ in large multi-floor buildings. Moreover, our GSM-based system effectively differentiates between floors in both wooden and steel-reinforced concrete structures, achieving correct floor classifications between 89% and 97% of the time. In contrast, in the wooden building, the 802.11-based fingerprinting system achieved correct classifications only 62% of the time due to a limited fingerprint size.

In the future, we plan to test applicability of additional positioning algorithms to GSM-based fingerprinting. We also plan to extend our system to a working prototype that will allow for accurate localization both indoors and outdoors.

Acknowledgments

We would like to thank our anonymous UbiComp reviewers and especially our shepherd John Krumm for their detailed and sharp comments. We would also like to thank Neil Ernst for his contributions to earlier versions of this work.

References

1. L. Aalto, N. Gothlin, J. Korhonen, and T. Ojala. Bluetooth and WAP push based location-aware mobile advertising system. In *MobiSYS '04: Proceedings of the 2nd international conference on Mobile systems, applications, and services*, pages 49–58. ACM Press, 2004.
2. P. Bahl, A. Balachandran, and V. Padmanabhan. Enhancements to the RADAR User Location and Tracking System, Microsoft Research, Technical Report, Feb. 2000.
3. P. Bahl and V. N. Padmanabhan. RADAR: An in-building RF-based user location and tracking system. In *INFOCOM*, pages 775–784, 2000.
4. J. Eberspacher, H.-J. Vogel, and C. Bettstetter. GSM switching, services and protocols, 2001.
5. E. Elnahrawy, X. Li, and R. Martin. The limits of localization using signal strength: A comparative study. In *Proceedings of the 1st IEEE International Conference on Sensor and Ad Hoc Communications and Networks*, Santa Clara, CA, Oct. 2004.
6. A. Haeberlen, E. Flannery, A. M. Ladd, A. Rudys, D. S. Wallach, and L. E. Kavraki. Practical robust localization over large-scale 802.11 wireless networks. In *Proceedings of the Tenth ACM International Conference on Mobile Computing and Networking (MOBICOM)*, Philadelphia, PA, Sept. 2004.
7. A. Hopper, A. Harter, and T. Blackie. The active badge system. In *Proc. of INTERCHI-93*, pages 533–534, Amsterdam, The Netherlands, 1993.
8. T. Kindberg and A. Fox. System software for ubiquitous computing. *IEEE Pervasive Computing*, 1(1):26–35, Jan. 2002.
9. J. Krumm, G. Cermak, and E. Horvitz. RightSPOT: A Novel Sense of Location for Smart Personal Objects. In *Proceedings of Ubicomp*, 2003.
10. K. Laasonen, M. Raento, and H. Toivonen. Adaptive on-device location recognition. In *Proceedings of the Second International Conference on Pervasive Computing*, pages 287–304. Springer-Verlag, 2004.
11. A. Ladd, K. Bekris, G. Marceau, A. Rudys, L. Kavraki, and D. Wallach. Robotics-based location sensing using wireless ethernet. In *Proceedings of the Tenth ACM International Conference on Mobile Computing and Networking (MOBICOM)*, 2002.
12. H. Laitinen, J. Lahteenmaki, and T. Nordstrom. Database correlation method for GSM location. In *Proceedings of the 53rd IEEE Vehicular Technology Conference*, Rhodes, Greece, May 2001.
13. A. LaMarca, Y. Chawathe, S. Consolvo, J. Hightower, I. Smith, J. Scott, T. Sohn, J. Howard, J. Hughes, F. Potter, J. Tabert, P. Powledge, G. Borriello, and B. Schilit. Place Lab: Device Positioning Using Radio Beacons in the Wild. *3rd Annual Conference on Pervasive Computing*, 2005. To appear.
14. L. Luxner. The Manhattan Project: AT&T Wireless invades the Big Apple with microcells. *Telephony*, 8(20), Feb. 1997.
15. N. B. Priyantha, A. Chakraborty, and H. Balakrishnan. The cricket location-support system. In *Mobile Computing and Networking*, pages 32–43, 2000.
16. A. Ward, A. Jones, and A. Hopper. A new location technique for the active office. In *IEEE Personnel Communications, 4(5)*, pages 42–47, Oct. 1997.
17. M. Youssef, A. Agrawala, and U. Shankar. WLAN Location Determination via Clustering and Probability Distributions. In *IEEE PerCom 2003*, March 2003.
18. Ekahau, http://www.ekahau.com.
19. Ubisense, http://www.ubisense.net.
20. Versus Technologies, http://www.versustech.com.

Learning and Recognizing the Places We Go

Jeffrey Hightower[1], Sunny Consolvo[1], Anthony LaMarca[1], Ian Smith[1], and
Jeff Hughes[2]

[1] Intel Research Seattle
Seattle, WA, USA
[2] University of Washington
Computer Science & Engineering
Seattle, WA, USA

Abstract. Location-enhanced mobile devices are becoming common,
but applications built for these devices find themselves suffering a mismatch between the latitude and longitude that location sensors provide
and the colloquial place label that applications need. Conveying my location to my spouse, for example as (48.13641N, 11.57471E), is less informative than saying "at home." We introduce an algorithm called Beacon-
Print that uses WiFi and GSM radio fingerprints collected by someone's
personal mobile device to automatically learn the places they go and
then detect when they return to those places. BeaconPrint does not automatically assign names or semantics to places. Rather, it provides the
technological foundation to support this task. We compare BeaconPrint
to three existing algorithms using month-long trace logs from each of
three people. Algorithmic results are supplemented with a survey study
about the places people go. BeaconPrint is over 90% accurate in learning
and recognizing places. Additionally, it improves accuracy in recognizing places visited infrequently or for short durations—a category where
previous approaches have fared poorly. BeaconPrint demonstrates 63%
accuracy for places someone returns to only once or visits for less than
10 minutes, increasing to 80% accuracy for places visited twice.

1 Introduction

Devices that can automatically figure out their geographic coordinates are becoming common. Many mobile phones are now location-enhanced due to U.S.
E911 and European E112 initiatives requiring location capability for calls placed
to emergency services. The Global Positioning System (GPS) covers most of the
earth's surface, and GPS chipsets are continually decreasing in cost, making it
feasible for them to be integrated into many mobile devices. Technologies like
RightSpot [1] and Place Lab [2] have shown that beacon-based location can
allow a device to compute its position with high availability throughout someone's day—including indoors and in environments like the "canyons" formed by
high-rise buildings where GPS is unreliable. Applications such as mapping and
way-finding are straightforward to build using any of these location technologies.

M. Beigl et al. (Eds.): UbiComp 2005, LNCS 3660, pp. 159–176, 2005.
© Springer-Verlag Berlin Heidelberg 2005

Many emerging location-enhanced applications, however, want colloquial place names like "Home," "Work," "Movie Theater," or "Tony's Pizzeria" instead of latitude and longitude coordinates. An example is a dynamic instant messaging (IM) client that can set its status message to its user's current place. Using place names as the IM status is likely more informative to IM buddies than raw coordinates like 48.13641N, 11.57471E. We call this disconnect between the coordinates that devices provide and the place names emerging applications desire as the problem of *moving from location to place*.

One step in the move from location to place is to use databases such as Yahoo! Yellow Pages, Microsoft MapPoint, or governmental map and census repositories. Each of these databases can translate a coordinate into a corresponding business name, street address, map image, geographic feature, political subdivision, or other label. This process is called *geocoding*. Applications like tour guides, recommender systems, and franchise store locators (*e.g.* "Where is the nearest McDonald's Restaurant to my current position?") have been built using geocoding. A shortcoming of geocoding is that without the context of a specific query, geocoded place names can be as challenging to interpret as raw coordinates—particularly if the names are shared with others or reviewed in hindsight in a log of the places someone went. For example, revealing to my spouse that I am currently in the residential area 142 meters north of the cash machine located at the corner of Broadway and Main, although a precise description of my position, is less useful than saying I am at home. The problem is that geocoded information, like a raw coordinate, does not correspond to someone's mental model of their personal routine nor to the terminology they use when discussing the places they go.

To start to overcome these challenges in geocoding, the research community has proposed ways of enabling people's mobile devices to automatically *learn* the places they go and then to *recognize* whenever they return to those places. This paper's contributions are on this topic. Note that this work is not about automatically assigning semantics or names (*e.g.* "home") to places, but in providing the mechanism for learning the physical destinations in someone's life and detecting whenever their devices return to those places.

Place learning algorithms take as input a sensor log gathered from a mobile device and produce as output a list of the places the device went. The sensor information collected about each of these places is called a *waypoint*. A recognition algorithm uses a place's waypoint to detect when the device returns to that place. Figure 1 illustrates the learning and recognition cycle. An effective learning algorithm can do two operations:

1. **Segment** a sensor log into times when the device was in a stable place and assign a waypoint.
2. **Merge** waypoints which are captured from repeat visits to the same place.

Likewise, an effective recognition algorithm has two capabilities:

1. **Recognize** when the device returns to a known place using a waypoint list.
2. **Recognize** when the device is *not* in a place. We refer to this state as mobile.

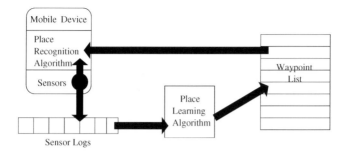

Fig. 1. The flow of data through the place *learning* and *recognition* cycle

This paper contributes a new place learning and recognition algorithm called *BeaconPrint*. BeaconPrint uses 802.11 and GSM radio response-rate fingerprints to learn and recognize places more accurately than previous approaches. We demonstrate BeaconPrint's effectiveness with a thorough comparative evaluation to three published place algorithms using one month of multi-sensor trace logs collected from each of four people. To supplement these algorithmic tests, we also conducted a survey study about the places people go. Because the data collectors for the algorithmic experiments were all members of our research team, the survey study allows us compare the places they went during the month to the number, type, and visit frequency of places reported by survey participants. We show that this comparison finds no obvious idiosyncrasies in the data collectors' habits, thus lending credence to the claim that BeaconPrint generalizes.

2   Related Work

Place learning algorithms can be divided into two classes: *geometry* and *fingerprint*. Geometric algorithms produce coordinates, circles, or polygons to describe the significant places the algorithm believes the user went. Examples of geometric place algorithms are recurring GPS dropout used in the comMotion system from Marmasse et al. [3], Ashbrook and Starner's GPS dropout windows plus hierarchical clustering [4], and the sensor-agnostic temporal point clustering contributed by Kang et al. [5]. Fingerprint algorithms, in contrast, produce a waypoint list with no geography. Fingerprint waypoints are a "signature" of each place which allows the device to detect when it returns to the place, but provides no direct information about where that place is geographically located. Fingerprint place algorithms include BeaconPrint, the graph clique-based GSM cell fingerprints of Laasonen et al. [6], and cell-ID matching which has been studied in depth by Trevisani and Vitaletti [7].

A variety of sensors can produce input logs for learning. These sensors range from traditional technologies like WiFi network interfaces and GPS receivers that are found on many mobile devices to sensors like accelerometers, barometers, or altimeters that are custom built or currently not found on most devices.

Although data from more exotic sensors may support accurate place learning, BeaconPrint shows that high accuracy is possible with commodity hardware. Microphones are a commodity sensor and there is promising work on using recordings of ambient audio as a sensor log [8]. However, continuous mobile recording of audio (or video for that matter) presents social and legal challenges that have hampered their adoption.

BeaconPrint is structurally similar to Krumm and Hinckley's NearMe location technology [9]. NearMe is a service allowing pairs of devices to compare the 802.11 radio signatures they hear to decide whether they are in physical proximity to one another. Although learning and recognizing places is a different task then determining proximity, the similarities between NearMe and BeaconPrint will be described in Section 3.3.

In evaluating BeaconPrint we compare it to the Ashbrook and Starner, comMotion, and Kang et al. algorithms. The following subsections discuss our implementation and use of each of these algorithms. A post facto discussion of each algorithm appears in Section 4 following the experimental results. We elected to exclude the GSM fingerprint approach of Laasonen et al. from our evaluation. This algorithm is clever but complex due to what we see as an artificial restriction. The complexity in the Laasonen approach seems to come about because programming interfaces on GSM phones only allow access to the unique ID of the single tower to which the phone is connected. This restriction is an artificial one imposed by the phone manufacturers and service providers. Industrial-grade or low-level GSM modems can see multiple nearby towers. Using only a single beacon requires significant complexity to build, merge, traverse, and interpret hand-off graphs—ultimately to approximate the capability that 802.11 and low-level GSM radios get for free: performing full parallel scans for all nearby radio beacons. BeaconPrint uses parallel scans to achieve high accuracy in learning and recognizing places with a significantly simpler approach.

2.1   Ashbrook and Starner's GPS Dropout plus Hierarchical Clustering Algorithm (A&S)

Ashbrook and Starner's algorithm [4], henceforth referred to as A&S, learns places people go in order to construct a Markov model predicting where they might go next. A&S exploits the variable availability of GPS in real environments to learn a person's places. It segments the GPS sensor log by marking positions at the beginning of every window of at least t minutes where the person's GPS receiver loses the satellite signal or indicates a speed continually below 1 mile per hour. Both of these situations indicate the person probably stopped or entered a building where the GPS signals cannot penetrate. These candidate positions are then merged using a variant of k-means clustering. The clustering is repeated hierarchically to identify sub-places. Clustering produces the waypoint list. Our experience agrees with their observation that choosing $t = 10$ minutes (9.6 actually) maximizes the number of correctly learned places.

As published, A&S does not explicitly discuss or evaluate recognition, however, it seems clear that using A&S waypoints for recognizing places means using live GPS data to lookup the nearest waypoint that is no further away than the radius at which the place was learned during clustering. If no place meets the criteria then the device is labeled as mobile. This distance-constrained containment search is the recognition approach used for evaluating A&S in this paper.

2.2   The comMotion Recurring GPS Dropout Algorithm

The comMotion system [3] is a GPS-equipped wearable or hand-held device which can present to-do lists or other information that is relevant to the person's current place, for example, a list of home chores when the person arrives home. Systems like comMotion are often called remembrance agents.

The comMotion system learns places using GPS in a different way than A&S. In comMotion, a place is a position where the GPS signal is lost three or more times within a given radius. The segmentation step extracts these timestamped GPS drop points, and the merge step groups them into places. The paper does not reveal what radius was used, however our iterative refinement experiments revealed 100 meters to be a good choice.

To perform recognition with comMotion for our experiments, we use live GPS data to lookup the nearest 3-time GPS drop point place that is no further away than the radius. If no place is found, the device is labeled as being mobile.

2.3   Kang et al.'s Sensor-Agnostic Temporal Point Clustering Algorithm (KSAC)

Both of the previous algorithms depend on properties of the GPS satellite signals to work properly. To avoid this dependence, Kang et al. designed a sensor-agnostic algorithm using temporal point clustering. We refer to this approach as KSAC. KSAC takes as input a stream of timestamped coordinates derived from any location system. It performs the segmentation and merging steps simultaneously using time-based clustering. For our experiments, we use the suggested clustering parameters of time $t = 300$ seconds and distance $d = 300$ meters.

KSAC's technology independence, although a good characteristic for an algorithm to have, presents the challenge of first turning sensor logs into coordinates. Using GPS alone provides poor results because GPS coverage is low and spotty in daily-life usage—a fact exploited by A&S and comMotion. Therefore, we duplicated the approach used in KSAC by first running all of our traces through the Place Lab location system (acquired from www.placelab.org) to produce coordinates. For recognition using KSAC, we ran our testing traces through the Place Lab system and used the coordinates it emitted at each time step to search for the nearest cluster within the cluster separation radius. If no cluster is found, the device is labeled as mobile.

3   The BeaconPrint Algorithm

Previous algorithms like A&S use exceptions experienced by the underlying location system to learn places. For example, A&S logically reasons that the loss of a GPS signal means the person entered a building, and entering a building means the person is at a significant place. Reactive approaches, however, can be sensitive to errors in the technology. For example, if a GPS signal is lost and later acquired in the same position on multiple days as someone's walk to work takes them into an urban canyon, A&S could erroneously identify this point as a place.

In contrast, BeaconPrint continually gathers statistics about the radio environment around the mobile device and uses this data to learn, merge, and recognize waypoints. This proactive approach allows BeaconPrint to recognize both indoor and outdoor places and be more robust to errors as our experiments will show. Although not completely sensor agnostic like KSAC, BeaconPrint uses as its sensors the commodity 802.11 or GSM wireless radios which are already built into most mobile devices.

WiFi access points and GSM towers both broadcast unique identifiers for the purpose of discovery and hand-off. For example, WiFi access points transmit periodic beacon frames containing the AP's unique MAC address. We refer to these fixed radio sources as *beacons*. Mobile devices can periodically scan for the IDs of nearby beacons. WiFi devices can scan without connecting to the network or listening to any data traffic and can see the IDs of access points even if the network is WEP encrypted. A timestamped log of these beacon scans is the input to BeaconPrint's learning phase.

BeaconPrint operates as follows: Define a time window w. Stable scans seen continuously for at least w indicate a significant place. A stable scan is one that contains no beacon IDs not seen in time w. The fingerprint (a histogram of all the beacons seen during w) is the waypoint that allows BeaconPrint to recognize return visits to the place. After constructing the waypoint list, BeaconPrint then identifies and merges similar waypoints (those inferred to have come from repeat visits to a single place). The recognition phase compares the live fingerprint seen by the device to histograms in the waypoint list. By examining the degree of the match, BeaconPrint is able to present a weighted and ordered list of device's most likely current places.

3.1 Learning

Making BeaconPrint work in practice requires a bit more logic than the basic outline presented above. The problem with the basic version is that it cannot distinguish beacons seen infrequently while a device is in the same physical place (*e.g.* a beacon that is only detected every 100th scan because of signal attenuation or multipath effects) from new beacons seen as the device is physically leaving a place. Consequently the basic version fails to learn some places and the ones it does find are erroneously divided into multiple places by the detection of low response-rate beacons. To fix this problem, we define a certainty parameter c with range $0 \ldots c_{max}$ and divide the window w into dwell increments of length $d = w/c_{max}$. If d time passes without seeing a new beacon, i.e., the scans are stable, then start collecting a fingerprint. This fingerprint's certainty c increments every additional dwell d that passes without seeing a new beacon. When

$c = c_{max}$, the fingerprint becomes valid. Seeing a new beacon decrements c. If c reaches 0, the fingerprint is recorded if valid or else discarded. Beacons are considered new if they are not seen for at least w and are not in the current fingerprint.

3.2   Parameters in BeaconPrint

BeaconPrint takes two parameters: window size w and confidence depth c_{max}. Window size is the adjustment offered by most place learning algorithms to specify how long the person must stay somewhere for it to be considered a place. Choosing w under 2 minutes works poorly in practice because spurious places such as stoplights and crosswalks where the person stopped only briefly will be discovered.

The other parameter, c_{max}, determines the dwell time and confidence. Choosing c_{max} too low results in the problems of the basic version where infrequently seen beacons cause places to be erroneously fragmented. Choosing c_{max} too high causes distinct places with a short physical travel distance between them to be incorrectly grouped together because an insufficient number of new beacons to end the fingerprint is seen during transit between the places. When the person starts moving and leaves a place, the algorithm should detect new beacons and end the fingerprint gathering within the time length of one dwell window $d = w/c_{max}$. Therefore, if r is the average arrival rate of new beacons seen when moving between places, this goal will be met if:

$$new~beacons~during~one~dwell~time > max~confidence$$
$$r \cdot \frac{w}{c_{max}} > c_{max}$$
$$c_{max} < \sqrt{rw}$$

Choosing $c_{max} = \sqrt{rw}$ works well in practice for any window size.

To investigate the rate r, we examined our trace logs for the new beacon arrival rate in portions of the log where the person was mobile. We first tried to determine mobility only considering portions of the log with a valid GPS lock indicating non-zero ground speed, however this approach proved unreliable because the amount of time with a GPS lock is very low with receivers carried by a typical person in his daily life. Instead, we determined mobility by extracting portions of the log where each data collector's ground-truth diary (see Section 4.1) indicated they were in transit between two places. This results in an r value of 0.0631Hz, 0.0055Hz, 0.0686Hz for WiFi, GSM, and both together. These values are used in subsequent experiments in this paper. For example, using GSM and WiFi with a time window w of 2 minutes (120 seconds) specifies a c_{max} of 3.

It may be possible to update r in real time based on beacon arrival rate. However, detecting when the person is mobile without supervised labeling is difficult. Although BeaconPrint itself detects mobility, the feedback loop created by using the algorithm to tune its own r value presents a challenge. Alternatively, a classification method such as the one provided by the Opportunity Knocks to infer and predict the person's mode of transportation (*e.g.*, car, bus, bike, or walk) [10] might make it possible to compute different r values for each mode and improve BeaconPrint further. It is not clear, however, that adding dynamism to r is even needed. If we repeat the rate analysis broken down by each individual person, the consistency of r across our four data collectors suggests that instead of online adjustments, it is appropriate to simply set r based on the beacon technologies in use (WiFi, GSM, or both) and perhaps according to the general beacon density of the region (*e.g.*, beacons per square kilometer in the greater San Fransisco Bay Area for all local residents). Examining these ideas in greater detail is future work.

3.3   Fingerprints: Merging and Matching

Place learning algorithms using fingerprints often choose signal strength as their metric. Instead, BeaconPrint follows the conclusions offered by LaMarca et al. [2] and constructs its fingerprint using a response-rate histogram where response-rate is (1-beacon loss rate). Response-rate is an aggregate statistic based on MAC layer characteristics, signal fading, multipath, and interference. LaMarca et al. showed that when a device is stationary, the percent of scans which see a particular beacon can be more effective in predicting the distance to that beacon than the signal strength values reported by the wireless network interfaces of both WiFi cards and GSM phones.

Choosing response-rate fingerprints adds the final piece of logic to the learning algorithm: When c_{max} reaches 0 and a valid fingerprint is recorded, beacons with less than c_{max} entries in the fingerprint histogram are discarded. This approach trims outliers and discards the new beacons which caused the fingerprint to end when the user left the place being fingerprinted.

In implementing the NearMe location server [9], Krumm and Hinckley studied four ways to detect if two wireless signatures are similar:

1. Number of beacons the fingerprints have in common.
2. Spearman rank-order coefficient of the ordered relative signal strengths.
3. Sum of squared differences of the signal strengths.
4. Number of beacons the fingerprints do not have in common.

BeaconPrint applies the first technique, extended to operate on response-rate histograms instead of simple sets. During the merging phase of BeaconPrint, if the overlapping set of beacons in the two fingerprints contains more than 68% of the weight of both histograms (68% is 1 standard deviation of a standard normal), then the fingerprints are deemed similar and merged. For each new fingerprint, all pairs of fingerprints are iteratively compared and merged until the set stabilizes.

During recognition, BeaconPrint considers the device to be in a place if more than 1 standard deviation of the weight in the observed fingerprint overlaps with any part of the place's fingerprint. The fingerprint currently seen by the device thus might match multiple learned places. In this case, the list of recognized places can be ordered by the weight of the shared beacons in each matching place fingerprint. If no fingerprints match, the device is labeled as mobile.

4   Algorithm Evaluation

To evaluate BeaconPrint, we compare it with the three algorithms described in Section 2.

4.1   Data Collection

To accurately evaluate BeaconPrint and overcome any startup effects, we collected a substantial amount of multi-sensor trace data as well as ground-truth about the places people actually went and the times they were there.

Sensor Logs We collected 24x7 GPS, WiFi, and GSM trace logs for one month from each of four members of our research team as they went about their normal lives. We choose members of our team as the data collectors instead of recruiting external participants because the data collection task required substantial effort as well as technical expertise to diagnose and fix any problems. Furthermore, the data is inherently sensitive making it challenging to recruit external volunteers. However, as we will describe in Section 5, we also conducted a small, in depth survey study of the places people go using recruited participants to compare our data collectors to people not on our research team.

Each data collector carried a backpack containing a laptop, mobile phone, and 16-hour battery. The laptop had attached to it a standard WiFi network card and a GPS unit which was modified to send data into and draw power from the laptop's PC card slot. As described previously, WiFi access points and GSM towers both have unique identifiers. Our data collection software scanned for these unique identifiers at 2Hz and kept a timestamped log of all the nearby beacons heard in each scan. GPS data arrived in a serial stream and was logged at 1Hz. The GSM scanning occurred on the mobile phone and was relayed to the laptop over a Bluetooth data link. In total, we collected 3.4GB of multi-sensor data amounting to over 1,440 hours of sensor logs. On later analysis we discovered that one of our data collector's laptops experienced periodic hardware failures and its logs were segmented and incomplete. This data was excluded from our analyses.

Ground-Truth To collect ground-truth, each data collector was given a clip-on watch and a small paper notebook to carry with them everywhere. In the notebook, they kept a diary of the name and time they entered and left every place they went during the month. At the end of the data collection these diaries were coded and each data collector used map software to indicate the coordinates of every unique place in their diary. These diaries and maps provide the ground-truth information about the coordinates of the actual places the data collectors went as well as the actual times they arrived and left those places. Finally, each data collector completed the survey study described in Section 5.

Data Collector Demographics Our data collectors are assigned the pseudonyms Adam, Bob, and Charles.

Adam is a parent of 2 children. Many of his places involve driving his kids to school, doctors, restaurants, and extra curricular activities. He usually walks to work but chooses to drive about one time in four. He stops for coffee on his way to work every day and typically goes out for coffee at least once more during the day. He usually eats out for lunch.

Bob is a challenging person for any place learning algorithm. He lives in an area of dense urban high-rises. The places he goes for errands and entertainment around his home are tightly clustered and close to one another. Bob typically takes public transit to work which is outside the urban area. He occasionally drives to work. He eats out for lunch at a wide variety of restaurants nearly every day. Bob frequently goes out for coffee, although less often than Adam.

Charles walks to work every day but frequently drives to specialty shops and other destinations located several miles from his house. He packs his lunch many days but is also a regular patron at a small set of restaurants near his home and work. Charles is a frequent traveler, particularly on weekends. During our logging he made two train trips to the same destination over 100 miles from his home and a plane trip to a destination over 600 miles from his home. Obviously Charles' log has a gap during the time he was in flight since radio technology is prohibited on airplanes.

4.2   Experimental Results

We divided each data collector's sensor logs in half. Each algorithm was given the first half of the log to learn the data collector's places. The second half of the log was then used to evaluate how well the algorithm could recognize based on the places it learned. Places which the data collector only visited in the second half of their log were time-spliced out. Table 1 summarizes the results of this experiment. It shows the percent of time each algorithm correctly identifies the data collector's actual place. For example, the percent of time an algorithm correctly identifies place p is the total amount of time the algorithm predicts p divided by the total amount of time the data collector actually spent at p. The total percentage appearing in the table is the aggregate of this statistic across all the data collector's places.

Because our data collectors, like most people, spend most of their time at home, at work, or in transit, Table 1 also shows the correctness statistics when home and work and then when all three of these periods are omitted from the analysis. Factoring out these periods reveals the effectiveness of each algorithm at recognizing less frequented places.

For the total percent of the time each algorithm was incorrect, we also analyzed the data further to understand why it erred. To present these results, the table shows a breakdown of the percent of time the algorithm made each of the four possible errors:

Wrong means the data collector was in a place but the algorithm reported they were in a different place.

Missed means the data collector was in a place but the algorithm reported they were mobile.

Spurious is the result of a learning error. A spurious error occurs when the data collector was in a place but the algorithm reported they were in another place which does not correspond to anywhere they actually went in learning. Merging or clustering errors are usually the cause of spurious recognition errors.

False Positive means the data collector was actually mobile but the algorithm reported they were in a place.

BeaconPrint performs well. It has the highest overall accuracy for all three data collectors in all three situations presented in the table. The percent of time it chooses the wrong place is also strictly the lowest. BeaconPrint is less accurate for Bob when compared to its performance for Adam and Charles, but the other algorithms are significantly worse on Bob's data. Bob's urban neighborhood has a density of nearly 2000 beacons per square mile. Beacon density in and of itself can be a good thing for a fingerprint algorithm like BeaconPrint, but density combined with unpredictable radio propagation is not. The concrete and steel canyons formed by urban buildings wreak havoc on the signals of GPS and other radio technologies. Unpredictable radio propagation makes it difficult to get a GPS lock and challenging to acquire clean beacon fingerprints with good place discrimination capability. Consequently, learning and recognition errors rise for Bob. Despite these challenges, BeaconPrint still performs much better for Bob than we anticipated.

BeaconPrint's improvement in the accuracy of recognizing places other than home and work is particularly notable as shown by the second and third sections of the table. To investigate these infrequent places further we examined the percent of time the algorithm was correct, broken down by the number of visits the data collector made to each place and the amount of time they spent in each place. These results are presented in Figures 2 and 3. Values in parentheses are the total number of places and amount of time our data collectors spent in places with the given visit frequency or dwell characteristics. The right-most set of columns on both graphs is obviously dominated by time spent at home and work.

From these graphs it is clear that BeaconPrint provides a significant improvement in the ability to recognize places visited infrequently or for short visits. These infrequently visited places are also quite numerous. When examined strictly by count, they make up the majority of the places our data collectors went. We believe BeaconPrint's ability to recognize places that are visited infrequently or for short durations is the most significant contribution of the overall accuracy improvements offered by the approach. We will examine this conclusion further in Section 5 in the context of our survey study.

Person Algorithm	Adam				Bob				Charles			
	BP	A-S	cM	KSAC	BP	A-S	cM	KSAC	BP	A-S	cM	KSAC
Full Analysis												
Correct	**96.39%**	**92.29%**	**90.50%**	**91.05%**	**85.12%**	**25.52%**	**49.85%**	**65.38%**	**91.13%**	**80.94%**	**79.33%**	**85.95%**
Incorrect	**3.61%**	**7.71%**	**9.50%**	**8.95%**	**14.88%**	**74.48%**	**50.15%**	**34.62%**	**8.87%**	**19.06%**	**20.67%**	**14.05%**
Wrong	0.25%	3.84%	2.18%	1.38%	4.68%	43.74%	6.29%	25.98%	0.38%	5.58%	4.10%	1.27%
Missed	0.98%	1.29%	5.41%	1.00%	5.81%	0.15%	40.44%	2.78%	2.17%	3.26%	6.90%	7.19%
Spurious	0.70%	0.01%	0.00%	1.44%	1.42%	24.42%	0.58%	0.05%	3.35%	6.46%	6.95%	3.34%
False Pos	1.68%	2.57%	1.91%	5.14%	2.97%	6.17%	2.84%	5.82%	2.97%	3.76%	2.71%	2.25%
Home and Work Omitted												
Correct	**72.26%**	**58.58%**	**43.52%**	**29.34%**	**60.41%**	**21.05%**	**40.10%**	**24.87%**	**68.19%**	**26.17%**	**23.90%**	**42.68%**
Incorrect	**27.74%**	**41.42%**	**56.48%**	**70.66%**	**39.59%**	**78.95%**	**59.90%**	**75.13%**	**31.81%**	**73.83%**	**76.10%**	**57.32%**
Wrong	1.98%	14.05%	7.96%	11.63%	1.72%	21.04%	4.20%	24.95%	2.14%	14.92%	12.81%	6.84%
Missed	5.63%	4.51%	31.50%	3.49%	16.30%	0.44%	45.33%	14.88%	9.32%	2.29%	15.85%	34.21%
Spurious	5.93%	0.00%	0.00%	12.13%	6.60%	18.10%	0.00%	0.10%	3.65%	35.50%	32.19%	3.63%
False Pos	14.19%	22.86%	17.02%	43.41%	14.97%	39.37%	10.37%	35.19%	16.70%	21.12%	15.25%	12.63%
Home, Work, and Transit Time Omitted												
Correct	**72.98%**	**60.77%**	**17.05%**	**45.64%**	**56.00%**	**29.02%**	**11.17%**	**28.61%**	**77.17%**	**20.35%**	**8.05%**	**32.49%**
Incorrect	**27.02%**	**39.23%**	**82.95%**	**54.36%**	**44.00%**	**70.98%**	**88.83%**	**71.39%**	**22.83%**	**79.65%**	**91.95%**	**67.51%**
Wrong	3.95%	29.69%	16.73%	23.20%	3.08%	37.73%	7.54%	44.60%	3.23%	22.55%	19.36%	10.34%
Missed	11.23%	9.54%	66.21%	6.97%	29.13%	0.79%	81.29%	26.61%	14.09%	3.46%	23.94%	51.69%
Spurious	11.83%	0.00%	0.00%	24.19%	11.79%	32.46%	0.00%	0.18%	5.51%	53.64%	48.64%	5.48%

Table 1. Percent of time each algorithm correctly identifies the data collector's places. BeaconPrint has the highest correctness and the least percent of the time choosing the wrong place

Correctness by Number of Visits

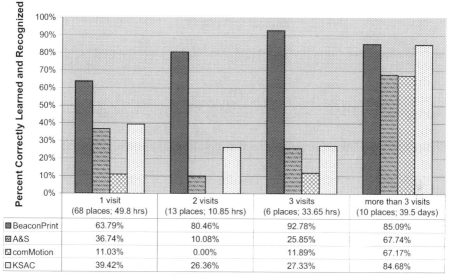

	1 visit (68 places; 49.8 hrs)	2 visits (13 places; 10.85 hrs)	3 visits (6 places; 33.65 hrs)	more than 3 visits (10 places; 39.5 days)
BeaconPrint	63.79%	80.46%	92.78%	85.09%
A&S	36.74%	10.08%	25.85%	67.74%
comMotion	11.03%	0.00%	11.89%	67.17%
KSAC	39.42%	26.36%	27.33%	84.68%

Total Number of Visits to the Place

Fig. 2. Success of each algorithm by the number of visits to the place

Correctness by Dwell Time

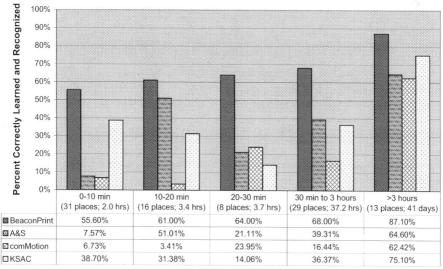

	0-10 min (31 places; 2.0 hrs)	10-20 min (16 places; 3.4 hrs)	20-30 min (8 places; 3.7 hrs)	30 min to 3 hours (29 places; 37.2 hrs)	>3 hours (13 places; 41 days)
BeaconPrint	55.60%	61.00%	64.00%	68.00%	87.10%
A&S	7.57%	51.01%	21.11%	39.31%	64.60%
comMotion	6.73%	3.41%	23.95%	16.44%	62.42%
KSAC	38.70%	31.38%	14.06%	36.37%	75.10%

Total Time Spent in the Place

Fig. 3. Success of each algorithm by time spent at the place

comMotion The comMotion algorithm was reasonably successful at learning and recognizing the 2 or 3 places our data collectors visited regularly, but worked poorly for other places. The requirement for the user to go to a place at least three times before it can be recognized is overly restrictive. The small amount of success comMotion appears to have in recognizing a one-visit place in Figure 2 is due to a coincidental learning error which turned out to be beneficial during recognition.

Although comMotion uses GPS loss to find places, we found that the availability of GPS during transit between places was far less continuous than com-Motion seems to assume. Bob, our data collector who lives in the urban high-rise area, would often be mobile for a substantial period without achieving GPS lock. He could travel from his home to the bus stop, ride the bus for 20 minutes, and then walk a few blocks to work with little to no GPS lock—not surprising since he lacked a clear view of the satellites for almost the entire journey. Adam and Charles fared a bit better, probably because both of them commute by foot in less urban areas.

A&S As in comMotion, the low availability of GPS limited the amount of available data, although this does not hurt the accuracy of A&S as much as might be expected. Filtering for GPS dropout windows and then also for GPS readings with velocity less than 1mph is a clever enhancement. For example, both Adam and Charles live in wood-frame houses where GPS had weak and intermittent but not lost coverage. Because of its velocity filter, A&S found these places quickly.

Hierarchical clustering of locations and sublocations did not prove useful. It was difficult to choose a constant pair of radii for the hierarchical clustering. Indeed, the approach yielding the highest accuracy was to only cluster locations (not sublocations) using the single radius of 200 meters—close to the sublocation radius proposed in the original paper. The success of single-level clustering is logical because our data collectors do not have readily identifiable groups of nearby places connected by longer commutes. Their places are dense in certain areas but there are many scattered places in between. To capture these weaker place hierarchies it may be possible to alter A&S to choose different radii for locations and sublocations in different regions of the map, however this is not a trivial change because it would require a different clustering algorithm. The published clustering algorithm depends on having a single constant radius per level.

KSAC The KSAC algorithm performed reasonably well in our experiments. Although its performance lagged behind BeaconPrint, it was able to recognize infrequently or briefly visited places somewhat better than A&S or comMotion because of its use of temporal clustering. KSAC does seem to have a weakness in its ability to distinguish mobility as seen by the high number of false positive errors. We believe this issue arises because its clustering tries to account for large regions resulting in a good set of place waypoints, but a lack of sharp demarcation between places.

5   Survey Study

The data collectors mentioned previously were all members of our research team. Therefore the question remains whether they, and hence the sensor logs they collected, are representative of a wider population. To address this issue and supplement the algorithmic evaluations, we conducted a survey study investigating the places people go.

We recruited 6 participants of varying ages and professions. Note that we use the term *participants* here to distinguish the people who participated in this survey study from the data collectors who wore the backpacks and gathered the sensor trace logs. The data collectors were also participants and completed this study bringing the total number of survey study participants to 9. Recruited participants consisted of 2 males and 4 females, ranged in age from 25 to 40, and were drawn from a variety of professions including homemaker, scientist, writer, and retail clerk. All participants were from the Seattle area. Participants received a US $75 American Express gift cheque as a thank-you for their participation.

The study asked participants to recall all the places they go at least twice a year (once per year for medical-related places) and within 50 miles of home. We used two techniques to help reduce the recall bias associated with survey studies. First, we used categorical prompting. We structured the survey as a packet where each page was a broad category such as restaurants, medical, shopping–food, shopping–non-food, etc. The head of each page then contained check-boxes for many subcategories which the participant could check off one-by-one as they completed the page to remind them about the types of places they go within categories (*e.g.*, Asian-fusion vs. French restaurants). Second, we allowed participants to complete the survey packet on their own time over the course of several days, thus allowing them the opportunity to fill in places periodically as they remembered more. By using a carefully designed prompting exercise and leisurely homework, we hope that we were able to gather a more complete set of places then would have been generated from a straight recall task with participants brought to our lab. However, we realize the list of places generated likely represents a lower bound, as participants may have forgotten about some places they go that met the criteria and may have deliberately left off other places. For each place, participants recorded the subcategory name, the name they use to refer to the place, the frequency with which they visit the place, and a description or address of its location.

We used participants' data to search for idiosyncrasies in our data collectors' places or habits that would cast suspicion on their data logs and hence our conclusions about the success of BeaconPrint. Fortunately, there are no suspicious mismatches to be found. In fact, the participants' survey data, the data collectors' survey data, the data collectors' diary records of the places they went during data logging, and even the BeaconPrint algorithm's predictions are

174   Jeffrey Hightower et al.

very consistent as shown by Figure 4. This graph demonstrates that places our
data collectors went are not distributed in visit frequency significantly different
from the places external participants report going. This comparison supports
the claim that there is no reason to believe the BeaconPrint results will not
generalize beyond the three data collectors whose sensor logs were used in the
algorithmic analyses. The fourth column of this graph shows no data for diaries
and BeaconPrint because sensor data collection only occurred for one month.

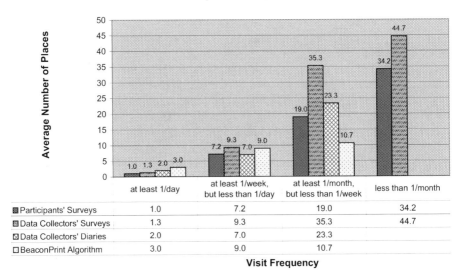

**Comparison of Reported and Actual Place Visit
Frequencies**

	at least 1/day	at least 1/week, but less than 1/day	at least 1/month, but less than 1/week	less than 1/month
Participants' Surveys	1.0	7.2	19.0	34.2
Data Collectors' Surveys	1.3	9.3	35.3	44.7
Data Collectors' Diaries	2.0	7.0	23.3	
BeaconPrint Algorithm	3.0	9.0	10.7	

Visit Frequency

Fig. 4. The average number of places visited by visit frequency. Participants in
the survey study reported an average of 72.3 total significant places

Analyzing Figure 4, we hypothesize that the data collectors might have reported more infrequent places (columns 3 and 4) because, being members of our
research team who frequently participated in our "hallway" discussions about
this work, they were primed to recall all the odd places they go once or twice
a year. The data collectors' diaries, which recorded where they actually went,
however, are quite consistent with the participants' surveys. BeaconPrint clearly
does well. The fact that the third grouping is lower for BeaconPrint can be
explained by the characteristics of the experiment. BeaconPrint's recognition
ability was only tested on the evaluation half of the month-long sensor logs, so
multiplying the value in this case by 2 is probably appropriate, thus raising it
to a comparable level.

6   Future Work

Armed with statistics about the amount of time BeaconPrint is correct, we plan to conduct additional user studies to understand the ways in which people respond to wrong, missed, spurious, and false positive errors. We hope to understand which types of errors are benign and which are egregious in the context of different applications and scenarios from the users' perspective. This new study will both inform our design of place-enhanced applications and help us focus future work on improving the BeaconPrint algorithm.

Algorithmically, we plan to extend BeaconPrint to support partially supervised learning of places. Active Campus Explorer (ACE) [11] has shown the value of allowing users to click or tap the screen of their mobile device to indicate their actual position when the location system is unsure. ACE uses this correction to improve its accuracy whenever the user is again near the corrected position. ACE has shown that these manual corrections have low cognitive overhead on users and are a well liked feature. We believe that manual correction techniques extend quite naturally to BeaconPrint and have the potential to significantly improve its accuracy by avoiding any ambiguity about when to collect a fingerprint for a place. We also imagine that the mechanism for manual correction in BeaconPrint could be combined with an interface for adding semantics or names (*e.g.*, "home") to the places BeaconPrint learns.

7   Conclusion

The BeaconPrint algorithm presented in this paper addresses the problem of automatically learning the places a person takes their mobile device and then being able to recognize whenever the device returns there. BeaconPrint uses 802.11 and GSM response-rate histograms to learn and recognize places using radio fingerprints. Using 802.11 and GSM radios as its sensors allows BeaconPrint to run on commodity hardware, since many mobile devices have these radios built in. BeaconPrint can begin to recognize a place after the first time the devices goes there. We evaluated BeaconPrint using 1 month of multi-sensor trace logs from each of three people.

BeaconPrint increases the accuracy of place learning and recognition to over 90%. When it does err, the percent of time BeaconPrint chooses the wrong place is also lower than previous approaches. The largest contribution of BeaconPrint, however, is its success in learning and recognizing places visited infrequently or only for short durations. People in our studies averaged 72.3 places they go at least twice a year (or once per year for medical-related places). Only 1 or 2 of these places are visited every day (usually home and work) and only 7 or 8 others are visited at least weekly. The other 63 places are visited infrequently. Although places visited most frequently are arguably the most personally significant, previous algorithms are generally quite poor at learning and recognizing anything except those most frequented places. Their accuracy with infrequent places averages 5-35%. BeaconPrint patches this deficiency by demonstrating an

accuracy rate of over 63% even for places someone returns to only once or visits
for less than 10 minutes, increasing to 80% accuracy for places visited twice.

References

1. Krumm, J., Cermak, G., Horvitz, E.: Rightspot: A novel sense of location for a
   smart personal object. In: Proceedings of the Fifth International Conference on
   Ubiquitous Computing (Ubicomp), Springer-Verlag (2003) 36–43
2. LaMarca, A., Chawathe, Y., Consolvo, S., Hightower, J., Smith, I., Scott, J., Sohn,
   T., Howard, J., Hughes, J., Potter, F., Tabert, J., Powledge, P., Borriello, G.,
   Schilit, B.: Place lab: Device positioning using radio beacons in the wild. In: Proceedings of the Third International Conference on Pervasive Computing. Lecture
   Notes in Computer Science, Springer-Verlag (2005) to appear.
3. Marmasse, N., Schmandt, C.: Location-aware information delivery with commotion. In: Proceedings of the Second International Symposium on Handheld and
   Ubiquitous Computing (HUC). Volume 1927., Springer-Verlag (2000) 151–171
4. Ashbrook, D., Starner, T.: Using GPS to learn significant locations and predict
   movement across multiple users. Personal and Ubiquitous Computing 7 (2003)
   275–286
5. Kang, J.H., Welbourne, W., Stewart, B., Borriello, G.: Extracting places from
   traces of locations. In: Proceedings of the Second ACM International Workshop
   on Wireless Mobile Applications and Services on WLAN Hotspots (WMASH 2004),
   Philadelphia, PA, ACM Press (2004) 110–118
6. Laasonen, K., Raento, M., Toivonen, H.: Adaptive on-device location recognition.
   In: Proceedings of the Second International Conference on Pervasive Computing.
   Volume 3001 of Lecture Notes in Computer Science., Springer-Verlag (2004) 287–
   304
7. Trevisani, E., Vitaletti, A.: Cell-id location technique, limits and benefits: An experimental study. In: Proceedings of the 6th IEEE Workshop on Mobile Computing
   Systems & Applications (WMCSA 2004), IEEE Computer Society Press (2004)
8. Clarkson, B.P., Pentland, A.: Unsupervised clustering of ambulatory audio and
   video. In: Proceedings of the IEEE International Conference on Acoustics, Speech,
   and Signal Processing (ICASSP). Volume 6., Springer-Verlag (1999) 3037–3040
9. Krumm, J., Hinckley, K.: The nearme wireless proximity server. In: Proceedings of
   the Sixth International Conference on Ubiquitous Computing (Ubicomp), Springer-
   Verlag (2004) 283–300
10. Patterson, D.J., Liao, L., Gajos, K., Collier, M., Livic, N., Olson, K., Wang, S.,
    Fox, D., Kautz, H.: Opportunity knocks: a system to provide cognitive assistance
    with transportation services. In Davies, N., Mynatt, E., Siio, I., eds.: Proceedings
    of the Sixth International Conference on Ubiquitous Computing (Ubicomp 2004).
    Volume 3205 of Lecture Notes in Computer Science., Springer-Verlag (2004) 433–
    450
11. Griswold, W.G., Shanahan, P., Brown, S.W., Boyer, R.T.: Activecampus—
    experiments in community-oriented ubiquitous computing. Computer 37 (2004)
    73–81

Visually Interactive Location-Aware Computing

Kasim Rehman, Frank Stajano, and George Coulouris

Computer Laboratory
University of Cambridge
15 JJ Thomson Avenue
Cambridge CB3 0FD
United Kingdom
{kr241,fms27,gfc22}@cam.ac.uk

Abstract. The physical disappearance of the computer, associated with Ubicomp, has led to a number of interaction challenges. Due to the lack of an interface users are losing control over applications running in Ubicomp environments. Furthermore, the limited ability for these applications to provide feedback makes it difficult for users to understand their workings and dependencies. We investigate whether an interaction paradigm, based on the visualising location-aware applications on a head-mounted display, is feasible and whether it has the potential to improve the user experience in the same way graphical user interfaces did for the desktop. We show the feasibility of the idea by building an Augmented Reality interface to a location-aware environment. Initial user trials indicate that the user experience can be improved through in-situ visualisation.

1 Introduction

Long-term use of indoor location-aware applications, has brought to light a number of usability problems. The disappearance of the traditional "interface" in the Ubicomp paradigm has resulted in users not being able to control or understand such applications, to an extent that makes them feel comfortable. This research proposes one solution to this problem.

Our group's research into indoor location-aware applications in the course of the Sentient Computing Project [1] has examined how we can support office workers in their daily interaction with computing, communication and I/O facilities by letting applications adapt to changes in location of users and things. Over the past years users have been supported in having phone calls forwarded automatically to their current location; having videos, notes and documents recorded along with the user's current context; being notified about events in the physical world etc. Notably, these applications have been designed for spontaneous walk up and use.

Contrary to what you might expect the user experience relating to such applications has remained suboptimal. For example, automatic actions often occur without users knowing why. Sometimes expected actions are not performed by the system for no apparent reason. What characterises such breakdowns in location-aware applications is that they are entirely unintelligible for most users.

These problems are not accidental but at the root of context-aware computing. Bellotti and Edwards [2], starting from the point of view that complex machine inferencing

M. Beigl et al. (Eds.): UbiComp 2005, LNCS 3660, pp. 177–194, 2005.
© Springer-Verlag Berlin Heidelberg 2005

based on human context is a "difficult proposition", recapitulate on four design principles that need to be adhered to. More specifically, they recommend that context-aware systems inform the user of *system capabilities and understandings*, and provide *identity/action disclosure* ("Who is that, what are they doing and what have they done?), *feedback* and *control*.

A number of other Ubicomp researchers have pointed out problems along these lines such as Rehman et al. [3], Bellotti et al. [4], Edwards and Grinter [5], Shafer et al. [6], Dourish [7], Dey et al. [8] and Odlyzko [9].

The more interesting part, however, is how to solve these problems. Location-aware walk-up-and-use applications in particular offer little facilities for feedback and control as opposed to PDA-supported location-aware applications.

In our attempt to tackle this challenge we decided to introduce visualisation into the location-aware environment. One of the research questions we are interested in is, can we reap benefits from visualisation in Ubicomp[1] in the same way the desktop benefited from its introduction in the form of graphical user interfaces (GUIs). Amongst the benefits of desktop GUIs has been the provision of a good mental model [10], the ability to achieve your goals through a number of predictable interaction steps, due to a small set of standard interaction facilities; and, very importantly, it *shows* us the system state at any one point in time. Each of these features seems relevant to the Ubicomp interaction problem. In the following we will present a platform for building location-aware applications that exhibit these features.

A head-mounted display (HMD) combined with Augmented Reality (AR) [11] makes it possible to give users the illusion that visualisations are co-located with devices, people and physical spaces: objects on which location-aware applications operate. We will show how location-aware applications can make use of such a facility to convey a mental model and provide feedback, referring directly to the objects of interest. Combining this with a personal interaction device, we can create a new visual interaction paradigm which allows for control as well.

Our main result is that introducing visualisation into Ubicomp, firstly, allows users to make a better mental model of the application, secondly, reduces the cognitive load associated with the application and, thirdly, gives them a more empowering user experience.

2   System Description

Before we present the platform we created to build visually interactive location-aware applications we will briefly introduce AR.

2.1   Augmented Reality

In its widest sense any system that connects the real and virtual world can be labelled "Augmented Reality". As such, even tangible interfaces are examples of AR. A narrower definition involves a system that uses an HMD, a tracker and 3D graphics. The

---

[1] We regard location-aware computing, or the more general context-aware computing as flavours of Ubicomp.

tracker continuously measures the position and orientation of the head. The system responds to the user's head movement by continuously shifting the virtual viewpoint it uses to display a 3D graphics scene on the *see-through* HMD. This makes the virtual scene *appear co-located with the physical world*. Achieving a good alignment, also called registration, is notoriously difficult and depends on good calibration of the HMD [12]. AR requires trackers with high accuracies. Even though these are often tethered there have been successful mobile indoor AR systems [13]. Figure 1 shows the equipment that needs to be carried around by the user in a typical mobile AR setup.

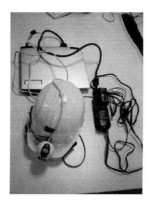

Fig. 1. Equipment required for the tetherless version of our system: a laptop, a helmet with an HMD and a camera, and the HMD electronics unit.

2.2   Architecture

Figure 2 shows the architecture of our system. The Ubicomp backend that runs our location-aware environment is called SPIRIT [14]. It stores a virtual world model in a database. This virtual world can be regarded as a mirror image of the real world. Every real world "smart" object and person has a virtual CORBA [15] proxy that provides an interface to their virtual state and capabilities. SPIRIT gives application developers access to these interfaces. SPIRIT's crucial property, however, is that the world model is a spatial model of the physical environment that is managed by SPIRIT. As smart objects and people move in the real world their locations and spatial relationships in the world model are updated. SPIRIT can naturally only update locations if the real counterparts are tracked by the Active Bat system.

The Active Bat [14] system used by SPIRIT is an indoor ultrasound location system. With this system Active Bats (Fig. 3) can be located anywhere in our laboratory within 3 cm 95% of the time. The Bat is a small trackable tag that is about 85 mm long. Two small buttons are located on the left side.

SPIRIT allows applications to subscribe to events. Using the spatial model of the physical environment, low-level Bat sightings are abstracted to high level sentient events

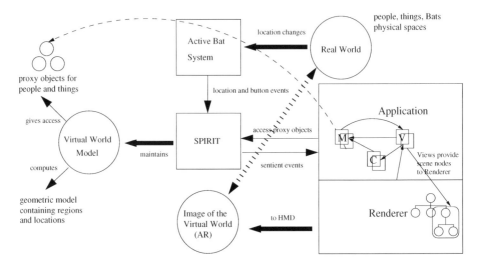

Fig. 2. How to bring an image of the virtual world into the real world. Solid arrows indicate system interactions. Dashed arrows show conceptual relationships between the virtual world, real world and the image of the virtual world. The important arrows have been made thick.

Fig. 3. The Active Bat

to be used by application developers. Example high-level events are: "Andy is close to Pete", or "Andy is in the same room as John". By using Bats to tag objects and people we can let our applications reason about the spatial relations of objects and/or users. Each lab member is equipped with a personal Bat that not only tracks them but can be used to initiate actions in the location-aware environment (by pressing its two buttons). Button press events are forwarded to SPIRIT in the same way as Bat movement events, which allows SPIRIT in turn to generate events such as "Andy's Bat's side button was pressed while being held close to the monitor". This allows application developers to introduce interaction into their location-aware applications.

The most important abstraction of the SPIRIT system is a physical region. For each object or person a set of regions is stored. These are predefined around the particular person or object, having different sizes and shapes. High-level events are generated by evaluating the overlap and containment of such regions. More on how to employ regions to compute spatial relationships can be found in [14].

The question we faced was how would a visually interactive location-aware application interface with the existing SPIRIT system. There are a number of issues here but our main concern was that we wanted to visualise parts of the virtual world, i.e. we wanted the user to see what is happening inside the SPIRIT system, rather than building an interface that receives messages from a particular location-aware application in the course of its execution. In the first case, visualisation and application are accessing the same data structures, in the second case the visualisation is a client of the application.

The architecture devised to fulfill this requirement was an object-oriented Model-View-Controller (MVC) architecture [16]. This implies that the application is modelled as a set of triples, each containing a Model, a View and a Controller[2]. Each domain object the application operates on is mapped to one such triple.

The visualisation essentially consists of constructing a 3D world on the user's HMD. This is achieved through a scene-graph-based 3D graphics package [17]. A component called Renderer provides a platform to build visually interactive location-aware applications on. It takes care of all AR-related operations in order to separate them from the core application logic. It also maps the view hierarchy constructed in the application to the scene graph; views are organised entirely hierarchically in MVC.

Models in the application are images of the actual virtual proxies. These Models are able to access the state and capabilities of the virtual proxies and can be regarded as equivalent from the application's point of view. The important connection is as following: Models are representatives of objects living in the virtual world and Views merely visualise them. The Views make up the 3D world the user sees through the HMD. Hence, the user sees an image of the virtual world overlaid on the real world. We can now relate the virtual state of a smart object directly to its physical embodiment.

We have conveyed a very high-level view of our system since in this paper we are mainly interested in studying the effects of our system on users; a more accurate description of our system for the purpose of reproduction can be found in [18].

3 Introducing Visual Interaction into a Location-Aware Application

In order to put our interaction paradigm into practice we chose following approach: We ported a location-aware application already deployed and used in our lab to our platform so that it could provide feedback via the user's HMD. The ultimate aim was to compare two versions of essentially the same application.

---

[2] The original MVC allows models to have multiple Views, but we only need one View per Model to generate the AR overlay.

3.1   A Typical Location-Aware Application

The application we chose to port for our user trial is the *Desktop Teleport* application already deployed in our lab. Many GUI environments allow you to have different Desktops, each containing a particular set of applications, documents and settings. In this location-aware teleport application, users can *walk up* to a computer, press a button on their Bat and have a Desktop that is running on a different computer "teleported" onto the current computer. VNC [19] is used in order to achieve this. VNC stands for Virtual Network Computing and allows users to access their GUI Desktop remotely from any computer. The computer running the Desktop locally contains a VNC Client that is listening to "connect Desktop" events from the middleware, which are initiated by the Bat button press. When it receives such an event it connects to a VNC server which then sends bitmapped images showing its current screen to the client. The server receives mouse and keyboard events in return. It is important to note that users can have multiple Desktops running simultaneously.

One use for this application would be to walk up to a random computer in the lab, click the Bat button and bring up your personal Desktop that contains your email inbox. After checking your email you can disconnect. All of this is done without having logged in or out.

The teleport application makes use of "active" regions defined around computers in our lab. When users enter one of these active regions, the Bat buttons invisibly gain functionality. The upper button cycles through the Desktops of the user, since she can have more than one running. The user can see a different Desktop on the screen every time this button is pressed. It is possible for the user's Bat to be in two teleport regions simultaneously. This could be the case if the user is, say, working on two computers that are next to each other and their teleport regions happen to overlap. The lower Bat button will then cycle through available machines.

Sometimes users choose to turn off teleporting, say, because they want the buttons to have some other functionality. Currently, this is being done by holding your bat at a specific location in space and pressing one of the Bat buttons.

The description of this application will immediately reveal a number of potential usability problems.

– One problem is that the Bat can *invisibly* take on different functionalities according to where in the physical space it is located (inside or outside a teleport region). With many applications running simultaneously this can become a considerable problem; in general, applications can turn any part of the physical space into an "active" region.
– Another problem is the different concept of the active region that system and user have. In the teleport application the design idea is that the user's Bat starts controlling the Desktop when she is standing in front of the computer. The SPIRIT system evaluates this by testing for a region overlap as described in Sect. 2.2. The user, on the other hand, does not use regions in order to understand the concept of "in front of a computer". The result is that user and computer will have slightly different ideas of where the teleport region is.
– Finally, we face the usual problems of applications without a feedback path. The "nothing happened" syndrome is notorious in our lab. Basically, error diagnosis by

the user is impossible and the only advice given to users is to try again and email support.

In many ways the application is typical for what we might expect from location-aware applications, should they become pervasive. It contains a mix of implicit (user location) and explicit (button press) interaction . It needs to deal with user settings (teleporting on or off). Furthermore, it involves a networked service (teleporting service). Finally, it uses location contexts that are more fine-grained than rooms.

3.2   Interaction Prototypes

One of our aims when introducing this interaction paradigm was to supply a set of widgets with it as well. The question was what kind of widgets will AR-based visual interaction in Ubicomp environments require? In a large survey of Ubicomp applications we found a number of patterns of interaction. The set of widgets [18] we built for these patterns is centred around the Active Bat as a personal interaction device. The concept of a personal interaction device that is always carried around by the user has been suggested in previous Ubicomp literature [20,21]. A big advantage such a device has is that you can use it to address the system (in Bellotti's terms [2]).

In the next section we will discuss two of our widgets in use in a real application: *Bat Menu* and *Hot Buttons*.

3.3   The First Interactive Application in Space

Using object-oriented analysis we identified all objects of interest and split them up into Models, Controllers and Views. The Bat buttons that had previously gained functionality invisibly were now labelled using AR. We employed our *Hot Buttons* widget which is similar to the way "hot buttons" work on mobile phones. Their descriptions change according to the context.

The teleport region, also previously invisible, was read from the world model and visualised as a polygon in space. The current machine was indicated by an outline around the actual monitor. Figure 4 shows what the user sees through her glasses when walking up to a computer. Users can now see where to place or where not to place their Bat in space in order to achieve what they want. We use stereoscopic see-through glasses in order to support depth perception, which is necessary when you are visualising regions in "thin air".

When the user walks into a teleport region, new labels appear on her Bat buttons, signifying the relevant functionality. They disappear when the user leaves the region. Inside the region the user has the ability to switch through her Desktops. As previously, this is accomplished by the user pressing the upper button on the Bat. We decided to visualise this interaction using our *Bat Menu*. A menu appears overlaid next to the Bat with each item indicating a Desktop by name. As the user presses the upper Bat button, Desktops switch through on the computer as before, but now she sees a red outline on the menu jumping from item to item. The current Desktop on the computer and the current menu item always match. The augmented Bat with the menu is shown in Fig. 5. The menu of Desktops is controlled by the button marked by the overlay "Desktop>>".

Fig. 4. Users see the teleport regions through their glasses. The regions are shown just below both monitors (The HMD is see-through, so the real-life scene is not present in the computer-generated image. Therefore, the composite must be simulated in order to show it here.).

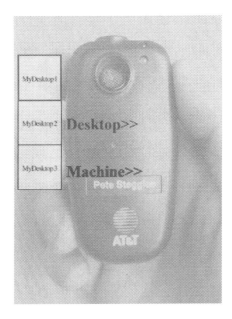

Fig. 5. The augmented view of a Bat while inside a teleport region. Square menu items show desktop names (here too, the composite picture is simulated).

Teleport-able machines (computers) will have a green outline overlaid around their actual monitor. Using the lower Bat button, labelled in green, the user can cycle through the machines, a bright green outline jumping from monitor to monitor indicating the current machine.

A big influence in designing the interaction was Norman's conceptual model [10] methodology. Its idea is that as a designer you create a model for the user by communicating to her (visually) how to use your product; in essence the designer is translating a user manual into visual design.

Applying it to our design meant that we had to make sure that in each use case the application always shows the user what is possible, how to achieve it and how to evaluate whether you have achieved it. As an example, users of our Bat Menu can instantly identify each of these.

4   User Evaluation

The visual and non-visual version of the teleport application were now compared against each other in a user trial. One feature not included in the trial was the ability to switch between machines that are located next to each other; this feature is generally not used in the lab. Instead you can now control the state of the teleporting service using the lower Bat button, no matter where you are standing.

The visualisation shows the teleport regions around the computer in which teleporting can be initiated using the Bat button labelled with the AR overlay "Desktop>>". The second button has an overlay label that reads "Teleporting is on" or "off", depending on whether you are inside our outside of the teleport region. Pressing it will toggle the label from one state to the other.

4.1   Method

The number of test subjects was chosen to be ten. Five of the test subjects can be regarded as novices and five as experts depending on their familiarity with location-aware applications.

The trial consisted of 5 parts. Each of the two experimental parts was preceded and followed by an interview part. The first experiment was a test involving the non-augmented teleport application, the second, the augmented teleport application. One might argue that performing these two parts in sequence will result in users being more familiar with the application when they use the augmented version of the application, but the experiment had to be done in one order and this was the most sensible one. Furthermore, the test subjects were given time to familiarise themselves with the application before they were tested.

The aim was not just to get their answers to questions but also find out *why* they gave particular answers or performed in a certain way. Therefore, we used a combination of short answer questions, and open questions that encouraged the test subject to talk; for the experimental part we employed user observation and thinking aloud techniques. The tasks consisted of giving answers to *what if* questions while using the application. Interviews were flexible with the evaluator drilling down to detail if the test subject had something interesting to say. The tasks and initial interview questions, however, remained the same for all. The guide used for the experiments/interviews is shown in Appendix A. We are only presenting our most important results. Details can be found in [18].

One premise we use for the interpretation of our observations is the mental model theory. Mental model theory [22] assumes that humans form internal representations of things and circumstances they encounter in everyday life in order to explain how they work. One important aspect is that these representations are "runnable" in the head, i.e. they can be used in order to predict the result of a particular interaction with the world. They are not always accurate, which is why humans can have misconceptions about the effects of their interaction. Nevertheless, a mental model can be updated to a more accurate one when a situation occurs where a misconception becomes obvious.

4.2   Lessons Learnt

Users Can Be Provided with a Conceptual Model of a Location-Aware Application   The conceptual model methodology [10] briefly introduced in Sect. 3.3 assumes that humans make mental models about applications or products we design and that designers can influence the formation of these[3]. Two questions we were interested in were:

1. What do the internal representations that users make of location-aware applications look like?
2. Can we, through our visualisations, influence the mental model they make of the location-aware application?

The basis for eliciting the mental models users built of the application are the *what if* questions (Appendix A), the explanation of how the application worked and an additional task given to the test subjects. The additional task was described as following:

> Imagine you want to provide a manual of the application for other users. Instead of a description can you draw a diagram for this purpose. Try not to use text if you can.

First of all, we can say that the mental model theory is suitable to explain our findings. Users are able to answer questions about what the effects of particular actions are using their mind only. When building these models users make certain assumptions about how things should work. For example, one test subject thought you need to point the Active Bat at the monitor in order to teleport. This, even though neither the Active Bat nor the monitor show any clues that a directional signal is used between them. Another test subject thought the teleport regions exactly coincide with the extent of the desks on which our computers stand.

Interestingly, we observed that such misconceptions were not at all limited to novices. In fact every test subject had some kind of idea of where teleporting would be active.

---

[3] We are using a broad definition of conceptual model here.

Especially, the case of the person who associated the desk extent with the teleport region for no logical reason, shows that users might need to have some visual idea of where this region is. So, *by trying to aim for invisibility we leave a gap in the user's mental model that is filled by self-initiative.*

Another observation is that mental models about the application can vary a lot. For example, one of the test subjects, in his explanation employed no metaphors at all. The drawing produced by him even includes a reference to a variable and a lot of text. So, in general we can say that this is a non-visual person. As a contrast another person produced a drawing in which he visualises the on/off button as a light bulb. His depiction is fairly concrete, like an image. This by the way was the only fully correct "manual" we received. Another person seemed to have a more procedural model. His "manual" includes a number of different cases that "work" or do "not work". He depicted four cases, varying the distance and position of the Bat to the monitor and also the teleport setting. Two other notable metaphors that were employed by the users were, viewing the Bat as a remote control and viewing the application as a state machine.

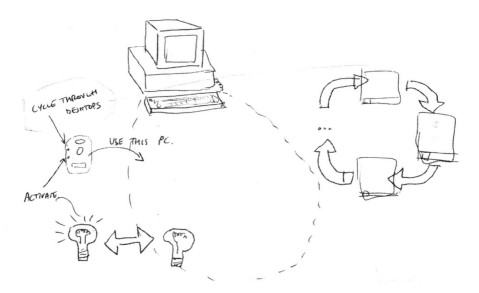

Fig. 6. Full marks for this diagram. The test subject has a good mental model of the application

We shall now examine how the visual interface affected the user's mental model of the application. Two "tricky" bits can be identified in this application. Firstly, the fact that teleporting only works if the user is standing in a particular region and, secondly, the fact that the teleporting state (on/off) influences the function of the first Bat button. Teleporting will not work outside the region but will only work inside it if teleporting is enabled. On the other hand, turning teleporting on or off will work independently of the location. This makes sense, since users want to turn teleporting on or off independently of their location.

It was found that the overall understanding of the application was much better during and *after* the use of the visualisation. When users were asked to explain how the application works before and after using the visual interface, in general their second explanation was much deeper and more detailed than the first one, especially with respect to the two above-mentioned non-straightforward concepts. The answers obtained in the interviews corresponded to the observations made during the experiments. Seven test subjects had problems working out the *what if* questions whereas nobody had problems with the visual version.

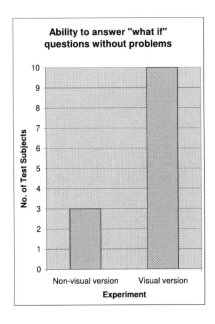

Fig. 7. All test subjects using the visual version could work out all answers.

Visualisation Reduces the Load Location-Aware Applications Pose on the User's Working Memory We stated earlier that users were able to answer all *what if* questions during the visual experiment. Partly, this is due to the increase in user understanding we identified afterwards.

However, the fact that the interface shows you your context, i.e whether you are inside a teleport region or not, we found was somehow disproportionately helpful in answering the *what if* questions. It seemed that thinking about whether you were at the right location "blocked out" thinking about whether teleporting was actually on or off, i.e. visualising *where* something will work, freed cognitive resources for other processing. Remember, that in order for the user to evaluate whether a teleport will be successful two conditions need to be fulfilled: the user needs to be in the teleport region *and* teleporting needs to be enabled. The fact that this error was so consistently performed struck us as odd.

After consulting some research on *systematic errors* the most plausible explanation is that what we had witnessed was a working memory overload. According to one theory [23], systematic errors are performed when the working memory goes beyond a threshold, but are not performed at all when it is below that threshold. This is one of the more unexpected results of this user trial. Even though we have been using location-aware applications for years in our lab the load some of them pose on the working memory is not mentioned when users are asked about usability problems.

Let us enumerate the items that need to be kept in the user's short term memory for our application: which Active Bat button to use for teleporting, where to stand, whether teleporting is enabled, how to enable it and whether the machine has a listening VNC client running on it; and all of this is just for one application. Looking at it from this perspective it becomes clear how a memory overload could occur.

Another observation was that only expert users could remember how many Desktops they have running at the beginning of the experiments. Many users in the lab have Desktops running for months because they forget about them. Since Ubicomp is supposed to support unstructured, often interrupted tasks, offloading memory requirements is desirable.

Visualising the Ubicomp System Could Create a New Kind of User Experience
We shall now examine the effects of introducing visualisation on the general user experience. This is not a full evaluation of how the user experience changes if you are experiencing all location-aware applications through an AR interface. Many more experiments with a non-prototypical system would be required for that. Nevertheless, we can obtain hints as to how the user experience will change if visualisation becomes more widely used.

Users were generally very happy with the visual interface. Nine out of ten test subjects made positive or very positive statements in this respect. One of the test subjects said that the Augmented Reality interface lets you know that "the application is not broken". She was an experienced user of location-aware applications and this seemed to be her biggest problem with location-aware applications in general. The remark says more about the user experience users currently have with "invisible" location-aware application than it applies to the visually enhanced version.

Interestingly, providing users with a better kind of location-aware application made clear to us what users had been missing, or rather been putting up with so far:

- Especially experienced users appreciated the fact that the Active Bat could give visual feedback. The only feedback received currently from our Bats is audio in the form of beeps of different pitches. One test subject explained that when she hears a beep or a sequence of beeps she has "no idea of what is going on".
- Another test subject said he would not rely on the teleport application currently deployed in our lab and would always have a backup if he planned to use it in order to teleport his desktop containing presentation slides to a presentation room (a popular use of the application).

– Finally, one misconception a user had of the existing teleport application was that he had thought the teleporting region was only a small region around the monitor. What was peculiar, was that he was a frequent user of the existing teleport application. He did not realise that the teleport region was a lot bigger, simply because he only uses the small region in front of the monitor.

What these examples show is a particular attitude towards location-aware applications. Apparently, users hardly explore them. They are conservative in the sense that they only use what they know works and even then they are in a constant state of uncertainty as to whether it is performing or not. This is, of course, not the attitude we as designers can allow the users to have. What needs to be done is to work on changing this user experience. We need to spend time thinking how we can give users the feeling that they can rely on, even play with, the applications without breaking them.

In this context, what was mentioned again and again was a kind of "coolness" factor experienced by users using the Augmented Reality interface to the location-aware application. Possibly, by generally introducing more enjoyable features into location-aware applications we can influence the user experience.

4.3   User Feedback

At the end of the experiments test subjects were asked what was the most desirable and worst feature of the system. The following gives a list of the most desirable features mentioned: Feedback, predictability, "coolness", explicit showing of location contexts and visualisation of the Desktops as a menu.

Most of these points have already been discussed in the previous sections. There is no clear cut definition for "coolness", but it is the adjective used by several test subjects.

The most undesirable features can be listed as: Calibration, bulkiness of hardware, slow update rate and the limited field of view.

Calibration relates to a short (10 s on average) process to be performed once for the experiment by each user. Test subjects had to adjust the HMD until they would see a virtual cube on a particular location. The slow update rate is not a property of the head tracker but comes from the Active Bat system (around 2 to 3 Hz). Hence, only location updates of the Active Bat overlay suffered from this problem. The rest of the application was running at 30 Hz, the update rate obtained by the tracker. The limited field of view is due to the HMD. Since it contains mini-monitors it uses to generate the virtual images, its field of view cannot wrap around the user's head.

Initially, we had expected that achieving accurate enough overlay for interaction with a location-aware application might be difficult. However, we were able to resolve this issue by careful pre-calibration of the HMD to an extent that misalignment was not mentioned as an undesirable feature by a single user. In general, we found that users had no problems fusing the virtual and real image, i.e the visualisations were in deed regarded as being co-located with the real world and not interfering with it.

It has to be said that undesirable features were hardly ever mentioned in the interviews. It was only after prompting test subjects that these were mentioned. This does not mean that these features are negligible. In fact most of these will become bigger problems when users have to wear HMDs for a longer period than a few minutes. On the other hand, we are not proposing to deploy this system at the present time in its present form. This is only a starting point and the future will show in which direction this research will develop.

5   Outlook

The limited display facilities we have in Ubicomp can prove to be a potential stumbling block in developing this research further. Not everyone feels comfortable using an HMD. Also, most real world locations are not fitted with an accurate tracking system. Before exploring a number of alternatives we would like to make clear to what extent our system is independent of the Active Bat system and the use of an HMD.

As Fig. 2 shows, our system receives updates about location changes and button presses in the form of sentient events. Such events can be generated using any location technology. Also, MVC makes no assumption about the display technology used. Any display technology can be used provided that a View object has access to the display. It makes architecturally no difference whether the display technology used is a PDA, projector, LCD display or an HMD. In each case a View object will be receiving updates from the Model and display-specifically mapping these to visualisations.

Let us look at the practical implications of different display and sensing technologies. Overlaying visualisations on movable objects (such as the Bats) is not possible without an accurate tracking system. However, if real world objects themselves provide a small (colour) display there is no need to track them to such a high accuracy[4]. The power consumption of such displays can, of course, be a limiting factor for years to come.

Nonetheless, other opportunities to visualise Ubicomp applications exist. Projector-based visualisation such as the Everywhere Display [24] appears promising. By combining a camera with a projector, interactive visualisations can be created on real world objects. Most notably, it allows us to visualise "active" regions as long as there is a display surface available, such as the floor.

PDAs can also be used to render visualisations. One of its more sophisticated uses would be to use it as a "portal" [13] to the virtual world. Wagner et al. [25] recently presented AR on a PDA. The PDA uses a camera and overlays virtual images on the live feed. The PDA could show users the same visualisations we have used.

Finally, less obtrusive displays than the one we used, almost indistinguishable from normal eyeglasses and better suited for day-long wearing, have been on the market for a couple of years now.

This discussion, however, should not distract us from the main point of the paper. The study of the effects visualisation has on users is to a large extent independent from what technology we use. The user experience after introducing visualisation did not improve because users were impressed by AR visualisations, but because they were feeling much more in control.

---

[4] The objects still need to be tracked in order to create location-aware behaviour, but the accuracy required can be far less, depending on the application.

6   Conclusion

The physical disappearance of the computer in the Ubicomp paradigm will continue to lead to usability problems. Users have difficulties in using hidden features of "smart" objects and in understanding what virtual implications their actions have, or in fact don't have.

Our hypothesis has been that we can increase application intelligibility by visualising such smart applications.

In order to test our hypothesis we built a system to upgrade location-aware applications with Augmented Reality visualisation capabilities. We stress that our prototype, while not of production quality or particularly comfortable is not a demo but a complete, usable system. We applied it to an application that is already deployed and used in our lab: Desktop Teleporting. For the first time a location-aware application had a chance to present its inner workings to the user. Most notably, we were able to show users spatial aspects (such as regions) of an application that operates in the physical world.

We then carried out a small-scale but carefully conducted user trial whose outcome validated our hypothesis. In nearly all test subjects we witnessed an increase in user understandability. On the basis of the mental model theory we were able to establish a link between our hypothesis and the result.

Most importantly, using Augmented Reality we were able to give our test subjects, for a limited time, a novel and much more empowering user experience. We believe that visualisation will be a fundamental component in making Ubicomp applications easier to understand and use. We hope and expect that this paradigm will be widely adopted in future computing environments.

7   Acknowledgements

The work described was conducted at the Laboratory for Communication Engineering (LCE, now part of the Computer Laboratory as the Digital Technology Group). We thank its leader Andy Hopper for his vision, encouragement and support. Our research has greatly benefited from the LCE's unique infrastructure, the cooperation with other LCE members and the group's constant drive towards inventing the future.

The psychology-oriented UI work done at the Computer Laboratory's Rainbow Group (current affiliation of the first author), especially by Alan Blackwell who also offered valuable comments on this paper, has been inspiring in drawing some important conclusions. A big "thank you" to our test subjects. Furthermore, the first author thanks Tom Rodden for an enlightening and challenging discussion on Ubicomp Design.

The first author was generously supported by AT&T Research Laboratories, Cambridge; Cambridge University Board of Graduate Studies; Cambridge European Trust; Cambridge University Engineering Department and St. Catharine's College, Cambridge.

A   Guide Questions to Be Used by the Evaluator

1. How many Active Desktops do you have?
2. Is your Teleporting on or off? Would you prefer to control it from your bat or a "SPIRIT Button" on the wall?
3. What do you know about Teleporting?
4. How does it work? (For novices delay this question, until they have explored the application)
5. *Evaluator*: identify concepts, conventions and prompt user
6. Can you Teleport to the broadband phones? Our phones are embedded computers. The aim of this question is to find out whether they believe that every computer in the Lab "affords" [10] teleporting.
7. *Evaluator*: Explain experiment.
8. Experimental Part I begins. *Evaluator*: Let user play with invisible application, observe difficulties.
9. *Evaluator*: Ask "what if" questions involving one Bat press, user movement and a Bat button press and combinations of the two. Experimental Part I ends.
10. Imagine you had to give another user a manual for this application. Can you make a drawing instead?
11. Experimental Part II begins. *Evaluator*: Let user play with visible application, observe difficulties.
12. *Evaluator*: Ask "what if" questions involving one Bat button press, user movement and a Bat button press and combinations of the two. Experimental Part II ends.
13. How does it work?
14. *Evaluator*: identify concepts, conventions and prompt user
15. Teleporting is best described as a property of: Space, Bat, Machine, "System", Bat System, other:

References

1. Andy Hopper. The Royal Society Clifford Paterson Lecture, 1999. Available at: http://www.uk.research.att.com/pub/docs/att/tr.1999.12.pdf.
2. Victoria Bellotti and Keith Edwards. Intelligibility and Accountability: Human Considerations in Context-Aware Systems. *Human-Computer Interaction*, 16(2, 3 & 4):193–212, 2001.
3. Kasim Rehman, Frank Stajano, and George Coulouris. Interfacing with the Invisible Computer. In *Proceedings NordiCHI*, pages 213–216. ACM Press, 2002.
4. Victoria Bellotti, Maribeth Back, W. Keith Edwards, Rebecca E. Grinter, D. Austin Henderson Jr., and Cristina Videira Lopes. Making Sense of Sensing Systems: Five Questions for Designers and Researchers. In *Conference on Human Factors in Computing Systems*, pages 415–422, 2002.
5. W. Keith Edwards and Rebecca E. Grinter. At Home with Ubiquitous Computing: Seven Challenges. In *Proceedings of the 3rd international conference on Ubiquitous Computing*, pages 256–272. Springer-Verlag, 2001.
6. Steven A. N. Shafer, Barry Brumitt, and JJ Cadiz. Interaction Issues in Context-Aware Intelligent Environments. *Human-Computer Interaction*, 16(2, 3 & 4):363–378, 2001.

7. Paul Dourish. What We Talk About When We Talk About Context. *Personal and Ubiquitous Computing*, 8(1):19–30, 2004.

8. Anind K. Dey, Peter Ljungstrand, and Albrecht Schmidt. Distributed and Disappearing User Interfaces in Ubiquitous Computing. In *CHI '01 Extended Abstracts on Human factors in Computing Systems*, pages 487–488. ACM Press, 2001.

9. Andrew Odlyzko. The visible problems of the invisible computer: A skeptical look at information appliances. *First Monday*, 4, 1999. Available at: http://firstmonday.org/issues/issue4_9/odlyzko/index.html.

10. D.A. Norman. *The Design of Everyday Things*. The MIT Press, 1989.

11. Steven K. Feiner. Augmented Reality: A New Way of Seeing. *Scientific American*, April 2002.

12. H. Kato and M. Billinghurst. Marker Tracking and HMD Calibration for a Video-based Augmented Reality Conferencing System. In *Proceedings 2nd International Workshop on Augmented Reality.*, pages 85–94, 1999.

13. J. Newman, D. Ingram, and A. Hopper. Augmented Reality in a Wide Area Sentient Environment. In *Proceedings ISAR (International Symposium on Augmented Reality)*, 2002.

14. A. Harter, A. Hopper, P. Steggles, A. Ward, and P. Webster. The Anatomy of a Context-Aware Application. In *ACM/IEEE International Conference on Mobile Computing and Networking (MobiCom-99)*, 1999.

15. Object Management Group. *The Common Object Request Broker: Architecture and Specification, Revision 2.0*, July 1995.

16. G. Krasner and S. Pope. A Description of the Model-View-Controller User Interface Paradigm in the Smalltalk-80 system. *Journal of Object Oriented Programming*, 1(3):26–49, 1988.

17. Josie Wernecke. *The Inventor Mentor*. Addison-Wesley, 1994.

18. Kasim Rehman. Visualisation, interpretation and use of location-aware interfaces. Technical Report UCAM-CL-TR-634, University of Cambridge, Computer Laboratory, May 2005.

19. T. Richardson, Q. Stafford-Fraser, K.R. Wood, and A. Hopper. Virtual Network Computing. *IEEE Internet Computing*, 2(1):33–38, Jan/Feb 1998.

20. R.W. DeVaul and A. Pentland. The Ektara Architecture: The Right Framework for Context-Aware Wearable and Ubiquitous Computing Applications. Technical report, The Media Laboratory, Massachusetts Institute of Technology, 2000.

21. Gregory Finn and Joe Touch. The Personal Node. In *Usenix Workshop on Embedded Systems*, 1999. Available at: http://www.usenix.org/publications/library/proceedings/es99/full_papers/finn/finn.pdf.

22. Donald A. Norman. Some observations on Mental Models. In Genter and Stevens, editors, *Mental Models*, pages 7–14. Lawrence Erlbaum Associates, Hillsdale, NJ, 1983.

23. Michael D. Byrne and Susan Bovair. A Working Memory Model of a Common Procedural Error. *Cognitive Science*, 21(1):31–61, 1997.

24. Claudio S. Pinhanez. The everywhere displays projector: A device to create ubiquitous graphical interfaces. In *Ubicomp*, pages 315–331. Springer-Verlag, 2001.

25. Daniel Wagner, Thomas Pintaric, Florian Ledermann, and Dieter Schmalstieg. Towards massively multi-user augmented reality on handheld devices. In *Third International Conference on Pervasive Computing (Pervasive 2005)*, Munich, Germany, May 2005.

DigiDress: A Field Trial of an Expressive Social Proximity Application

Per Persson, Jan Blom, and Younghee Jung

Nokia Corporation
P.O. Box 100, FIN-00045, Nokia Group, Finland
{per.persson, jan.blom, younghee.jung}@nokia.com

Abstract. In May 2005 Nokia Sensor application (www.nokia.com/sensor) was launched, allowing mobile phone users to create digital identity expressions, seen by other users within Bluetooth range. This paper describes the design and mass-scale longitudinal field trial of a precursor prototype called DigiDress. 618 participants voluntarily used the application for an average of 25 days. The identity expressions created were both serious and playful, revealing and non-revealing. Factors influencing the identity expression included strategies for personal impression management, privacy concerns, and social feedback. The application was used with both acquainted and unacquainted people, and viewing the identity expression of people nearby was one major motivation for continued use. Direct communication features such as Bluetooth messages were not commonly adopted. DigiDress acted as a facilitator for 'real' social interaction between previously unacquainted users. Privacy concerns and their alleviations, as well as use barriers, were identified.

1 Introduction

With the prospect of small, wearable, power-effective and cheap computing devices equipped with some form of short-range radio, there has been increasing interest in how such devices can support encounters between collocated people. With appropriate software, handheld devices and mobile phones equipped with radios such as WLAN or Bluetooth, are able to broadcast information to and fetch information from nearby users directly without connection to a network or server. This type of technology creates a digital 'sphere', 'field' or 'aura' surrounding each user [1], leading to interesting possibilities for social interaction. The overall question for research in this area, which could be termed *Social Proximity Applications* (SPA), could then be formulated as follows: 'In an encounter between spatially proximate people, how can information in *digital* realm support and augment existing social behavior, practices and experiences taking place in *real* space?' The present paper describes a field trial that was performed to evaluate DigiDress, an SPA allowing digital identity expressions within user's proximity. Prior to setting out the design and the specific research questions, however, let us examine what previous work has been done in this application domain.

M. Beigl et al. (Eds.): UbiComp 2005, LNCS 3660, pp. 195-212, 2005.
© Springer-Verlag Berlin Heidelberg 2005

1.1 Previous Research on Social Proximity Applications

One type of SPAs is concerned with providing awareness of who is nearby. The Hummingbird radio device [2], carried by members of a closed group, emitted a notification when a group member was in 50-100m proximity and displayed the name of that member. More recent systems, for instance Jabberwockey (http://www.urban-atmospheres.net/Jabberwocky/), do not restrict themselves to pre-defined groups, but open up for awareness of unacquainted users as well (e.g. fellow commuters encountered during one's route to work via the Bluetooth radio of mobile phones).

A second type of SPAs allows users to create a more or less sophisticated identity expression, broadcast to proximate users to facilitate social interaction. NewsPilot allowed journalists in a broadcasting house to jot down the stories they were working on at the moment, which would then be shared with fellow journalists in range, supporting ad-hoc collaboration [2]. HOCMAN was a WLAN-based system for motor bikers, giving out a signal when another HOCMAN biker was encountered on the road, in addition to automatically exchanging HTML homepages that could later be browsed locally [3].

In the third type of SPA systems, some sort of intelligence is embedded in the exchange of data between collocated users, with the purpose of giving recommendations or supporting collaboration. The simplest system of this type comprises so-called dating applications in which the user fills out a personal profile, which will then be compared with the personal profile of another proximate user. If there is a 'match', users will be notified about it, possibly with a picture of the counterpart (e.g. proxidating.com, dreamlove.it and bedd.com). Serendipity is another example in the enterprise domain, although the actual profile match takes place on a server [4]. Similar but with a different purpose, WALID [1] allowed users to define tasks or errands they wanted to be done. Whenever two WALID devices met, their software compared each others' lists and suggested a trade of tasks if there was a match. Social net [5] collected time logs of co-present users and then compared such lists across two proximate users to find common acquaintances of newly acquainted users.

The fourth type of SPA systems involves proximity messaging, one-to-one or one-to-many. Cybiko's Wireless communicator application was a good example of this.

1.2 See and Be Seen: DigiDress Design Rationales and Principles

DigiDress application (DD) aimed to complement existing social practices rather than replacing them. At its core, DD aspired to augment one of the most basic social processes when two or more people gather: *see and be seen*. People express what they are or what they want to be through clothing, personal possessions and behavior. Even electronic products can convey personal identity [8]. Social encounters thus involve elements of identity expression, facilitating mutual evaluation of and inferences concerning personality type, sense of humor, ethnicity, class, taste and other factors [6, 7]. DD aimed to augment this reciprocal process by allowing users to create media rich digital identity expressions, in addition to finding others' identity expressions nearby and browsing them with mobile phones. Consistent with gazing behaviors in public spaces, it should not be possible to *push* the digital identity expression onto others, but the access should be based on the principle of *pulling* information from nearby users. Another important principle, also derived from the sociology of public spaces [6], was to make the identity expression available to others before being allowed to access the identity expressions of others. At the same time, it should still be possible to take a sneak peak at another individual's identity expression without revealing one's own interest to that individual. Lastly, giving and receiving social feedback on identity expression should also be possible in the digital realm, since such a mechanism exists in real social space. Although these design rules were derived from social research, they were congruent with the principles of 'profile exchange' defined by [9].

Many of the SPAs mentioned above were intended for a quite specific target group or situation of usage (e.g. dating, task exchange, encounters among colleagues). In contrast we wanted DD to be an open expression tool suitable for a wide range of social encounters, social relationship types and contexts of use, particularly encompassing acquainted and unacquainted users in public or semi-public spaces.

Our work started with the following basic research questions:

1. What contents will users create with an expressive proximity application and what factors will influence the content creation?
2. How will users find and view others' identity expression and how will the proximity aspect influence the experience and behavior? How will DD experience be different from the experience of non-proximate expressivity systems such as personal web pages on the Internet?
3. Will the interaction in the digital realm trigger or facilitate social behavior in real social space?
4. Given the public nature of DD identity expression and viewing those expressions, will users experience privacy concerns?
5. What potential use barriers will there be for this type of application?

2 Description of the DigiDress Prototype

Usability tests in lab environment or focus groups based on usage scenarios were not thought to capture the issues arising from the social experiences of using DD over an extended period of time. In order to answer our research questions, we had to create environments in which participants would be motivated enough to voluntarily use the application in real social situations, giving rise to genuine social consequences. Among other things, this involved making a stable, easy-to-use prototype, deployed on a platform that would be widely spread among mobile users in order to achieve a critical mass of users, which is in fact a general comment for many SPAs (see [1]).

Series 60 platform (www.series60.com) provided such a possibility, with four phone models (Nokia 7650, Nokia 3650, N-Gage, Nokia 6600) being commercially available at the time of the trial, fall 2003. All of those devices were equipped with Bluetooth, with a range of approximately 10-20m depending on environment. Trial participants were able to install DD on their own S60 phones without having to carry a separate prototype hardware. Furthermore, designing the DD software according to the style of S60 user interface would spare users having to learn new interaction principles before taking the application into use. The following section describes the features of the DD prototype.

Creating identity expression. Emphasizing identity expression, the editor was at the core of DD. Creating 'a DigiDress' on the mobile phone should be a media-rich, yet easy process, with templates assisting the creativity of the user.

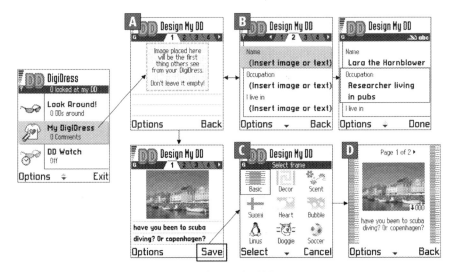

Figure 1. Creating and editing a DD page.

The editor comprised 4 tabs (Figure 1A). Tabs 1 and 3 allowed users to add free text and one image. Tabs 2 and 4 contained fields, each of which could be filled with either text or image (B). We provided suggestions for headings, in order to stimulate the imagination of the users, trying to balance light information with more serious and professional content.

- Tab 2 headings: Name, Occupation, I live in, Three items I cannot live without, Favorite food/drink, Favorite phone model, Favorite TV program.
- Tab 4 headings: Favorite motto, Person I admire, In five years I will, I laugh, I get upset, If I met Jorma Ollila I would, My contact information.

User could ignore the headings, change them or create new ones. While saving a DD, user was asked to choose one of 12 graphical frames (C), which would cover the margins (D). If no content was added to a tab or a field, that tab or field would not show up in the viewer mode (D). Since all but one of the supported phone models had camera, creating and adding images was an intuitive feature. Although users had to create a DD before viewing others' DDs, the obligatory content was minimized to the image in Tab 1 since this was the main element to be shown in the 'Lookaround' list on others' phones. The DD became immediately available to others when saved for the first time and later whenever the application was launched. At any time, users could come back and modify their DD. Having multiple DDs and easily switching between them was considered, but after some design iterations it was deemed too complex, causing more confusion than benefits considering the trial.

Lookaround. This feature (Figure 2) scanned the environment for other DD users and Bluetooth devices, and presented them in a list. The identification of users was not based on phone numbers, but on the unique Bluetooth device identifier (MAC address). If the identified device was running DD application, the Tab 1 image and the first 45 characters of text were automatically fetched and listed (Figure 2E). From the list, user could choose to open the full DigiDress (F). By scrolling sideways in the viewer (F), the full contents of the DD could be browsed. From the viewer, user could also save the DD locally, send Bluetooth messages, add public comments or view the comments this user had received from other users (G). If the device did not have DD application running, only the Bluetooth name of the device was listed.

Lookaround and viewing DDs were conducted without prompting the DD owner for authorization. As long as the DD application of any given user was running in the foreground or in the background, other users within Bluetooth range could fetch that particular DD. Thus, the DD owner did not have to actively use the application (or the phone) at the time of someone else downloading his/her DD. Neither were owners made aware that another user was downloading the DD pages. The only trace of someone's viewing the pages were provided in **My Popularity** feature, which listed the number of 'views' the DD had received as well as the timestamp of those. This rather 'public' design of the system aimed to be in line with the design principles presented above, mimicking existing social practices in public spaces.

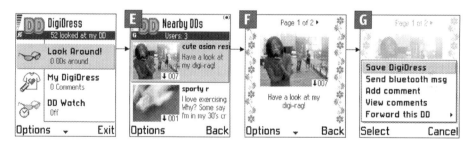

Figure 2. Lookaround, result list and viewing another user's DD.

Bluetooth messages. Bluetooth messages were simple and private text messages between two users (Figure 3J). Recipients, who were notified with a sound signal and a visual notification, could reply to an incoming message but not store them.

Comments. Comments provided a more public form of communication. Received comments were automatically stored in a list (Figure 3H and I). This list was available not only to the page owner, but could be accessed by any visitor to a DD (Figure 2G). In this way comments worked as a proximity 'guestbook'. Page owner could delete any comments, and also add own comments.

DD watch. The DD watch feature (Figure 3K), allowed users to set a time interval for automatic Lookarounds. If a DD device was found nearby, a sound notification would be delivered.

Leaving the DD application could be done in two ways. By 'shutting down', the application was closed and the pages were not made available to others anymore. In this mode, the device would be treated as any other non-DD device when scanned for. 'Exit' on the other hand, merely pushed the application into the background, allowing the user to interact other applications on the phone. In this mode, DD was still viewable by others and the user could still receive comments and Bluetooth messages. In combination with Lookaround logic and DD availability described above, the application hoped to avoid most of the privacy pitfalls of [10], e.g. obscuring the nature of an application's disclosure potential or requiring excessive configuration to manage privacy.

Phone-to-phone distribution. DD application also allowed users to distribute the software to non-DD users via Bluetooth or infrared. This was thought to facilitate the uptake of the application which was critical to the success of DD.

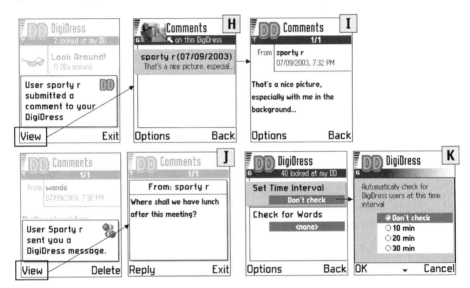

Figure 3. Comments, Bluetooth messaging, and DD watch.

3 User Trial Method

To maximize the saturation of DD, the most important criteria for the user trial was to find an environment with high density of the four phones compatible with DD application. At the time of the trial, employees of Nokia and the office sites in which they worked, provided the most saturated environment for the supported phones, in addition to including mobile-savvy and motivated users. Although such a setup would be slanted to professional environments, a company internal trial gave us a chance to establish a DD 'eco-system' to study the real application usage.

Recruitment. We aimed for voluntary adoption of the application, based on interest rather than trial 'enrolment'. In principle, the software was made available for download from the corporate intranet, along with the basic information on how to get started. No other training sessions or material were provided to users. First invitation to download the application was e-mailed to a selected group of 25 employees on September 15th 2003. Three days later, a mass e-mail invitation was sent to 1800 individuals using the compatible phone models. Four days after that, DD trial was featured on the corporate news service on the intranet portal. For reasons of confidentiality, users were instructed not to distribute the application to individuals not working for the company.

Logs. The DD prototype was equipped with a logging functionality that tracked its usage, e.g. number of application exits, amount of content in the DD, number of lookarounds performed, number of DDs found, downloaded and collected, number of messages/comments sent and received, etc. In total 36 such parameters were checked by the prototype. This data was inserted into a mobile text message (SMS) and automatically sent to a specified phone number every 72 hours (intervals were shorter during the first 72 hours after installation). A log SMS was also sent when distributing the application to another phone. If DD was not running at any of the times above, the message would be sent upon switching on DD, after which the order would resume the 72 hour interval. All log SMS sending took place in the background without interfering the user. During installation, users were informed about the logging functionality. The log SMS messages were all sent to a dedicated phone number. We used a Nokia 9210i Communicator to collect those messages and then exported them to PC for further analysis. SMS-based logging provided a unique opportunity to monitor application uptake and usage during the trial. Since the employer covered the phone bills of all employees, costs associated with the SMS logs was not likely to be an issue. This report includes data received from DD users between September 15 and December 12, 2003, which makes the user trial period 89 days.

Interviews. Since the SMS messages revealed the sender's phone number, we were able to identify the formation of DD communities and the most active users. 10 such users, 3 females and 7 males in Helsinki metropolitan area, were contacted and interviewed at the end of the trial period (not to interfere with their application usage). Interviews were individual- and group-based. Occupation ranged from sociologists and designers to marketing and corporate communication managers. Interviews were performed in English and lasted approximately 90 minutes, covering usage, motivations and general perceptions of DD.

Collection of created DDs. For content analysis, 46 DigiDresses were collected by the researchers in their everyday office life primarily at two major corporate office sites in Helsinki metropolitan area. This was done directly via Bluetooth, or indirectly via multimedia messaging service (approximately 50 users were e-mailed and requested to send their DDs). The DDs were subject to content analysis by two of the authors.

4 Results

During the trial period 618 users installed DD on their phones. 36,7% received it from another phone and the rest downloaded it from the website. Log files were received from phone numbers representing 23 countries, Finland being the dominant one (81% of total sample), indicating where DD was used. Number of installations per day was greatest in the beginning of the trial period with peaks of over 90 installations per day in conjunction with our mass e-mail and the corporate news flash.

Although the installation pace slowed down after the first four weeks, and never exceeded 10/day, it never stopped completely. This suggests that interest in the application was maintained by word of mouth.

Use span refers to the number of days from the first log file (installation date) to the last log file sent to us from a given individual. This gave us a rough estimation of how long participants showed interest in DD application after installing it. The average use span was 24.7 days (of a total of 89 days trial), with the standard deviation being 25.7. Approximately 20% of the population shut down or uninstalled DigiDress already after one day and never came back. See 'Use barriers' section for discussion on reasons. Users visited the application on average 16 times during the trial, which amounts to 0.7 visits/day of use span. This was measured by the number of 'exits' and 'shutdowns'. In all, these figures indicate relatively high activity levels with the application.

4.1 Creating and Managing Identity Expression Through DigiDress

4.1.1 Contents Created

Analyzing the last log file sent by each user having created a DD, on average 2.3 images and 100.6 characters were added, including the obligatory image on the first page. These figures show the amount of data in created DDs, but not the nature of the content. For this we had to analyze the 46 collected DDs. All but 2 of the collected DDs were in English, although users were predominantly Finnish. This might have been caused by the fact that the corporate language is English. Moreover, the DD prototype was only provided in English, which might have influenced users. In total, the 46 DDs contained 321 content-filled fields in tab 2 and 4, which mounts up to almost 7 filled fields per DD.

It is difficult to fully capture the rich, humorous and intelligent content created by users in a research publication. However, we found three dimensions to describe the characteristics of the DD content. First, *serious* vs. *playful* content was one distinct dimension. Some users presented themselves in a sober manner, often with the intent of enabling professional networking inside the company (e.g. Figure 4). On the other hand, many DDs contained light, playful and often humorous material. In these DDs, jokes, puns and comical use of imagery were common (Figure 5 and Figure 7). High degree of playfulness could involve play with real or fictitious identities, one's own or others'. One user pretended to be 'King of Bavaria' and provided information to fit with this character (e.g. "Three things I can't live without: crown, throne & BMW"). One user created her DD as if the owner of it was the Kanga character from Winnie the Pooh (Figure 6). In the interview she stated (Female 3): "*I like Winnie the Pooh characters a lot. I made a test on the Internet, where you can test which one of the animals you are, and I was the Kanga.*" When scoring each of the 46 collected DDs on the seriousness-playful scale (1 to 5), the average rating turned out to be 3.1 (standard deviation 1.1), i.e. almost at mid-point.

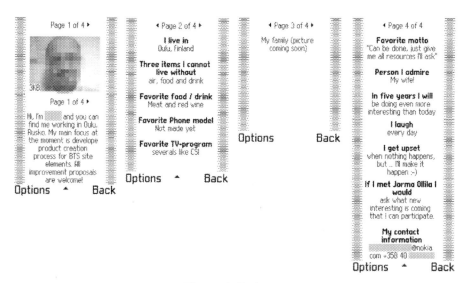

Figure 4. Serious DD.

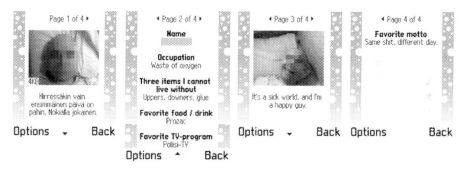

Figure 5. Playful DD.

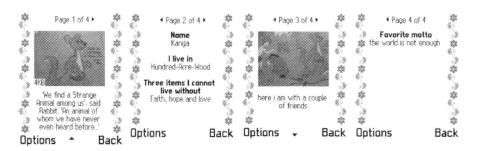

Figure 6. Assuming fictitious identity in a DD.

The second extracted dimension characterized how users *revealed* or *held back personal information* about themselves. At the one end of this dimension, users distinctly revealed personal features, facts, interests, preferences, personality traits, habits and even a facial image (40% of the collected DDs seemed to have recognizable facial image of its owner). This did not necessarily mean that the user's traceable identity (home address, phone number etc.) was revealed, but a clear sense of personality of the DD owner could nevertheless be detected. From the researchers' point of view, it seemed like the facts mentioned were true and honest. Pictures from travels, summer cottages or babies were common. Pride of oneself, one's life or accomplishment seems to have been one motivation. At the other end of this dimension, the DD owner explicitly withheld such information or even tried to conceal it in various ways. From our ratings of the 46 DD sample, revealing and holding back were equally common (on average 2.9 on a 1 to 5 scale with an SD of 1.1). Third, the content analysis also made it clear that users had quite different conceptions on what type of *audience* they expected for their pages. *Audience specific* DDs typically required a series of inferences based on quite specific knowledge about the DD owner or the subject matter for the reader to fully understand the intended meaning:

Male 1 [describing his DD pages]: *The front image is from popular culture stuff that I really enjoy. Which are Wallace and Gromit animations. And cheese is a really basic pun. Cheese is English for 'smile you're in a photograph' and cheese is also one of the main things in this character's life.*
Interviewer: *So you have to be a Wallace and Gromit fan to understand this?*
Male 1: *Yeah this is an inside joke.*

At the other end of this dimension, DDs presented information so general that almost any adult could understand its meaning (e.g. Figure 7).

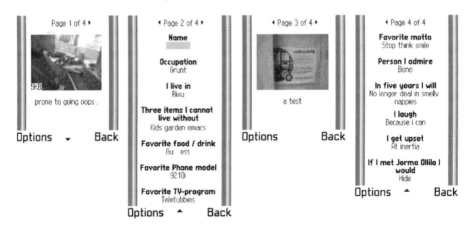

Figure 7. Audience general DD.

When rating the DDs on the specific-general audience dimension there was a clear advantage to the general end (3.4 on a 1 to 5 scale; SD 1.0). This suggests that users expected viewers to be not only familiar colleagues, but also unacquainted users and even strangers, possibly envisioning usage not only in office space but also in more socially open environments such as lunch canteens and cafeterias.

4.1.2 Factors Influencing Content Creation and Management

The interviews revealed motivations for and factors influencing the DD content creation. As expected, many of our interviewees considered DD to be a tool for *identity expression and impression management*. The social consequences of showing the DD page to others were experienced as real, as testified by an interviewee working in a building with a colony of DDs from acquainted and unacquainted people (Female 2): "*I thought it's quite important actually what you have in there [the DD]. Cause I didn't have enough time to think of funny answers. It's really the impression you want to give, I would like to do it properly and really think.*" For instance, playful content seemed to have been a way for people to avoid being categorized as 'boring' and 'uninteresting' (Male 6): "*I was thinking that other people would view it [the DD]. I don't want to have it boring, like: 'Profession: engineer' or 'I like: mashed potatoes and fish'. So then I added 'Three things I cannot live without: women, airplanes, and beer' [to my own DD].* "

The *assumed audience* also influenced the DD content. This related not only to general vs. specific audience, but also to the corporate environment in which the trial was set. Many interviewees believed that their DD content would have looked different had the application been used outside the corporate context. On the one hand office environment may have made content less playful than otherwise (Male 4): "*I want to be as honest as possible but I have to take into account the context. I cannot create a totally surrealistic DD that's accessible in an office environment.*" At the same time the corporate context created a reasonably safe social environment, encouraging somewhat more personal content (Male 2): "*Since you are within Nokia, you could leave personal info. Contact [info] especially. People can see it. But if it was public, I would not probably put those things.*"

Privacy concerns surely affected the ways user created DD content. By describing general, playful or fictitious content, for instance, users could express their personality in interesting ways without revealing too much personal data. Discussing the fact that she avoided putting her real name on her DD page, Female 2 stated that "*one option would be like [Female 3 – the Kanga DD] has done: she's not saying her proper name; she doesn't have a picture of herself. Just invent an imaginary thing. Whether it's funny or bizarre.*"

Another factor came from the *design of the application* itself. Although our pre-filled subject headings on tab 2 and 4 (see Figure 1B) were meant as *inspiration* for content creation and not *compulsory*, the design of editor gave the impression that these fields 'had to' be filled in. Moreover, the possibility to change the headings was hidden deep down in the application. This was commented by Male 2: "*It [pre-filled subject headings] is good. You see what you can do with it. But the thing is that you don't realize in the first place that you can change them. You may feel that you have to put something in so it's quite annoying. You don't have to in fact, but you feel that way.*" These design flaws clearly propelled users to follow the content specified by the subject headings: in our 46 DDs sample, only 21 of 321 fields headings (or 7%) could be considered to be new or user self-created. The headings surely influenced the content in the system as a whole.

Explicit and implicit *feedback from other users* also affected the DD content (Male 4): "*Part of the fun of using the DD is maintaining the different profiles [DD pages].*

Getting feedback from others and tweak in more." Via the 'My Popularity' feature, DD provided users with a indirect but still valuable social feedback. Female 1, for instance, realized that her playful DD received more views than a more serious version, which made her stay with the playful one. For most of the interviewees, the DD content was not static but constantly evolving. This was also reflected in our log files. 73.4% of the total user population modified their DDs at least on one occasion. Among these users, the average number of modifications was 2.9, the standard deviation 3.3 and the maximum value 44.

Finally, some interview participants reported that *watching others' DD pages* affected their content creation. Female 3, for instance, explained that "*when you see other people's DD's, you get more courage of the kinds of things you can put there.*" Since DD and the ways in which pages were shared with others over Bluetooth were new phenomena to the users, there were no established conventions about appropriate/non-appropriate content types. The users, as a community, seemed to have developed such practices by observing the behavior and content creation of others. The emergence of these habits, conventions, do's and don'ts was likened to the evolution of sub-culture specific language or web pages (Male 1): "*It's like a language you're learning. It's language specific to some certain...like culture. You might learn new things later that if you do this then you signal that you're part of this culture. Like Web pages, they are evolving all the time. So this must be the same thing.*"

4.2 Lookaround: Detecting Proximate Users

Interviews revealed a relatively homogenous path of events following the installation of the application. Here is one typical description, provided by Male 3: "*Originally I got a mail from you, and forwarded the application to all my colleagues I knew. It created a buzz immediately. People installed it on to their phones, we played around with it a bit, went to have lunch, put the search [DD watch] on, found some people in the canteen.*" After creating the DD, the application was typically first explored together with colleagues after which usage spread into more open environments such as lunch canteens, where it was more likely to see and be seen by unacquainted users.

The Lookaround feature was of course at the core of all of these activities since it provided the means to discover nearby users and their DDs. Among the participants using the feature at least once during the trial (79.7% of the sample), the average number of 'Lookarounds' was 11.3 (standard deviation 16.9). On average 0.5 lookarounds were performed per day, assuming the average use span of 24.7 days. Figure 8 depicts the use of the lookaround feature on each day of the use trial, among the entire use population. We have not been able to identify the mid-trial peaks (e.g., Nov 3rd). They could indicate some corporate event. The figure suggests, however, that interest and active usage of DD was maintained over the course of the trial period. The average time required to generate the results of each Lookaround was 44.0 seconds. An average of 24.7% of the Lookarounds were cancelled.

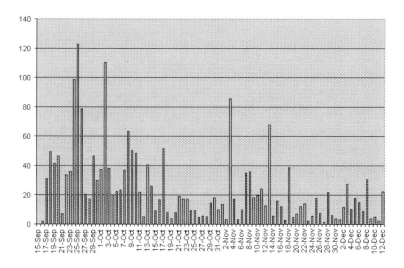

Figure 8. Number of times Lookaround feature was used. Log files were sent from users' phones every 72 hours. The increment from the preceding to the present message in the value of the variable has been divided by the number of days present in the gap between the present and the preceding message. The figures in the diagram thus represent averages for one particular use day.

It is difficult to know why users cancelled, but the time for Lookaround process to complete was dependent on number of nearby Bluetooth and/or DD devices. This suggests that users were not too keen on waiting to get the complete results. This was also expressed in the interviews (Male 3): "*The search process [Lookaround] is really slow. It's very annoying. [---] If you're in a bus, trying to find out if there are other people, it takes a lot of time. That's been the biggest turn-off for myself.*" The logs showed that on average 0.4 DD users were found for every Lookaround. From a trial point of view this 'saturation' is satisfactory although we do not know if lookaround were used in situations where the user was sure of the existence of a nearby user, or if the feature was used in more opportunistic situations ('is there a DD around?'). Locally, however, low saturation may have been a problem contributing to the figure of 20% 'early quitters' who used DD for a day or less. Not finding other DD users in Lookaround was a standard complaint among the interviewees (Female 2): "*My experience usually is that there is no one around. It is very funny and surprising when you find someone.*" This excerpt describes the turnoff for many users not finding anyone, but also great enjoyment when DDs were found in the list, motivating further usage. When asked to find a metaphor for what it feels like to use Lookaround, our interviewees suggested 'eavesdropping', 'spying with a good intention' and 'fishing'.

209 out of 618 participants used the automatic scan feature, DD watch. This shows that many users were eager to find other DDs without having to remember to perform lookaround consciously. Saving other users' DDs also turned out to be rare. Only 7.4% of the participants had at least one saved DD. Although some of our interview-

ees considered saving good DDs as important, the average use of this feature was low.

4.3 Social Interaction: See, Identify, Approach and Be Approached

The contents of DDs have already been described. Our interviewees characterized the DDs of other users with words such as "funny", "intelligent", "interesting", "boring", or "hasty". Viewing found DDs also involved the social guessing game of identify the owner of a DD in the immediate physical proximity, as well as matching the content with the appearance or behavior of that individual (Male 1): "*It's funny when you see the guy, the actual physical person and then you see his DD; how the hell do these connect? Because in web pages you never know who the person is. And also guessing who the hell the person is.*" This excerpt is interesting in two respects: it describes the ways in which the DD content gave new or different information about its owner, and thus may have influenced the social inferences made about that person. Negotiating between the appearance of the person and the DD content probably influenced the viewer's interpretation of both. Secondly, the comment clearly describes the different experiences of watching DDs and web pages: With DD, the physical person was likely available for visual inspection.

Lookaround feature was a 'socially safe' exercise, in the sense that the owner of the viewed DD was not made aware of the process. Some of our interviewees clearly expressed satisfaction with staying in this 'lurker mode' and not continuing to engage in direct communication through Bluetooth message or comments (Male 2): "*I started to use it with some colleagues and that's mainly it in the beginning. And then you start to look around during the lunchtime and these sorts of things. To see what people have been doing. But I never used this comment feature. [---] Just interested in looking around and see what people have been doing. [---] So it is a means to get to know someone without getting involved with him.*"

This attitude was consistent with usage of other features. Only 15.7% of the users had received comments, and only 11.2% sent comments to others. Among those that had received at least one comment, the average number was 1.3, SD being 0.7, and the maximum value 4. Sending Bluetooth messaging was more popular, with 19.8% of the users sending at least one. Based on these figures it could be assumed that users did not have much usage for direct communication via the application. Another speculative reason could be the short communication range provided by Bluetooth, making messaging suitable only for particular contexts.

Although the overall usage of direct communication was low, it facilitated face-to-face social interaction between unacquainted users as evidenced by the following episode (Female 2): "*I had a very interesting experience. Last Friday I and one of my colleagues were sitting in the coffee area of my floor. And there was nobody nowhere, no people. And I had my phone on the table. And suddenly I received that funny sound. And I was like: 'what'? And someone sent me a comment like 'hello funky kanga'. And I was like: 'who might it be'?, because no one was around. And after a couple of minutes a couple of guys came from some meeting room. We didn't know who they were but they were looking at us. And they went and came back, and one was asking: 'Who is kanga?'*"

Incidentally, the person coming back to Female 2 turned out to be another of our interview participants in another session. He also brought up this event, describing it from the other perspective: (Male 5): *"We had some fun with that, we were sitting in a meeting room so it was [Male 4] and myself. We were looking around and suddenly: hey there was a DD also. [---] They were sitting outside the door. It was Friday and we sent them a little note and then we got a note back. Because obviously she didn't know. First of all we didn't know if it was a he or she. That was quite fun. That was really funny [laughing]."*

These excerpts report not only the ambivalence in identifying the owner of the DD (he or she?), but also how the application became a tool – or an excuse – for approaching a unacquainted user. Here was a case of someone stepping out of the lurking mode to engage in digital and later real social interaction. Based on 10 interviews only, however, it is difficult to judge the commonality of this phenomenon.

Comments and Bluetooth messages provided direct communication channels to the user. The 'My Popularity' feature, offered a more implicit feedback channel. Most of our interviewees regarded this feature in positive terms since it proved to the user that their DD had in fact been viewed by others. One interviewee in one of the group sessions (Male 4) had missed this feature, but when instructed to check it in the interview he was overwhelmed by the popularity his DD had attracted:

Male 3: *How many people have downloaded your DD [turning to Male 5]*
Male 5: *It says '26 looked at my DD'*
Male 4: *[Looking at his phone] 65! [astonished]*
Male 3: *I have 48 also.*
Male 5: *Man!*
Male 4: *I think pretty many people have been peeping my DD. 65, hell what is happening?*

Since each DD download was marked with a timestamp, users were able to speculate about the context in which their DD had been viewed. At least one of the interviewees reported having done so (Female 3).

4.4 Privacy Concerns and Alleviations

The concept of DD, as well as many of the social experiences associated with it, were new to participants. This also meant that the social implications of making one's DD publicly available to nearby people may not have been fully understood at the beginning of the trial. At least Female 2 learned about these issues after some time: *"When I was doing my profile, I was thinking: 'I'll put a few pictures of myself'. I wasn't really thinking properly. It was too early. I didn't properly realize that everyone will be able to see this picture."* It is possible that this user set up DD on her own, without being able to find anyone around her: without using Lookaround and finding another user nearby, it was difficult to appraise the implications of one's own DD and how it will be seen/accessed by other users. Informing the user about the social consequences of creating a DD should be more highly prioritized in future versions [cf. 10].

Being able to view a DD without the owner's consent concerned some users in the interviews. Male 4 suggested that viewing a DD should always be preceded with a request to its owner. This was challenged by the two other users in the interview:

> Male 4: *I would always have this opt in functionality. If someone is requesting my DD: 'User this and this is requesting my DD'. If it's male, no way. If it's female, then perhaps. [---]*
> Male 3: *It makes it too complicated if you have to approve those.*
> Male 4: *But there should be an opportunity for those narrow-minded people who do not want to, who want to keep things under control.*
> Male 5: *To get this [DD application] flying, I think part of the fun is the aspect of browsing around. If everybody blocks the thing, it's going to harm this.*

Accommodating Male 4's privacy concerns would compromise the satisfaction of the open information space created by the 'non-request design' of the DD prototype. As the complaints of Male 4 were not common, the design of the DD prototype seemed to have been appropriately balanced in this respect.

Another related concern was the shift DD created vis-à-vis the perception of the mobile device. The mobile phone and its content have traditionally been seen as genuinely private. Unless users explicitly hand over the phone to someone else, the content has 'stayed with the user' and the user has always been in charge of controlling the access to the content. DD challenged this in the sense that other users were allowed to fetch data from the device without the owner's immediate awareness. Male 4 compared this feeling with someone invading his personal space: "*This is a private device. Someone is basically violating my area.*" Female 2 also recognized this feeling, but in the end pointed out that DD-like applications will change those traditional perceptions of the mobile phone: "*I had web pages for many years and I didn't care about the fact everyone can see those. Maybe... as it [the mobile phone] is the personal device, it feels different. But, of course it is a question of education and thinking differently.*" Just like peer-to-peer file sharing systems changed the perception of the PC, so perhaps will future commercially successful SPA shift the view of the mobile device.

Our interviewees identified a number of alleviations to the various privacy concerns. We have already described the ways in which users adapted their DD content to balance expressivity and privacy concerns. One interviewee (Male 6) also pointed out that the personal content he put on his DD, such as phone number and home address, were already publicly available in various databases (at least in Finland), and putting it on his DD did not increase the risk of someone misusing that information. Also the office test environment seemed to have a remedying effect, in so far as users could rest assure that only colleagues could see the pages (Female 1): "*In this environment you are more secure. You know the people.*"

4.5 Use Barriers

As discussed above, low saturation of DD users nearby turned users off and posed perhaps the biggest barrier for users to adopt DD. If applications like DD are to succeed, they need to be launched on a widely spread platform, preferably be freeware and preinstalled and be subject to a coordinated marketing campaign.

The slow and occasionally unreliable Bluetooth performance was reported by users as a barrier. For instance, whenever a user engages in any Bluetooth communication, the device (and the DD) becomes invisible to other devices. In terms of saturation, however, Bluetooth is the only realistic alternative at the moment.

Another barrier identified by our interviewees was that our prototype required users to have the application running in order to make the DD available. Forgetting to turn it on in social situations or after phone re-boot seems to have been common, leading to fewer DDs available for others, which decreased motivation for using the application. One innovative user (Male 5) managed to install a separate auto-start application for DD. This radically changed his way of using DD. Auto-start of DD on phone re-boot should be implemented in future versions.

Before the trial we feared that Bluetooth would not provide users with enough range to create rich user experience we aimed for. Fortunately, none of our interview participants expressed any concern in this respect. In fact, Bluetooth provided the appropriate distance by which users most often had visual access to the other part, which was deemed to be valuable in the case of DD (Female 2): "*Making it shorter doesn't make sense. But if it were the whole Nokia house [Nokia headquarters in Espoo, Finland], it would be chaos. It increases the complexity and how you think about it. Instead of now...the real proximity... you know that it's just the people who you see. It's more controllable than the bigger range.*"

5 Discussion

The method of this trial had several limitations. It confined the potential usage of the application to professional context. The number of collected DDs for content analysis was small in comparison to the number of participants. Both interviewees and the collected DDs were selected from the most active users, providing limited understanding of e.g. why the application had so many early quitters. Nevertheless, the large number of users and the long use span suggest that DD generated positive user experience, and that the basic concept was on the right track. The study also revealed a number of design flaws. The expressivity of the DD and its editor should be strengthened. The field headings triggered users' creativity, but it must be made clearer to the user that headings can be ignored, changed and that new ones can be swiftly created. Also the DDs should display traces of social feedback from other users (e.g. by placing comments from other users directly into the DD pages). Future versions of DD must explain in simple way the principles according to which people have access to others' DD content (only in proximity, both users must run DD and have Bluetooth on, no request required, no differentiated access control between trusted and non-trusted peers etc.). Such explanation has to be done in the application itself (without interrupting the usage), in help files or marketing messages. Making the DD effortlessly available to others without having to remember to launch the application or to turn Bluetooth on, should be provided. This should also boost the critical mass of SPA content in public locations, facilitating the adoption of these types of applications. Most of these issues (and many others) have been addressed in the design of Nokia Sensor application (www.nokia.com/sensor). Unleashing the creativity and social curiosity of users outside the office environment, Nokia Sensor will hopefully tell us the real potential - and concerns - with this kind of technology.

6 Acknowledgements

DD prototype used WILD Bluetooth middleware developed in Nokia Research Centre. Special thanks to Seamus Moloney, Jussi Moisio, Tero Reunanen and Kimmo Rosendahl, who contributed and implemented the prototype. Funding for DD concepting and prototyping was provided by Nokia Venture Organization.

References

1. Kortuem, G. and Segall, Z.: Wearable communities: augmenting social networks with wearable computers. Pervasive Computing, IEEE , Volume: 2 (1) (2003), pp. 71 – 78
2. Redström, J., Dahlberg, P., Ljungstrand, P. and Holmquist, L.E.: Designing for Local Interaction. Proc. Managing Interactions in Smart Environments (MANSE), Springer Verlag (1999)
3. Esbjörnsson, M, Juhlin, O. & Östergren, M.: Traffic encounters and Hocman: associating motorcycle ethnography with design, Personal and Ubiquitous Computing, vol. 8 (2), (2004)
4. Eagle N. and Pentland, A.: Social Serendipity: Mobilizing Social Software, IEEE Pervasive Computing, Special Issue: The Smart Phone, April-June 2005, pp 28-34
5. Terry, M., Mynatt, E.D., Ryall, K., Leigh, D.: Social net: using patterns of physical proximity over time to infer shared interests, CHI '02 extended abstracts on Human factors in computing systems (2002)
6. Goffman, Erving, Behavior in Public Places. Notes on the Social Organization of Gatherings, New York, The Free Press (1963)
7. Willis, P.: Common Culture. Symbolic work at play in the everyday cultures of the young, Boulder & San Francisco, Westview Press (1990)
8. Blom, J., Monk, A., Theory of Personalization of Appearance: Why Users Personalize Their PCs and Mobile Phones, Human-Computer Interaction, Vol. 18, No. 3, 193-228, (2003)
9. Kortuem, G., Segall, Z., & Thompson, T., Close Encounters: Supporting Mobile Collaboration through Interchange of User Profiles, Lecture notes in computer science, Vol. 1707, Springer, (1999)
10. Scott Lederer, I. Hong, K. Dey, A. Landay. Personal Privacy through Understanding and Action: Five Pitfalls for Designers, Personal and Ubiquitous Computing 8 (6), Nov. 2004.

Control, Deception, and Communication: Evaluating the Deployment of a Location-Enhanced Messaging Service

Giovanni Iachello[1], Ian Smith[2], Sunny Consolvo[2], Gregory D. Abowd[1],
Jeff Hughes[3], James Howard[3], Fred Potter[3], James Scott[4], Timothy Sohn[5],
Jeffrey Hightower[2], Anthony LaMarca[2]

[1] College of Computing and GVU Center
Georgia Institute of Technology, Atlanta, GA, USA
`{giac, abowd}@cc.gatech.edu`
[2] Intel Research, Seattle, WA, USA
`{ian.e.smith, sunny.consolvo, jeffrey.r.hightower,`
`anthony.lamarca}@intel.com`
[3] Department of Computer Science and Engineering
University of Washington, Seattle, WA, USA
`{jeffdh, jamesh, fpotter}@cs.washington.edu`
[4] Intel Research, Cambridge, UK
`james.w.scott@intel.com`
[5] Computer Science and Engineering
University of California, San Diego, La Jolla, CA, USA
`tsohn@cs.ucsd.edu`

Abstract. We report on a two-week deployment of a peer-to-peer, mobile, location-enhanced messaging service. This study is specifically aimed at investigating the need for and effectiveness of automatic location disclosure mechanisms, the emerging strategies to achieve plausible deniability, and at understanding how place and activity are used to communicate plans, intentions and provide awareness. We outline the research that motivated this study, briefly describe the application we designed, and provide details of the evaluation process. The results show a lack of value of automatic messaging functions, confirm the need for supporting plausible deniability in communications, and highlight the prominent use of activity instead of place to indicate one's location. Finally, we offer suggestions for the development of social mobile applications.

1 Introduction

Social mobile applications are a category of mobile computing applications that support individuals and groups in interacting with their social milieu. These applications, which include mobile voice and messaging, person finders, and geographic recommendation systems, are characterized by a common set of requirements and concerns, especially related to availability, privacy and management. We are particularly interested in location-enhanced applications, because our own observations, ethnographic literature and market research surveys all suggest that location plays a fundamental

M. Beigl et al. (Eds.): UbiComp 2005, LNCS 3660, pp. 213-231, 2005.
© Springer-Verlag Berlin Heidelberg 2005

role in accomplishing everyday communication and coordination tasks. For example, English [7] and German [10] studies agree that one of the most frequent uses of SMS is to coordinate and schedule meetings, for which location plays a significant role.

We are interested in understanding how people use location and place to communicate with each other, considering the phenomenological characteristics of place and the cultural baggage that is associated with it, including notions of presence, privacy, activity and cultural geography. One application we have recently developed is Reno, a peer-to-peer, location-enhanced service for cell phones that allows users to communicate their position to others. Considerable preparations have preceded the deployment of Reno. We first performed an Experience Sampling Method (ESM) study [4]; the communication strategies suggested by the participants of that study led to the development of a prototype, which was piloted with members of this research group [30]. The pilot study confirmed the potential usefulness of the application, and exposed some of the consequences engendered by the communication of one's location.

In order to minimize disruption of people's activities, Reno supports automatic 'pull' and 'push' disclosures of the user's location, which raise questions regarding the balance of usefulness, management effort and control, as well as safety and privacy concerns. These issues were not specifically addressed in the pilot study, which focused instead on the role of location in interpersonal communication. We thus set out to investigate the concerns and practices engendered by Reno, with special attention to the need, motivation and risks associated with artifacts acting on the user's behalf, and the widely acknowledged need for plausible deniability in interpersonal relations [5, 15, 17]. This article reports on the findings of a real-world deployment of Reno with two families with teenage children and their friends. In the remainder of this article, we briefly describe Reno, provide details of the study process and results, and offer some remarks useful for developing social mobile applications.

2   Reno

The version of Reno we used in this study is the latest in a series of successive designs, refined after the pilot study [30], interviews with users and a cognitive walkthrough performed by two expert HCI professionals. Reno is a location-enhanced messaging application for Nokia Series 60 phones that allows the user to request the location of other users and to tell his/her location to them.

Before using Reno to disclose a location, the user must define place names (*e.g.*, "School" or "Home") and assign them to physical locations. The program will offer the name whenever the user subsequently visits that location. When sending a location, either as a reply to a request or by the user's initiative, Reno offers a selection of nearby place names, as computed by the location algorithm. Location sensing is performed using cell tower connection patterns, similar to the technique described by Laasonen *et al.* [18]. The physical location (cell tower) of the user is never sent by Reno: only the place name or activity defined by the user is (Fig. 1). Reno also provides a customized, pre-defined list of activities that may be used instead of place names for replying to messages. One of the aims of this design is to minimize the need for typing on the phone for messages involving location disclosures: if the place name is already defined, only two interaction steps (selections) are necessary for

Fig. 1. A usage scenario for Reno. The application presents a list of likely locations and a static list of activities when replying to request. (Drawing by K. Truong)

replying to a location request. All basic tasks require three or fewer selections to be completed (excluding typing new place names).

Reno has two automated features: the *Instant Reply List* and *Waypoints*. Reno will automatically reply with the current most likely location to any request coming from a person on the *Instant Reply List* (which is a user-defined subset of the Reno contact list). If the location is undetermined, Reno transmits "Unknown Location." *Waypoints* cause Reno to trigger a location disclosure whenever the user enters a specific, pre-defined location (to avoid bursts of messages when the user briefly leaves and returns to the same location, there is a two-hour timeout). To set up a Waypoint, the user must indicate both the location of interest and the recipient of the message. Users can see how many times Reno disclosed their location automatically using an audit tool called *Activity Report*.

Reno uses SMS messages to communicate. The messages consist of two parts: a human-readable sentence, followed by compressed information, a checksum and a 'magic' string used for message recognition. Human-readable messages increase the opportunities for using the application with people not using Reno.

3   Hypotheses

Before engaging in an actual deployment of Reno, we performed a pilot study [30], to identify fundamental issues requiring further investigation. The short duration (5 days) and the choice of participants (the researchers with some family and friends) did not provide a firm basis for the collected evidence. Moreover, we refrained from addressing privacy questions in that study because the specific skills and knowledge of the participants would not support general observations. In this study, we set out to test the following hypotheses:

1. Automatic disclosures are not problematic with appropriate corrective measures.
2. Deception and denial practices will occur with Reno.
3. Activity, as well as place, will be used by participants in their communications.

The selection of the first two research questions resulted from an analysis process balancing the need for and usefulness of automatically disclosing location to others and the privacy concerns of the application's stakeholders [12]. The third question was motivated by the observation of the pilot participants' uses of location disclosures.

3.1   Automatic Location Disclosure Is Not Problematic

This hypothesis is particularly interesting due to the ongoing debate about the trade-offs between automatic technology and people's concerns about its impact on privacy and social relations. Research in the mid-90's on the management of availability for receiving calls on cell phones suggested that caller identity, the stated urgency, and topic of the communication could be used to decide on a case-by-case basis whether to answer the phone [27]. Other research used rule engines to automatically decide, on the user's behalf, whether to disclose personal information such as location [11].

However, recent work in information security has highlighted the importance of optimistic security for controlling access to information in organizations [26]. Optimistic security employs social pressure to achieve self-restraint, and simple technical means and *ex post facto* redress to prevent unauthorized access, instead of creating complex security and access control policies upfront. This approach could be used for limiting unwanted access to location information. Our objective is to understand whether lightweight mechanisms are good enough for users of social mobile applications, or whether more complex technical solutions are really necessary.

3.2   Denial and Deception Practices Will Occur

To the best of our knowledge there has been no real-world study of deception and denial in location-enhanced applications, except for Benford *et al.*'s, which however relates to the unusual situation of a mixed-reality game [2]. However, commonsense observation and social science research [5, 7, 15, 17] indicate that these practices are essential for protecting one's environmental privacy ("being left alone"), simplifying interaction and meeting others' expectations. Acceptance of ubicomp applications require that these practices be understood and accommodated.

In our ESM study, participants stated that they preferred not to deceive outright, but rather use denial strategies (*e.g.*, not answering) instead. So, we built various ways for achieving deception and denial with Reno (*e.g.*, using inaccurate names to label locations, not labeling the location, responding with an activity, or ignoring requests). We hypothesized that users would deny disclosing their location in some instances by delaying replies, time-shifting answers, and ignoring requests, but not by outright deception. Participant selection was crafted to expose potential tensions [15].

3.3   Activity, as Well as Place, Will Be Used

In the pilot study, we observed that participants used location as a proxy for other messages, including their current activity and availability, their future movements, and for predicting arrival times. This observation mirrors ethnographic literature on the use of mobile phones, which points out that even though people often begin cell phone conversations with telling or asking about location, what they really communicate are activity and availability [31]. In this study, we set out to understand how people use place and activity, by providing an option to tell their current activity instead of their location with Reno and characterizing instances of use.

4   Demographics and Process

We enrolled two families with teenage children by posting ads on high school bulletin boards in Seattle. We asked the parents and two children from each family to participate. We then asked each child to contact one friend or schoolmate, so that we could observe usage within parent-child and peer relationships. We chose families with children 16 or under to expose coordination and dependence dynamics, as well as a need for independence. Participation requirements included: use of a cell phone for adult participants (to reduce novelty effects), adults not in Information Technology-(IT) related occupations, at least one parent working outside the home, and children attending school outside the home (to guarantee a minimal amount of mobility).

The need for entire families, the proximity of the holiday season and busy lifestyles made recruitment challenging. Maximum compensation was USD160 per participant, for a total involvement of 10 hours over 3 weeks. Compensation was tied to participation in the interviews and to the number of email surveys completed, to encourage active participation without impacting the usage of the application.

We enrolled 11 participants (6 female). The ages of the parents were between 48 and 52. All were employed full-time outside of the home; two were architects, one was a program director for social services and the fourth was a traveling salesperson. Six teenage participants were 16 years old, and one was 14 years old. All attended one of two schools. All participants had lived in the Seattle metropolitan area anywhere from 9 to 25 years (avg. 14.2).

Participants were representative of a large segment of the US population regarding their familiarity with IT. All owned a computer and used a PC both at home and at school/work, and all but two used email and the web frequently. No adult used Instant Messaging (IM), whereas all teenagers did (5 out of 7 did so frequently). Adult participants all owned cell phones, as well as 4 teenagers—consistent with statistics of cell phone use in the US[1]. Adults did not use Text Messaging (SMS) on the phone regularly. Of the teenagers who owned cell phones, one reported sending more than 100 messages per month, another reported 21–40 messages per month, and two reported less than 10 messages per month (also consistent with SMS use statistics).

Fig. 2 depicts the social networks involved in this study. Lines connect participants who knew each other before the study and indicate the self-reported assessment of how often the two participants meet each other in person (if the paired responses differed, we defaulted to the most frequent). The adults are depicted in darker circles. The two families and their friends formed two substantially distinct social groups although some of the children attended the same school and knew each other. Participants 1–5 formed Group 1, while participants 6–11 formed Group 2.

---

[1] 72% of US adults and 56% of teenagers owned a cell phone at the end of 2004. Sources: Harris Interactive Survey, The Yankee Group 2004 Mobile Users Survey.

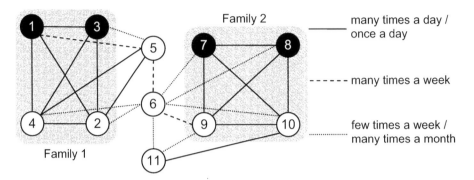

Fig. 2. Graph depicting how often participants see each other. (Adults in darker circles.)

After a screening phone interview and the selection of the two families, we invited each participant for a 60 minute introductory session, in which we explained the study goals, demonstrated the application, and administered demographic surveys and release forms. We also asked participants to compile lists of activities they would likely engage in and places they would visit during the following weeks. These lists were pre-coded into the software as shortcuts to reduce the negative impact of typing.

Deployment started one week thereafter. Participants participated in a short training session at our offices and were provided with a Nokia 6600 phone with Reno preloaded. We transferred the SIM cards and contact lists of the participants who had GSM phones and who agreed to do so (5 out of 11 participants). Participants used Reno for a period of 14 to 18 days. Every other day, participants were sent an email survey with questions about their use of Reno including whether they had left the phone behind; why and when they had requested or disclosed a location; and whether they had ignored requests, delayed responding, responded with something other than their actual location or communicated about location by other means than with Reno.

The software performed extensive logging of user activity. At startup and every 24 hours thereafter, the program sent status messages to the investigators via SMS, containing statistics such as cumulative running time, messages sent and received, cumulative time in unlabeled locations, and up to four samples of the participant's location disclosures per day. Finally, the phone kept an internal log of communication activity, creation/deletion of places and contacts and of application malfunctions.

We interviewed each participant for 30–45 minutes after one week of use and for one hour at the end of the study. The interviews were recorded and transcribed for further analysis. We asked participants how they had used the application, both in specific instances and generally. The answers to the email surveys and the status and sample messages sent back by Reno were used as a basis for these interviews, to increase the quality of recollection and provide the opportunity to give situated comments on Reno. We did not directly address privacy or plausible deniability issues until the latter part of the final interview, to avoid influencing their responses.

Waypoints and the Instant Reply List were enabled after one week of deployment, when participants came for the mid-study interview. We chose not to alternate the presence of automatic features between groups (that is, providing automatic features to one group the first week, and to the other the second week) to lower the learning curve by providing simpler functions initially and more complex ones later on. Participants were asked to indicate what Waypoints they would like other participants to create for them and on whose Instant Reply List they wanted to be. These requests were then summarized and sent to each participant in a follow-up email inviting them to set up at their discretion the automatic features others had requested.

In the email reminder for the last interview, we offered participants the opportunity to continue using the application for one additional month, with a token compensation but without the duty of filling out the bi-daily email surveys. Despite the appeal of high-end phones (especially for the teenagers), and the desire by one mother to continue using Reno, both groups declined this offer. Usability issues deriving from OS-application integration were among the main reasons for not continuing to use Reno. These issues included lack of integration with the normal SMS application of the phone (some participants in Group 1 at first did not differentiate between the two), reliability of the Java implementation, and Java UI quirks such as the 'Exit' item on all context menus (which quits the application without warning) and security prompts at each startup of the application.

5   Results

Excluding test messages and messages sent by accident, participants sent a total of 347 messages, of which 212 were disclosures (including 34 automatic disclosures). Fig. 3 depicts the volume of messages exchanged over the two-week period between each couple of participants. Outgoing arrows from participants 5, 8, 10 and 11 indicate Reno messages addressed to people outside of the study. Fig. 4 shows the volume of messages sent over the two week period. Note that most of Group 1 started two days later than Group 2. Participants added an average of 4.1 persons to their Reno contact list (which was separate from the phone's standard contact list), excluding test entries (min 1, max 10, median 4).

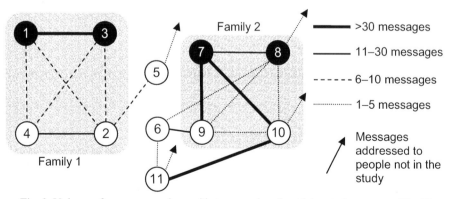

Fig. 3. Volume of messages exchanged between pairs of participants (compare to Fig. 2).

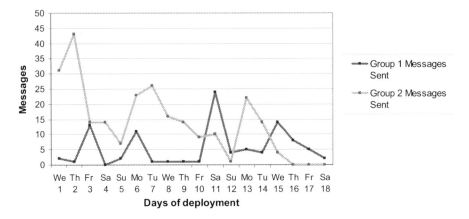

Fig. 4. Daily messages sent; group aggregate.

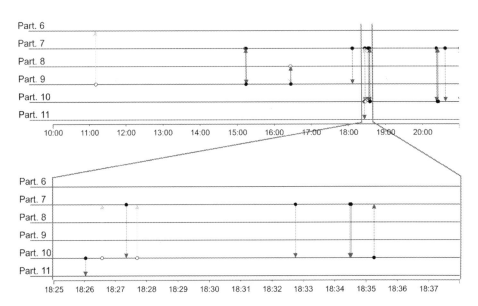

Fig. 5. Messages exchanged by Group 2, on Tue, December 7th. The upper graph shows time span 10:00–21:00. Lower graph zooms in on 18:25–18:38. Light arrows indicate location requests. Dark arrows indicate disclosures.

Use of Reno was concentrated in short bursts around specific events. Fig. 5 shows a sample of use, specifically by Group 2 on Tuesday, December 7th, with a detail of 13 minutes in the late afternoon. Participant 10 was waiting for her mother to come home. This snippet shows three types of messages. The disclosure at 18:26 from participant 10 to her friend (participant 11) was an *awareness* disclosure—"Relaxing." At 18:26 and 18:27, she asked where her mother (participant 7) was because the mother was late—a *waiting* message, to which the mother replied that she was at a store (18:27). The second request may have been sent before the daughter received her mother's reply, due to SMS transfer delays. The mother then sent 3 *unprompted status* messages: at 18:32 still from the store; at 18:34 she informed the daughter that she was finally "driving" and on her way home (the same message was sent twice, perhaps because she pressed the send button multiple times). The daughter then replied with another awareness message to her mother that she was "studying" (interestingly, different from the message she sent 9 minutes earlier to her friend).

5.1   Automatic Features Are Not Needed

At the outset of this study, we hypothesized that participants would find Instant Replies and Waypoints useful and not invasive, and that these functions just needed to be fine-tuned. However, observed behavior and interviews suggest a radically different conclusion: the participants *did not want* automatic features. The main motivation for the Instant Reply List was to reduce the burden of replying to a large number of messages each day. When asked about the amount of messages sent and received daily, no participant mentioned being overwhelmed by the number of requests.

Only three participants enabled any automated features. When the other participants were asked about their reasons for not configuring Waypoints and the Instant Reply List, only one cited potential privacy issues. All others indicated that 1) they were not completely confident of how the features would work in practice (even though we provided them with extensive training and documentation on the features); and 2) they did not feel a subjective need for setting up Waypoints or the Instant Reply List.

Regarding the Instant Reply List, three participants said that they preferred to control what they tell to others, to avoid confusing the recipient with potentially erroneous disclosures ("I felt like sometimes it [Reno] would be wrong;" [part. 9] "it's just like, y'know, the phone is taking over" [part. 6]).

Participants of the ESM study opposed unsupervised "broadcasting" of messages to others. We introduced Waypoints to verify this in practice. Two of the three participants who had set up Waypoints feared that repeated messages may disturb the recipient ("Cause I thought—well, this could get really obnoxious." [part. 7] "With this pinging all the time—after a while you would quit checking it" [part. 3]). Our participants thought that the other person would not be interested in receiving constant updates about their whereabouts ("So, you control [manual disclosures], I guess is what I'm saying. And—and that sort of process is very important." [part. 3] "I sure don't want to just keep receiving messages when somebody's at some place. Therefore, I don't really want to just send 'em just for the heck of it either." [part. 8]). Reno was used for prompting attention and awareness of oneself: the expressiveness of communication draws on the intentionality of that communication, and automatic notifications do not achieve the same intentional effect as manual messages. Teens seemed particularly concerned by this: no teen set up Waypoints or Instant Replies.

The lack of value of automated features may be caused by the small size of the social networks who participated, each comprising 5–6 users; however, there is reason to question whether social location disclosure applications would be used with much larger groups. In Smith *et al.*'s study on communication within social groups [29], adults' social network size was approx. 20. In our ESM study, participants confirmed that they would share their location with no more than 23 other people, with an average of 11 people. Teenager social networks size may be larger (in Smith's *et al.* study it averaged 59), but the same study suggests that people with large social networks are willing to invest the effort to manage them. These considerations indicate that automatic functions are *not* a priority for social mobile applications.

These observations contradict some of the preliminary findings of the pilot study, where Waypoints had been useful to participants for a variety of purposes. Pilot study participants were, however, the designers of the application, who had tailored the application to meet their personal needs and knowledge. Real-world evaluation demonstrated that the actual need and perceived usefulness of both automatic features was much lower. Especially the teenagers did not choose to adopt automatic features, and one voiced strong concerns of his parents using the technology to put a leash on him. On the contrary, two adult participants suggested uses of Waypoints and Instant Replies at work, such as using the Instant Reply function to track the whereabouts of employees and Waypoints to receive notifications about the arrival of "scarce resource" consultants at a construction site, in order to arrange unplanned meetings (an ambush-type function [23]). Both participants suggested that the use of this technology could be mandated in employment contracts. While these comments suggest possible uses for automatic location disclosure, they refer to controlled organizational settings, and are aimed at improving workplace coordination and efficiency.

5.2   Control and Environmental Privacy

Seven participants out of 11 (three adults) valued being able to withdraw from a communication and avoid invasions of their and other's personal space, something that is commonly called *environmental privacy* ("you know, I really don't want anybody calling me during a meet [*sic*]" [part. 6] "I didn't want to call him [the son] during class." [part. 7]). Seven participants (two adults) reported that they would intentionally ignore messages to signal unavailability or comply with social etiquette and this protocol was understood by the initiator of the communication. ("I don't always carry my cell phone with me… On purpose." [part. 8]) We found similar results in our ESM study. Reno messages were used by parents to prompt their children during school hours without "get[ting] her in trouble" [part. 3]. All our teenage participants mentioned that school policy prohibited them from using cell phones during class (however, only two teens left their phones in their lockers—all others silenced the phones in class and reported no problems using them there.)

An interesting distinction between teens and adults is revealed: while the concerns with disturbing a teenage recipient relate to the risk of causing potential trouble (in class), the concern with adults is related to interrupting or disturbing *the parent*. These observations are consistent with ethnographic studies that point out the appealing features of text messaging for teens in controlled environments [14, 20]. Participant comments on automatic features related interestingly to environmental privacy, as two participants expressed concern about using Waypoints to avoid "driving her crazy just hearing [the incoming messages]" [part. 3].

5.3   Control and Deception

It is widely acknowledged in social psychology that interpersonal relationships and communication involve significant amounts of deception, from harmless lies told to simplify communication and respond to expectations, to sophisticated constructions to achieve specific goals [4]. Common sense, as well as psychological and sociological studies [15, 17], suggests that teenagers in particular lie to adults for various reasons, and on a variety of topics including their past or present location, whom they are with, and what they are doing [17]. We set out to measure the number of occurrences of:

– delayed answers (*i.e.,* the user knowingly delays answering even if s/he could);
– time-shifted answers (*i.e.,* the answer describes a past or future location, but not the current location);
– ignored requests; and
– explicit deception (*e.g.*, deliberately sending an inaccurate location).

This was done by keeping a log of disclosures in which the disclosed location differed from the most likely location as calculated by the phone, and by asking specific questions in the email surveys and interviews. Participants reported three cases of deception delivered through Reno: one case of time-shift and two inaccurate disclosures. In the first case, a participant was supposed to pick up another person, and replied "Driving" to a location request, though she still was in the office and that option was available when she replied. In her account, she was "actually walking out of the door" and thought "it would be good for [the other participant] to know that I was on my way at least and driving". The second case involved one participant who was home shopping online and replied with "Running errands" as a simple way "of just [letting] them know—I'm just kind of doing some things that aren't too important—if you need me." In the third case the same participant replied "Running errands" instead of his actual location, while he was shopping for Christmas presents to avoid curiosity and accountability; during the interview, he commented: "if I say I'm Christmas shopping, then they'll want to know for who [*sic*] and where."

All in all, these three accounts of deception (out of 212 disclosures) expose a much lower amount of deception than we had expected given social psychology literature. For example, in an influential study on the topic, DePaulo *et al.* indicated that children use some form of deception in up to 30% of the social interactions with their parents and parents use deception in 8% of interactions with their children [5]. There are several plausible explanations for such a discrepancy. First, the definition of social interaction is not clear; in the DePaulo study, for example, social interaction appears to refer to an entire conversation, and it may be questionable whether a single Reno message constitutes a social interaction. Second, participant self-selection may have produced social networks with a high degree of reciprocal trust. Third, while we stressed the confidentiality of interviews to all participants, the teenagers might not have felt comfortable discussing cases of deception with us.

A simpler explanation, however, might lie in the contingent context of the deployment: the study was executed during a busy part of the school year, just before Christmas vacation, and most participants had very regular schedules packed with extracurricular activities. Most teenage participants did not drive or did not have a car—they *needed* their parents to know their location when they were not at school or at home, so they could be ferried from one activity to the next. Furthermore, each family spent both weekends of the study together, a circumstance which reduced the chance for children to be in unusual or unallowed places. From the methodological perspective, the question ensues of whether a two-week deployment is sufficient for gathering statistically plausible data about such an elusive phenomenon.

While most participants claimed that they would not have a problem disclosing their location to close friends and family, many participants were also acutely aware of privacy issues (the terms "spyware" and "bear collar" were brought up spontaneously by four participants). When asked specifically about privacy concerns, participants suggested that their experience with Reno had not caused concern for various reasons, including the facts that they exchanged location with close family and friends, that location disclosures were intentional and that *place names* were fully under their control: "The person's picking the place. *Of course* it's [the place name] expected. *They* put it on the list." [part. 1]

One of the teenagers expressed concerns that his parents might use Reno to track his whereabouts, and to prevent him from visiting certain friends. Although he used Reno very little because he found calling more convenient, during the interviews he demonstrated a very accurate mental model of the application. He mentioned that his parents (who were not among the study participants) might use the Instant Reply feature as a "punishment," and that they might check his phone regularly to ensure that they were on the list. He reported deceiving his parents about his location in normal phone conversations, and claimed that he would associate different names to the same location and use them based on who was requesting his location, as a deception strategy within Reno.

In summary, we did not gather sufficient quantitative information for verifying our hypothesis on deception, but the qualitative observations provide compelling evidence that the application would allow participants to modulate their disclosures as they felt appropriate, even if this involved deceitful communication. Many participants understood the implications of subjective place naming and the automatic functions. As mentioned above, however, control and usefulness, and not privacy concerns, were the main reasons why participants chose not to use automatic functions.

5.4 Privacy and Social Relations

The results of our field study allow us to draw some conclusions on the characterization of privacy in social relations. Participants viewed privacy concerns as interrelated with broader requirements for control and application utility. While participants unanimously said they would not reply to location requests from unknown people, many teens pointed out that they would feel comfortable telling their location to any of their acquaintances who would go to the trouble of asking. This assertion should be taken with a grain of salt, given that it refers to hypothetical situations, but it demonstrates an expectation of self-restraint and social control that would prevent just any person from asking the location of another.

Self-restraint manifested itself in different ways across participants. Most adults were quite conscious that in a working environment, increased efficiency could justify mandatory use of the application. In the relationship with their children, they valued the ability to inquire their location, but they also considered it inappropriate to spy on their children, even if they felt it was legitimate ("And you know, it's pretty cool sometimes, as a parent, to know where your teenager is […]—but then you're big brother and I don't know what I think about it." [part. 8]). Most teenagers assumed that none of their peers would request their location (or ask to be on their instant reply list) whom they would not disclose their location to. However, not all teens are alike: participant 5 suggested he would use automatic replies to spy on friends as well.

In view of the great fluidity of these relations, the boundary-setting process of personal privacy, compellingly described by Palen and Dourish [25], is supported much better by optimistic security (which exploits self-restraint and redress mechanisms) than preventive access control. Reno is designed to support such fine-grained control on what the application discloses to others and provides audit functions (the Activity Report) to verify the performance of the automated features. However, the Activity Report was not used by any of our participants who activated Waypoints or the Instant Reply List, suggesting that auditing may be more effective when integrated within the core application interface.

5.5   Activity Vs. Place

In the pilot study we had observed that location was often used as a proxy for conveying other messages, such as status, estimated time of arrival (ETA), or reminders [30]. In response to these findings, we introduced the option of responding to a location request with an activity instead of with a place. Of the aggregate 212 disclosure messages sent, 52% indicated a place and 48% indicated an activity.[2] Most participants, both heavy and occasional users of the application, roughly displayed this breakdown.

To facilitate the naming of locations, we preloaded customized lists of locations for each participant. For this purpose, participants were asked to indicate up to 10 places by choosing among 15 suggested names or supplying their own. A similar questionnaire produced a list of five activities, which appeared in addition to the current location(s) when the user was selecting a message to send with Reno (Fig. 1).

Table 1 shows the number of place names and activities that were defined by the participants before the start of the deployment, names that were added subsequently, how many physical locations were labeled with place names, and how many place and activity names were actually used in messages. Participants added many new place names in addition to those they initially indicated in the questionnaires. Table 2 shows the places and activity names used by one teenage participant. Participants labeled an average of 2.9 locations (min 0, max 9, median 3) with place names (we excluded our office if it had been labeled during the training session).

Participants used 20 unique place names to tell their location: 13 place names were proper names of specific places, understandable by a person living in Seattle. These names are potentially available from a phone directory and could be retrieved based on the user's location. Most remaining place names can be categorized in what Schegloff groups in the set of R_m names or "relation to members," i.e., names that have value in relation to the members taking part in the communication (e.g., "Home," "School:" these names are relative to the speaker and must be understood by the recipient) [28].

---

[2] "Car" and "In Car" were considered places in this analysis.

Table 1. Place and activity names defined, used for labeling locations and actually disclosed. Identical names are counted once for each participant who used them.

		Names	Locations Labeled	Actually used
Places	**Initially defined**	95	11	9
	Added during use	22	21	18
Activities	**Initially defined**	57	N/A	34
	Added during use	6	6	6

Table 2. Place and activity names used by participant 10. First column: names indicated before deployment; Second column: names added during the deployment. Text in angle brackets is descriptive of the actual text removed for participant anonymity.

	Labeled Places	**Used Activities**
Initially Defined	Home School	Soccer Studying Relaxing
Added During Use	<participant brother's name>'s bball practice Library <neighborhood name> <abbreviation of the proper name of a place>	Hip hop Making lunch

Participants used 13 unique activity names when sending Reno messages. Users could not add activities to the activity list, but three participants (all teenagers) labeled *physical locations* with activity names instead of place names. Six locations were labeled with the activity that was taking place there (*e.g.*, "Hip hop," "Horticulture"). This shows that activity can be used as an R_m term for indicating location. On the other hand, activities can be more vague than place names and may thus be used in plausible denial dynamics. The participants who labeled locations with activities explained that the recipient of the disclosure already knew their location and that they wanted to be more descriptive (this agrees with other published research [31]): participant 10 regularly sent two replies to each request: one with her location and another with her current activity. This demonstrates that activity and place are often used jointly or interchangeably for achieving communication goals and that the choice of what to disclose is a function of, at least, the activity being accomplished with the communication—an extended form of the selection process described by Schegloff [28]. This has design implications, as activity may be added to location-enhanced people finders or messaging applications as a general-purpose fallback option.

6   Informing the Design of Social Mobile Applications

Although it is risky to infer general design guidelines based on relatively small-scale studies, some observations we made agree with other published research cited throughout this article. The mutually supporting evidence fortifies the credibility of our conclusions.

6.1   Don't Make Automated Functions a Design Priority

Automated features designed to streamline and facilitate communication should not be a design priority. Although the pilot study suggested promising applications for Waypoints, the participants in the field study described in this article unanimously preferred to maintain control over the messages their phones transmitted. Few participants used Waypoints even for very routine activities (such as leaving work or arriving home). Most participants felt that the time spent sending the message was well worth the gain in precision and purposefulness. This contradicts the mainstream view in the ubicomp community that increasing information overload demands "intelligent" technology to take up the role of an "electronic assistant" for the user. Quite the contrary, the main value participants saw in Reno was the lightweight interaction it afforded, which made it easy to use during *interstitial activity* (*i.e.*, those times, such as waiting for a bus, between sanctioned activities).

6.2   Lightweight Messaging: A Hit Social Mobile Application?

All participants viewed Reno as an enhanced messaging application, rather than strictly a location-enhanced service. They appreciated the convenience of quickly requesting location and adapting that request to inquire about availability and current activity, without having to type lengthy messages and having to make disruptive phone calls. We know that: "What are you doing?" and "Where are you?" are often-asked questions—which leads to the question of how a pre-coded set of common inquiries and replies could support lightweight routine communication tasks (*e.g.*, "Where are you?" "What are you doing?" "Busy," *etc.*) The Nokia 6600 message templates are a step in this direction, but the text messaging application could provide context-sensitive interpretation to facilitate responses (for example, it could present a list of activities in reply to a "What are you doing?" message). Such an 'intelligent' messaging application seems very promising, especially if coupled with simple location and activity sensing. Lightweight messaging would fill the value gap for people not accustomed to typing on the phone or in situations that do not afford distractions.

6.3   Explicitly Support Plausible Deniability

While supporting deception may appear an unethical proposition for designers to follow, we are convinced, by overwhelming literature and by our observations that people want to deceive, or deny replies, from time to time, for purposes that are important to them. Cases of outright deception about location occurred relatively rarely, both in the ESM study and in the deployment; however, participants in both studies indicated that in those instances having the option to deceive, "stretch the truth," or deny a reply would be important. They affirmed that they might lie about their location in order to preserve their individual privacy, or as a way of achieving positive, longer-term, social effects. All this supporting evidence led us to conclude that communication technology should support plausible deniability (*e.g.*, by preserving imperfect sensing and communication). Participants who felt a need to achieve deniability demonstrated the ability to do so with Reno by tailoring place names, the auto-

matic features and outgoing messages. This suggests that these qualities may be sufficient to enable plausible deniability and thus avoid the related acceptance problems.

7   Related Work

The telecom industry has hailed Location-Based Services (LBS) as the next killer app
after the unexpected success of SMS. Ubiquitous person finders targeted at corporate
customers were commercially launched by KDDI in Japan in 2002 [16]. DoCoMo
introduced person-to-person LBS in the form of location-augmented iMode websites
[24], amidst mounting privacy concerns [13]. Child-tracking applications are available in the United Kingdom [22]. A more general cell-phone based person-finder
application has been developed by Kivera Inc. for AT&T Wireless (now part of Cin-
gular). The system, called Find People Nearby (formerly known as Find Friends)
allows the user to build a buddy list, and to locate other subscribers in any area covered by AT&T. The user can then call the person, send a message or invite him/her to
a meeting point chosen from businesses in the AT&T Yellow Pages. Although AT&T
does not disclose usage statistics, the success of this application has been arguably
limited [3]. Probable causes include the lack of interoperability with other providers
as well as usability issues.

   Reno overcomes the former limitation by leveraging the universal interoperability
afforded by SMS. Moreover, users of Find People Nearby cannot label locations,
whereas Reno provides tools for creating and using meaningful place names, instead
of hard-to-understand geographical or urban coordinates [9]. In Find People Nearby
the user must grant permission to be located by a friend, similarly to the Instant Reply
List; after granting permission, however, the system automatically discloses the location in the form of urban coordinates. Thus, the user cannot choose on a case-by-case
basis whether to reply and what to disclose. This detracts from the tool's flexibility
and curtails control and denial practices.

   Schegloff provided an early account of how people formulate place in everyday
conversations, and described it as a *selection problem* among several, formally correct
alternatives [28]. He suggested that at least three factors influence the selection of a
place name: location references (relative to one's current position, physical or otherwise), membership to specific social group(s) and the activity being accomplished
with the place formulation. We have adopted this description and, in fact, the location
and activity names that our participants chose can be categorized according to it.
Recent studies on the formulation of place using mobile communication technologies
include Laurier's account of how location is used to express much more than geographical position [21], and Weilenmann's account of the use of place to express
activity and availability [31]. These studies report on "ethnographic" observation of
already existing practices, whereas we have tried to study the use of place and activity
with an emerging technology. While the agreement of our observations with these
studies corroborate the credibility of our data, the novel ways people used Reno hint
at how the formulation of location and availability might change with the widespread
use of mobile social applications.

   Lederer *et al.* [19] report that people decide whether to disclose information about
their activities and location based on the identity of the requester more than on the

situation in which this happens. Both the ESM study [4] and the present study confirm this, and, in addition, highlight that users provide either the information that they think will be most useful to the requester, or none. Barkhuus and Dey investigated the balance between security and management burden and suggest that people are willing to forgive some control over their personal location information if the application is useful to them [1]. Our experience with Reno shows that users display similar feelings towards automatic disclosure of location information—what these authors term "active context-awareness." The imprecise nature of cell-phone tower-based localization can be viewed as both a problem and an advantage. In location-based games such as 'Can You See Me Now?' [6], the imprecise nature of location sensing is exploited by the designers to enrich the game by creating uncertainty. In Reno, imprecision and ambiguity afford a space for privacy.

Finally, Laasonen *et al.* show how cell-phone tower localization can be used in combination with user-based labeling schemes [18]. We have taken their concept of *areas* (clusters of sensed cell towers) to define signatures for a specific place. GSM phones, even when stationary, switch between cells and these patterns can be exploited to achieve increased precision. In addition, our software can sense whether the user has been moving across numerous cell boundaries; this knowledge is used to obtain more accurate signatures. We preferred cell tower-based sensing over GPS, because of its better performance in buildings and dense urban environments, and over WLAN-based positioning, due to the more simple hardware configuration.

8   Conclusions

We set out to understand how and why people choose to disclose their location information with a social mobile application, by probing three salient questions: how people relate to automatic disclosure mechanisms, what denial or deception techniques they would adopt, and how place and activity names are used. However, the results of our study required us to step back and reconsider our assumptions, which were based on our own common sense considerations and a straightforward interpretation of Weiser's idea of calm technology. The agreement of our observations with a great deal of published literature in related fields supports our claims and empowers our conclusions drawn from a relatively short field study.

Our participants did not use automatic functions and provided strong evidence suggesting that, even in a "complete" social network, automatic functions would be unnecessary in the face of loss of control. Although the low rate of deception prevents us from drawing firm conclusions, our participants did not voice any concern of being unable to use Reno within denial or deception practices, thus supporting our claim that the control provided by Reno is sufficient for achieving plausible deniability. We observed that activity was often used instead of place when responding to a request for location. This, combined with the praise for the ease of use and unobtrusiveness of Reno, hints at a vast untapped potential for simplified mobile messaging.

Acknowledgements

We thank for their collaboration and help Wendy March, Tony Salvador, John Sherry, Gillian Hayes and Jehan Moghazy. Thanks to Khai Truong for the usage scenario picture. We also thank our anonymous reviewers and all the participants of our user studies. This work was funded in part by Intel Corp., the NSF through the GRFP and Georgia Institute of Technology. Human subjects research is covered by Georgia Tech IRB protocol H04232.

References

1. Barkhuus, L., Dey, A.: Location-Based Services For Mobile Telephony: A Study Of Users' Privacy Concerns. In: Proc. Interact 2003, IOS Press (2003) 709–712.
2. Benford, S., Seager, W., Flintham, M., Anastasi, R., Rowland, D., Humble, J., Stanton, D., Bowers, J., Tanadavanitj, N., Adams, M., Farr, J. R., Oldroyd, A., Sutton, J.: The Error of Our Ways: The Experience of Self-Reported Position in a Location-Based Game. In: Proc. Ubicomp 2004, LNCS 3205, Springer Verlag (2004) 70–87.
3. Brown, K.: On The Trail Of Location Services. Wireless Week, March 1, 2004, Reed Business Information (2004) 18.
4. Consolvo, S., Smith, I., Matthews, T., LaMarca, A., Tabert, J., Powledge, P.: Location Disclosure to Social Relations: Why, When, & What People Want to Share. In: Proc. CHI 2005, ACM Press (2005) 82–90.
5. DePaulo B.M., Kashy D.A.: Everyday Lies in Close and Casual Relationships. Journal of Personality and Social Psychology 74 (1), American Psychological Association (1998) 63–79.
6. Flintham, M., Anastasi, R., Benford, S. D., Hemmings, T., Crabtree, A., Greenhalgh, C. M., Rodden, T. A., Tandavanitj, N., Adams, M., Row-Farr, J.: Where On-Line Meets On-The-Streets: Experiences With Mobile Mixed Reality Games. In: Proc. CHI 2003, ACM Press (2003) 569–576.
7. Grinter, R. E., Eldridge, M.: 'y do tngrs luv 2 txt msg?' In: Proc. ECSCW '01, Kluwer Academic Press (2001) 219–238.
8. Hancock, J.T., Thom-Santelli, J., Ritchie T.: Deception and Design: The Impact of Communication Technology on Lying Behavior. In: Proc. CHI 2004. ACM Press (2004) 129–134.
9. Harrison, S., Dourish, P.: Re-place-ing Space: The Roles Of Space And Place In Collaborative Systems. In: Proc. CSCW '96, ACM Press (1996) 67–76.
10. Höflich, J. R., Rössler, P.: Mobile schriftliche Kommunikation – oder: E-Mail für das Handy. Die Bedeutung elektronischer Kurznachrichten (Short Message Service) am Beispiel jugendlicher Handynutzer. Medien & Kommunikationswissenschaft 49, Nomos-Verlag (2001) 437.
11. Hull, R., Kumar, B., Lieuwen, D., Patel-Schneider, D.F., Sahuguet, A., Varadarajan, S., Vyas, A.: Enabling Context-Aware and Privacy-Conscious User Data Sharing. In: Proc. MDM'04, IEEE Press (2004) 187–198.
12. Iachello, G., Abowd, G.D.: Privacy and Proportionality: Adapting Legal Evaluation Techniques to Inform Design In Ubiquitous Computing. In: Proc. CHI 2005, ACM Press (2005) 91–100.
13. Informa Telecoms & Media: What the Operators Are Doing. Mobile Location Analyst, Oct 2003 (2003). Available online: http://www.baskerville.telecoms.com.

14. Ito, M., Daisuke, O.: Mobile Phones, Japanese Youth and the Replacement of Social Contact. In: Ling, R., Pedersen, P. (eds.): Front Stage/Back Stage: Mobile Communication and the Renegotiation of the Social Sphere, Conference Proceedings, 22–24 June 2003, Grimstad, Norway.

15. Jensen, L., Jensen, J., Feldman, S., Cauffman, E.: The Right to Do Wrong: Lying to Parents Among Adolescents and Emerging Adults. Journal of Youth and Adolescence 33 (2), Kluwer Academic Publishers (2004) 101–112.

16. KDDI: GPS MAP, a Location Service For Mobile Phones. Available online: http://www.kddi.com/english/corporate/news_release/archive/2002/0718/.

17. Knox D., Zusman, M.E., McGinty, K., Gescheidler, J.: Deception of Parents During Adolescence. Adolescence 36 (143), Libra Publishers (2001) 611–614.

18. Laasonen, K., Raento, M., Toivonen, H.: Adaptive On-Device Location Recognition. In: Proc. Pervasive 2004, LNCS 3001, Springer Verlag (2004) 287–304.

19. Lederer, S., Mankoff, J., Dey, A. K.: Who Wants to Know What When? Privacy Preference Determinants in Ubiquitous Computing. In: Proc. CHI 2003, ACM Press (2003) 724–725.

20. Ling, R.: The Social and Cultural Consequences of Mobile Telephony as Seen in the Norwegian Context. Telenor R&D Report R 9/2002, ISSN 1500-2616 (2002).

21. Laurier, E.: Why People Say Where They Are During Mobile Phone Calls. Environment and Planning D: Society and Space 19, Pion (2001) 485–504.

22. Mapamobile: Available online: http://www.mapamobile.com/.

23. Mynatt, E., Tullio, J. (2001) Inferring calendar event attendance. In: Proc. ACM Conference on Intelligent User Interfaces (IUI 2001), ACM Press (2001) 121–128.

24. NTT DoCoMo: iArea: Location Based Services. Available online: http://www.nttdocomo.com/corebiz/imode/services/iarea.html.

25. Palen, L., Dourish, P.: Unpacking "Privacy" for a Networked World. In: Proc. CHI 2003, ACM Press (2003) 129–136.

26. Povey, D.: Optimistic Security: A New Access Control Paradigm. In: Proc. New Security Paradigms Workshop 1999. Ontario, Canada, ACM Press (1999) 40–45.

27. Reichenbach, M., Damker, H., Federrath H., Rannenberg K.: Individual Management of Personal Reachability in Mobile Communication. In: Yngström, L., Carlsen, J. (eds.): Information Security in Research and Business, IFIP TC11 13th International Conference on Information Security (SEC '97), Chapman & Hall (1997) 164–174.

28. Schegloff, E. A.: Notes on a Conversational Practice: Formulating Place. In: Sudnow D. (ed.): Studies in Social Interaction, The Free Press (1972) 75–119.

29. Smith, H., Rogers, Y., Brady, M.: Managing One's Social Network: Does Age Make a Difference? In: Proc. Interact 2003, IOS Press (2003) 551–558.

30. Smith, I., Consolvo, S., Hightower, J., Hughes, J., Iachello, G., LaMarca, A., Abowd, G.D., Scott, J., Sohn, T.: Social Disclosure Of Place: From Location Technology to Communication Practice. In: Proc. Pervasive 2005, LNCS 3468, Springer Verlag (2005) 134–151.

31. Weilenmann A.: "I Can't Talk Now: I'm In A Fitting Room": Formulating Availability And Location In Mobile Phone Conversations, Environment and Planning A 35, Pion (2003) 1589–1605.

Place-Its: A Study of Location-Based Reminders on Mobile Phones

Timothy Sohn[1], Kevin A. Li[1], Gunny Lee[1], Ian Smith[2], James Scott[3], and William G. Griswold[1]

[1] Computer Science and Engineering
University of California, San Diego, La Jolla, CA, USA
{tsohn,k2li,gulee,wgg}@cs.ucsd.edu
[2] Intel Research, Seattle, WA, USA
ian.e.smith@intel.com
[3] Intel Research, Cambridge, UK
james.w.scott@intel.com

Abstract. Context-awareness can improve the usefulness of automated reminders. However, context-aware reminder applications have yet to be evaluated throughout a person's daily life. Mobile phones provide a potentially convenient and truly ubiquitous platform for the detection of personal context such as location, as well as the delivery of reminders. We designed Place-Its, a location-based reminder application that runs on mobile phones, to study people using location-aware reminders throughout their daily lives. We describe the design of Place-Its and a two-week exploratory user study. The study reveals that location-based reminders are useful, in large part because people use location in nuanced ways.

1 Introduction

Everyday we use special messages in order to help us remember future tasks. These messages, known as reminders, take many forms, such as post-it notes, emailing oneself, to-do lists, and electronic calendar alerts. For example, a student may send himself an email to remind himself to bring a book for class the next day.

Reminders can be more helpful when rich contextual information is used to present them at appropriate times in appropriate places. [7]. A grocery list reminder is more helpful while passing the supermarket en route home from work, rather than while at work or after getting home.

Several context-aware systems [8,10,19] have prototyped reminder applications [7,19], but the evaluation of applications built on these systems has only been conducted in limited areas. In a recent pilot study on location-based reminders, we found that the reminders that people wanted extend beyond life in the research lab into all aspects of their personal lives [18]. In particular, people often set reminders because the current context, both physical and social, prohibited completing the activity at the time. Therefore, our ability to understand the role of contextual reminders in a per-

M. Beigl et al. (Eds.): UbiComp 2005, LNCS 3660, pp. 232-250, 2005.

son's natural setting depends on a ubiquitous system being available consistently in a person's life.

A compelling platform for pervasively deploying context-aware reminders is mobile phones. Mobile phones with location-sensing capabilities are becoming state of the art, and several location-aware applications are available for use. The ubiquity of mobile phone networks enables pervasive location sensing, while the always-carried and always-on nature of phones mean that reminder creation and notification are permanently available to users. These factors allow a reminder system to be omnipresent in the everyday life of a user. In addition, reminder notifications on mobile phones do not require any extra hardware, and gives people a familiar device for in situ interaction.

Yet, the suitability for phone-based context-aware reminders is unclear. The sensing capabilities of phones are limited in the types of context and their accuracy of sensing. The limited input capabilities of mobile phones, combined with the tendency towards use while committed to another task, suggests a simplistic user interface that permits posting a reminder in a few key-presses. Can potentially inaccurate, one-dimensional reminders (*i.e.* using location) prove useful, and if so, how? Are the phone's capabilities in data entry, notification, and viewing adequate?

These technical and social limitations motivate the focus on location as a context cue. Recent advances in computing and location-sensing technologies are enabling high coverage location-sensing opportunities [15,16] to use in building location-aware applications. Most of these systems require some initial configuration, but can then provide pervasive location sensing throughout a person's daily life. Using one's location to trigger reminders is a potentially valuable piece of context that can improve the way people use reminders. Our aim is to find how location-based reminders are used when available throughout a person's day. Of course there are types of reminders in which location is not useful, but our focus is on those that could benefit from the additional location information. How and why does location figure into the relevance of a reminder for a person? How important is positional accuracy and timeliness to the usefulness of location-based reminders?

In the following sections we describe the design, implementation, and deployment of a location-based reminder application, named Place-Its, for mobile phones. This simple application, with the mobile phone as a platform, permitted the integration of location-based reminders into peoples' daily practice. We then report on a 10-person user study involving Place-Its over a two week period. The study participants found location-based reminders to be useful, despite relatively low location accuracy. In particular, participants found value in having the application always naturally on-hand for posting and receiving reminders, along with pervasive location sensing. Also, the participants used location-based reminders in numerous ways, including several in which the location served as a convenient proxy for other kinds of context. Finally, we conclude with a discussion of implications for future research.

2 Related Work

The idea of using location information in context-aware applications is not new. Much work has been done in the past in context-aware prototypes that have all shown location to be a useful element of context.

The Forget-me-not project was one of the pioneering efforts in the area of context-aware reminders. Forget-me-not employs a small PDA-like device that associates different items of interest with icons to help the person remember various tasks they need to attend to [17].

ComMotion is a more recent example of a context-aware system, supporting reminders that utilize location as contextual information [19]. Using GPS technology for location-sensing, people could set reminders around certain locations, with given time constraints. When the person was near that location and the timing constraints were satisfied, they would be alerted with an audio alert.

Cybreminder [7] took these ideas a step further, developing a reminder application based on the Context Toolkit [8] that focused on using a variety of context information, including location, to determine when best to trigger reminders. This project focused on abstracting hardware technology away from the developer. Thus, it was able to create a fully featured reminders application taking into account a variety of contextual information. This toolkit relies on the existence of special sensing hardware that limits its ability to be deployed ubiquitously.

Focusing on a different aspect of reminders, Stick-e notes [5] explored the post-it metaphor in the digital rather than physical world. Stick-e notes were placed at particular locations using GPS enabled PDAs, and could be made visible to others, thus emulating the affordances of physical notes in a digital environment.

Unlike the previously mentioned systems, ActiveCampus [10] examines mobile computing restricted to a university campus setting and provides a location-based reminders system using 802.11 radios to provide location sensing. A reminders feature is integrated into the system where people can set reminders to be triggered at predefined locations on campus, typically buildings.

The wearable computing research community has also had a number of projects exploring reminder notifications through extra hardware. Memoclip uses a small wearable computer that relies on location beacons distributed in the environment to trigger location-based reminders [4]. The reminder bracelet involves a bracelet worn on the wrist of the user that subtly alerts the wearer of upcoming events, as entered into their PDA calendar, using temporal information only [11]. The Sulaweski framework discusses a spatial reminder service that uses GPS and infrared to approximate a person's location and delivers reminders accordingly [20]. Memory glasses is another project that attempts to augment user memory by using subliminal cues [6]. The wearable remembrance agent used a heads up display to provide context-relevant information [21]. While some of these systems use implicit reminders, with some type of context or activity inferencing, they all find that subtle cues are effective. Like the systems mentioned above, these wearable solutions also focus on exploring new services that can be provided using location as context.

In the ethnographic space, Kaasinen performed a study examining people's needs for location-based services, using existing tools and methods [13]. People were given

GPS enabled devices and typical tasks to perform, with the focus being on their expectations for location-based services. The participants found the scenarios given to them to be unrealistic, as they felt the given situations did not reflect the real needs of people. They also expressed concerns about how location-aware systems might cause drastic changes in human interaction. Antifakos et al. examined the effects of imperfect memory aids when used to help recall. They found that displaying uncertainty helped to improve recall rates, especially in cases where uncertainty was high [3].

These pioneering efforts have generally not permitted evaluation in the context of people's normal lives. This is because they either used additional hardware, such as GPS receivers, that people typically do not carry around (taking both cost and inconvenience into account), or because they are restricted to a predefined area such as the campus of a university. GPS itself provides restricted location sensing, only operating in outdoor regions where line of sight with multiple satellites is available, whereas most people spend their days largely indoors, and even while outdoors GPS may not be available in areas such as "urban canyons". Studies conducted on university campuses typically use radio technology for location-sensing, requiring that beacons be placed in the environment, something that currently is not sufficiently available outside such settings [10]. Other location-sensing technologies, not listed here, could be used for a reminders application but possess similar restrictions, requiring special hardware [12]. Wearable computing solutions also require special hardware to provide many of the developed services. As a result of these constraints, it has been difficult to examine how location-based reminders could be used when integrated into someone's daily routine. The study here takes advantage of research done in client-side GSM-based location-sensing technology as well as the popularity and low cost of mobile phones to study location-based reminders, free of the aforementioned restrictions.

3   The Place-Its Application

Place-Its is designed around the post-it note usage metaphor, and named for its ability to "place" a reminder message at a physical location (i.e., a place). It usefully deviates from the metaphor in that notes can be posted to remote places. Although a person is home for the night, he can post a note at work to be retrieved the following morning upon arrival. To convey how Place-Its is used for location-based reminders, the following is a scenario based on Place-Its' actual usage by one of the participants from our study (screenshots next page).

Jill is currently busy at work, and remembers she needs to call her mom. She knows she will have free time when she gets home, so she conveniently creates a Place-It note (Figure 1a) that will trigger on arrival (Figure 1b) and remind her to call her mom (Figure 1c) at home (Figure 1d). Jill glances and sees that she has two other notes that are still posted (Figure 1e). After work Jill has dinner with her friends and arrives at home later that night. As she walks into the house, her phone vibrates and displays a message (Figure 1f), reminding her to call her mom. Immediately, she makes the call.

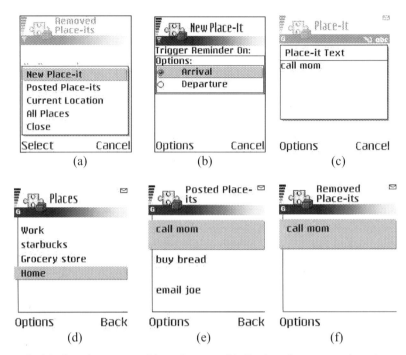

Figure 1. (a) Creating a new Place-It note; **(b)** Setting the note to be triggered upon arrival; **(c)** Typing the text of the note; **(d)** Posting the note to 'Home'; **(e)** Showing all posted Place-It notes; **(f)** The reminder is triggered when Jill arrives at the home and the note is removed.

The three components to a Place-It reminder note are the *trigger*, *text*, and *place*. The *trigger* identifies whether the reminder should be signaled upon arrival or departure of the associated *place*. The *text* is the message associated with the note. Reminders are created with a message, and then posted to a location on the person's list of places. People could use the phone's predictive text input for entering their reminder texts to ease the burden of typing on the phone's keypad.

A person can view all posted reminder notes at any time (Figure 1e) and can delete or edit any of the fields associated with the note. After a reminder note is posted on a place, when the trigger (arrival or departure) occurs, the note is automatically removed and put in the Removed Place-Its list. Once a note is removed, it can be edited, and reposted to the same or a different location.

We had three main design principles for the Place-Its application. First, it must be an always-on service, to ensure that reminder notifications are always possible and users can have confidence that they will get their requested reminders. A reminder system that is only available a small percentage of a person's day is ineffective if the message needs to be delivered outside the operational time frame. Second, the application must be easily deployable. Requiring people to carry extra pieces of hardware can hinder their integration of the reminder tool into their daily activities. The application is best deployed through a familiar artifact that people already use or carry on a daily basis. Last, for several reasons, we purposely omitted features to set time-based reminders. This choice simplified the interface, omitting at least one step from the reminder creation process. It is also consistent with current reminder applications, which permit using just one kind of context (typically time). This was also a natural way to force all users to use location as their primary source of context when creating the reminder, even though they were not accustomed to it.

3.1 Mobile Phone Platform

Mobile phones offer a way to meet our first two design goals. Mobile phones are emerging as viable platforms for deploying personal ubiquitous computing applications. Multimedia, communications, and general computing capabilities are all converging to the mobile phone platform. Phones are also deployed and carried by over a billion people across the world, making them ideal for application deployment. Since people already carry mobile phones with them for communication purposes, they are unlikely to forget the device or have it hinder their normal activities. Mobile phones also present a convenience factor. Because people typically keep their phone handy for answering calls, they also can quickly create and receive a reminder note on their phone anywhere at anytime. Finally, the public use of a phone is, in the most part, socially acceptable. Given these advantages, our aim was to deploy an application designed for the phone platform, taking care to exploit these advantages where possible.

Place-Its is targeted at the Symbian Series 60 platform and was written using Java 2 Micro Edition (J2ME), with the Connected Limited Device Configuration (CLDC 1.0) and Mobile Information Device Profile (MIDP 2.0) APIs. The application contains a small portion of C++ code to access GSM cell tower information on the device. All development and deployment was done on the Nokia 6600 phone, chosen for its large screen and good developer support.

3.2 Location-Sensing

Achieving pervasive location sensing is essential for Place-Its to be useful. The Global Positioning System (GPS), with all its strengths and weaknesses, is the most widely used location technology today. However, it is not widely available on mobile phones, although it is beginning to emerge on certain models.

Another option would be to take advantage of the recent efforts by telephony providers to support accurate location sensing on mobile phones to meet E112/E911 requirements [1,2]. A by-product of this effort is the development of commercial pay-for-use location-based applications. It is possible to use a provider-based location mechanism for Place-Its, however these services are only emerging, without much support for independent developers to access location information directly. Per-use charging schemes would also cause high costs to be incurred by applications such as Place-Its, which need to continually monitor the user's location.

Looking to perform all location computations on the client device to avoid any charges by the provider, a better solution is Place Lab, a location system that relies on mapped radio beacons in the environment to provide location estimates [16]. Place

Lab for the mobile phone platform can use both GSM and Bluetooth radio technologies for location sensing. All computation is done on the client device, preserving people's location privacy. Previous studies have shown that Place Lab achieves approximately 100 meter accuracy and 100% coverage in urban areas. However, the initial requirement for cell tower location mappings is problematic since if a person moves outside of a mapped area, location capabilities are no longer available. Because it is costly to map every possible region where a person will go, we chose not use Place Lab. However, as the number of mapped regions grows, Place Lab would be a good solution for location-based applications like Place-Its.

We chose to use the location technique employed by Reno [22] for marking and detecting places, inspired by the ideas of Laasonen et al. [15], but simplified somewhat for our purposes. The key observation made by Laasonen et al. is that one can think of a place as a clique in a graph. This graph starts out as a set of nodes representing GSM cell towers. Edges are added to the graph between nodes as the phone observes a transition from one cell tower to another. A transition A-B means that a mobile phone was associated with cell A and now is associated with cell B. By using this strategy, the graph of nodes that a mobile phone associates with can be constructed.

When a mobile phone is stationary in one place, it does not stay always associated with the same cell tower; it "hops around" or, in the graph sense, traverses a set of edges on the graph. In a given location, the small set of nodes, a clique, that are traversed is typically quite stable for a mobile phone that is not moving. We watch for cyclic transitions such as visits to the sequence of nodes, A, B, C, A. The Reno location algorithm considers this the clique A, B, C. Reno's algorithm basically defines a place as the sequence of nodes visited in a cycle when that cycle has been repeated more than once. For example, if the sequence of nodes A, B, A C, B, A is observed, the algorithm considers the current place to be defined by the clique A, B. (C was not visited more than once.)

When trying to discriminate places, the algorithm simply takes the set of nodes seen recently (within some time window determined by hand tuning) and looks for cliques that overlap this recent list. For simplicity, the algorithm ranks the possible places (cliques) based on the amount of the clique that is "covered" by the recent nodes. This favors small cliques over large ones, but in practice causes few problems.

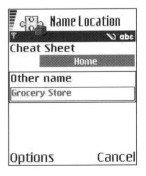

Figure 2. Once Place-Its is able to determine a unique location signature, the person can name the location by typing it in, or using a pre-defined "Cheat Sheet".

Once a place is determined, the person is able to label that place with a unique name (Figure 2). An advantage to this approach is that places can be identified wherever a person goes independent of any extra hardware or external data. A disadvantage is that a place must be previously visited and marked by the person before any reminder messages can be associated with that place.

4   User Study

In this section, we describe an exploratory user study of Place-Its performed with ten participants, over a two-week period in Winter 2005. We studied location-based reminders in the daily lives of people with different occupations, to analyze behavioral and usefulness factors for location-based reminders through a mobile phone interface. As an initial study, we emphasized naturalness over experimental controls, enabling us to observe genuine behaviors that could set directions for future research, as well as inform application design and future experiments. In this section we describe our experimental set-up, and in the subsequent two sections describe our results gathered from the study.

4.1   Participants

We recruited participants through mailing list postings and advertisements, seeking a group that used a variety of methods for creating reminders using other tools, had experience with mobile phones, and would manifest a variety of location-based reminder behaviors. The ten chosen participants consisted of students and working professionals, ages 18-45, three women and seven men (see Figure 3). Five of the ten participants were undergraduate or graduate students at different universities in the area. The other five were full-time working professionals. None of the participants had been exposed to using location technology for creating and delivering reminders before. Each of the participants had a GSM service provider, allowing them to use

Participant	Age Range (Gender)	Occupation	Current Reminder Method
A	18-21 (M)	Undergraduate	post-its, notepad
B	18-21 (F)	Undergraduate	paper planner
C	22-25 (M)	Graduate	email, notepad
D	22-25 (F)	Graduate	None
E	22-25 (M)	Graduate	electronic calendar, email
F	25-35 (M)	Professional	PDA
G	35-45 (M)	Professional	email, visible items
H	22-25 (M)	Professional	post-its, electronic calendar, phone alarm
I	25-35 (M)	Professional	electronic calendar, PDA
J	22-25 (F)	Professional	post-its, email, electronic calendar, phone

Figure 3. Demographic information about each participant and their current method of creating reminders. A-E are students and F-J are working professionals

our application and location detection algorithm, while maintaining their communication capabilities with minimal hassle.

The dominant reminder habits of the participants fell into four broad categories. Three used personal information management tools for their reminders (e.g., Microsoft Outlook, PDA), three used mainly email, and another three wrote their reminders down in a notebook or on post-it notes. The last participant did not use any of these methods, relying purely on memory.

4.2 Methodology

We conducted our study in three steps, a pre-study questionnaire, a two week long deployment, and post-study interview. Our pre-study consisted of a basic questionnaire regarding demographic information, mobile phone usage habits, and current methods of creating reminders. To help the participants personalize their Place-Its application, we asked each to provide, in advance, up to ten frequently visited places where they might want to set a reminder during the study. These pre-defined "Cheat Sheet" lists were put on the phone for the participants, enabling a participant to define a new place without having to type it in using the phone's keypad (Figure 2). The person was still required to visit that location and mark the place before they could label it.

We provided each participant with a Nokia 6600 to use during the study. However, they transferred their personal SIM card to the new phone for the duration of the study, thereby transferring their address book and allowing them to use the same phone number and phone network account. Since the phone was unfamiliar to some participants, we also conducted a basic phone tutorial. We explained our application, using the adapted post-it note usage metaphor. Each participant was told that before a reminder could be posted at a location, they had to have visited the location and named the place. Reminder notifications would be triggered by a phone beep and vibration, and would conform to the profiles of the phone. If the phone were in silent mode, a notification would not occur. Our participants were aware that we would be logging usage data on the device for analysis after the study completed. We asked the participants to incorporate the application into their daily lives and routines, using the application to set reminders as the need arose. After one week, the participants filled out a mid-study questionnaire by email regarding their experiences with Place-Its and the types of reminders they were posting.

Near the end of the two weeks the participants were sent a post-study questionnaire by email regarding their experiences with location-based reminders and the Place-Its application. The study concluded with each participant returning the Nokia 6600 and a 30 minute personal interview discussing their questionnaire responses.

5 Observations and Initial Classification

There were 89 reminders created overall, of which 67 (75%) reminders were arrival trigger reminders and 22 (25%) reminders were departure trigger reminders (See

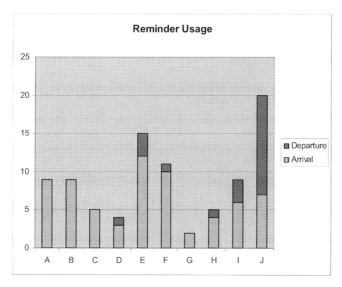

Figure 4. Reminder usage for each participant. 89 total reminders were created, 67 were arrival reminders and 22 were departure reminders. Participants A-E are students, and participants F-J are working professionals.

Figure 4). One of the main reasons we found for the smaller number of departure reminders is that many participants, after trying departure triggers for certain types of reminders (e.g., bring the book when you leave), found that the reminder came to their attention several kilometers away from where the reminder was needed. The problem is that a unique clique (see Section 3.2) could not be determined quickly enough as a person moved away from a location. Thus, departure reminders were generally not used and the tasks were accomplished with arrival reminders instead (e.g., pack book when you get home). This type of adaptive behavior is described further in Section 6.

Nineteen reminders (21%) were re-posted one or more times for a total of 63 re-postings. Reposting reminders occurred because either the reminder was triggered at the wrong location or the note was triggered at the right location, but could not be attended to at the time. Participant <I> reposted several reminders more than forty times to the same location to provide motivation to study every time he came home. Participant <E> occasionally visited a coffee shop close to the university campus on weekends. <E> posted a reminder on campus to be removed during the week when he went to campus, but it was falsely triggered during a visit to a nearby coffee shop. He therefore re-posted the reminder.

Although participants could post reminders wherever they had defined a place, 32 (36%) reminders were posted on a person's home and 39 (44%) reminders were posted on a person's workplace/campus. All of the participants reported in the post-study interviews that the majority of their desired reminders involved either the home or workplace/school. On one or two occasions, participants forgot to mark a place they had visited, preventing them from posting a reminder to that location when they wished. For example, <I> wanted to set a reminder for a place he went to once a week. During the first week of the study he forgot to mark that place, thus was unable to set a reminder for the following week. If the study was conducted for longer period of time, these initial setup issues would have a lower effect. A technical solution would be for the application to automatically log time stamped cell tower observations. A person could define a place at a later time by correlating a visited location with a specific time, and then the application could retrospectively reconstruct the clique from the cell tower logs.

The time lapsed between the posting and removing of a reminder varied from minutes to days. We can discern no patterns, whether across the subjects, places, etc., suggesting that there is little time-based correlation between when a person remembers to post a reminder and when the person's location permits the activity to be performed.

5.1 Self-Reported Usage Data

We implemented an on-device multiple-choice questionnaire that would appear on screen after a reminder notification. The questionnaire consisted of 4 questions that could be answered quickly with a few key presses. Where are you in relation to where this reminder should be delivered? Was this reminder notification expected? Did you remember this reminder before the notification? Has receiving this reminder changed what you are about to do? The responses to these questions helped us gather feedback about the timeliness of reminder notifications and behavioral changes with regards to the reminder. We did not always offer a questionnaire after each reminder notification to avoid it becoming an annoyance. If the questionnaire screen was shown (about 50% of the time), the participant had a choice to ignore the questionnaire, or to proceed with answering the questions. If the participant did not respond to the questionnaire within a two minute time interval, the form would disappear from the screen. 49 (36%) questionnaires were acknowledged, and of those, 34 (69%) were answered.

Figure 5 shows a table of the 34 questions and the number of responses in each category. The dominant responses in Figure 5a show that most reminders notifica-

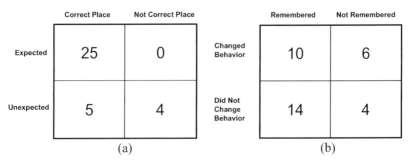

Figure 5. (a) Number of self reported responses about whether the reminder notification was expected and whether it was delivered at the correct place. **(b)** Self reported responses about if the reminder was remembered before the notification, and if the reminder changed what the participant was going to do.

tions were given at the correct place and the notification was anticipated. However, there were some reminders in which although the location was correct, it was delivered unexpectedly (e.g., on arrival instead of departure). Only four responses indicated that the reminder notification was not at the correct place, and hence unexpected. In Figure 5b, the horizontal dimension is whether the participant remembered the reminder before getting the notification. The vertical dimension represents if after being reminded, any behavioral changes occurred because of the reminder notification. The expected value of a reminder application is in reminding people about things that they have not otherwise remembered, and this is represented by 6 out of 10 non-remembered reminders causing a change in behavior. It is interesting though, that in 10 out of 24 cases where a reminder was for something that the user had already remembered, a change in behavior was nonetheless reported. This indicates that the Place-Its application was valuable as a motivation cue, beyond its memory-aid intent..

5.2   Classifying Place-It Note Usage

Psychology researchers have identified three general classes of prospective memory tasks: time-based, event-based, and activity-based [9,14]. Our application enables reminders in the event-based and activity-based classes. We classified the ways Place-It notes were used into 6 sub-categories, to analyze their function and use (See Figure 6). This is not meant to be a definitive classification of every reminder that a user might want to create, but simply provides an idea of how our application was

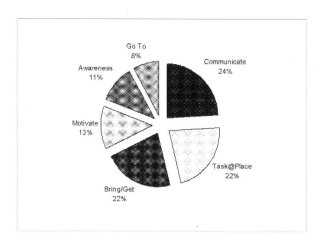

Category	Communicate	Task@Place	Bring/Get	Motivate	Awareness	Go To
Description	email, call, talk to a person	a task that can only be done at a specific place	Bring/get an item from a place	motivate to do a task	being aware of an activity	go to a place
Example	"Talk to Ken"	"Start Baking!"	"Bring Book"	"Study Greek"	"Check the time"	"Go to grocery store"

Figure 6. A classification of Place-It note usage into 6 categories.

used for the duration of the study. Some reminders could be interpreted to be in two or more categories; in these situations, participant feedback was used to disambiguate. The *goto* category maps directly to the activity-based class of reminders from psychology literature. The other categories are varying types of event-based reminders.

There are several noteworthy points in the frequency of the different types of reminders. The largest category is *communicate* reminders. These reminders involve emailing, calling, or talking to another person. This is somewhat surprising, since many forms of communication are not place-specific. An email can be sent from any location with Internet connectivity. Using mobile phones, calls can be made at any time as well. User feedback informed us that such reminders were typically created because, at the moment where the idea of communicating came to the user, they did not have enough time to actually perform this communication. This implies that location is being used as a reminder cue for other kinds of situational context (e.g., inactivity or cessation of an activity), which we expand on later.

Another surprise, given the inaccuracy of the location technology for departure reminders, was that *bring/get* reminders were tied for the second largest type. Participants considered this type of reminder important enough that they adapted to the limitations of the technology. Participant F created a reminder, "Bring metal case" to be triggered on arrival. Due to receiving the reminder, he would pack the metal case soon after he arrived home, thus not forgetting it when he left for work the next day.

Another unexpected significant type of Place-It usage was *motivate* reminders. These reminders did not necessarily have a high priority at the time of creation, but would sometimes increase with priority as time went on. They existed solely to motivate the person to perform a certain task such as "Study Greek" or "Go to the gym". Participant <I> would always re-post his motivation reminders after they were removed, considering them of low priority at the time of removal; however, as time for his Greek exam drew near, the motivation reminders became helpful in his time management.

6 Post-Study Responses and Discussion

6.1 Mobile Phones Offer Available, Convenient Reminder Creation and Delivery

Mobile phones provide a means of creating and delivering reminders that makes them attractive to users. We found that 8 of our 10 participants appreciated the consistent availability of location-based reminders through their mobile phone, and lessened their use of other reminder tools in favor of Place-Its.

Quote 1 <participant J>: *"Since I was out of town, I would think of things on the drive that I had to do when I got back and I'd put reminders on the phone. Even though I did remember what I had to do without the help of the reminder, it was a relief knowing I would've been reminded had I forgot."*

Participant <J> normally uses post-it notes or an electronic calendaring system to send herself reminders. However, in this situation, neither of these means were accessible to her, thus <J> found it useful to use Place-Its to create her reminder. In addition, having a reminder that would trigger after she came back to town was useful because Place-Its would interrupt her to display the reminder. With <J>'s current methods, it's possible had <J> forgotten the task, the reminder would have been overlooked. In our post-study interview <J> explained that she stopped using her current methods of reminders in favor of Place-Its due to its availability.

Quote 2 <participant E>: *"There are certain activities that my calendaring application is not particularly good at reminding me about. Especially to do something when I'm not near a computer. So getting reminders for these types of activities was a welcome behavior... [examples are] grocery shopping, and also when I'm leaving work I'm on my way out, done for the day, not liable to be checking email."*

The two methods that <E> uses for reminders are an electronic calendar for all reminders, and email messages for critical ones. Neither of these two methods allow <E> to trigger reminders when away from a computer, while Place-Its provided an always-available application. One of the successes was that on the way home, <E> was reminded to go grocery shopping, which would not have happened otherwise.

Quote 3 <participant F>: *"I didn't use my PDA much... it's much bulkier compared to just being able to use the phone"*

Although <F> normally uses his PDA for reminders, during the course of the two-week study, <F> found it more convenient to use the phone. <F> still carried his PDA with him by habit and used it for other functionality, but preferred Place-Its for reminders due to both its location capability and the fact that the phone was always within short range to use.

The convenience of mobile phones encouraged four participants, who may not have bothered to create a reminder in the past, to enter a Place-It for the sake of not forgetting it. As an interesting side note, some people found that entering a reminder helped reinforce their own memory to perform the task. One person said:

Quote 4 <participant B>: *"I would pull my phone out to silence it for class and [looking at it] would remember that a reminder would be coming."*

An important concern regarding the phone platform is the text input method. Many of the participants found text entry to take too much time even with predictive input support, so would resort to one or two word phrases. Those who wanted to input a grocery list found it easier to use Place-Its for the reminder to go to the grocery store, and have a separate paper list for the actual items. One possible solution to overcome these methods would be to use the voice and picture capabilities found on many phones today. This would enable quick voice memos, or snapshot pictures that would stimulate a person's memory about a reminder.

6.2 Location Provides an Indirect Cue for Other Context

The kinds of reminders posted and the way that they were posted strongly suggests that the location itself is not always important, but it is just a convenient proxy for context that is not as easily sensed or readily available.

Quote 5 <participant E>: *"I'm busy at work, so I don't want to make the call now, but I want to remember to call my sister when I get home"*

During the workday <E> was typically too busy to take the time to make a call to his sister. However, the phone call was of enough importance that he didn't want to forget about it. Since <E> knew that he would have more free time when he gets home, he set the reminder location for his home. The location itself was not important, but <E> knew that time will be more likely to be available when no longer at work. Motivational reminders are often similar in that the location has been chosen to catch the person in a particular frame of mind (or change a person's frame of mind). The location may afford that frame of mind, but in many reminders the "relevant" location was akin to "no longer at work or on the road."

Certain locations imply access to tools that may be used by the person in completing a specific task. These tools may offer services not innately tied to the location, but in the person's mind, the task can be completed there.

Quote 6 <participant F>: *"I was in another building at work, when I thought to myself I should create a status report e-mail to send to my boss concerning my progress on a recent project. Even though I would be back in about an hour, I decided to post the Place-It on the phone. When I came back to my building, the beep went off right as I got back to my desk. Looking at the Place-It, the e-mail then became the next thing I did."*

<F> needed to write an email at a time when he did not have access to the tools he needed to compose one. Knowing that he has a computer back in his office and that he will be there shortly, he set a Place-It for his office. Sending the email is not something that is innately tied to his office; he could very well send one from any place where he has computing facilities for email access. However, he is able to take advantage of some knowledge about his schedule for the rest of the day to set a reminder for a location known to provide the services he desires in a timely manner.

Similarly, location can also imply the presence of other people, but without a reasonable guarantee:

Quote 7 <participant C>: *"I made a reminder for myself to ask a lab mate about a class, and I got the reminder just as he walked into the lab... I set the Place-it for the lab because I figured he would be there."*

<D> was really looking for his lab mate when he set this Place-It, but realized that his labmate would probably be in the lab at some time. Using this foresight to his advan-

tage, he set a Place-It there, knowing that it would draw his attention at a place where he would probably be able to find the person of interest. Although many context-aware systems have supported buddy alerts, this behavior demonstrates how setting reminders on locations can be used to alert the user when someone of interest is nearby, without the explicit ability to sense when buddies are nearby. Given the nature of certain relationships between people, it is often likely to find someone of interest at a particular location within a large but acceptable time range. By using this knowledge, one can use a location-based reminder to essentially create a person proximity reminder.

Activity inference is another context-aware feature that has long been desired and seems to be supported to some degree by location-based reminders, with some help from the user. A general statement of the challenge is to determine what the user's goal is in a long-running activity. Consider inferring the activity, *going to Kevin's house.* When asked to explain the thought process behind setting a Place-It on departure from work to "call Kevin," <J> responded:

Quote 8 <participant J>: *"I set the place-it for departure because I knew when I would go to the guys' place after I left work. Even if I didn't go there directly, I knew I would go there pretty soon."*

When she set this reminder, <J> had some notion of what her activity would be later in the day when she left work. She knew that her schedule entailed going to the guys' place eventually and very likely when she left work. This allowed her to use a departure reminder as a mechanism for aiding the system in adequately inferring her activity. In this case, leaving work meant it was probable that she was heading to Kevin's place.

As cited earlier, departure reminders often have high accuracy requirements. Indeed, they can even require predictive power—really activity inference: which of the several times that someone leaves their office during the day is the last time, so that they should be reminded to bring a book? Inaccuracy almost becomes a feature: who wants to be reminded all afternoon? Time-constrained reminders could have helped, but our users used arrival reminders as a proxy—you cannot leave a place until you have arrived, after all.

6.3 Location-Based Reminders Are Useful

In light of the above remarks, it is understandable that participant comments regarding location-based reminders were generally positive. Two participants (F, J) requested to be future research subjects because they found Place-Its to be helpful in their daily activities. They also asked if we could build a version of Place-Its for their current mobile phone to use on a regular basis. Six participants (A, B, C, D, E, H) considered location-based reminders to be useful to them, and their use of Place-Its to be enjoyable. The remaining two participants (G, I) did not find location-based reminders to be helpful, stating that their lives revolve around a set time schedule. They only desired time-based reminders or did not need any reminders at all.

During our post-study interview we asked each participant to describe any problems they experienced with Place-Its. These responses generally fell into two categories. Four participants had problems with the application being too easy to exit, or crashing. They were sometimes unaware of these events, and hence missed reminders. More significantly, the other six participants said the location algorithm used by Place-Its was sometimes not accurate enough for their reminders. The participants would get the reminder, but not necessarily at the right location. This degree of this perception lessened over time as the participants adapted their behaviors. One participant, not surprisingly, asked for time-constrained reminders.

Due to the way location-based reminders were used and the relative inaccuracy of location-sensing in Place-Its, we cannot claim location itself is essential context, even as we find it to be useful for triggering reminders. More than anything, its ready availability admits opportunistic use by those who can map their relevant (but unsensed) context to anticipated, coarse, location cues. Indeed, the two participants who work by a set time schedule are achieving similar results by mapping their relevant context to time cues and modifying their behavior. Providing location-triggered reminders expands the palate of context affordances that people can appropriate to guide their activities, accommodating a wider range of personal organizational styles.

7   Conclusions and Future Directions

The prevalence of mobile phones and the pervasiveness of their networks makes them a promising platform for personal ubiquitous computing. Our findings from a two-week deployment of Place-Its help validate that location-based reminders can be useful even with coarse location-sensing capabilities. Notably, location was widely used as a cue for other contextual information that can be hard for any system to detect. On the whole, it appears that the convenience and ubiquity of location-sensing provided by mobile phones outweighs some of their current weaknesses as a sensing platform. This bodes well for the use of mobiles phones as a personal ubiquitous computing platform.

Our study revealed unexpected uses of location-aware reminders. We found that Place-It notes were often used for creating motivational reminders to perform activities that would vary in priority over time. This is similar to using post-it notes in highly visible areas for motivation. The locations for motivational reminders were often set at frequently visited places, such as 'home'. We also found that a majority of the uses for Place-Its involved communicating with people through a variety of media (*e.g.* email, phone). Communication is typically not tied to specific locations, implying that location is being used as a cue for other kinds of situational context.

As a first study, the results presented here are preliminary. Our results suggest a few application modifications that are worthy of further investigation. First, given the limited text entry mechanisms available on mobile phones, a way of associating audio messages or pictures with reminders could offer greater convenience, encouraging unique and more opportunistic use. Second, with an understanding now of how location affords certain classes of reminders, it would be interesting to investigate how adding time-constrained notifications changes user behavior. Third, research into more accurate and faster location sensing on mobile phones should reduce the need for users to adapt their reminders to the capabilities of the application.

Finally, to both account for the effects of inaccurate location sensing and naturally support the use of recurring reminders, we propose a change to the user interface. Rather than the application automatically removing a Place-It when it is detected and presenting it as an explicit reminder notification, the application would continuously display a list of nearby Place-Its as to-do items, sorted by proximity to the current location. The user would then explicitly pull down a Place-It when it is no longer relevant, rather than repost it if it is still relevant. Alerts could still be provided when location certainty is high.

Acknowledgements

Thanks to Candy Lam for help in performing this research. We also thank our anonymous reviewers and the participants in our user study. This work was funded in part by a gift from Intel Research.

References

1. http://www.europa.eu.int/comm/environment/civil/prote/112/112_en.htm
2. http://www.fcc.gov/911/enhanced/
3. Antifakos, S., Schwaninger, A., Schiele, B. Evaluating the Effects of Displaying Uncertainty in Context-Aware Applications. *Proceedings of the Sixth International Conference on Ubiquitous Computing (Ubicomp 2004)*, Springer-Verlag (2004) 54-69.
4. Beigl, M. MemoClip: A Location-Based Remembrance Appliance. *Personal and Ubiquitous Computing* 4(4), pp. 230-233.
5. Brown, P.J. The Stick-e Document: A Framework for Creating Context-Aware Applications. *Electronic Publishing* 8(2&3) 259-272.
6. DeVaul, R. W., Pentland, A., Corey, V. R. The Memory Glasses: Subliminal vs. Overt memory Support with Imperfect Information. *IEEE International Symposium on Wearable Computers*.
7. Dey, A.K. and Abowd, G. D. CybreMinder: A Context-Aware System for Supporting Reminders. *Intl. Symposium on Handheld and Ubiquitous Computing*, pp. 172-186. (2000)
8. Dey, A.K, Salber, D., Abowd, G.D. A Conceptual Framework and a Toolkit for Supporting the Rapid Prototyping of Context-Aware Applications. *Human-Computer Interaction, 16*. 2001.
9. Einstein, G.O. and McDaniel, M.A. Normal Aging and Prospective Memory. *Journal of Experimental Psychology: Learning, Memory, and Cognition*, 16, pp. 717-726. (1990)
10. Griswold, W.G., Shanahan, P., Brown, S.W., Boyer, R.T. ActiveCampus: Experiments in Community-Oriented Ubiquitous Computing. *IEEE Computer* 37(10), 73-80.
11. Hansson, R., Ljungstrand, P. The Reminder Bracelet: Subtle Notification Cues for Mobile Devices. *Extended Abstracts of CHI 2000*. ACM Press, New York, 2000; 323-324.
12. Hightower, J., Borriello, G. Location Systems for Ubiquitous Computing. *IEEE Computer* 34(8), 57-66.

13. Kaasinen, E. User Needs for Location-aware Mobile Services. *Personal and Ubiquitous Computing*, 2003. 7(1), 70-79.
14. Kvavilashvii, L. and Ellis, J. Varieties of Intention: Some Distinction and Classifications. *Prospective Memory-Theory and Applications.* Lawrence Erlbaum Associates, New Jersey.
15. Laasonen, K., Raento, M., Toivonen, H. Adaptive On-Device Location Recognition. *Proceedings of the 2nd International Conference on Pervasive Computing* (Pervasive 2004), Vienna, Austria, April 2004.
16. LaMarca, A., Chawathe, Y., Consolvo, S., Hightower, J., Smith, I., Scott, J., Sohn, T., Howard, J., Hughes, J., Potter, F., Tabert, J., Powledge, P., Borriello, G., Schilit, B., Place Lab: Device Positioning Using Radio Beacons in the Wild. *Proceedings of the 3rd International Conference on Pervasive Computing (Pervasive 2005)*, (Springer-Verlag). (2005)
17. Lamming, M. and Flynn M., "Forget-me-not: Intimate Computing in Support of Human Memory", *Proceedings of FRIEND21 '94, International Symposium on Next Generation Human Interface*, 1994, 125-128.
18. Li, K.A., Sohn, T., and Griswold, W.G. Evaluating Location-Based Reminders. Technical Report CS2005-0826, University of California, San Diego.
19. Marmasse, N., Schmandt, C. Location-aware information delivery with *comMotion. Proceedings of the 2nd International Symposium on Handheld and Ubiquitous Computing.* (2000), Bristol, England, 157-171.
20. Newman, N. J., Clark, A. F. Sulawesi: A Wearable Application Integration Framework. *Proceedings Of the 3rd International Symposium on Wearable Computers*, 1999, 170-171.
21. Rhodes, B.: The wearable remembrance agent: A system for augmented memory. In: *Proceedings of the 1st International Symposium on Wearable Computing*, Boston, MA, 1997. IEEE Press, 123-128.
22. Smith, I., Consolvo, S., Hightower, J., Hughes, J., Iachello, G., LaMarca, A., Scott, J., Sohn, T., Abowd, G. Social Disclosure of Place: From Location Technology to Communication Practice. *Proceedings of the 3rd International Conference on Pervasive Computing (Pervasive 2005)*, (Springer-Verlag). (2005)

Time, Ownership and Awareness: The Value of Contextual Locations in the Home

Kathryn Elliot, Carman Neustaedter, and Saul Greenberg

Department of Computer Science, University of Calgary
Calgary Alberta CANADA T2N 1N4
Tel: 1-403-220-6087
{elliotk, carman or saul}@cpsc.ucalgary.ca

Abstract. Our goal in this paper is to clearly delineate how households currently manage communication and coordination information; this will provide practitioners and designers with a more complete view of information in the home, and how technology embedded within the home can augment communication and coordination of home inhabitants. Through contextual interviews, we identify five types of communicative information: reminders and alerts, awareness and scheduling, notices, visual displays, and resource coordination. These information types are created and understood by home inhabitants as a function of *contextual locations* within the home. The choice of location is important to the functioning of the home, and is highly nuanced. Location helps home inhabitants understand *time*: when others need to interact with that information, as well as *ownership*: who this information belongs to and who should receive it. It also provides them with *awareness* of the actions and locations of others. These findings resonate and further elaborate on work by other researchers.

1 Introduction

As computing devices become smaller, inexpensive and wirelessly interconnected, they will be embedded within our everyday environments [4,5]. In this new genre of ubiquitous computing, researchers suggest that the home can be augmented by making it more connected to other places, and more aware of its inhabitants [5,9,11]. The home can somehow display information so that people can access it anytime and anywhere. Example information includes the well-being of distant family members, schedules of home dwellers, weather forecasts, recipes, videos and music. Benefits touted for such pervasive information include increased feelings of connectedness to loved ones, better time management and more entertainment options [7,10,19].

Our own focus is in *communication and coordination information for the home,* i.e., information that people use to communicate and coordinate with household members (including themselves) and with the outside world, where the home serves as the communication center. We include within this category any communication item used within the home or taken from the home into the outside world. For example, notes, lists, newsletters, schedules, calendars, voice mail, email, snail mail, and instant messages are all pieces of home communication information.

M. Beigl et al. (Eds.): UbiComp 2005, LNCS 3660, pp. 251-268, 2005.

The vast majority of households already cope with large quantities of this information, mostly through a variety of tacit mechanisms. The technological opportunity is to somehow augment the home by supplying this information for display and interaction through digital forms. Designers and researchers are even now proposing how we can do this, e.g., [7,19]. However, without a great deal of care, inappropriate designs could lead to information overload [8], ineffective uses, and mismatched audiences. Understanding how such information is currently managed in the home will help us make more educated design decisions.

Several researchers have already begun to explore various aspects of communication in the home, e.g., [1,2,3,7]. In particular, Crabtree et al's study identifies "prime sites" in the home for introducing ubiquitous technology to support communication [2,3]. They found that space in the home "...does not simply 'contain' action then, but is interwoven with action in various functional ways." [15] That is, information-related places in the home fall into three categories based on the type of activities that take place there: places where information lives, places where information is left or displayed for others and places where information is created or reworked.

Our own study, described below, uses a different method and takes place in a different culture. Yet it validates these findings: we saw the same types of places, and the same interweaving of space and action. While valuable as a replication, our results also add to this previous work in three important ways:

1. We describe what types of communication information are present in the homes we studied, for which information systems can be designed;
2. We discuss how places (sites) are initially selected and established, as well as how they are grouped throughout the home; and,
3. We extend the notion of places by investigating what the location of a piece of information tells people about it, and how this meta-data and context helps household members cope with and organize communication information. That is, information spaces are not only interwoven with action and activity (as Crabtree et al. describes [2,3,15]), but are also interwoven with *time, ownership* and *awareness*.

The paper unfolds by first describing how we used contextual interviews as the basis for our study. Subsequent sections summarize our interpretation of our interviews; we describe the types of communication information seen in the homes, and articulate the role locations have on information and interaction. These are illustrated by examples drawn from the study. After comparing our results to related work, we conclude with implications for future home information systems.

2 The Study

We used semi-structured contextual interviews to gain a thorough understanding of how households and individuals currently handle communication information in the home: what communication information is present and manipulated by inhabitants, and the role meta-data about each message plays in how it is handled.

Participants. We recruited and interviewed 29 people (16 female, 13 male) within the context of 10 different households, all in the same large Canadian city. We intentionally selected diverse households to provide a broad range of household size, composition and demographics. We interviewed roommates, common-law partners, divorced parents with shared custody, married parents with young children, working couples with teenagers and retired couples with adult children. Participants included 5 teenagers, 16 young-mid adults (ages 20–39) and 8 middle-aged adults (ages 40–60). For pragmatic reasons, we did not interview children under the age of 12. Homes ranged widely in size and architecture from small one bedroom apartments to large houses. Participants were from a wide variety of backgrounds: students, retirees, programmers and office administrators. Most were moderately technically inclined.

Method. We used a series of semi-structured interviews that took place in each household's home context. We asked all members of the household to show us what communication information they used, and where this information was located in the home. We provided a deliberately vague and open definition of communication information so that we could see what they considered it to be. We toured the home and photographed this information within their locations.

Guiding Questions. We found that people would naturally provide a four part answer when generally asked about a specific piece of communication information:

1. *What is it?* What is this information about, what is it related to?
2. *Whose is it?* Who needs to pay attention to it? Should I pay attention to it? Is it mine? Who else needs to see it?
3. *What needs to be done with it?* What actions need to be taken?
4. *When do I/others need to interact with it?* Is it urgent? At what point in time will I/others need to interact with this information?

For example, a typical statement would be "Well, that's a phone message *(question #1)* for my mom *(#2),* and she needs to call them back right away *(#3)* so she needs to see it when she comes home. *(#4)* ". Our goal for an interview was to understand a person's explanation about the type of communication information, its medium, and its location. These explanations suggest what meta-data people use to help them decide how to handle the information they come across. Depending on what participants showed us and their responses, our interview questions then focused on understanding what kinds of information were present, why participants had chosen the various information locations, and when participants would typically access or interact with the information.

Analysis and Results. We analyzed interviews and observations, using an open coding technique to reveal similarities and differences between participant households. In general, we found that in spite of the diversity of our participant demographics, household compositions and home architectures, there were many commonalities.

We discuss our results in the remainder of this paper. Due to lack of space, we do not provide full details of our analysis. Rather, we present our main findings and use actual examples drawn from our participants as well as related work to illustrate what we saw. The next three sections outline the specific types of communication information found in the home, identify the media used to handle each type of communication information, and investigate the fundamental role that *locations* play and how they help people cope with communication information. For simplicity, from this point forward we use the terms *communication information* and *messages* interchangeably. In Section 6 we will describe how these results and analysis confirm and extend related work.. This is followed by its implications to practitioners.

3 Communication Information Types

In analyzing our data, we saw many similarities in the kinds of communication information present in the home, in spite of the diversity of the homes, their layouts, and the people within them. We found five categories of communication information in the home distinguished in terms of how the information was used or its intended purpose:

1. *Reminders and Alerts* are intended or used as a memory trigger.
2. *Awareness and Scheduling* information provides knowledge of the activities and whereabouts of household members.
3. *Visual Displays* are to be shared or admired.
4. *Notices* provide household members with information about activities or people outside the home.
5. *Resource Coordination* information is used to coordinate the sharing of common household resources.

These five categories are not mutually exclusive; a single piece of information may fall into several groupings. For example, a shared grocery list could be both a to-do list (Reminders and Alerts), and a way to coordinate sharing of duties (Resource Coordination). Finally, these categories describe and contain all of the instances of communication and coordination information we saw in our participant households. Every household we interviewed had at least one and usually many more examples of each category. The categories are discussed below in detail.

Reminders and Alerts. The most common type of information present in the home is *Reminders and Alerts*. This category includes anything intended or used as a memory trigger, e.g., to-do lists, reminder notes or emails, instant messages, or warning tags. We saw three sub-types of this information: *reminders* that remind people about things they know but may forget, *to-do* lists that contain a list of things that must be done and *alerts* that remind or inform people of critical information.

This category is highly time-sensitive. The goal of messages in this category is to convey information at the right time, whether this time is related to the urgency of the message (e.g., a reminder to call the shop right away, since it closes early), or to its relevancy (e.g., remembering to return a DVD on your way to work, or remembering what errands you need to run on the way home).

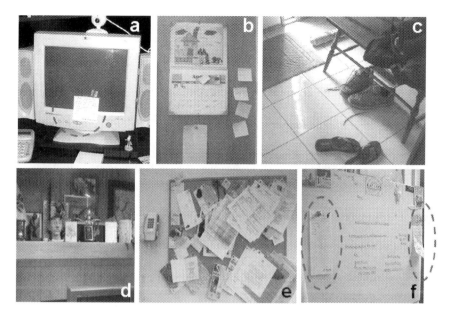

Fig. 1: Information Types

An example of this category is visible in Figure 1a. Here, a mother wanted to remind her son that he is to put dinner in the oven when he arrives home from school. She placed this note on the son's computer monitor because there is some urgency to it. To foreshadow the role of locations, she knows that her son will see this at the right time, as his routine on coming home is to go to his computer to check his email. An example of an alert is a post-it note stuck on a container of food in the fridge, alerting a roommate with allergies to the presence of nuts. It is an alert as the roommate needs to see the message before she considers eating it.

Awareness and Scheduling. The 2nd most common type of communication information present in homes concerns Awareness and Scheduling. *Awareness information* is used to maintain an understanding of the presence and activities of household members, e.g., this information is used to know who is currently home. *Scheduling information* includes items such as one's calendar activities or time schedule, e.g., what time someone will be returning to the house. Both awareness and schedule information involve knowing details about the day-to-day routines of household members.

While Awareness and Scheduling information is not as time sensitive as Reminders and Alerts, it is critical to the smooth functioning and micro-coordination of the household and the comfort of its inhabitants. Its goal is to provide people with knowledge of the whereabouts and activities of others. For example, we saw that this information is particularly important for families with children, where parents need to coordinate who drives the children to their various activities. A more mundane example is knowing or deciding when dinner will be served. While some of this information is left explicitly (e.g., as a note in a central common location such as the kitchen table), other times it is left implicitly through routine actions and gathered peripherally (e.g., the presence or absence of cars or shoes).

Figure 1b illustrates a common scheduling artifact, a family calendar. On this calendar, events for members of the household are explicitly written down so that they are not missed or forgotten. Using the example above, this may include a ride schedule so parents know who needs to be picked up and where. Figure 1c shows an entryway to the house where guests leave their shoes, and how the presence or absence of shoes acts as an implicit awareness message. Since members of this household enter through the garage, they know that shoes in the front entrance mean that guests are present in the home; they may even be able to identify guests from their shoes.

Visual Displays. Household members often set up information to be shared, noticed and/or admired. Examples include the display of birthday cards, postcards, pictures, awards, or children's artwork. We call this category of information Visual Displays.

As an example, Figure 1d shows a mantle in a family room containing pictures, birthday cards, awards and medals, as well as children's artwork and souvenirs. These are all pieces of infrequently updated information that the family wishes to display in a public location, where it attracts the attention and comments of both household members and guests. Other examples include awards on the mantle, postcards on the fridge door, birthday cards on the hall table, and funny comics in the computer room.

Notices. The goal of Notices is to provide household members with information about activities or contacts outside the home. The most common example of this category is phone messages. Notices also include newsletters, forms or notices from school, letters, etc. This information may be very time sensitive (e.g., a school notice that needs to be signed right away, or an urgent phone message) or not at all (e.g., the latest church bulletin). The defining characteristic of a notice is that it comes from something outside the home. Figure 1e shows a family bulletin board covered in notices and newsletters from work, school and children's activities. Phone messages are seen in the top left hand corner of the board. This information keeps the family aware of what is happening with their outside activities and contacts. As with Visual Displays, this category of information is often shared between home members and publicly displayed; however, its content is more practical and more frequently updated.

Resource Coordination. This final category includes any information used to manage the sharing of a common resource. For example, Resource Coordination items may include contact information, financial data, charts for sharing chores, bills to be split among roommates, or notes on food that is not to be eaten by others. Items from this category are less common, but still present in every home. Figure 1f illustrates how two roommates coordinate the sharing of groceries: on the left of the fridge door is a shopping list; on the right side is a receipt for the recent grocery purchases.

In summary, understanding the types of information is the first step to knowing how to handle a particular piece of information. Information type is part of the answer to our first question: *'what is it?'* We will see that this is not enough: other factors come into play to help people understand information and how it should be handled.

Information Media. People choose many different kinds of paper-based and electronic media to communicate these five information types. When people have a choice of media to use, we found that the information type did not usually determine the medium selected for a message. Instead, the selection of medium was based on the convenience and comfort level of the medium for the sender and recipient.

Placement of information also plays a large role; the affordances of where the message needs to be placed will determine the media used. If (say) a note needs to be left at the family computer, appropriate media choices could include a sticky note (for sticking on the monitor), or typing a note into an opened text editor on the display.

The medium by itself rarely helps household members answer any of our guiding questions. The answer to these questions, and the ability to cope quickly with the information, is provided by richer means—*contextual locations*—as described next.

4 Contextual Locations

Every household we looked at had a set of key locations (places) that inhabitants used for displaying, interacting, organizing and coping with communication information. We found that these places within the home were more than they initially seem to be. No matter what the answers were to *what is it, who is it for, when do they need it* or *what needs to be done* for a given piece of information, when we asked people "How do you know?" they would almost always reply with some variation of "Well, because it is on the fridge" or "…in the doorway" or "…on her placemat". *People use placement to filter and manage communication information in their homes.*

These places provide household members with important meta-data about the communication information located there. This meta-data includes **time** information, **ownership** information and **awareness** information. Places are what enable people to answer our guiding questions for each message: *whose is it, what needs to be done with it,* and *when do I/others need to interact with it.* In this way, space is interwoven not only with action [15], but also with this rich context and meta-data about the messages placed there. We call these places **Contextual Locations**, since they provide the information in them with context, and therefore richer meaning.

We will first describe how places for information are initially selected. We then describe the ways these chosen contextual locations afford time, ownership and awareness to the information placed there.

Location Placement in the Home. We consider contextual locations to include any place where communication information was placed. These could be static (e.g., the kitchen table) or dynamic (e.g., a day planner carried in a purse). The number of locations in a home varied widely. One participant household had only four locations they used for communication information, while another had 23 separate locations. The average number of locations per household was just over 15; in fact, 60% of our households had between 13 and 17 locations.

The number of distinct communication information locations per household appears to be determined by two separate factors. The first is the house size: we found that the larger the home, the more locations present. The smallest home we studied had the fewest locations and the largest had the most. The second factor is the number of independent adults in the household. The presence of children does increase the number of locations, but not as significantly as the presence of another adult. For example, a household consisting of a divorced mother and her 15 year old son had far fewer locations than a similar sized home inhabited by two adult roommates. However, couples tended to have fewer locations than two unmarried friends or roommates, because they typically had very entwined lives.

The number and placement of these locations is part of the home ecology, where it is a shared household understanding that develops over time. To illustrate, one participant household contained a group of roommates who had been living together for only a few weeks. While each had a good understanding of places for their individual information, the shared locations were not yet well formed or understood. Insufficient time had passed for meaning and use of these locations to evolve.

Through their everyday routines, households implicitly select locations in order to provide answers to the four information questions. These locations develop social meaning over time, and become a strong shared language in the home. People rely on their knowledge of home routines (their own and those of others) as well as the placement of main traffic paths and common areas to find suitable places for information.

Pathways and Routines. Information locations tend to group themselves along pathways through the house [2], for instance the path from the front door to the kitchen. Since these are routes most of the household will pass through over the course of the day, they are chosen as places to leave the information people need to or want to see. Part of this is derived from familiarity, where people know the routines of other household members—what they do when they come home, where they go, where they leave things like keys or purses—and use this knowledge in deciding where to leave messages. As Tolmie et al. [18] found "Routines are resources for action, and knowledge of others' routines can be resources for interaction."

In one of our households, the teenage son enters through the front door, passes through the kitchen, and then goes down to the basement. Parents leave notes for him on the kitchen counter since he has to pass by it on his way to the basement stairs. Knowledge of his routine, as well as the pathway he takes from the entrance way to the basement, meant that this was the logical place for this information. *Households use their knowledge of routines and pathways to select information placement.*

Once these locations are established however, they themselves become an element in daily routines. For example, many of our participants would describe locations they would explicitly check for information as part of their routine upon arriving home. These would include locations such as the answering machine or the kitchen table. *Information locations may create or establish new routines.*

Constellations. Areas also tend to be grouped. One communication area will normally cause other ones to form nearby, since it is often convenient to have different kinds of communication information in close proximity. We call these location groupings *constellations,* since they consist of many unique locations linked by common activities or subjects. For example, if the kitchen counter is used to organize coupons and flyers, other locations such as the family grocery list will usually be nearby. Constellations are most often present in common, frequently visited areas of the house, such as the kitchen, family room, entrance way, etc.

In addition, communication media and technology such as phones and computers also attract communication information. Since this technology is less portable, information typically comes to them. Since locations group together as we described above, constellations will often form around these areas. For example, for obvious reasons phone messages usually go next to the phone. Calendars are also usually near the phone, so that people can check their schedules when making plans with others. Other types of information, such as school newsletters, are needed near the calendar as they augment its information. This creates an information constellation around the phone. *Information locations tend to group themselves so that other relevant information and useful technology is nearby.*

Location Attributes and Proximity. The attributes of a location affect both how suitable it is for information display and the kinds of information left or placed there. For instance, it would make very little sense to organize school handouts by pinning them up on the wall in the bedroom. Information would not be at hand when it was needed, and important events or letters might get missed. It is much more likely that these handouts will be stacked in piles on the kitchen counter, because it is flat, and they can be moved around easily. As a common, frequently visited place, the kitchen counter is a location where everyone who needs this information can get at it.

There is also the issue of relevance—information related to something needs to be near it, so the media will be chosen to adapt to the location, as discussed earlier. Phone messages will often be left on sticky notes near the wall phone; shopping lists on the fridge will be magnetic, etc. *Places in the home will be repurposed as information locations to meet people's need for organization.*

Visibility Versus Practicality. The fitness of a location for communication often dominates other seemingly more practical factors. For example, it may be more practical to put new information in a location that has the space for it instead of an already heavily used information-crowded location. But this is not done. For example, there may be ample space in the basement for school handouts or church newsletters, but because the basement is not a commonly frequented place, information might be missed. Instead, it is added to the already busy central bulletin board. While it takes up much needed space, competes for attention, and gets in the way, it is more easily accessed. A second example would be placing a DVD that needs to be returned on the first stair leading down to the entryway as all household members will see it (and perhaps trip over it) as they go by, even though it might be less hazardous to leave it by the TV. *Location has such great value in terms of providing organization and relevance that it overrides more practical considerations.*

5 Time, Ownership and Awareness

The above attributes and groupings described how people choose locations to communicate with members of their household; these locations become part of the household's shared language. Next, we will see how choice of location adds valuable information to each message as meta-data regarding *time, ownership* and *awareness*.

Fig. 2: Urgent message from mother to son   **Fig. 3**: Envelopes to be mailed placed with keys

5.1 Time

One primary way locations add information is in timing, where time attributes—urgency, relevance, when it needs to be seen or used, the dynamics of the information—are all conveyed by the location in which the information is placed. This helps people answer the question *when do I/others need to interact with this information.*

Urgency and Relevance. There is a definite correlation between location choice, and when information will be needed or when it should be seen. One of the most frequently stated reasons for location choice by our participants was the need for the information to be seen at a certain time. This time could be when one eats breakfast, or leaves the house in the morning, or sits down to watch TV. People use their knowledge of the routines of themselves and others to know where to put information so that it is seen in a timely way.

Household members use this knowledge to convey urgency in a message, to make sure information is at hand when needed and to provide a type of priority system for themselves and others. For example, messages from a mother to her teenage son were usually left near the computer upstairs, where the mother knew it would be seen at some point. However, as seen in Figure 2, she would place urgent notes on the TV screen instead, as she knew her son would surely see it as soon as he returned home, since the first thing he does after school is watch TV.

This information also works for recipients of information. Household members know when there may be messages for them at certain locations. For instance, upon arriving home from school or work, people typically have a set of places they will check either implicitly or explicitly for information. If there is nothing in these locations, they assume there is nothing they need to address.

As another example, the placement of information is very frequently used to create timely reminders. Figure 3 shows how household members leave things that need to be mailed with one person's wallet and keys (e.g., the letter tucked into the wallet), itself a part of the key rack constellation, so that he sees them when he picks up his keys to leave in the morning. This type of reminder, done by leaving things where they will be noticed at the right time, was common to all households. *Locations provide a vital means for people to convey time-related relevance and urgency.*

Information Dynamics. We also found that information will change location over time as its dynamics change. This includes relevance to other messages, whether or not actions associated with that information have been taken, whether the message is still useful, and its temporality (e.g., is it a new message or an old one).

We saw that as information becomes less relevant or is dealt with, it is often moved to a new location. For example, when bills first arrive in the home, they are usually sorted and left for the person who pays them. This person will then open them, and move them to a 2nd location, for example, the computer, in order to remember to pay them online. Once the bills have been paid, they are moved to a 3rd location for storage, a filing cabinet for example. This is true of much information that moves through the home—postcards and pictures may be placed in one location until everyone has looked at them, then in another place for long term storage or display.

Fig. 4: Information dynamics

For example, in one household, members left phone messages as sticky notes on the outside of a cupboard door above the main household phone (Fig. 4a). After dealing with a message, the member may throw it out. However, if the member needs to keep the message, e.g., contact information that one does not wish to lose, it may be placed on the inside of the cupboard door for a kind of longer term common archive (Fig. 4b). The household knows that messages on the inside of the door are there for storage, while those on the outside still need to be dealt with. *In this way, locations provide a sense of the dynamics of the information.*

5.2 Ownership

One of the most important and most pervasive ways in which we saw location used was to implicitly or explicitly attach ownership to information. Not all information within the home is relevant to all members, so households use locations to define who information belongs to. This allows people to not only manage complexity, but to answer the questions *whose information is this* and *what needs to be done with it.*

Spaces. Each location within the home has an owner—this could be either the person who the space explicitly belongs to (e.g., a child's bedroom) or an implicit owner (e.g., Mom always works in that spot at the kitchen table, so it has become her spot). The knowledge of who a space belongs to is used to not only decide where to leave messages, but also gives members an understanding of which messages belong to them, and which information they are expected to act upon. Ownership of the space implies ownership of the information and responsibility for it.

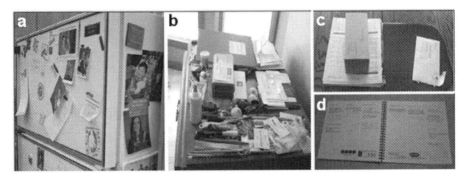

Fig. 5: Spatial Ownership

We found four main subtypes of location ownership within homes: public spaces, public subset spaces, personal spaces, and private spaces. *Public spaces* are those owned by everyone in the home. For example, the main house phone or the fridge door are usually considered public spaces, and messages affixed or near it may be for anyone. Figure 5a shows a fridge door used as a public space, where everyone can see it, place items on it, and interact with those items.

Public subset spaces are those that are public, but only to a subset of household members. Couples within a mixed household or parents in a family home typically have public subset spaces: spaces that are public and shared by them, but that do not belong to others in the home. Figure 5b shows a desk shared by parents in one of our participant homes. The parents leave a shared calendar for each other to see and use, but they know that their two adult sons do not look at, write on or otherwise interact with it. The sons know that this calendar is just for their parents because it is located in their parents' space. However, if they have events that they want their parents to note, they may leave a note for them with the calendar.

The other two types of spaces belong to individuals, where information within them are understood to be for the owner only. The first type is *personal spaces*: publicly visible spaces intended for only one individual. These could be the door to a bedroom, a placemat at the kitchen table, etc. Other members of the house will leave information in these places for the owner, and the owner will leave information there for themselves. Figure 5c shows one person's 'personal placemat' containing items placed there by that person for their own use. Yet because it is publicly accessible, others may leave things there for this person to see and act upon.

The final type is *private spaces,* intended for only one individual and not publicly visible or usable by others: day timers, purses, bedroom bulletin boards, etc. Information left in private spaces by its owner are usually personal reminders, personal scheduling and contact information. Its owner typically does not expect others to see information in these locations, such as the personal agenda of one household member illustrated in Figure 5d.

Knowing who the space belongs to gives household members a quick way to understand whether or not the information located there is something they should pay attention to. It also helps them decide where to leave information that others need to be aware of or take action on. *Spatial ownership (implicit or explicit) indicates or implies information ownership or information action responsibility.*

Spatial ownership may also vary by time or activity. For instance, O'Brien et al. [14] found that users of a technology would often 'own' or control the space around it. For example, someone watching TV in the living room temporarily controls that space, and may displace other activities taking place in that room, such as a noisy board game, or someone wishing to study. We found that if this shift in ownership is routine, information placement may become a part of it. In Figure 2, we saw our earlier example of a mother leaving an urgent note for her son on the screen because she knows that he will watch TV soon after he gets home from school. He owns the TV space at this specific time, so notes needing to be seen at that time and pertaining to him will be left there. He also knows that notes stuck on the TV screen at this time are his. *Spatial ownership may have routine variations based on time and activity.*

Visibility and Privacy. We also found that the visibility of the different locations within the home implies not only information ownership but also the privacy level of the message. Information that household members do not need or necessarily want others to see will be placed in locations that are less visible and therefore more private. Information to be shared with others (e.g., awards, pictures, messages to all) is put in the highly visible and publicly accessible locations. Household members use this in order to protect their own privacy and to protect that of others when it is needed. For example, a husband may leave a message for his wife from the doctor tucked in her purse, rather than on the kitchen table where their houseguest may see it. They use this knowledge to know when information has been placed somewhere for sharing, or when this information is more personal and sensitive. *The visibility of the location of a piece of information implies its privacy level.*

Actions. The location of a piece of information implicitly attaches intended or expected actions to it. Often information is placed in a certain location so that a member of the household will know they are expected to do something with it (also observed by Crabtree et al. [2]). Using previously mentioned examples, this may be a letter to be mailed placed by car keys, or a stack of bills to be paid placed by the computer.

Seeing a message in a certain location lets people know what they are expected to do with it. This may be a simple reminder to oneself, as in the example of a person putting a video to be returned by the door, so they can see it as they leave and infer that it is ready to be returned. This is one direct way space is interwoven with action, as in Crabtree et al's Coordinate Displays [2, 3].

Location ownership indicates responsibility for these actions. People will place information for others in locations that "belong" to that person as a request for action. For example, a child may place a school notice for their parent to sign on the parent's desk. Personal reminders are often left in personal or even private locations. Action triggers placed in public areas, such as the DVD return example above, can be taken care of by any household member. *The location of information implies intended actions and responsibility for those actions.*

5.3 Awareness

Finally, locations include meta-data for communication information by providing awareness information for family members. Awareness information for home inhabitants is very important to people for scheduling, coordination and comfort, as described by Neustaedter et al. [13].

Presence The presence or absence of an object from its routine location provides information, especially awareness information. For instance, many of our participants mentioned knowing whether or not someone was home by the presence or absence of their cars in the garage or on the street. What shoes were in the entry way or what keys were on the key rack was also frequently cited as a way of knowing who was around, including whether or not guests were there.

Figure 6 shows how one of the participant households evolved a particularly rich system for handling awareness information. Each member of the household would wear different colored slippers while in the main floor of the house, as it was tiled and cold on bare feet. These slippers would be left in the main entryway (Fig. 6a) when the wearer was not in, or at the foot of the stairs when they were upstairs in the carpeted area of the home (Fig. 6b). In this way, family members always knew who was home, and their general location in the house. *The presence of an object in a routine location can provide information to household members.*

Fig. 6: Slippers indicate presence and location.

Monitoring The above assignment of actions through locations combined with the information gathered through the presence or absence of artifacts also works as a form of internal monitoring. Household members know whether others have completed their tasks because they can see what information is present in which locations. This is discussed by several previous authors, e.g. [6,7,18]. Harper et al. [6] calls this workflow control or workflow management. While the home is definitely not as work oriented as the office, there are still jobs that must be done to keep the household running smoothly. One example is a wife seeing that her husband has not paid the bills yet since they are still in a pile on the corner of the desk, instead of being filed. She knows he has been busy, so she takes on the job of paying them herself. He then knows she has done this because the bills have been moved. A second example [6] is parents placing their teenager's cell phone bill in the doorway to his bedroom to make sure he sees it. Once they know he has been home and has therefore seen it, they can then ask if he has paid it – he has become accountable for it because they know he has to have seen it. *Household members use locations to monitor and help each other.*

6 Confirming and Extending Related Work

The findings of our study confirm and extend what others have seen. The most relevant related work is by Crabtree et al. [2, 3], whose publications motivated us to find out more about the value of locations in the home. Our approach and Crabtree et al's differed. We used contextual interviews as opposed to participant logs; we studied different household types, and we were working with North American families rather than British ones. In spite of these methodological and participant differences, we found that the concept of contextual location we observed in our households goes hand in hand with the three activity places described by Crabtree et al. [2, 3]. Our idea of ownership and how it is exploited extends their idea of *coordinate displays*, i.e., places where information is left for others. Our idea of constellations are particular ways that their *ecological habitats* (places where information lives) are formed and used. Their notion of *activity centres* (places where information is created or worked with) are another way of describing the act of manipulating information within these locations. All are enhanced by our explanation of why people choose to leave things in certain places. Thus, part of our work confirms their findings. This confirmation is valuable to practitioners as it validates and adds richness to Crabtree et al's results and generalizes the work to a broader audience.

However, we stress that we have built upon Crabtree et al's previous work in three significant ways. First, we identified the types of communication information present in the home, i.e., reminders and alerts, awareness and scheduling, notices, visual displays, and resource coordination. While they show instances of these in their examples, we classify them as generalizable categories that developers can design for.

Second, we described how these places are initially selected by the household (constellations, pathways and routines), and how they are distributed through the home not only in space but in time. This is important as designers can now not only determine what types of places should contain ubiquitous computing technology, but also where these places could be located within the home.

Finally, Crabtree's notion of space being interwoven with action [2,3,15] is extended by *contextual locations* to describe space as being interwoven with not only action and activity, but also with time, ownership and awareness. Our work looks to explain why inhabitants would select one coordinate display (for instance) over another coordinate display, and what these choices mean. This provides a more complete picture of the management of communication information in the home.

We have also confirmed and added richness and nuance to other related work concerning the specific ways such locations help us. Hindus et al. [7] and Harper et al. [6] described how the presence or absence of articles in specific locations, (e.g., a bill to be paid) is used by family members to monitor and help each other complete the tasks needed to keep the household running smoothly. Taylor and Swan investigated organizational systems in the home, and saw that the locations of informational artifacts could act as a trigger for conversation or serve as a physical point of reference for planning. We expand those ideas, looking at what these different locations can mean to household members, along with how they are established [16] [17].

7 Practitioner Implications and Design Opportunities

Our work is intended to provide a more complete view of home communication information management than has previously been reported. Our study found that communication in the home involves a rich and highly nuanced use of information, routines, and locations. All findings have implications for the design of ubiquitous or context-aware technologies for augmenting communication and coordination in the home, and for practitioners who want to better understand the home environment.

Existing Communication Technology. Our results point towards problems or weaknesses in existing technologies. While we did see many instances of electronic communication being used in the home, and these were included in our study, they were almost always supplemented by some sort of paper media – a sticky note reminding someone to read an email or respond to a phone message, a printed schedule from a web page etc. Electronic media currently cannot be situated in the home in the same way as paper media, and thus do not have the same value to household members.

For example, although email has many advantages over regular paper-mail, it has trouble replacing it because it does not provide the same physical affordances seen in our examples [6]. Other current communication technologies, such as electronic messaging, file and reminder systems also do not currently have the location affordances needed to fully replace physical ones. For example, while there are many commercial reminder programs available and in use, they do not include the location meta-data that home users need, and thus are poor replacements for (say) the scribbled note left with car keys or atop shoes. Filing systems on personal computers are impoverished as locations. A person may file something in a folder, and then quickly forget where it is. And since a person cannot flick through digital files to look for a picture on a handout she remembers, or know that it is in the stack near the coffee maker, it is hard to quickly re-find it. In addition, because of its history as an office machine, the PC is not currently well designed for domestic use, and is usually placed in an area that is isolated from the family's main activity centres [12].

Of course, electronic systems can contain the same raw information, and provide many advantages over paper based systems: distribution over a network, searching and sorting capabilities, etc. Yet none have the meta-data we saw in contextual locations readily available. There is no way of attaching urgency, relevance or awareness information to these types of electronic messages. Exploiting ownership is difficult, as ownership boundaries are rigid and access is often limited by passwords. This loses the richness of visible locations, be they personal or shared, as well as the ability to monitor other household acts for awareness. Thus the benefits gained by integrating existing technology into home communication are currently tempered or minimized by their inability to use or replace the physical affordances of locations.

Design and Research Opportunities. Given the richness of existing practices of communication within the home, design of appropriate technologies appears daunting. For example, it is hard to imagine technology that can replace the richness and flexibility of the sticky note, with its ability to be conveniently placed at any location. Yet opportunities abound. The types of communication information we identified can help designers target areas where the most value can be received from new systems, and what kinds of information these new systems could integrate.

Knowing the value of locations will provide designers with new uses and goals for current technology. For example, a movable projector system as described in [10] could be used to display electronic messages in location-appropriate places. This kind of system would allow designers to go beyond physical world functionality, for instance by adding in the ability to place messages appropriately in particular home locations from work. It could even be an extension of a current instant messaging application. Another possibility includes the integration of displays and sensors into already meaningful home locations, so that electronic messages could be automatically displayed in appropriate locations. Messages could even migrate if, for instance, a person for whom there is an urgent message is sensed near a different display than the one initially chosen for the message. These 'smart' messages thus know about contextual locations and exploit routines and understandings already in place.

The Value of Location. It is now obvious that having all information available through some kind of monolithic computer application accessed through a conventional display misses all the nuances of location placement. People will not know where the information is, will not know what they have to deal with at the moment, and will not be reminded at appropriate times. Locations are used on such a large scale within the home that they cannot be ignored. It is key to how people deal with the ever-growing information pool they have available to them. Locations need to be valued not just as a place in which to work with or to display information, but also as a spatial means of providing it with context, value, and interaction opportunities. This means that if and when designers look at integrating technology systems into the home, they need to provide this meta-data either through physical locations, or through some kind of digital replacement. As home inhabitants add meaning when they select the locations over time, locations cannot be hardwired into the home except in obvious cases, e.g., the fridge door or the telephone as a likely neighborhood.

Locations are not the only solution for design dilemmas; however, they do provide a very rich, intuitive way for people to cope with information. People already understand the semantics of location within the home. It would be more difficult to move into a design that did not support this very natural tendency, especially in the home environment where people are resistant to change and to technology.

These recommendations are intended as preliminary and general suggestions based on our study results. Future work includes developing more specific recommendations to further increase their value to designers and practitioners.

To Conclude. We offer four main contributions from the results of our study that add understanding to how people currently handle communication information in the home. First, we validate Crabtree et al's assertion [2,3,15] that information spaces in the home are interwoven with action and function. Second, we identified five types of communication information in the home. Third, we discussed how information places within the home are chosen, distributed and selected. Finally, we articulate our concept of *contextual locations:* the vital role that location plays in providing meta-data to household members that allow them to easily decide how to handle communication information. This meta-data, related to *time, ownership* and *awareness,* allows people to quickly deal with the vast quantities of information present in the home.

Our results are significant for they offer designers and practitioners a more complete picture of information management and routines in the home. We hope that our work will sensitize designers to the compelling implications that locations have for the design of future home information systems. We offer design avenues for communication information and have shown that it is important for future home information systems to either support locations or provide additional meta-data that locations typically provide. We have laid a foundation of knowledge which clearly suggests what will not work and should inspire methods that do work. Our own future research directions include extending our understanding of locations to include emotional, social and aesthetic aspects of home life and using these results to design ambient and interactive devices to support communication information in the home.

We acknowledge TRLabs, Alberta Ingenuity, iCore and NSERC for funding.

References

1. Crabtree, A., Hemmings, T. and Mariani, J. **Informing the Development of Calendar Systems for Domestic Use.** *Proc. ECSCW'03,* Helsinki, Finland, (2003).
2. Crabtree, A. and Rodden, T. **Domestic Routines and Design for the Home.** *Computer Supported Cooperative Work,* Vol. 7. Kluwer Academic Publishers (2004), 191-220.
3. Crabtree, A., Rodden, T., Hemmings, T. and Benford S. **Finding a Place for UbiComp in the Home.** *Proc. Ubicomp'03.* Springer-Verlag (2001), 208-226.
4. Dourish, P. **Where the Action Is.** MIT Press (2001).
5. Edwards, W.K. and Grinter, R.E. **At Home with Ubiquitous Computing: Seven Challenges.** *Proc. UbiComp'01.* Springer-Verlag (2001), 256-272.
6. Harper, R., Evergeti, V., Hamill, L. and Strain, J. **Paper-mail in the Home of the 21st Century.** *Proc. Okios Conf Digital Tech. in Home Environments.* (2001)
7. Hindus, D., Mainwaring, S.D., Leduc, N., Hagström, A.E., and Bayley, O., **Casablanca: Designing Social Communication Devices for the Home.** *Proc CHI'01* (2001), 325-332.
8. Intille, S. **Change Blind Information Display for Ubiquitous Computing Environments.** *Proc. ACM UbiComp'02,* (2002).
9. Intille, S. **Designing a Home of the Future,** *IEEE Pervasive Computing,* (2002), 80-86.
10. Intille, S., Lee, V. and Pinhanez, C. **Ubiquitous Computing in the Living Room.** *Proc. Ubicomp'03, Video Program.* (2003).
11. Kidd, C., et al. **The Aware Home: A Living Laboratory for Ubiquitous Computing Research.** *Proc. CoBuild'99,* LNCS, Vol. 1670, Springer-Verlag, Berlin (1999), 191-198.
12. Mateas, M., Salvador, T., Scholtz, J. and Sorensen, D. **Engineering Ethnography in the Home.** *Proc. ACM CHI '96,* (1996), 283-284.
13. Neustaedter, C., Elliot, K., Tang, A. and Greenberg, S. **Where are you and when are you coming home? Foundations of Interpersonal Awareness.** Report 2004-760-25, Dept Computer Science, University Calgary, Alberta CANADA T2N 1N4. (2004).
14. O'Brien, J., Rodden, T., Rouncefield, M. and Hughes, J. **At Home with the Technology: An Ethno. Study of a Set-Top-Box Trial.** *ACM TOCHI* Vol. 6(3) (1999), 282-308.
15. Rodden, T., Crabtree, A., et al. **Between the Dazzle of a New Building and its Eventual Corpse: Assembling the Ubiquitous Home.** *Proc. ACM DIS'04.* (2004), 71-80.
16. Taylor, A., and Swan, L., **Artful Systems in the Home,** *Proc. ACM CHI* (2005), 641-50.
17. Taylor, A., and Swan, L., List Making in the Home, *Proc. ACM CSCW* (2004), pp. 542-5.
18. Tolmie, P., Pycock, J., Diggins, T., MacLean, A. and Karsenty, A. **Unremarkable Computing.** *Proc. ACM CHI'02,* (2002), 399-406.
19. Venkatesh, A. **Computers and Other Interactive Technologies for the Home.** *Communications of the ACM,* Vol. 39(12). ACM Press (1996), 47-54.

Living for the Global City:
Mobile Kits, Urban Interfaces, and Ubicomp

Scott D. Mainwaring, Ken Anderson, and Michele F. Chang

People and Practices Research Lab
Intel Corporation
2111 NE 25th Ave., JF3-377
Hillsboro, OR 97124 USA
{scott.mainwaring,ken.anderson,michele.f.chang}@intel.com

Abstract. Using ethnographic methods, 28 young professionals across the global cities of London, Los Angeles, and Tokyo were studied to understand in some detail what items they carried with them (their mobile kits) and how they used these items to access people, places, and services (through various urban interfaces). The findings are analyzed in terms of these cities as existing sites of ubiquitous information and communication technology (ICT) use. More specifically, findings are considered with respect to the prospects in these cities for ubicomp as a paradigm of trusted, environmentally embedded computing, as opposed to a wearable computing paradigm of individual self-sufficiency. Overall, at least for the young professional class studied, practices of urban interfacing were remarkably similar across all three cities studied, suggesting that ubicomp systems might be developed to address the range of urban concerns and to unburden and empower urbanites.

1 Introduction

The term *ubiquitous computing* can be understood in a variety of ways. Loosely, it can refer to a state of affairs in which information and communication technology (ICT) is everywhere, used by everyone, for many purposes in many contexts, most often taken for granted, unseen, part of daily life. From this point of view, ubiquitous computing is already a reality in the most developed parts of the world, particularly in "global cities." These are culturally, economically, and politically prominent world metropolises like London, Los Angeles (L.A.), and Tokyo, primary nodes in the interconnected, increasingly information-based global economy [e.g., see 8, 30]. And though it is clearly overstating the situation to claim that *everyone* in these cities is using ICTs, if taken to mean personal ownership and use of devices like personal computers and mobile phones; it is not an overstatement if ICT use is viewed more broadly to include, for example, buying a subway ticket from a vending machine or placing a call to a mobile phone.

This paper reports on an exploratory ethnographic study of ubiquitous computing in this sense as practiced and encountered in London, L.A., and Tokyo. The sheer size of these places (see table 1) necessitated narrowing the focus of the study to a

M. Beigl et al. (Eds.): UbiComp 2005, LNCS 3660, pp. 269–286, 2005.

tractable scale. We chose to look at young professionals, many in fairly freelance or autonomous employment situations, as they went about their lives in the city, staying mostly clear of the time they spent at home or at work to focus instead on their travels and use of non-home, non-work, "third places" [23]. We sought to approach ubicomp not as a theoretical possibility, but as a set of existing practices from which we could learn and infer opportunities for future value, either in reducing barriers and costs or increasing benefit. We also sought, with some skepticism, to assess the notion that places like London, L.A., and Tokyo actually form a coherent category – that they are essentially a single, distributed place, despite their apparent differences. Was ubicomp realized fundamentally differently in these three places, with different implications for future direction, or could one usefully design ubicomp for "the city"?

Table 1. Population and density of the three global cities studied

	London	Los Angeles	Tokyo
Urban Region	Greater London (City & 32 boroughs)	L.A. County (L.A. & 87 other cities)	Tokyo Metropolis (Tokyo & 26 other cities)
Population (2004)	7.6 million	10.1 million	12.4 million
Area	1580 km² 610 mi²	10518 km² 4061 mi²	2187 km² 844 mi²
Density	4810 per km² 12459 per mi²	960 per km² 2487 per mi²	5670 per km² 14692 per mi²
Transit Ridership	34% (see note 1)	7% (see note 2)	63% (see note 3)

1. Daily travel in Greater London, 2003. Excludes walk/bicycle trips at 23%. http://www.tfl.gov.uk/tfl/ltr2003/market-share.shtml

2. Journey to work data, LA county, 2000. Excludes walk/other trips at 4.5%. http://www.publicpurpose.com/ut-jtw2000la.htm

3. Annual passenger journeys, Tokyo-Yokohama metro area, 2000. http://www.publicpurpose.com/ut-tokmkt.htm

A stricter reading of ubiquitous computing contrasts with the notion of wearable computing. The wearable paradigm involves empowering the individual through augmenting the body with ICTs such as cameras and microphones, heads-up displays, eyes-free input devices, and personal databases and automated agents. The individual bears the burden (in bulky, battery-laden near-term implementations, quite literally) of this technology, but also exercises control and autonomy, and in the extreme is self-sufficient despite whatever resources the environment does or does not provide. In contrast, the ubicomp paradigm involves augmenting the environment with networked sensors, displays, and services in an unobtrusive but empowering way. The individual is freed from having to carry, maintain, and manage ICTs, which instead plentifully stand ready as needed to adapt themselves to the individual and his or her context. Rather than being dependent upon what they carry, individuals in this paradigm become dependent upon their environment, into which they place their trust and from which they consent to be sensed and adapted to.

Urban life has features of both paradigms. Urbanites typically carry a large array of objects (many of them technological) with them in their bags, purses, wallets, and pockets. These containers are private domains over which they exercise control, and their contents provide a measure of self-sufficiency and reassurance, particularly when they are confronted with the unexpected, challenging, or threatening. But urbanites also live in heavily technologically augmented environments offering all manner of amenities, public and proprietary, free and commercial. Much of what they carry with them are interface tokens required to gain access to, conduct transactions with, and use and enjoy their chosen slice of the urban environment. These tokens have co-evolved with the environment itself, such that the contents of a wallet can be considered a microcosm of the world its bearer inhabits. And sometimes these tokens can be dispensed with partially or entirely, as when one sets out for a night on the town, carrying just the bare essentials, trusting that fun will be had.

In investigating everyday life in London, L.A., and Tokyo, we sought to understand how these two paradigms balanced and interacted in the lives of our study participants. We paid close attention to what they carried with them, how, when, and why it was used, and how it reflected who they were and wanted to be, as well as how it reflected the character, realities, and potential of the encompassing city. We observed the environments through which our participants traveled, shopped, worked, and recreated, and analyzed our participants' attitudes toward them, whether of fear, trust, engagement, disengagement, resignation, delight, or some combination. In short, by understanding in detail how some residents of each of the three cities practiced ubicomp in the loose sense, we aimed to better understand ubicomp in the stricter, paradigmatic sense, with its associated issues of trust and the practical co-design of the personal and the environmental.

2 Related Work

Our overall approach is one of lightweight ethnography [10, 18, 19], in which methods from anthropology are adapted for more rapid turn-around and applicability to issues of technology use and design, while seeking to remain true to the core ethnographic concern of understanding everyday practice and experience from the perspective of another culture. Our approach is related to what Marcus [17] has called multi-sited ethnography, in which the traditional ethnographic focus on a single field site is shifted to encompass multiple global sites and their interrelationships, though it is less self-reflexive and open-ended, and does not explicitly explore interconnections *between* London, L.A., and Tokyo.

A number of studies in the computer-human interaction (CHI) and computer-supported cooperative work (CSCW) literatures have looked at what people in cities carry with them and why. Much of this has been in the context of understanding mobile work and workers [e.g., 14, 26, 31]. Our study seeks to extend this beyond the work domain, into everyday urban routines [see also 13, 34]. The emerging field of urban computing [24, 25] shares these interests, seeking to apply technologies of ubicomp and mobile computing to enhance social spaces in cities, beyond utilitarian concerns of efficiency and commerce.

An important set of studies and analyses have illuminated the profound impact of widespread mobile phone adoption across many social domains, from political organization to adolescent development [e.g., see 2, 11, 12, 29]. For the people and places we studied, mobile phones were a fundamental infrastructure underlying much of what we observed. Given this large existing literature, we focused not so much on mobile phone usage per se and the varieties of social interaction it affords (and blocks), but on the larger mobile kits, of which mobile phones were an important part, and the wider set of everyday transactions they support.

We have been strongly influenced by the work of sociologist Christena Nippert-Eng, who has studied how people use objects, spaces, and routines to manage boundaries between home and work in their lives [21]. In more recent research on Chicago-area professionals' conceptions of privacy, Nippert-Eng and her associate Jay Melican used wallets and their contents as an entry point for conversations with their participants on boundaries between public and private, disclosure and concealment [Nippert-Eng and Melican, personal communication]. Though we did not have our participants sort their wallet contents into "private" and "public" piles, we did adapt their methodology to leverage wallets (and more generally, whatever was being carried) as conversational resources as well as data in itself.

Cooper and colleagues [5] also looked in depth as wallets, using semi-structured interviews about the contents of 55 UK adults' wallets to inform the design of e-wallets as wearable technology. Their findings regarding wallets are generally consistent with ours, though based on a broader, larger, and older sample; and as might be expected, there were some discrepancies as well (e.g., they reported more emotional attachment to the wallet and variability in its contents than we found). We have reported on implications of our study for the notion of e-wallets elsewhere [15].

In her multi-year and ongoing Portable Effects project [33], Rachael Strickland has documented the "nomadic design practices" of many people through inventories of what and how they carry (many of these collected as part of interactive museum exhibits in the San Francisco Bay Area). Like her, we see our participants as vernacular designers of their mobile kits, creatively balancing personal, cultural, and infrastructural constraints. As predicted by this point of view, we found participants' practices and materials to be idiosyncratic and expressive of their identities, but also exhibiting important regularities and identifiable genres.

At a macroscopic level, London, L.A., and Tokyo are major topics of study in their own right, generating multiple histories, economic, cultural, political analyses, not to mention tourist guides, blogs (see [28]), and commentary [e.g., 9]. L.A., in particular, has captured the imagination of a group of urban theorists, resulting in an emerging field of "Los Angeles Studies" [20]. Furthermore, their comparison and interrelationships as embodied in the "global city" concept continues to attract attention, following from the seminal work of Sassen [30]. Though much of this work is clearly beyond the scope of ubicomp, scholarship is increasingly recognizing the crucial role of ICTs in the past, present, and future of these world cities. We found this macro-level work valuable in providing a background for our mainly micro-level investigations of every-day ICT use in context.

Our current more micro-level work is also in many respects a continuation of our previous exploratory work on the various meanings that ubiquitous infrastructures can have for the people enmeshed in (or reacting against) them, and their implications for the design, adoption, and appropriation of ubicomp systems [16]. We sought both to enlarge the scope of this work beyond a U.S. and home life focus to more global and mobile contexts, as well to zero in on the details of interacting with ubiquitous infrastructures in everyday life.

3 Study Design and Methods

The study was designed to address the following questions regarding the notion of global cities as sites of ubiquitous computing:

☐ Mobile kits. What do people carry with them? How is the carrying (multiple items, multiple choices) managed? How are these items perceived or valued?

☐ Urban interfaces. How do people use the city and the environments and services it offers? In what situations are items from the mobile kit involved, and how are they used?

☐ Global differences. In terms of mobile kits, urban interfaces, and their interaction, what differences (if any) between global cities matter? To what degree is it warranted to talk of "the global city" or "urban computing" as if they were unitary domains?

As is common in ethnographic work, we selected participants for theoretical interest and for trust relationships with the researchers rather than to serve as a statistical sample. As we were primarily interested in learning about differences between the different cities to be studied and had limited resources to cover any particular city, we decided to focus on a particular life stage and social class of participants: young professionals, aged 22 to 32, without children, transitioning into the workforce after completing their higher education. We expected (and found) this group to be tech savvy, mobile, and confronted with novel challenges as they adapted to a new life stage. They were also of theoretical interest as a group that it seemed could in principle choose to purchase and carry a wide variety and quantity of stuff if they so desired, but also a group that could choose to carry very little and rely on resources in the urban environment that was in many ways designed for and friendly to them. (Thus we might expect substantial variability of mobile kits based on personal preference and circumstances of employment, relative to other groups who might be more constrained in terms of what they were expected and able to carry.) At a more practical level, we also had relatively easy and trusted access to them through our academic and professional contacts in the study cities, many of them former students or classmates of our contacts. Thus, many of our participants were graduates of elite universities, notably: the Royal College of Art (London), USC (University of Southern California, in L.A.), and Keio University SFC (Shonan Fujisawa Campus, near Tokyo). And many were in the design and media industries; freelancers were relatively over-represented.

It is worth noting that by focusing on this particular lifestage, class, and to some degree occupational milieu across the three cities studied, we may have biased the study away from finding differences between the cities. For example, it may well be that the lifestyles of elderly residents, immigrant groups, or children vary considerably more across our study sites than do those of elite young professionals. We do not wish to suggest that other groups merit any less attention from the ubicomp community, and indeed may merit more. Nevertheless, we believe our study design was a reasonable initial approach to the research questions at hand, and that it is not a priori apparent that this group would have limited variability. Furthermore, our goal was not a comprehensive survey of ICT use across all people in all cities, but an interesting first pass through the "global city" looking at an influential group of urbanites with similar needs and concerns which *could* in principle be met in different ways in different urban contexts. We welcome and look forward to additional cross-cultural comparisons of ubicomp practices.

In addition to selecting individual participants, designing this study also involved selecting cities to "participate" in the research. Whereas individual participants were selected to form a fairly homogeneous sample, London, L.A., and Tokyo were chosen for diversity within the category "major world city." According to the Loughborough Globalization and World Cities (GaWC) rankings [1], each of these is one of the 10 "alpha" world cities, and London and Tokyo (along with New York and Paris) are in the first tier of these. Although similar in these terms, there are fairly obvious differences between them – widely dispersed on different continents and economic communities, different cultural origins, different levels of multiculturalism, different transportation infrastructures, and population densities (see Table 1). Of these, we were particularly influenced by differences in common modes of transportation, as we expected this would have a large influence on everyday urban practices. For this reason, we chose L.A. and its famous (or infamous) automobile culture over first-tier New York as the U.S. city in our sample.

A total of 28 individuals participated, 12 in London, 10 in Los Angeles, and 6 in Tokyo. Participants took part in a four different activities:

1. An initial interview, including a survey of their "mobile kit", i.e., everything they were carrying with them – in their car, pockets, bags, wallets, hands, etc.
2. One or two days of diary keeping, focused on use of any of the aforementioned items. Various methods were experimented with, including notebooks, voice recorders, and GPS-enabled camera phones (see [22]).
3. A "shadowing" session in which a researcher accompanied them on a shopping, commuting, or other trip through the city.
4. A final interview, including a review of their diary, and a discussion of positive and negative images of future technology.

Interviews took place for the most part in public places such as restaurants and cafes; we had limited access to homes and workplaces. Participants were thanked for their participation with cash gifts, and promised that their data would be treated confidentially.

4 Three Global Urbanites

In this section, we present brief sketches of one participant from each of the cities we studied, not because one individual can represent the range of themes and issues we encountered even in our small sample, but only to give some sense for the concrete cases we encountered. In the subsequent section, we turn to more general findings.

Fig. 1. Some study participants and their mobile kits. Alex running an errand near Covent Garden, London (left); Jenna's silvery mobile kit (minus iPod), Los Angeles (center); Sumi umbrella shopping in a Ginza department store, Tokyo (right)

4.1 London

Alex, 23, grew up in the U.S. and Australia and moved to London four years ago thinking that he would get a job in theatre, one of his passions. That has never quite happened, and he now finds he can only attend the theatre two or three times a year due to the expense. He commutes by bike (unless the weather gets really nasty) 20 minutes from his apartment in South London to his job providing technical support in media production; it's actually faster than the Tube (the London subway), doesn't go on strike several times a year (though he feels penalized when his colleagues use this as an excuse not to show up for work), and most importantly lets him breathe much better air. Recently he's also been working part-time as a personal assistant for a New York "VIP" (a Very Important Person he declined to name), looking after a luxury apartment being leased for a year to facilitate the VIP's frequent trips to London. The apartment serves as a very handy central "base," where Alex can drop off his bike and bag on his way back home and go out, unencumbered, on foot.

Alex's mobile kit consists of a wallet, an iPod ("the newest model since I'm a geek"), and a Sony Ericsson Bluetooth-enabled mobile phone, all of which are kept in his pockets so he can easily check that he has them whenever he leaves a place. A small shoulder bag holds two key rings (one for his bike, his apartment, and his notebook computer which he keeps chained to his bed in case of burglary; the other for the VIP's apartment), gridded paper notebook and pen (for capturing ideas for his blog), food (an apple and a "superfood" bar), sunscreen lotion, and a book for leisure reading. (He was also carrying two CD cases for Broadway musicals. Although he had ripped the CDs themselves to his iPod, he needed the cases for their booklets so he could read the lyrics while listening.) In his hand was usually a water bottle (see Fig. 1, left).

Sleek, minimalist style is important to Alex. He goes so far as to hide his iPod ear bud cord under his shirt so that it emerges discretely from his collar. He hates having things in his pockets, but does so for security, as mentioned. Stylish techno gadgets are a source of pride, as well as having a central role in his daily activities. To connect to his phone he bought a Bluetooth adapter for his computer at work, so that he can send SMS (Short Message Service) messages with the computer keyboard. The iPod is sometimes the focus of his attention, as when he spent an afternoon in a large, hidden park near his flat listening to his Broadway CDs, but more often is set to random play to provide the "soundtrack to my commute" and other travels.

4.2 Los Angeles

Jenna is in her mid-20's and lives near the beach in Santa Monica. She works for a prestigious non-profit media company, which requires frequent travel – she had just returned from New York City before we interviewed her. When she's not away, each workday she drives her Honda sedan 16 miles inland to her office near Hollywood, where she spends much of her day emailing and phoning clients. Her mobile kit, which she carries in a small shoulder bag, consists of a Calvin Klein wallet, a Palm Tungsten PDA in a metallic case, an iPod, an LG clamshell mobile phone, and a key ring (6 keys, wireless key fob for her Honda, and an ornament bearing the logo of her employer). Each of these is entirely or at least partially silver – her fashion statement (see Figure 1, center).

Jenna loves her work and respects her employer, but feels that it's only realistic to prepare for the possibility that she could lose her job (and access to her online work files) with short or no notice. She makes it a point to keep her client database, painstakingly acquired over time, separate from the data on her work (employer's) PC; it resides only on her PDA, which she never leaves at work for fear that someone might gain access. In the event she loses her current job, she will still have her client database – a valuable resource for her next job.   (The PDA is also used more publicly to display photos, often to people she meets during her business trips.)

Data loss is also a concern regarding her mobile phone. The current one is a recent replacement for one she had lost, along with many phone numbers stored on it. Because of this, she has resolved to store fewer numbers on her phone – "only people who really matter to me". Thus, her work PC, PDA, and cell phone are all compartmentalized domains that she goes to some length to keep separate, and which represent in some sense varying (increasing) levels of intimacy.

Jenna's use of her car was also noteworthy for its different zones. In addition to being a mechanism for her commute, it serves in some way as an extension of her apartment. The trunk serves as a laundry hamper (holding plastic bags of dirty laundry and laundry soap at the time of our surprise inspection, on their way, eventually, to a Laundromat), recycling center (collecting empty water bottles waiting for a trip to a recycling drop-off point – she does not have curbside recycling service), and pantry or refrigerator (holding cases of full water bottles; these move to the front seat or her bag for use, and then make their way to the floor of the back seat where they collect before being transferred to the recycling bin in the trunk).

4.3 Tokyo

Sumi, 23, recently graduated from Keio SFC and moved to Tokyo, renting an apartment with a roommate and joining a venture company as a part-time clerical administrator. Though paid part-time, she works full-time as a means of advancing in her career. Indeed, this strategy just paid off and she has accepted a full-time position at a major multinational bank beginning the next year. She currently has about a 30 minute commute to work (10 minutes walking, 20 minute on the train), but her life is played out in many ways beyond this (temporary) home/work axis. Although serious about developing a career, rather than focusing on her workplace relationships, she values and spends much time cultivating face-to-face her close network of (mostly female) friends from college – and indeed relies upon them, more than libraries and professional courses, to support her continuing business education. Relationships with friends often bring her to outlying cities like Shonandai and Yokohama, though she stays connected continuously through email on her *k-tai* (mobile phone). (Like many of our Japanese participants, Sumi uses her k-tai mostly for email, although she sometimes downloads coupons to it from the i-mode Gurunavi restaurant search engine, or emails them to it after finding them from her PC. She continually checks her k-tai to see if she's gotten mail.)

Sumi's mobile kit is carried in one of seven bags she switches between based on fashion, supplemented by (on the day we interviewed her) a paper shopping bag with with a little-known logo on it re-purposed to hold a newspaper, her day planner, and a CD player she's had since sophomore year in high school. (This reused shopping bag greatly surprised our Japanese colleagues, as it seemed very out of place with Sumi's overwise *ojyousama* [upper class young woman] persona; it may be a new trend.) The main bag holds her wallet, k-tai (accessorized with a strap she got several years ago by being stopped on the street in Yokohama to appear on *Piiko's Fashion Check* TV show), key case (parent's house in Kobe, apartment, company van, office desk), tissues, make-up (usually a pouch, but the day's bag was too small for this so she only had lip gloss), and a book.

Sumi shifts between her upscale *ojyousama* upbringing and a more practical role as a *shakaijin* (working adult). For example, in her shadowing session in Tokyo's glitzy Ginza district she went umbrella shopping in a number of department stores with truly astonishing assortments of umbrella styles on display (see Figure 1, right); finding none to her liking, she moved on to browse in Prada and Barney's New York. But ultimately she ended up purchasing a new day planner in a quite ordinary Sony Plaza store in the subway station. Sumi works to construct her new identity in conjunction with her social network of like-minded women; often they turn outside of Japan for role models, following with great interest American television shows like *Ally McBeal* and *Sex and the City* (available in Japan on DVD and on pay TV services).

5 Overall Themes

5.1 Mobile Kits

What people carried with them was, overall, remarkably similar across all three cities. Wallet (with cash, credit card, debit card, ATM card, ID, transit pass or license), mobile phone, keys, and a bag to carry stuff in were universal. A work-related scheduling device – be it a traditional paper day planner (most common), PDA, or occasionally data downloaded to an iPod – were nearly universal, though their forms were more variable. Other common categories included:

Body items. Tissue, lip balm, eye drops, glasses or sunglasses (even in famously cloudy London!), and for women, a make-up kit.

Cocooning items. By this we mean items that allow escape from one's current environment through creating a kind of "bubble" in which outside distractions are shut out. These include music players like the nearly ubiquitous iPod and its earlier incarnations (see [3, 4]), but also books, magazines, mobile phone email and games, "anything to avoid staring at stranger's shoes on the Tube" as one London participant put it. But cocooning could also be seen as unfortunate and anti-social; in particular, images of friends or children sharing the same space but not paying attention to each other were often selected as representing fears of future technology.

Experience-capture items. Less common, but highly valued by their users, were notebooks, sketchbooks, stand-alone cameras, and cell-phone cameras. Sometimes these were in service of an explicit activity, like journal keeping or blogging, but often they were for informal sharing with friends (camera phone photography was often deemed nonserious in this sense).

Professional tools. This could include work-related books, files, and especially notebook computers; often they were simply shuttling between home and work, but sometimes they were being taken into the field to a client site, etc., or carried about in case a client was encountered. Because of their importance to the bearer's livelihood, these items were often closely guarded and worried about – theft or damage were seen as serious dangers.

Emergency items. Rarely these were actual weapons like pepper spray; more often these included battery chargers (sometimes the emergency of running out of power could be anticipated, but often these were carried "just in case") and emergency food rations. We did not encounter supplies for medical emergencies in our sample.

Junk. A large and diverse category, including actual trash waiting for an opportunity to be thrown out; but also receipts (some but by no means all of which were being purposely saved for reimbursement or reconciliation with monthly statements), left-over transit or phone cards with small amounts of money on them, and sometimes items that surprised and embarrassed their bearers as their purpose had been forgotten.

Management of all these ensembles of containers, devices, certificates, and objects was an ongoing concern. Different styles could be discerned, for example, whether the wallet had defined compartments with a place for everything and everything in its place (more common than not) or was a haphazard amalgamation of items to be sorted through at time of use. (In either case, there is an opportunity here for techno-logical augmentation, so long as it is not seen as insulting the abilities of the wallet keeper.) Often style itself was the point, as with participants who had multiple bags and wallets to suit different fashion contexts or personal moods, or even for single-bag owners who often invested considerable time and trial-and-error over years to find the "right bag for me."

The importance of the body in the management, perception, and valuing of urban kits is difficult to over-estimate. The category of "body-related" items was alluded to above, but this could be extended to include the fit of wallets and other items in pock-ets (avoiding uncomfortable and unsightly bulk sometimes gave rise to secondary or tertiary wallets annexed to the carried bag), the way bags are worn while walking or placed while sitting, the importance of bodily contact providing reassurance that critical items are safe in one's possession, and the positioning of cell phones and transit passes to be ready-at-hand, to name but a few. There was a general delight in being unburdened and unencumbered, whether that meant stashing items away in one's car (or VIP apartment one is tending, in Alex's case), or positioning an RFID (radio frequency identification) transit card in one's pocket so that it can be read by a subway wicket without breaking one's stride, or leaving everything behind but your keys and some cash to run out to the corner store.

The question of how people value and perceive the items they carry is complex and often idiosyncratic and contradictory. For example, Nippert-Eng and Melican [personal communication] found that cash was seen both as public (not something I'm attached to, something meant to be traded away in the public realm) *and* private (posing personal risk to me should I lose it, and in general none of anyone else's business) by their informants. Mobile kits were not *so* private that our participants balked at showing them to us in considerable detail and discussing them rather openly. Only a few rushed past certain areas in their wallets or compartments in their bag that were clearly not open to inquiry. Of course, we gave participants advance warning that we were researching what they carried and why, so they could adjust what they brought to the interviews if necessary. The car inspections in L.A. were the exception to this rule, and generated somewhat higher levels of discomfort, par-ticularly when this involved looking into trunks and glove compartments – closed furniture, in effect. And many items had a "cash like" quality of being meant for public (or at least semi-public) transaction, in Nippert-Eng and Melican's sense.

Nevertheless, mobile kits are valued in part because they *are* private, related to one's identity, and one's very body. Often our participants would say that either their day planners or their mobile phones were the most private things they were carrying, not because these held what was perceived to be sensitive information that could be clearly damaging should it fall into the wrong hands (unlike, say, the credit cards and identity cards in their wallets), but because these items embodied their personal histo-ries, who they knew, how they spent their time – who they *were*, in some sense. And in crowded urban environments, privacy can be a precious commodity indeed, and valued as an end in itself. Just as elements of mobile kits were used to cocoon, the mobile kit itself formed a personal space which one could control and put effort into managing.

5.2 Urban Interfaces

Perhaps the primary urban interface, not surprisingly, is money. Our participants used the city to earn money, to spend it, and sometimes to invest it (as in some cases of spending money on the alcohol required to socialize with ones work colleagues, who could provide future returns). Much urban infrastructure is designed around these economic activities. We have reported elsewhere on implications of our study for e-wallets and opportunities for technology to address issues such as receipt management, self-monitoring and self-control over temptation, and automated payment [15]. The intersection of ubicomp and money, like the intersection of ubicomp and cities, is a large topic for a fuller investigation in its own right, and compared to urban computing, is surprising by its absence from the agendas of the ubicomp research community. Here we just reiterate its global importance, and the high stakes it introduces: when it is not just one's notebook computer on which one's livelihood depends, but one's interactions with embedded sensors, displays, and disembodied processes running behind the scenes, the demand of robustness and trustworthiness placed by users on such systems will be high indeed. From such a perspective, which is indeed a bit paranoia-inducing, the appeal of the wearable as opposed to the ubicomp paradigm is not hard to imagine. It is likely to be an uphill battle to get mission-critical functions out of users' mobile kits and into the environment itself, unless this can be demonstrated to increase safety, cost-effectiveness, and user control.

But urban interfaces are certainly not *just* about money – even when they are (even mostly) about money. Looking at how our participants made use of their cities, a number of important classes of activity are worth calling out, though this is by no means a comprehensive list.

Traveling. Like money, not surprisingly a major and universal concern, particularly in densely populated areas where other people are often as much obstacle as resource. Our participants optimized their commutes, being able to tell us in detail how long it took (or could take), and what they did along the way. In transit-oriented cities, this often involved making use of amenities at major transfer stations, as well as the stations at which the commute began and ended; these transfer stations are logical nodes for the deployment of ubicomp technologies, as is already happening in Tokyo with JR East's experiments with Suica smart card transactions within its stations. In the car-oriented culture of L.A., along the way meant in one's car – which is also an excellent candidate for early deployment of ubicomp technologies, and a particularly nice one given the essentially captive audience and the ability of the platform to generate its own power. Travel obviously extends beyond commuting, becoming a precondition for a huge variety of urban interactions that city makes possible – if you can make your way to them! These include both place-based and people-based interactions, which despite the ubiquity of ICTs in these cities, are still primarily embodied experiences, ICTs being used primarily to coordinate rendezvousing in space rather than replacing it.

Networking. This includes creating, collecting, and maintaining personal contacts, often for one's work – but as in Sumi's case, work networking and networking among close friends can be closely related. Often networking is deliberate and self-conscious, with certain places affording match-making and relationship building, but sometimes it is quite serendipitous if not downright unlikely – on multiple occasions in our shadowing of participants, they unexpectedly "ran into" people they knew well. Through practices of self-selection of places and routes, even these largest of world cities can sometimes resemble to their inhabitants small towns. This has interesting positive and negative consequences, as place-based social-networking systems like Dodgeball [7] demonstrate; chance (or half-chance) encounters can be wanted or unwanted, and often both at once depending on whose perspective is taken. None of our participants had used such services, relying instead of personal networks of email and phone calls; the key artifact for networking, besides the cell phone, was the business card, which surprisingly has tenaciously resisted being replaced by some digital version. (The closest phenomenon we encountered to this was the appearance QR codes [27] – barcode-like glyphs – intended to be read by cell phone cameras which had begun to appear on avant-garde business cards in Tokyo.)

Mapping. This often takes the form of literal map use, as the complexities of navigating these cities is more than anyone but a highly trained taxi-driver could do from memory (see [32]). Nearly all Londoners in our sample carried their *A to Z Street Atlases*, focused on pedestrian and Tube navigation, just as nearly all Los Angelinos had their more car-oriented *Thomas Guides*. Personal atlases were far less common in Tokyo, where they had been incorporated into more of a ubicomp than a wearable paradigm: maps they were embedded everywhere in the environment, at subway entrances (nicely rotated such that straight ahead was always up), in print advertising, on store business cards, and increasingly on k-tai screens. But by mapping we want also to include practices of collecting places, often in the form of store business cards or loyalty cards, sometimes in the form on annotations on the *A toZ* or equivalent. We found this to be a widespread way of personalizing and making sense of the city, the place-holders often being sources of considerable pride, demonstrating the bearer's mastery of the environment.

Tracking. This was more of a latent than an often realized practice. Our study methodology, which included both self-monitoring and diary/blog keeping as well as being "shadowed" by a trusted stranger, prompted our participants to consider various future possibilities for tracking their own or others behavior. The reaction was surprisingly positive, despite the obvious privacy concerns; most participants could see at least some circumstances where automated tracking might have more benefit than risk. These often included business-related cases such as receipt tracking, but monitoring one's own spending was often entertained to be potentially useful, as was (particularly in Tokyo) the idea of learning the wise habits and skillful actions of an admired other.

Cocooning. As mentioned in the discussion of mobile kits above, disconnecting from the city and finding private space for oneself was a widespread if problematic activity, often technologically mediated. However, it often involved some measure of using the city itself, not just an interaction between one and one's mobile kit. For example, Alex's bike riding and the bike paths being actively promoted by the London government are a form, for him, of escape from the city; the random shuffling of the iPod enhances the experience, but it is not primary to it – the (relatively) fresh air and sense of speed and freedom seem more fundamental. Related to this, London has embarked on an ambitious and controversial plan to reduce traffic in its central areas through "congestion charging" enforced by mobile CCTV (closed-circuit television) checkpoints and automated billing of violators through the mail [6]. For better or worse, this is very much along the lines of the ubicomp paradigm (in a rather communitarian/authoritarian form) rather than any sort libertarian wearable scheme; and it appears to be working surprisingly well. It can be regarded as a ubicomp deployment to create a kind of giant cocoon within central London itself, creating an escape, at least partially, from the noise and pollution of the less regulated city.

Browsing. Finally, there is a mode of interfacing with the city that (at least at first approximation) requires neither money nor ones urban kit – if one disregards transit costs and infrastructural maintenance and support. This is the cheap thrill of simply walking (or driving or "cruising", in L.A.) around and browsing the myriad of sensory, social, and informational experiences the city has to offer. In Japanese, there is a term *tachiyomi* meaning "to read while standing in a shop, not buying" – a popular activity across all three cities, at least for our target population. Much of the delight of cities is *tachiyomi* generalized to all sorts of experiences, with a somewhat subversive sense of having gotten something for nothing as a finishing touch. Of course there is a danger that too much *tachiyomi* that does not ultimately lead to enough buying will put bookshops out of business. Ubicomp has the potential to ruin *tachiyomi* experiences by monitoring behavior, regulating spaces, and charging for access; but it also has the potential to deliver wonderful new forms of urban experiences through shared displays and public interactive systems that don't require everyone to pay in order to play.

5.3 Global Differences

From this one modest study, it would be foolish to try to draw any definitive conclusions about such a philosophical question as whether London, L.A., and Tokyo are fundamentally similar or fundamentally different. And it is too easy, though probably true, to say that they are both. For the purposes of ubicomp, however, the question is a practical one – what differences matter, and are there useful similarities?

To take the latter question first, overall we generally more struck by the similarities between the practices and concerns of our participants regardless of city and culture rather than the differences, and feel that our data suggest some useful global opportunities for ubicomp. At least, this is a hypothesis we would like to advance, and look forward to other studies to confirm or reject it.

All of the major categories within mobile kits and urban interfaces discussed in the preceding sections appear to cut across all three cities, at least to a first order of approximation. Perhaps we should not have been surprised by this, given the population within each city that we targeted and the processes of globalization that urban theorists have pointed to rapidly at work shaping the, as the argument goes, convergent evolution of each megalopolis. Yet we were surprised – at the ubiquity of wallets bulging with receipts and unexplained clutter, the widespread acceptance of plastic money, the similar vision of social network based professionalism being striven for by young Japanese and young Americans, the similarity of problems faced by commuters stuck in traffic in L.A. and those stuck in the Tube under London. Similar forms and similar problems suggest the possibility of similar solutions.

That being said, there are important differences. Infrastructure is one of them. For example, car-based ubicomp is likely to look far different than pedestrian- or transit-based ubicomp. Indeed, one could argue that car-based ubicomp isn't ubicomp strictly speaking at all, but rather a form of wearable computing, if one can imagine that one "wears" a car while driving or riding it in (not such a farfetched idea). In any case, car-based systems are probably easier to deploy and are already an area of great interest to the automotive industry.

The infrastructures underlying technology diffusion and deployment are also likely quite different across London, L.A., and Tokyo, though this matter of practical politics, of how innovation happens or is thwarted by particular communities, is beyond the scope of our investigation. But there is something at work that is producing real-world smartcard payment systems in Japan, congestion charging in London, and the relatively backward state (in terms of SMS, email, and internet services) of mobile phones in L.A.

It would also be foolhardy to disregard important cultural differences between the US, the UK, and Japan. Though these do not necessarily preclude the success of similar technological paradigms across all of them, they do almost guarantee that the meaning and connotations of these technologies will differ, and that they will be culturally constructed in interestingly different ways. We are only suggesting that the cultural construction could proceed from fairly similar starting points. For example, business cards are important artifacts of social networking in all three locales, but anyone who has observed the differences of respect and decorum involved in business card exchange in the East compared to the West can see that these cards *mean* something different in Tokyo than they do in L.A. or London. The same is bound to be true of ubicomp artifact (and indeed can already be seen in the case of the different mobile phone cultures in all three cities).

6 Summary

Globalization theorists may be on to something, in positing the emergence of global cities, co-dependent, convergently evolving, and interlinked through a worldwide information economy. This phenomenon is relevant to ubicomp because these world cities are major centers of ubiquitous computing (broadly conceived), among all the other things they are major centers of. Ubicomp is already a lived experience in these cities, and at least for a class of elite young professions, similar lived experience in interesting and perhaps surprising ways.

In exploring with a handful of study participants the detailed of this lived experience, we uncovered some general trends that appear to cut across cities as widely separated in space and culture as London, L.A., and Tokyo:

☐ People are skilled at using their bodies and mobile kits to connect their private identities to the public spaces and urban interfaces they navigate as part and parcel of daily life in these cities. Ubicomp design should seek to leverage these skills, allow for this flexibility. It should also seek to help people cocoon, creating spaces in the city of escape and rejuvenation. It should work along with wearable technologies (like wallets, or e-wallets should technologies like mobile phones and iPods move in that direction) to allow people to record, collect, and track their environments and their own behaviors.

☐ Responsive, display-rich, trustworthy environments are a source of delight, even at small scales. They can afford *tachiyomi* – browsing/experiencing/enjoying without pressure to buy. Ubicomp may be able to unburden people – of expanding mobile kits, and the physical, cognitive, and emotional burdens they can produce, such as the constant vigilance of people checking that they still have their wallet, keys, mobile phone. Ubicomp may be able to reduce fear, if it can be trusted.

☐ Cultural differences are important, but global cities share much in common that can be designed for – a shared baseline of expectations and experiences. The details may differ (for example in car- vs. pedestrian-based implementations), and the culturally constructed meanings certainly will, but there are useful commonalities that can be leveraged.

We present these hypotheses in the spirit of calling attention to some phenomena ripe for consideration and testing by the ubicomp community. In addition to the question of global cities and whether they constitute a coherent domain for design, we also hope that future research will look at the needs and experiences of other, less privileged populations in this cities; at urban environments left off the globalization grid; and at better methodologies for conducting this kind of research, to facilitate tracking and self reflection.

7 Acknowledgements

Mizuko Ito at USC and Keio SFC played a primary and indispensable role in designing, facilitating, translating, and analyzing the data from this project. We are also most grateful to our research colleague Daisuke Okabe at Keio SFC who arranged, conducted, provided technical support for, and analyzed much of the Tokyo fieldwork. Thanks also go to research assistants Rachel Cody and Heidi Cooley (USC), and Keio SFC Kunikazu Amagasa, Aico Shimizu, and Noriko Watanabe (Keio SFC); to our research participants for sharing their everyday lives and mobile kits with us; to Paul Dourish, Christena Nippert-Eng, Jay Melican, William Gaver, and Nancy Ledbetter for their advice and assistance; and to our anonymous reviewers.

8 References

1. Beaverstock, J.V., Smith, R.G., and Taylor, P.J. (1999). A roster of world cities. *Cities, 16*, 445-458.
2. Brown, B., Green, N., and Harper, R. (2002). *Wireless world: Social and interactional aspects of the mobile age.* Springer.
3. Bull, M. (2001). The world according to sound: Investigating the world of Walkman users. *New Media and Society, 3*, 179-197.
4. Bull, M. (2002). The seduction of sound in consumer culture: Investigating Walkman desires. *Journal of Consumer Culture, 2*, 81-101.
5. Cooper, L., Johnson, G., and Baber, C. (1999). A run on Sterling – Personal finance on the move. In *Proc. ISWC '99*, 87-92.

6. Dix, M. (2002). The Central London Congestion Charging Scheme–From conception to implementation. Paper presented at the IMPRINT-EUROPE Thematic Network Seminar, Brussels.
7. Dodgeball. http://www.dodgeball.com
8. Hall, P. (2002). Christaller for a global age: Redrawing the urban hierarchy. In A. Mayr, M. Meurer, and J. Vogt (Eds.), *Stadt und Region: Dynamik von Lebenswelten* (pp. 110-128). Leipzig: Deutsche Gesellschaft für Geographie. (Available online at http://www.lboro.ac.uk/gawc/rb/rb59.html)
9. Haynes, M. & Rogers, J., Eds. (2004). *Smoke: A London peculiar.* http://www.smokelondon.co.uk
10. Hughes, J., King, V., Rodden, T., and Andersen, H. (1994). Moving out from the control room: Ethnography in system design. In *Proceedings of CSCW'94*, 429-439.
11. Ito, M., and Okabe, D. (2003). Mobile phones, Japanese youth, and the re-placement of social contact. Presented at Front Stage - Back Stage Confrence, Grimstad, Norway. http://www.itofisher.com/PEOPLE/mito/mobileyouth.pdf
12. Ito, M., Okabe, D., and Matsuda, M. (Eds.) (2005). *Personal, Portable, Pedestrian: Mobile Phones in Japanese Life.* MIT Press.
13. Jain, S.S.L. (2002). Urban errands: The means of mobility. *Journal of Consumer Culture, 2,* 419-438.
14. Luff, P. and Heath, C. (1998). Mobility in collaboration. In *Proceedings of CSCW '98*, 305-314.
15. Mainwaring, S.D., Anderson, K., and Chang, M.F. (2005). What's in your wallet? Implications for global e-wallet design. In *Extended Abstracts of CHI 2005*, 1613-1616.
16. Mainwaring, S.D., Chang, M.F., and Anderson, K. (2004). Infrastructures and their discontents: Implications for ubicomp. In *UbiComp 2004* (LNCS 3205, pp. 418-432). Springer.
17. Marcus, G. (1995). Ethnography in/of the world system: The emergence of multi-sited ethnography. *Annual Review of Anthropology, 24,* 95-117.
18. Mateas, M., Salvador, T., Scholtz, J., and Sorensen, D. (1996). Engineering ethnography in the home. In *CHI 1996 Conference Companion*, 283-284.
19. Millen, D.R. (2000). Rapid ethnography: Time deepening strategies for HCI field research. In *Proceedings of DIS '00*, 280-286.
20. Monahan, T. (2002). Los Angeles studies: The emergence of a specialty field. *City & Society, 14*(2), 155-184.
21. Nippert-Eng, C. (1996). *Home and Work: Negotiating Boundaries through Everyday Life.* University of Chicago Press.
22. Okabe, D., Anderson, K., Mainwaring, S.D, and Ito, M. (2005). Location-based moblogging as method: New views into the use and practices of personal, social and mobile technologies. Paper presented at Hungarian Academy of Science conference: Seeing, Understanding, Learning in the Mobile Age (Budapest).
23. Oldenburg, R. (1989). *The Great Good Place: Cafes, Coffee Shops, Bookstores, Bars, Hair Salons, and Other Hangouts at the Heart of a Community.* New York: Paragon House.
24. Paulos, E., Anderson, K., and Townsend, A. (2004). UbiComp in the urban frontier. Workshop at Ubicomp 2004. Proceedings online at http://www.urban-atmospheres.net/UbiComp2004/
25. Paulos, E. and Goodman, E. (2004). The familiar stranger: Anxiety, comfort, and play in public places. In *Proceedings of CHI 2004*, 223-230.
26. Perry, M., O'Hara, K., Sellen, A., Brown, B., and Harper, R. (2001). Dealing with mobility: Understanding access anytime, anywhere. *ACM TOCHI, 8,* 323-347.
27. QR Code. http://www.qrcode.com

28. Reed, A. (in press). 'My Blog Is Me': Texts and persons in UK online journal culture (and anthropology). *Ethnos.*
29. Rheingold, H. (2002). *Smart Mobs: The Next Social Revolution.* Perseus.
30. Sassen, S. (1991). *The global city: New York, London, Tokyo.* Princeton, NJ: Princeton University Press.
31. Sherry, J., and Salvador, T. (2002). Running and grimacing: The struggle for balance in mobile work. In B. Brown, N. Green, and R. Harper (Eds.), *Wireless world: Social and interactional aspects of the Mobile Age* (pp. 108-120). London: Springer Verlag.
32. Skok, W. (1999). Knowledge management: London taxi cabs case study. In *Proceedings of SIGCPR 99,* 94-101.
33. Strickland, R. (1998). *Portable effects: A survey of nomadic design practice.* Tech Report TR1998-003, Interval Research Corp. http://www.portablefx.com
34. Tamminen, S., Oulasvirta, A., Toiskallio, K., and Kankainen, A. (2004). Understanding mobile contexts. *Personal and Ubiquitous Computing, 8,* 135-143.

From Interaction to Participation: Configuring Space Through Embodied Interaction

Amanda Williams[1], Eric Kabisch[2], and Paul Dourish[1]

[1] Donald Bren School of Information & Computer Sciences, University of California, Irvine
Irvine, CA 92697-3425, USA
{amandamw, jpd}@ics.uci.edu
http://www.ics.uci.edu/
[2] Arts Computation Engineering, University of California, Irvine
Irvine, CA 92697-2775, USA
ekabisch@uci.edu
http://www.ace.uci.edu/

Abstract. When computation moves off the desktop, how will it transform the new spaces that it comes to occupy? How will people encounter and understand these spaces, and how will they interact with each other through the augmented capabilities of such spaces? We have been exploring these questions through a prototype system in which augmented objects are used to control a complex audio 'soundscape.' The system involves a range of objects distributed through a space, supporting simultaneous use by many participants. We have deployed this system at a number of settings in which groups of people have explored it collaboratively. Our initial explorations of the use of this system reveal a number of important considerations for how we design for the interrelationships between people, objects, and spaces.

1 Introduction

One common characterization of ubiquitous computing is that it engenders a move "off the desktop," implying the migration of information processing beyond traditional computational settings in desktop PCs and into the broader environment. In our work, we have been considering this transition, but from another perspective. Instead of thinking about ubiquitous computing in contrast to the desktop it leaves behind, our main focus is on the space into which computation will move. What sorts of impacts on space result when it is populated by ubicomp technologies?

The topic of augmented environments is one that has occupied ubicomp researchers for some time [3, 23, 30]. In general, these approaches have considered specific spaces and the ways in which they can be made responsive to aspects of human activity. However, our concern here is more generally with the ways in which social action is embodied, and embedded, in space. Our fundamental concern is with the ways in which we encounter space not simply as a container for our actions, but as a setting within which we act. The embodied nature of activity is an issue for a range of technologies. For example, researchers investigating interaction through video-

M. Beigl et al. (Eds.): UbiComp 2005, LNCS 3660, pp. 287–304, 2005.

conferencing technologies have noted that gesture loses much or all of its effectiveness across video connections, because in the everyday world, gesture happens not on a two-dimensional plane (such as a video screen) but rather in a three dimensional space [16]. Gestures unfold in a space around and between the bodies of communicative partners, and this mutual relationship between bodies, gestures, and space is intrinsic to how gestures work. Similarly, the ways in which spaces can be explored depends on our presence within it and the fact that we are not merely observers but participants in a spatial environment [10, 11].

Space and social action, then, are tightly entwined. The spatial organization of activities makes them intelligible to others; for example, people's mutual orientation in conversation [22], as they walk down the street [26], or as they stand in line [8], provides others with the means to see and interpret what is going on. In other words, this relationship goes beyond simply space and action; rather, it speaks to, first, the mutual configuration and arrangements of bodies, artifacts and activities in space, and, second, the social and cultural practices by which actions are both produced and interpreted. Objects and activities take their meaning from the ways in which they are embedded into systems of practice; through these practices, people configure space for each other and render particular objects and activities "seeable" [12, 13, 18].

This complex relationship is the basis of our inquiry. In particular, we are interested in the ways in which the migration of computation into the everyday environment might reconfigure the relationship between people, objects and space; first, by making spaces responsive to activities in ways not previously possible, and second, by presenting new challenges for the interpretation of actions and objects in space. In other words, how will people be able to make sense of computationally enhanced spaces, and how will they be able to make sense of each other in those spaces?

We have been exploring these questions through the development and evaluation of a collective dynamic audio installation called SignalPlay. In this system, a series of physical objects with embedded computational properties collectively control a dynamic "sound-scape" which responds to the orientation, configuration, and movement of the component objects [21]. The system and its component objects – chess pieces, building blocks, bongo drums, an antique compass, and a toy light saber – are large enough that they cannot all be used by a single person at once; spread through a space, they create a sonic environment which is experienced and transformed collectively by multiple people. SignalPlay has been exhibited a number of times, generally in gallery spaces, and we have observed people's interactions with and through the system. In this paper, we will explore some of our early experiences with SignalPlay, and set out an initial framework for describing and understanding people's encounters with augmented objects and augmented spaces.

We will begin by discussing some current work that explores similar technological and design concerns and which examines the collective configuration of space, particularly in gallery settings. After a brief presentation of the design of SignalPlay, we will discuss our observations of its use and the framework for interaction that is emerging from our analysis. Finally, we will discuss some of our further investigations and the potential implications of this work.

2 Related Work

Our investigations were informed by several areas of previous work, including uses of complex audience spaces as a focus for embodied interaction, use of representational objects in tangible interaction, studies of the collective experience of exhibits and gallery spaces, and considerations of how people come to understand a space that they inhabit.

2.1 Tangible Interaction with Sound

Art practice has long explored ideas of computational sensory feedback based on physical interaction. These ideas appear in 1950's and 1960's explorations such as a photoelectric and microphone controlled sound system designed by Billy Klüver for a series of performances held in October 1966 under the title *Nine Evenings: Theatre and Engineering* [4]. Installation and performance artists such as Myron Krueger and David Rokeby have continued to explore the use of sensor technologies with real-time sound generation. Our use of chess pieces as an interface device evokes a 1968 game of chess played by John Cage and Marcel Duchamp in which the movement of pieces controlled a composition of light and sound.

Work on the use of gestural user interfaces for electronic instruments includes that of the Hyperinstruments group at MIT Media Lab. The *Beatbug* system [34] in particular focuses on users' ability to manipulate musical system behavior at different levels of collaboration and complexity using simple toy-like objects. In contrast, SignalPlay uses music as a means of exploring a novel interface; we do not think of it purely as a musical instrument, but as an experience. It draws on the idea of tangible bits [20] and phicons [32] for the physical design of the objects. Unlike the metaDESK phicons, however, SignalPlay's objects can be thought of not only as non-representational icons that stand in for a digital interaction possibility, but also, and more noticeably, they are more literal icons (and in some cases what Ullmer and Ishii refer to as "actualities") that represent real-world objects with known interactional rules.

In this sense, SignalPlay bears some resemblance to *ensemble* [2], in which common wardrobe items are augmented to turn the childhood game of dress-up into a music manipulation activity. As well, the Cardboard Box Garden [7] uses physically embodied audio spaces to investigate the augmentation of familiar objects with computational capabilities.

2.2 Gallery Studies

Partly because SignalPlay was deployed in a gallery space, it is in many ways related to the *Ghost Ship* installation described by Hindmarsh et al. [19]. In the *Ghost Ship* exhibit, interactive components were distributed throughout a gallery space such that visitors could interact knowingly with a component in their immediate proximity; but sometimes unbeknownst to them, they might also influence other components in the exhibit. Our system is heavily audio-based, while theirs used video images, yet both installations elicited strikingly similar expressions of confusion, surprise and playfulness. These detailed studies of interaction and collaboration in a public place, using close video analysis, informed our methods of observation.

The Ghost Ship study is one of a number of detailed studies of interaction in gallery and exhibit spaces conducted by researchers at Kings College London [17, 33]. A central feature of these studies is that they turn their attention away from HCI's traditional focus on how a single individual might interact with an exhibit, and focus instead on how a group of gallery-goers might interact around a particular object or exhibit. The issue here is not simply that most people visit gallery and exhibit spaces in groups, although this is true [14]. Rather, drawing on a range of studies into the role of objects in the collective production of orderly action, they focus on the ways in which people's actions essentially "configure" the space for each other. People encounter spaces as ones that are populated with others, and exhibits as visible sites of other's activity. Detailed studies of video records show the ways in which people attend to each other's interactions with exhibits, which in turn shape aspects of their own encounters with them. Encounters with exhibits are collective experiences, and individual actions around them are organized with regard to the presence, orientation, activities, and gaze of others. The Kings College group has used these observations in support of design activities [17].

2.3 Understanding Space

In an evaluation of the Sotto Voce system [1] it is noted that mutual eavesdropping through the system, and consequent lack of sound attenuation with distance, could affect couples' spatial interaction with each other. However, the role of sound in shaping understandings of space is not extensively addressed in the ubiquitous computing literature. Anthropology and urban studies have addressed the topic as it relates to spaces on the scale of cities. Dourish and Bell [6] discuss space as infrastructure, shaping and shaped by peoples actions in it and beliefs about it. They present an example of auditory organization of space: children in the British Commonwealth memorize the sounds of London's churchbells through a nursery rhyme, and aural map of the city. Indeed, most European cities of the early modern era generated informative ambient soundscapes, conveying not only neighborhood, but time, significant events and power structures, and encouraging or forbidding certain actions [9]. The aural "landscape" is one of the ways in which the city takes on a shape; similarly, patterns of movement, religious activity, historical patterns of migration and habitation, etc, all serve to shape landscapes and make them collectively intelligible [27]. Dourish and Bell argue that ubiquitous computing technologies and the infrastructures upon which they depend similarly offer an infrastructure through which space can be encountered and understood.

In his discussion of context-aware technologies, Svanaes [29] notes that space "comes into being through interaction" and discusses simple technological probes aimed at highlighting how people come to understand augmented space. It may be informative to think of SignalPlay as just such a probe.

3 System Design and Implementation

We take two lessons from these studies. First, at a broad level, they demonstrate the complexity of the relationship between technologies and spatial encounters. Interactive technologies are encountered not simply in their own right, but also as elements in spaces populated by other technologies and people, and which is a site of social action and social meaning. Second, that, although gallery spaces are outside the primary traditional domains of ubiquitous computing application, the exploration and creative engagement that they encourage can provide us with a site for exploring these questions.

Our goal, then, was to create a system that we could use as an experimental testbed for understanding how people explore and understand ubicomp technologies as spatially situated phenomena. The primary criteria were that, first, that the system should be distributed in space; second, that it should allow for simultaneous use by multiple individuals acting independently or in concert; and third, that it slowly disclose its operation. Our prototype system, SignalPlay, addresses these goals by using augmented objects as collective controls for a complex audio space. Deployed in gallery settings, it allows us to explore the ways in which people individually and collectively explore the intersection between spatiality and activity.

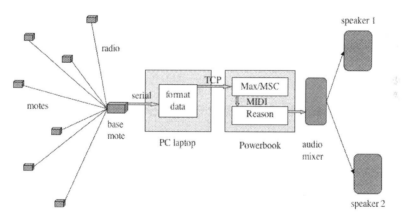

Figure 1: System Diagram of SignalPlay

3.1 Infrastructure

SignalPlay was implemented using Crossbow Mica2 motes running TinyOS. These 1-3/4" x 2-1/2" devices are small enough to be embedded into toys, and are capable of forming ad-hoc networks via radio. The motes were fitted with sensor boards that included accelerometers, magnetometers, light sensors, thermistors, and microphones.

The sensor data from each mote was transmitted at regular intervals of 50, 100 or 200 milliseconds, depending on the reaction time required, to a receiver mote, which was attached by serial connection to a PC laptop. A Java application read and formatted the sensor data and sent it via TCP/IP to a Macintosh laptop, which parsed the sensor data and generated the audio content based on changes caused by user manipulation of the object. The object behaviors and music content were programmed in Max/MSP and Reason. These two programs communicated with each other via MIDI, and the spatialized audio was output through a multi-channel sound interface.

3.2 Interface Objects

We designed or selected specific objects based on their capacity to elicit certain behaviors and on their relation to the theme of "play." On the one hand, the objects must, through their physical affordances, suggest how they should be handled; on the other hand, their effect upon a complex audio environment is difficult to convey through form alone.

The objects were three giant chess pieces (a rook and two pawns), five oversized building blocks, two bongo drums, a navigational compass in a wooden box, and a Star Wars lightsaber.

The three chess pieces sat on the ground amid a "chess board" of six disjoint squares, designed to cue the participant to move the pieces around the space, but with gaps and shifts in the grid arrangement to indicate that rule-based chess was not required. Each piece was about two feet high. A mote was placed inside each chess piece such that moving and setting down the chess piece triggered its behavior.

Five 12" cube building blocks were arranged on and around several small pedestals. Each had a hole in the top under which a light sensor is placed. The expected behavior of stacking blocks on top of one another dropped the light reading below a set threshold and the system responded to that stimulus.

The bongos had holes in the top, at the center of the drumming surface, with light sensors inside each drum. In striking the center of the drums the user could affect the light readings and thereby controls a bass line in the system. The system behavior was sensitive to which drum was struck and how long the light source was obscured. Our augmentations did not greatly affect the sound of simply drumming on the bongos.

The box-mounted compass was hinged in two directions, allowing it to swivel when tilted. A mote was attached to the outside of the box and readings from the attached accelerometer and magnetometer were used to control sound. When the compass was at rest or the compass lid closed it was silent. By opening the lid, the user activated its sound and controlled various parameters of a waveform synthesizer by moving, tilting and rotating the compass.

The lightsaber was an off-the-shelf plastic Star Wars lightsaber fitted with a mote mounted to the handle. It sounded upon sensing motion and was silenced after several seconds at rest. When swung by a participant, the speed at which it moved dictated the enacting of sampled sounds.

SignalPlay was deployed first at the opening event for a new research building at the UCI campus, and subsequently in a gallery space for several days. The installation, both at the building opening and in the gallery space, was arranged such that the chess set occupied territory – indicated by the squares placed on the floor – that was roughly central to the piece. Blocks were placed as a group to one side. The bongos, compass, and lightsaber were placed on two small pedestals to the other side. During the gallery showings the room, approximately 15'x18', was shared with another installation. The two installations were spatially distinguishable, but not separated; a set of three interactive sculptures was mounted on the wall while SignalPlay was placed on the floor and other horizontal surfaces.

There are several salient features of the design of the objects and the space that we wish to highlight here. First, the actions initially elicited by SignalPlay's objects do produce discernable effects on the system, but other effects can be gradually revealed through use over time. Second, the size and design of each object makes it difficult to operate more than one object at a time, making collaboration necessary to reveal all behaviors of the system. And third, the spatial distribution of the objects throughout a single room provided enough space for participants to play individually, but also allowed enough visual and auditory awareness to coordinate with others.

Figure 2: (a) Antique compass with attached mote. (b) A participant poses with the lightsaber. To the left is one of the chess pieces. Behind and to the right are the bongos. (c) Another participant stacks blocks.

3.3 Sound Controls

Each interface object affects the system in a readily apparent way through discrete sound events (*direct controls*) that occur in immediate response to participant interaction. In addition, most of the objects have effects on a system-wide level (*systemic controls*), thereby changing the ways in which the sounds of other objects are processed. Through this second mode of feedback, participants begin to engage in a process of interaction not just between themselves and the system, but also indirectly (and directly through social behavior) with other participants. Participants may thus play with the system individually, affect the response of other people's instruments, or play in concert.

The systemic control of sound feedback is currently based on control of tonal harmony (keys, scales and intervals), tempo, and timbre. For all of the objects except the lightsaber, we base the direct sounds on a globally specified pitch we call the *tonal center*; if the tonal center is changed, their sounds are transposed in pitch by the same interval. These objects, except for the compass, are also governed by a *scale* of specified intervals relative to that tonal center. The object sounds base their tonal harmony on a *set* of pitches defined by the tonal center and scale intervals. However, object sounds are not confined only to pitches within that set, but can also deviate by a chosen interval from specific pitches within the set.

Most of the directly controlled sounds have an associated tempo, be it the rate at which samples and notes are triggered, the delay and decay times of signal processing modules, or the enacting of dependent processes. Interaction with certain objects causes system-wide tempo changes that affect these parameters. For instance, a transient "hit" on the bongos will trigger that instrument's sound while instead holding your hand continuously over the light sensor will cause the tempo to speed up or slow down (depending on which drum you trigger).

The object behaviors form a continuum from simple and direct control to complex and systemic control in the following order: lightsaber, compass, bongos, chess pieces, and blocks. The lightsaber uses only direct controls with no affect on a system-wide level. This allows its behavior to be very easily understood. The compass is affected by the tonal center but not the pitch sets. The rest of the objects have direct controls with an increasing level of system controls. In addition, there are sounds that are not related to the physical objects; these are based entirely on systemic changes and have no direct control.

4   Exploring and Interpreting Space

We deployed SignalPlay in four showings. The first was the building opening noted above; the other three were showings at the Arts, Culture and Technology building at UCI. During the building opening and two of the gallery showings, we video-recorded people's interactions with the exhibit and received informal feedback from them during and after their interactions with SignalPlay. The video was a mix of handheld, manual recording, allowing close-ups of participant interaction with the system, and stationary video taken at a vantage point from which the entire installation could be viewed. The observations presented here are the results of an initial analysis of these video materials.

As is clear from the earlier description, SignalPlay is both inherently collaborative (since it is physically too large for a single person to explore) and responsive to transformations in its physical configuration; our goal, then, was to use it as a basis for understanding aspects of the interactions between people, actions, and artifacts in augmented spaces. One starting point for this analysis is Ullmer and Ishii's [32] MCRpd interaction model for representational tangible interfaces. Based on the model-view-controller approach to graphical user interface development, MCRpd presents a framework for tangible interaction in which the "view" component is distributed between the digital and the physical. A physical controller cum physical representation affects a digital model, which may output a digital representation.

They point to audio from a speaker as an example of digital representation, and chess pieces and chess boards as examples of physical representations.

We distinguish between two aspects of people's experience in forming an understanding of SignalPlay. The first is learning to *control* the system through the objects; they second is learning to "read" or *interpret* the sound output of the whole system as being a result of purposive human action. These two attributes are analytically distinguishable, as suggested by the MCRpd model, but not separable in practice. We interpret participants' perceptions of SignalPlay to be inextricably bound with their actions within it [25]. Control and interpretation are tied to participants' interactions with each other and with the space they inhabit. As we have illustrated above, people encounter ubiquitous computing technologies in socially-organized settings. Even when they are alone, they act nonetheless in spaces that have social and cultural meanings and interpretations. These factors – not just how people encountered the system along with others, but also how they encountered it in terms of sedimented understandings and metaphors – were significant aspects of our observations.

In what follows, we will discuss some of the experiences of SignalPlay drawn from the video materials. We organize these into three related topics. First, we consider individual interactions with the devices, and how both the material and metaphorical aspects of the artifacts shapes interaction. Second, we move from an individual to a collective level, discussing how people used aspects of the system to play not simply with the technology but also with each other. Finally, we approach the question of "reading the space" and discuss the ways in which learned how to interpret the actions of the system as the outcome of the embodied practices of actors.

4.1   Modes of Object Interaction

Our first consideration is the ways in which individuals encountered the system, and how the properties of the artifacts out of which it was constructed – both material properties and metaphorical properties – shaped and constrained their interactions.

Objects were designed to evoke certain behaviors by resembling everyday artifacts; however we also wanted to invite exploration by making it evident that these objects were augmented. Physical cues indicated that the objects were not exactly what they represented: the chess set was incomplete, the chess board strewn across the floor in a not-quite-grid, and the motes' antennae poked out of the blocks. As participants learned to exploit the digital augmentation of SignalPlay's toys, their engagements with the objects varied, reflecting different forms of engagement both with the objects themselves and with the effects that they controlled. We observed three major categories of use: iconic, intrinsic, and instrumental.

Iconic interaction entails interacting with a physical icon in the ways afforded by the object it represents. Examples of iconic interaction with objects in SignalPlay include moving chess pieces from one square to another, stacking the blocks, beating on the bongos, or holding the compass in front of oneself while walking around the room. For example, a few participants, while playing with the chess pieces, limited themselves to legal moves, never moving the rook diagonally or the pawns more than one square over. Iconic use, then, is shaped primarily by the metaphors suggested by the physical objects themselves; they are appropriated as augmented versions of their traditional analogs.

Intrinsic interaction takes advantage of the intrinsic physical characteristics of an object. For example, because our chess pieces were hollow, a pair of participants (playing together) proceeded to stack them on top of one another. This mode of play had nothing to do with the object's status as a physical icon of a chess piece, but rather responded to the physical configurations of the objects themselves. Turkle and Papert [31] report a wonderful illustration of intrinsic interaction in their dicussion of *bricolage* among elementary school students learning engineering concepts. Given an assignment to propel a small robot forward using a motor, many of the children used the motors to drive wheels; one boy, however, used a motor to drive a robot around directly by the force of its vibration. He did not think of the tool as an instance of the category *motor*, but rather as a thing that vibrates in such a way that might move a small robot around. Similarly, the idea to tilt our compass does not come from its "compassness", but rather from the fact that it happens to swivel in an interesting way when tilted.

Figure 3: Stackable chess pieces

In comparison to the two earlier modes of interaction, instrumental interaction is not focused on the physical objects themselves, but on the effects that they engender; people engaged in instrumental interaction reach "through" the objects, focused on using them as controllers of a digital system. In the case of SignalPlay, users took advantage of the ways in which the musical sounds were influenced by manipulation of the object, treating it similarly to a musical instrument. For example, we observed a participant "playing the compass" by a combination of tilting, swiveling his wrist, and closing and opening the lid. A pair of women played with the blocks by a combination of stacking and covering light holes with their hands or other objects. Instrumental interaction may exploit the intrinsic physical features of the augmented object, (as in covering light holes) or it may be externally the same as the iconic interaction (as in stacking the blocks), or it may constitute a combination of the two; the critical aspect of instrumental interaction is the user's understanding of the object and system.

Our observations of participants' play revealed in each object a different interrelation between these three modes of interaction. For example, the lightsaber had been augmented simply to make the sounds that might be associated with it through the Star Wars films; it did not affect any other sounds in the system. In this case, instrumental interaction did not differ significantly from iconic interaction; it acted just as a lightsaber is "supposed" (or might be expected) to act. In contrast, iconic interaction with the compass, triggered only a subset of the possible sounds. The intrinsic interaction of tilting the box allowed participants greater control over the pitch of the compass's sound. Participants generally understood the lightsaber right away, and we observed numerous instances where a participant might pick it up, play for just a few seconds, and quickly put it down or try to hand it off to another person. In the case of the augmented compass, we found many instances of extended interaction over several minutes, frustration, exploration, discovery and failure.

Figure 4: "Playing the compass" by tilting, closing and opening.

Initial Conditions and Sequential Experience. Participants' interaction with SignalPlay proceeded in an approximate sequence. A tentative poke may lead to engaged iconic interaction. Further exploration may involve intrinsic interaction, then confident use of the object as instrument. Instrumental interaction may then lead a participant to exploit more of the object's intrinsic characteristics. This sequence describes only a general trend. Participants' behavior could be influenced by their initial experience, which helped determine *which* exploratory actions they tried.

A man who tried raising and lowering the compass had some success affecting pitch change in that manner. When he subsequently played with the bongos, failing to make them trigger a sound by drumming them, he then tried to raise and lower them as he had with the compass. This action is not particularly afforded by the bongos, either physically or instrumentally.

We logged numerous instances of participants playing while a friend watched, sometimes right at their shoulder, pointing and suggesting actions. As the crowd grew, we logged an increasing number of participants watching and being watched by strangers who simply stood back and did not interact with the person at play. Mutual watching informed participants' understanding of how to control the system through objects; as watching increased, participants tended to become less tentative and more engaged. Some participants, after watching for some time, skipped iconic interaction altogether, imitating a more experienced participant's instrumental interaction.

Space and Modes of Interaction. In the case of the compass, when people thought of it iconically, they tended to cover more space, walking about the room holding the compass. When they started thinking of it more instrumentally, they were more likely to play it standing stationary and changing only direction and tilt. We saw this transformation take place in the case of one man who was bent on understanding the compass; though he roamed the room at first, after five minutes playing with it he was controlling the sound confidently and with his feet planted in one spot.

Playing with the blocks or the chess pieces as a collocated set reinforced the iconic nature of the objects. This became evident during one of the gallery showings when two participants moved the blocks and bongos onto the chess board into the middle of the room, disrupting the objects' clearly demarcated territories. Their treatment of the objects changed drastically as a result of this move. One covered the light hole on the bongo with one hand, swinging the lightsaber with the other and using it to cover a light hole on one of the blocks. Meanwhile her friend, as she bent to set it down a chess piece with one arm, covered the second light hole on the bongos with her other hand. Other participants followed their lead and adhered far less to iconic interaction than previously. That this disruption of the exhibit's spatial setup had such a noticeable effect on participants' object interactions indicates that their understanding of the system is affected not a little by how they think of it within the space of the gallery.

4.2 Collective Encounters and Interpretation

People tended to encounter SignalPlay in groups. One interesting set of issues, then, concern the ways in which it mediated collective experiences. People respond both the technology and to the setting within which it is encountered – in our cases, a technological demonstration or a gallery space. These settings lend meaning to the technology, as something to be explored and understood, but not necessarily to be used as a tool. These contexts shape and limit forms of engagement; the socially understood settings both "script" people's encounters with the technology (time-limited, to be shared with others, not to be taken away, etc) as well as making the space and the technology "legible" (in terms of, for example, how the various elements of our system could be seen as part of a single "piece" but distinguishable from others nearby.)

Playing with Others. Like Hindmarsh et al's *Ghost Ship*, the interactional capabilities of SignalPlay manifested themselves fully when the gallery space was crowded. Crowds lent themselves to group play and observation of participants by other participants, both of which encouraged instrumental interaction.

The chess set is a case in point. Due to the size and dispersal of the chess pieces, one person could not move them rapidly enough to make the tonal change obvious. At one showing, once the workings of the system were explained to the participants, two pairs of women gravitated towards the chess set, which had previously generated interest only in a couple individuals. These two groups remained engaged for longer than the previous solo players and, in attending to the objects' capacity as sound controllers, departed more from the iconic cues of the chess pieces; illegal moves were made more readily and conventions of turn-taking were discarded. One pair was quite aware of their departure from iconic interaction, commenting that "no one can win this game!" and cracking jokes about how they should have a chess timer

In later gallery showings that lasted longer and drew larger crowds, participants would roll a chess piece around the edge of its base, or hold it up and swing it, triggering chord changes in quicker succession than they would have if making chess moves. Indeed, it was during games of "speed chess", and other interactions that triggered rapid change, that the effect of the rook on the tonal center of the system became evident. Those of us who do not have perfect pitch depend on our imperfect memory in order to hear intervals. A single person engaging in iconic interaction with the objects in SignalPlay, then, typically does not reveal the systemic sound effects of some of the objects because of this temporal aspect of the system. On Hindmarsh's *Ghost Ship*, space was the key element in understanding the exhibit, since video images taken in one part of the room were displayed to other people in another part of the room. This was true for SignalPlay, since moving the rook in one part of the room would affect the tonal center for other objects scattered about the space, however time was also a critical factor. In SignalPlay, systemic sound controls were most evident when several users interacted at the same time, triggering objects in quick succession.

Peripheral Awareness and Mutual Monitoring. Unsurprisingly, participants' attention might be drawn to one another due to loud talking or sudden motions. Co-presence and peripheral awareness of companions' locations proved to be a crucial component in visitors' understanding of *Ghost Ship* [19]. In SignalPlay as well, awareness of people in space was a necessary step towards an understanding of system sound in space. However, participants' awareness of each other in the *Ghost Ship* installation was based on vision more exclusively than in SignalPlay, where awareness of others' actions did not necessarily depend on the direction of ones' gaze.

Participants frequently monitored each other through the system. For instance, a girl playing with the blocks demonstrated awareness of her friend playing with the compass, turning towards the camera, widening her eyes and smiling when the compass sound suddenly changes in quality. Additionally, participants are aware of each others' awareness, and explorations took on a certain aspect of performance. Two girls playing with the blocks dance to the music, and people playing with the lightsaber adopt dramatic poses.

This mutual monitoring through audio was not deliberately designed into the system, but rather the result of simple, but public interaction. Grinter et al [14] noted a similar phenomenon in the Sotto Voce system: the system was meant to allow pairs of museum visitors to share audio content regarding the exhibits, but it was used in addition to monitor the location of companions. In this case the information shared is not so explicit, but it is shared more widely, to strangers and friends alike.

4.3 Reading the Space

Finally, here, the experiences with SignalPlay also highlight our concern with the ways in which actions in space become readable and interpretable to others. We encounter spaces as particular kinds of places [15]; as public or private, as spaces of work or leisure, as rowdy or dignified, etc. In our deployments, we were particularly interested in the "legibility" of space and technology – that is, in how people could learn to read it or interpret it, and in particular how they could read the system's activity as being a consequence of their own and others' actions.

A direct physical mapping between the gallery space and SignalPlay's audio output would identify the sounds as coming from the speakers, located in certain corners of the room. On only one occasion, however, did a participant actually indicate the speakers as the source of the sound, an 8-year-old boy who wanted to know how we got the sounds from "there" (the bongos) to "there" (pointing at speakers). Though he knew intellectually where the source of the sounds were physically located, interactionally he mapped the sounds to the space quite differently. Seconds after he pointed out the speakers, the rook was moved, triggering the associated sound. Looking up from the bongos, he pointed towards the chess set. In this section, we examine how our participants might come to understand SignalPlay's audio output in space as something more than a simple physical correspondence. Participants' interpretation of the SignalPlay space was built upon their awareness of people in space, as previously discussed, as well as a strong association between sounds and objects, objects and territory, and awareness of each other's sound-producing actions.

Transferring Focus to Objects. We saw numerous instances of participants examining motes that were attached externally to the lightsaber and compass. However, we also saw a man peer inside the compass box, despite the visible mote. We also noted a woman who put the compass up to her ear, as if expecting the sound to emanate directly from it. These were the most noticeable illustrations of the general tendency to focus on the physical objects as the source of the sounds and regard the digital system as transparent. Universally, when a participant's attention was attracted by a sound associated with a certain object, they turned not towards the physical source of the sound – the speakers – but to the causal source of the sound, the object.

Physical Objects Demarcate Space. At one point during one of the gallery showings, a participant separated one of the blocks from the set, placed it on the floor next to one of the sculptures from the other installation sharing the room, and ran an Ethernet cable from that sculpture into the hole on top of the block that allowed light to reach the light sensor inside. This breached the grouping of the blocks, expressed by keeping them all in the same territory, not to mention the spatial distinction between the two installations. The displacement of that block proved to be an exception that proved the rule; it drew looks, comments, and jokes from other participants.

Different objects elicited different spatial behaviors. The lightsaber, compass and bongos tended to "wander" but return home. A participant might roam around the room with the lightsaber, poking their friends and swinging it around. Participants commonly walked around with the compass, and in fact that movement can be considered an example of iconic interaction encouraged by the compass. However, participants almost always put them back exactly where they found them.

The chess pieces on the other hand, were placed on a chess board, a clearly demarcated piece of territory. Though they were moved around, they were rarely moved off of the chess board. The blocks, for the most part, stayed on the pedestals on which they were originally placed. Territory was not marked for the blocks, any more than it was for the compass, which traveled more. The key difference was that while the iconic interaction with the compass required movement through space, the blocks encouraged stacking in place. Thus the interactional properties of the objects affected how participants fit them into the space of the exhibit.

Sounds and Sound-Producing Action. Sounds in SignalPlay are caused by visible action, allowing watchers to associate a sound with an object and the person controlling it, and thereby making the system's audio output interpretable. During a gallery session, three women off camera are discussing "the bong" and in order to clarify its source to them another participant simply picks up the rook and moves it. This demonstration makes explicit a usually implicit process of monitoring other participants' actions and associating them with system sounds.

These three aspects of interaction – with the artifacts themselves, with others, and as a means of reading space – are not separate behaviors; they arise in concert with each other. Here they provide us with a starting point for understanding the relationships between people and activities in augmented spaces, and how ubicomp technologies transform the legibility of actions in space. Although gallery settings differ from office, domestic, or mobile settings in which ubicomp technologies may be deployed, those settings are also populated by people and by technologies, and ones that must be interpreted and transformed through practical engagement. Our data illustrate that the collective, spatial, and sequential aspects of encounters with ubicomp environments are critical factors in how those technologies will be put to collective use.

5   Conclusions and Implications

Our world is both physical and social. While we might distinguish between these as analytic concerns, they are fundamentally intertwined as practical matters. Just as it is impossible for us to encounter space independently of its physical characteristics, it is equally impossible for us to encounter it independently of its social character and organization. This social character means that spaces are not "given"; they are the products of active processes of interpretation. The meaningfulness of space is a consequence of our encounters with it. For ubiquitous computing, this is an important consideration. We are engaged in the development of technologies that are rapidly moving out of traditional computational settings – laboratories and workplaces – and into everyday environments. Ubiquitous computing research is actively concerned with domestic environments, with technology in leisure settings, with mobile technologies, and with a range of computational embeddings in space. The research challenge, then, is to understand how it is that computationally augmented spaces will be legible; with how people will be able to understand them and act within them.

Taking this perspective highlights some aspects that are traditionally hidden in the ways in which we think about ubiquitous computing and interaction. Our traditional focus, drawn from decades of research on HCI, is on how people might interact with technologies. However, as we can see from observations with SignalPlay, this is a narrow perspective. Instead, we have been looking at how people engage with space and with each other through the technologies that we provided to them. Rather than focusing on interaction, we focus on participation; how people collectively act in space, and through that participation, achieve concerted social action.

Our SignalPlay deployments scarcely scratch the surface of this topic. They were limited in both scope and duration, and so provide only a brief snapshot of the ways in which people engage with augmented spaces. Nonetheless, the experiences are telling. A number of broad observations are particularly notable.

First, it was notable that people sought to understand the system not as a whole but in terms of the individual actions of different components. That is, although the different physical objects in SignalPlay embodied different controls and inputs for a single distributed system, people interacted with the system instead as a series of individual elements. In cases where, as we described, people essentially focused on the objects themselves as sound-producing (rather than sound-controlling), this was particularly clear. We are used to interacting in a world of non-communicating objects, with individuable characters and natures. This remains a primary element of people's encounters with these technologies. Objects take on meanings and interpretations in their own right rather than as elements of a "system." This suggests, then, that user's experiences and interpretations of ubiquitous computing systems will often be of a quite different sort than those of their designers, because of the radically different ways in which they encounter these systems. Narratives or design models based around a "systems" model should be tempered by alternatives constructed in terms of individual objects with unique identities, histories, and properties.

Second, one particularly interesting area for further exploration is the temporal organization of activity. In previous explorations of technologically augmented spaces, the primary focus has been on how computational power could transform the structure of those spaces for interaction, collaboration, or communication. For example, using video technologies to "link" spaces produces a "warping" of space for communication. However, our experiences with SignalPlay drew our attention to the ways in which information technology can transform the temporal structure of space and interaction. We currently lack good design approaches for understanding the temporal aspects of technologies; not just the sequential organization of interaction, but aspects of pace and rhythm. The temporality of interaction and encounters with technology is a neglected aspect of interaction design and an important part of our ongoing work.

Lastly, ubiquitous computing technologies are ones through which people encounter and come to understand infrastructures. As Star [28] notes, infrastructure is "sunk into" other technological systems and systems of practice. Mainwaring et al [24] have noted that infrastructure may itself be a site for negotiating social roles or for marking social categories, but our concern here is more the ways in which infrastructure manifests itself as an aspect of experience. The presence or absence of infrastructure, or differences in its availability, becomes one of the ways in which spaces are understood and navigated. At conferences or in airports, the seats next to power outlets are in high demand, and in a wide range of settings, the strength of a cellular telephone signal becomes an important aspect of how space is assessed and used. As we develop new technologies that rely on physical but invisible infrastructures, we create new ways of understanding the structure of space [29]. Again, this departs from the ways in which we normally think and talk about ubiquitous computing systems as designers, where our focus is primarily on the technologies and less on the spaces that those technologies occupy. Our design models must address space not as a passive container of objects and actions, but as something that is explicitly constructed, managed, and negotiated in the course of interaction; and at the same time, we need to be conscious of ways in which new infrastructures provide new ways of encountering space.

SignalPlay is an initial examination of people's interactions with and through computationally augmented objects and spaces. Our focus is less on technical innovation and more on uncovering behaviors and understandings that will inform future work. This includes augmenting a new interdisciplinary research building with a sensor network infrastructure that will support ambient displays of presence and activity, and enhancements to SignalPlay itself, incorporating network topology and radio signal strength in order to tie the system more closely to physical space. More broadly, our research in this area further develops the 'embodied interaction' paradigm, which concerns itself with how technologies and artifacts take on meaning for their users through their embedding into systems of practice [5]. This relationship between people, objects, and activities, cast in terms of the ways in which practice evolves, is a central consideration for future developments in ubiquitous computing.

Acknowledgements

This work was supported in part by the National Science Foundation under awards 0133749, 0205724 and 0326105, and by a grant from Intel Corporation.

References

1   Aoki, P., Grinter, R., Hurst, A., Szymanski, M., Thornton, J. and Woodruff, A.: Sotto Voce: Exploring the Interplay of Conversation and Mobile Audio Spaces. Proc. ACM Conf. Human Factors in Computing Systems CHI (2002), 431-438.
2   Anderson, K.: 'ensemble': Playing with Sensors and Sound. Ext. Abstracts ACM Conf. Human Factors in Computing Systems CHI (2004), 1239-1242.
3   Burrell, J., Gay, G., Kubo, K., and Farina, N.: Context-Aware Computing: A Case Study. Proc. Intl. Conf. Ubiquitous Computing Ubicomp (2002), 1-15,
4   Dinkla, S.: From Participation to Interaction: Toward the Origins of Interactive Art. In: Leeson, L.H. (ed.): Clicking In: Hot Links to a Digital Culture, Bay Press. (1996), 279-290.
5   Dourish, P.: Where the Action Is, MIT Press. (2001)
6   Dourish, P. and Bell, G.: The Experience of Infrastructure and the Infrastructure of Experience: Meaning and Structure in Everyday Encounters with Space. Working paper (under review) (2005).
7   Ferris, K., Bannon, L.: "...a load of ould Boxology!" Proc. Conf. Designing Interactive Systems DIS (2002), 41-49.
8   Garfinkel, H. and Livingston, E.: Phenomenal Field Properties of Order in Formatted Queues and their Neglected Standing in the Current Situation of Inquiry. Visual Studies, 18(1), (2003), 21-28.
9   Garrioch, D.: Sounds of the City: The Soundscape of Early Modern European Towns. Urban History, 30(1), (2003), 5-25.
10   Gaver , W.: The Affordances of Media Spaces for Collaboration. Proc. ACM Conf. Computer-Supported Cooperative Work CSCW (1992).
11   Gaver, W., Smerts, G., and Overbeeke, K.: A Virtual Window on Media Space. Proc. ACM Conf. Human Factors in Computing Systems CHI (1995).
12   Goodwin, C.: Professional Vision. American Anthropologist, 96(1), (1994), 606-633.

13   Goodwin, C.: Seeing in Depth. Social Studies of Science, 25, (2003), 237-74.
14   Grinter, R., Aoki, P., Hurst, A., Szymanski, M., Thornton, J., Woodruff, A.: Revisiting the Visit: Understanding How Technology Can Shape the Museum Visit. Proc. ACM Conf. Computer-Supported Cooperative Work CSCW (2002), 146-155.
15   Harrison, S. and Dourish, P.: Re-Place-ing Space: The Roles of Place and Space in Collaborative Systems. Proc. ACM Conf. Computer-Supported Cooperative Work CSCW (1996).
16   Heath, C., Luff, P.: Disembodied Conduct: Communication Through Video in a Multi-Media Office Environment. In Proc.ACM Conf. Human Factors in Computing Systems CHI (1991) , 99-103.
17   Heath, C., Luff, P., vom Lehn, D., Hindmarsh, J.: Crafting Participation: designing ecologies, configuring experience. Visual Communication, SAGE Publications (2002), 9-33.
18   Hindmarsh, J. and Heath, C. : Sharing the Tools of the Trade: The Interactional Constitution of Workplace Objects. Journal of Contemporary Ethnography, 29(5), (2000), 523-562.
19   Hindmarsh, J., Heath, C., vom Lehn, D., Cleverly, J.: Creating Assemblies: Aboard the *Ghost Ship*. Proc. ACM Conf. Computer-Supported Cooperative Work CSCW (2002), 156-165.
20   Ishii, H., Ullmer, B.: Tangible Bits: Towards Seamless Interfaces Between People, Bits and Atoms. Proc. ACM Conf. Human Factors in Computing Systems CHI (1997), 234-241.
21   Kabisch, E., Williams, A., Dourish, P.: Symbolic Objects in a Networked Gestural Sound Interface. In Ext. Abst. of ACM Conf. Human Factors in Computing Systems CHI (2005).
22   Kendon, A.: Studies in the Behavior of Face-to-Face Interaction. Peter de Ridder Press, Lisse, Netherlands (1977).
23   Koile, K., Tollmar, K., Demirdjian, D., Shrobe, H., and Darrell, T.: Activity Zones for Context-Aware Computing. Proc. Intl. Conf. Ubiquitous Computing Ubicomp (2003), 90-106.
24   Mainwaring, S., Chang, M., and Anderson, K.: Infrastructures and their Discontents: Implications for Ubicomp. Proc. Ubicomp (2004).
25   Robertson, T.: The Public Availability of Actions and Artefacts. In: Computer Supported Cooperative Work, 11, (2002), 299-316.
26   Ryave, A. and Schenkein, J.: Notes on the Art of Walking. In: Turner (ed.), Ethnomethodology, London: Penguin (1974), 265-274.
27   Smail, D.L.: Imaginary Cartographies: Possession and Identity in Late Medieval Marseille. Ithaca: Cornell, (1999).
28   Star, S.L.: The Ethnography of Infrastructure. American Behavioral Scientist, 43(3), (1999), 377-391.
29   Svanaes, D. Context-Aware Technology: A Phenomenological Perspective. Human-Computer Interaction, 16(2-4), (2001), 379-400.
30   Truong, K., Abowd, G., and Brotherton, J.: Who, What, When, Where, How: Design Issues of Capture & Access Applications. Proc. Intl. Conf. Ubiquitous Computing Ubicomp (2001), 209-224.
31   Turkle, S. and Papert, S.: Epistemological Pluralism and the Revaluation of the Concrete. In: I. Harel & S. Papert (eds.): Constructionism. Norwood, NJ (1991), 161-192.
32   Ullmer, B. and Ishii, H.: Emerging Frameworks for Tangible User Interfaces. In: Carroll (ed.): Human-Computer Interaction in the New Millenium, Addison-Wesley, (2001), 579-601.
33   Vom Lehn, D., Heath, C. and Hindmarsh, J.: Exhibiting Interaction: Conduct and Collaboration in Museums and Galleries. Symbolic Interaction, 24(2), (2001), 189-216.
34   Weinberg, G., Aimi, R., and Jennings, K.: The Beatbug Network – A Rhythmic System for Interdependent Group Collaboration. Proc. NIME (2002).

Scanning Objects in the Wild:
Assessing an Object Triggered Information System

A.J. Bernheim Brush, Tammara Combs Turner, Marc A. Smith, Neeti Gupta

Microsoft Research,
One Microsoft Way,
Redmond, WA, 98052
{ajbrush, tcombs, masmith, neetig}@microsoft.com

Abstract. We describe the results of a field deployment of the AURA system which links online content to physical objects through machine readable tags. AURA runs on commercially available pocket computers using integrated barcode scanners, wireless networks, and web services. We conducted a real world deployment with twenty participants over five weeks. The results from our field study illustrate the importance of moving beyond demonstrations and testing system design assumptions in the real world, as our field study highlighted several places that our seemingly reasonable design assumption did not match with real usage. Our experience deploying AURA highlighted several key features for mobile object triggered information systems including handling groups of items and a robust offline experience.

1 Introduction

For almost every manufactured or packaged object on Earth there are volumes of information available online, from personal reviews to manufacturing details. The challenge has been bridging the gap between physical objects and the collection of relevant online information about them. The rapid development of mobile computing devices, wireless networks, and sensors means that all the elements are present for the creation of mobile *object triggered information systems* that allow people to use a cell phone or PDA with a sensor to scan an object and access related information and services. These systems can be thought of as a new type of mouse for the physical world that enables users to "click" on the objects around them.

Our Advanced User Resource Annotation (AURA) system [14] integrates a wireless Pocket PC with a barcode reader so that users can scan books, CDs, DVDs, packaged grocery products and other barcoded objects and then view, store and share related metadata and annotations. The AURA system can support many different sensor technologies and scenarios of use including accessing reviews for products, doing just-in-time price comparisons, creating an inventory of collections of objects such as CDs or books, and sharing information about objects with others. We developed and deployed a set of core application features (scan, identify, retrieve, store object metadata, annotate, publish, etc.) and then evaluated the platform in a field study to test our design assumptions. As Sellen stressed at a workshop on application-

M. Beigl et al. (Eds.): UbiComp 2005, LNCS 3660, pp. 305–322, 2005.

led research in ubiquitous computing [5], we believe these types of field studies are critical to evaluate ubiquitous computing applications because it is impossible to anticipate exactly how design assumptions will play out without real usage experience.

We deployed AURA to twenty people internal to our organization for five weeks and collected data about their experience using surveys, ethnographic observation, and usage logs. We studied how participants used AURA in their homes, offices and on regular shopping trips. The ways in which participants used AURA and the problems they experienced, sometimes quite mundane, shattered a number of our design assumptions and highlighted several important features for object triggered information systems including handling groups of items and having a robust offline experience.

2   Related Systems and Research

The AURA project[1] shares the goal of bridging the gap between the physical and the online worlds with many other research and commercial systems. Perhaps the earliest object triggered information system to bridge this gap was the electronic tags research of Want et al. [17] where electronic tags on items such as books and posters linked to online information and actions. Several more recent systems were primarily designed for use at the desktop including the failed Cue Cat [6] commercial venture and the WebStickers project [11]. In formative evaluations of WebStickers the length of the barcode reader cord was frequently criticized highlighting the importance of mobility.

With advances in mobile computing devices and wireless networks a variety of mobile object triggered information systems have been developed. Products like Socket OrganizeIT [16] and Delicious Library [7] target consumers that wish to inventory their collections of books, music and other barcoded items. Mobile services such as Amazon Japan's Scan Search described at Gizmodo [9] let users take pictures of barcodes with camera phones. Camera phones in Japan also include software for reading QR Codes, two dimensional barcodes that often appear on Japanese advertisements [13]. Of the mobile systems, our focus on authoring and sharing information makes Konomi's QueryLens [10] one of the most closely related projects to AURA. QueryLens used PDAs with barcode readers to allow users to scan items and author queries, view and share information about particular objects.

Another set of object triggered information systems focus on usage in retail environments. Many different aspects of the shopping experience have been studied including preparing shopping lists [12], trying to decrease shopping time [3], and offering comparative pricing based on a user's current product selection [8]. Two systems similar to AURA are the Pocket Bargain Finder [4] system that allows users to shop in a physical retail store, find an item of interest, scan in its barcode and search for a potentially lower price among a set of online retailers and the discontinued Beeline Shopper [2] system that provided a barcode scanner and software for creating grocery lists and recommendations on healthier alternatives.

---

[1] Although they share the same name, our project is not related to Project AURA at Carnegie Mellon University: http://www-2.cs.cmu.edu/~aura/.

Although our system has a goal of building online communities around collections of scanned objects that differentiates it from several of the systems, many of the core features (e.g. scanning and viewing related online information) have been explored in these closely related systems. Thus the primary contribution of this paper is our field study. While Konomi deployed QueryLens on a small scale at a university festival, we are unaware of a similar field study of a mobile object triggered information system with a large group of users over several weeks.

3 The AURA System

The following illustrates a typical usage scenario AURA was designed to enable:
> *While shopping at his local bookstore, James scans a new book he is considering purchasing using the barcode scanner attached to his Pocket PC. His AURA client application queries the appropriate resolution service to identify the book James scanned and presents information about the book including links to reviews and pricing at several online sites. James decides he wants to remember the book and clicks the "Add to My AURA" button. This adds the book to his list of AURA items. James then makes a private comment on the book to remind him of the price at the bookstore.*

Other scenarios of use for AURA include accessing reviews of products, creating an inventory of collections of barcoded objects, and sharing information about objects with others. In the remainder of this section we present the design of the AURA client application and web portal.

3.1 The AURA Client Application

Our current implementation of the AURA client application runs on Windows Mobile 2003 ("Pocket PC") devices with an additional hardware barcode scanner (the "Socket In-Hand Barcode" scanner) inserted in either the Compact Flash (CF) or Secure Digital Input Output (SDIO) expansion slots of the device. Network connectivity in the form of WiFi (LAN) or Cellular (WLAN) connection is essential for many key features, although minimal functionality is available in an offline mode.

Users scan barcoded objects by positioning the external barcode scanner approximately 6-12 inches from the object and initiating a scan. Scanning is most convenient when users map a Pocket PC button to invoke the scanner, but a scan button is also available in the user interface. Users have visual feedback from the laser or LED targeting beam on the barcode reader that helps them position their scanner. If the scanner acquires the barcode's data, the user hears an audio tone signifying a successful scan. Although we currently focus on barcodes, the architecture is extensible, allowing other sensors technologies such as RFID, GPS, WiFi, IR or Bluetooth beacons, accelerometers, images, audio, etc. to be used to generate information to identify objects. After a successful scan, in online mode the client immediately tries to resolve the barcode and provide information about the object. In offline mode, the client adds the barcode to the scan history. Later, when the user reestablishes a con-

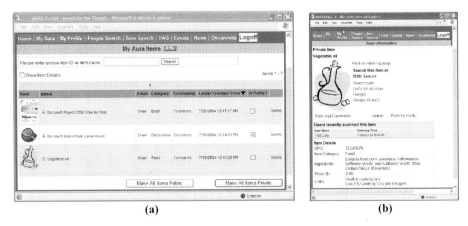

(a)   (b)

Fig. 1. In (a), an example AURA Web Portal page showing the user's list of scanned items. In (b), an Item Information page with item details

nection he or she can view the history of scans and select barcodes to send for resolution.

To resolve a barcode, the AURA client attempts to match the sensor data pattern against a collection of regular expressions stored in "resolution service definition files" which associate varying sensor patterns with "payloads" - applications and web services that offer metadata in exchange for an identifier. We have implemented some initial resolution service definition files that map the fourteen digit ISBN codes that appear on most books; the twelve digit UPC codes printed on many North American packaged goods; and our own seven letters and number scheme for identifying artwork in our organization's collection to related information and search queries. We make use of a combination of private and publicly available Internet-based services such as Amazon's ISBN web service and various search engines to connect objects to online information about them. New resolution service definition files can easily be added with AURA's extensible architecture. For example, new patterns might be defined to match against a library's ten digit barcode standard and map to the web interface for searching the library's catalog. We consider this open backend architecture a critical feature of AURA and an important differentiator from commercial systems that carefully control what information can be accessed about objects.

After AURA resolves an object, the client displays a limited version of the web portal's item information page for the object. This page shows information about the object that could include description, price, and links to search engines. In the interests of privacy, we designed the system so that all information about an object scanned by the user is initially kept local to the mobile device (and the selected resolution service) and not shared with the web portal. Users can choose to upload the details of scanned objects to the web portal with a single additional tap.

3.2 The AURA Web Portal

The AURA Web Portal provides a range of services to manage private and public collections of objects scanned and explicitly uploaded by users. The home page includes features targeted at encouraging sharing and community building. It displays lists of the most recently scanned and annotated items, the most popular items and the most recently scanned public items of the users that have scanned the most items.

When a user uploads information about an object to the portal, a record is created that represents the object and associated meta-data. The resulting item record is initially listed on the user's item list, shown in Figure 1(a), as a private item and is not visible to other users. Users can choose to explicitly make items public to others using the check box associated with each item. The item list page also has several features to facilitate sharing items with others through email and RSS. Each item offers an "Email" link that composes an email containing the item's metadata, constructed links, and annotations. The page is also exposed as RSS 2.0, allowing blog aggregators to collect and display item details in applications like email browsers.

Clicking on the name of an item in the list opens an Item Information page with item details. This page, shown in Figure 1(b), includes a list of URLs for searches and content related to the item. For example, a book item will have a link directly to the page for the book on an online book ecommerce site. The Item Information page also has links for making private and public ratings and comments that will be associated with the item. Any public annotations and ratings on public items are visible to all other users of the system and may be displayed on the homepage and search pages.

4 AURA Field Study

To study how people use AURA, we conducted a five week field study from July 7, 2004 to August 11, 2004 with twenty participants. Our field study was motivated by these research questions:

- How do people use the system? Our design assumptions were that people will use AURA mostly for information access and comparison shopping.
- Do people find the system functional and useful? Our assumption was that the benefits of AURA outweigh the frustration of carrying an external scanner and coping with items AURA can not identify.
- Does the privacy model meet users' needs? Our design assumed a conservative privacy model to limit the chances that a user would make an item public by mistake.
- How do people use the sharing features? Our design assumed that the ability to share object information with others was important.

In the rest of this section we first describe our methodology and then our study findings organized by our research questions.

4.1 Methodology

We recruited participants from an internal company email distribution list for people enthusiastic about Pocket PCs. Based on a screening survey that asked about users' experience with Pocket PCs and the devices they owned we selected twenty participants (16 male, 4 female). We did not know the participants before the study and to the best of our knowledge they did not know each other. We chose participants that owned and used a Pocket PC with either cellular or WiFi connectivity to the Internet so that we could evaluate AURA with people already familiar with connected handheld devices. Our selection criteria were driven by a desire to avoid the sometimes nontrivial usage problems associated with connecting a mobile device to wireless networks. We recognize the self-selection effects on our user population and plan to replicate the studies with less technically savvy users as the technology evolves.

Each participant started the study by attending a training session where we loaned them a barcode scanner and assisted them in installing the AURA client software on their device. We also gave the participants an overview of the system and led them through a training guide to practice using the core features of the system: scanning, uploading, and commenting.

During the first four weeks of the field study participants used AURA as they wished. We then asked participants to complete two specific tasks, with the goal of stimulating sharing through ratings and comments since there was greater likelihood that they would scan similar items. The first task, emailed at the beginning of the final week of the study, instructed participants to take AURA home and scan at least five items on their refrigerator shelves. Thirteen of the twenty participants completed this task. The second task, sent at the end of the final week of study, instructed participants to scan at least five items on their bookshelves over the weekend. This final task was unfortunately sent after people had probably gone home for the weekend, which may have contributed to the fact that only five participants completed this task. However, it is also possible that the low participation rate could have been caused by a lack of perceived value from AURA or by fatigue from the long field study, which finished at the beginning of the next week. At the end of the study all participants were compensated with a coupon for a free coffee. We also held drawings for a fifty dollar Amazon gift certificate each of the last three weeks of the study. Any participant that scanned at least one item during a week was eligible for that week's drawing.

4.1.1 Data Collected

During the field study we collected data using surveys, experience sampling, ethnographic observations, and logging usage of the AURA Web Portal.

Pre-Survey: We surveyed the participants before the field study to gather information about personal technology usage and shopping habits. Nineteen of the 20 participants completed the pre-survey. The majority of pre-survey respondents (78%) used their Pocket PC's several times a day and most for more than 30 minutes a day (68%). Twelve of the nineteen respondents (63%) primarily used the WiFi network to connect to the Internet and the remaining seven (37%) primarily used the Cell network. Almost 90% of participants stated they did a significant amount of shopping for their household with on average two shopping trips for groceries and other retail items in a week. This was important to us since we wanted participants who were likely to engage in retail shopping.

Post-Survey: On the post-survey we asked participants about their experience using AURA and their ratings of existing and potential features. All 20 participants completed the post-study survey.

Experience Sampling Method (ESM): To explore the motivations and settings for our participants' use of AURA at the moment they scanned and uploaded objects we used event contingent experience sampling [1]. We presented participants with an experience survey after every fifth item they uploaded to the Web Portal. The survey asked participants why they scanned an item, what they planned to do with information about the item, where they were, and who they were with. To keep the survey easy to complete, we provided a list of possible responses, but always included the option of "other." Participants completed 173 experience surveys out of the 231 times (75%) we presented the survey to them. Of our twenty participants, eighteen participants completed at least one experience survey.

Ethnographic Field Observations: We conducted ethnographic field observations for eight of our twenty participants, four men and four women. For each of these eight participants the same researcher first conducted a semi-structured interview in their office and then later accompanied the participant on a shopping trip to a retail store selected by the participant. Although we selected the participants to observe before they started using the system, picking the four women and randomly selecting four men, we were pleased that these participants turned out to represent well the different levels of engagement our participants had with AURA.

Usage Logs: We instrumented the Web Portal to record details of each user's uploaded items (due to our privacy model we can only log information about items explicitly uploaded by participants). We also logged comments and ratings made by participants on uploaded items.

4.2 How Do People Use the AURA System?

We explored how our participants used AURA by examining the number of items they uploaded, what they scanned, why they scanned the objects, and where they were when they scanned. While usage varied considerably among participants, many encountered problems scanning objects that could not be recognized by AURA. Among objects AURA did recognize, books and music were popular and the experience survey results suggest participants were often scanning at home to inventory a collection of objects.

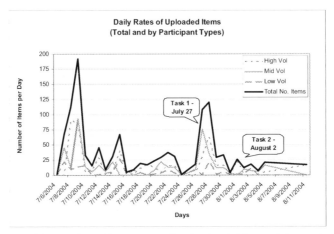

Fig. 2. Daily rate of the number of items scanned and uploaded by participants during the field study. There was self-directed usage until Task 1 was introduced on July 27 where we see a usage spike

4.2.1 How Many Items Did Users Scan?

During the five week field study our participants uploaded a total of 1,156 items (excluding items uploaded during training) out of an unknown number of scanned items. As shown in Figure 2, we saw a novelty effect with much of the activity occurring shortly after the beginning of the study and following the first task request. There was a wide range in the number of items scanned and uploaded by different study participants from 1 to 199 (median = 48.5, mean = 57.8, SD = 55.6). To understand the experience of different types of study participants, we classified them into three groups based on the number of items they scanned and uploaded.

- **High volume scanners:** the three participants who scanned and uploaded 100 or more items during the course of the study. One of these participants was part of the ethnographic observation.
- **Mid volume scanners:** the seven participants who scanned and uploaded 51 – 99 items during the course of the study. Three of these participants were part of the ethnographic observation.
- **Low volume scanners:** the ten participants who scanned and uploaded 50 or fewer items during the course of the study. Four of these participants were part of the ethnographic observations.

Table 1 presents statistics about the participant types including days active, number of items uploaded, and number of public and private items. Figure 3 shows that the number of items uploaded by individual users follows a power law distribution. Overall, participants were active on average five out of a total of thirty-five days in the study, with the high volume participants active an average of fifteen days. All high volume participants and one mid-volume participant scanned and uploaded items each of the five weeks of the study. The other sixteen participants were less consistent in their involvement. The median for mid and low participants was scanning at least

Table 1. Statistics about items uploaded by participants during the field study

Activities	Activity by Participant Types (N) Median (SD, Mean)			
	High (3)	Mid (7)	Low (10)	All (20)
Days Active	15 (1, 14)	5 (2, 6)	4 (2, 4)	5 (4, 6)
Total # of Items	170 (26, 172)	69 (7, 66)	15 (13, 18)	49 (56, 58)
Public Items	60 (70, 81)	8 (20, 18)	7 (11, 10)	10 (37, 24)
Private Items	88 (83, 91)	55 (20, 48)	8 (7, 8)	16 (43, 34)

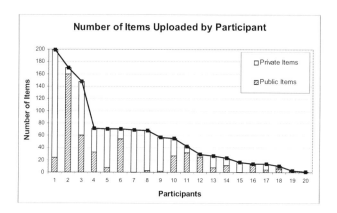

Fig. 3. Number of items uploaded by each participant

one item during three weeks of the study. The number of items uploaded by the high, mid and low participant groups was significantly different based on an ANOVA. (F(2, 17)=158, p < 0.01, follow-up Bonferroni analysis all p < 0.01). The number of days active of the high participants compared to the other two groups was also significantly different. (F (2, 17) = 36.3, p < 0.01, follow-up Bonferroni analysis all p < 0.01).

Of the 1,156 total items uploaded (685 private items, 471 public items), we found that about a fifth of the items had ratings or comments associated with them. Overall, participants made slightly more ratings than comments, with 130 ratings and 116 comments. For both ratings and comments, participants made considerably more public contributions than private ones. Nine percent (107) of the total items received public ratings compared to 2% (23) that received private ratings. Similarly, participants made public comments on 8% (90) of the total items uploaded and private comments on only 2% (26) of uploaded items.

4.2.2 What Did They Scan?

The usage log data showed us what types of items participants uploaded to the AURA web portal. Twenty-four percent of the items uploaded could not be recognized by the resolution services for UPC and ISBN currently implemented in the AURA system.

The percentage of unresolved objects (24%) is no doubt artificially deflated because it does not capture those objects that were unrecognized, but not uploaded. Given the questionable value of uploading unrecognized data it is possible that many more objects were not recognized by our system. We discuss frustration with unrecognized objects in Section 4.3.2.

To categorize the items recognized by the resolution services, three researchers first independently put the items in categories and then resolved any differences through discussion. The top three categories of recognized objects were Print Media items (books and newspapers) with 23% of items, followed by Music and Video items (19%), and Grocery items (18%). These three categories accounted for 60% of uploaded objects. The other categories of uploaded items were Household items (8%), Computer Software (4%), Consumer Electronics (2%), Office Products (1%) and Company Art (1%).

4.2.3 Why and Where Did They Scan?

The data from the 173 experience surveys gives us insight into why participants scanned items and where they were. The primary reason participants reported for scanning and uploading an item was to "inventory a collection of items" (61%). Other less popular responses included: "make a note of the item for later review" (10%), "do a price comparison" (10%), and "order it online" (3%). Respondents chose the "other" response option 16% of the time. Post-survey responses corroborate these results. When asked what they used AURA for, the only option to receive a median response of "Often" was "to inventory a collection of items."

When asked how they would use information about the items they scanned and up-loaded, the most common responses on the experience survey were "do nothing" (34%), and "get more information about this item" (27%). Respondents also chose the "other" response option 24% of the time. Less popular responses were "buy this item" (8%) and "email this item to someone else" (8%).

Participants told us on the experience surveys that they were primarily scanning in their homes (67%). However, several participants did try AURA in other locations. Fourteen of the twenty participants (including all high volume participants) scanned items in two or more locations and seven participants scanned in three or more. After the home, the participant's office was the next most popular scanning location reported on the experience survey (13%), followed by other people's offices (5%), grocery stores (4%), bookstores (4%), DVD/Video stores (2%), and somebody else's home (1%). Respondents chose the "other" response option 5% of the time. Post-survey responses agreed with the experience survey results. When asked how often they used AURA in these locations, only "your home" received a median response of "Often", while work, grocery and bookstore had median responses of "Sometimes." All other locations had a median response of "Never."

Table 2. Responses to post survey questions about participants' experience with AURA. Responses on a 5 point scale (1 = Strongly Disagree … 5 = Strongly Agree)

Post Survey Questions	Reactions by User Type Median (SD, Mean)			
	High (3)	Mid (7)	Low (10)	All (20)
1. Found AURA easy to use	5 (1, 5)	4 (1, 3)	4 (1, 3)	4 (1, 4)
2. Enjoyed using AURA	5 (0, 5)	4 (1, 4)	4 (1, 4)	4 (1, 4)
3. Found AURA useful	4 (1, 4)	3 (1, 3)	4 (1, 3)	4 (1, 4)
4. The benefits of the system out weighed any frustrations experienced	4 (2, 4)	3 (1, 3)	4 (1, 3)	3 (1, 3)
5. The external barcode scanner was easy to use	5 (0, 5)	4 (1, 3)	3 (1, 3)	3 (1, 3)
6. Remembered to carry barcode scanner with me	5 (0, 5)	4 (1, 3)	4 (1, 4)	4 (1, 4)
7. Found it easy to scan items	5 (0, 5)	4 (1, 4)	4 (1, 3)	4 (1, 4)
8. Enough items resolved to make AURA useful	3 (2, 3)	3 (1, 3)	3 (1, 3)	3 (1, 3)

4.3 Do People Find the AURA System Functional and Useful?

From the usage log data, post-survey responses and our observations we believe our participants had a mixed reaction to their use of AURA. Perhaps not surprisingly our three high volume scanners had the most positive reaction. On the post-survey the median responses for high volume scanners were "Strongly Agree" for the questions related to ease of use and enjoyment (Table 2, Q. 1 & 2), and "Agree" that they found AURA useful and that the benefits of the system out-weighted any frustrations experienced (Table 2, Q. 3 & 4). All questions shown in Table 2 were positively phrased and asked on a 5 point Likert scale from Strongly Disagree to Strongly Agree.

Mid volume scanners were the least enthusiastic on the post-survey with median responses of "Neutral" when asked if they found AURA useful and whether the benefits of the system outweighed any frustrations experienced (Table 2, Q. 3 & 4). In this section we discuss the some of the main factors that contributed to our participants' problems using AURA: challenges while scanning, frustration with unrecognized items, issues with connectivity and offline mode, and lack of value when shopping for low engagement objects.

4.3.1 Challenges when Scanning

During interviews and shopping trips with the eight participants observed in the field the researcher saw that participants found the external barcode scanner cumbersome and that it was harder for some participants to carry their device with the barcode scanner attached. The researcher observed and participants verbalized that it was difficult to manage both their mobile device and a shopping cart or basket. Participants that brought along others on their shopping trip found it convenient to have the additional person who could manage the shopping cart while they scanned items.

Issues with the external barcode readers were also reflected to some degree in the post-survey responses. The median response of low volume scanners (half our participants) was "Neutral" when asked if the external barcode scanner was easy to use. In contrast, the median response for mid volume scanners was "Agree" and high volume scanners was "Strongly Agree" (Table 2, Q. 5), so those participants may have had fewer problems.

During the observations three participants forgot the external barcode scanners at work or home. In these cases, we loaned them one to make the observation possible, but wondered how common this might be. While potentially difficult to illicit on a survey, where people might be reluctant to fully disclose, we did see that four participants responded "Disagree" and three responded "Neutral" when asked whether they remembered to carry the barcode scanner with them.

The act of scanning also sometimes posed challenges for the participants, as they had to learn to position the scanner at the appropriate distance and orientation to achieve a successful scan. The barcode scanners we used require fairly bright lighting conditions, and have a hard time with barcodes printed on shimmering and curving surfaces (like drink cans). The researcher also observed that many participants had turned their device's volume off, either by mistake or because they did not want to be heard scanning, and thus did not receive any audible feedback about successful scans which may have contributed to usage difficulties.

Some participants mentioned a fear of being seen scanning items in stores. They disclosed different reasons for this including: not wanting to be seen as stealing information, not wanting to be seen by or as a store employee, and general shyness. In practice, the researcher found that once participants were in the store and with someone else, most participants were not as embarrassed as they thought they would be.

4.3.2 Frustration with Unrecognized Items

We knew before the field study that there were several types of items that our existing resolution services could not resolve, including items that are not national brands or in stores that maintain their own private barcode numbering schemes. However, our belief was that by handling the UPC and ISBN identifiers AURA would do a reasonable job recognizing most of the items likely to be scanned by participants, particularly books, music and items in major chain stores.

Unfortunately, during the observations the researcher saw that participants were noticeably frustrated when items that they scanned did not resolve and unrecognized items occurred more frequently than we hoped. For observed participants the existing set of resolution services functioned best in book stores and was less useful in grocery stores where many of the scanned items were not recognized. When asked on the post-survey data if enough items resolved to make AURA useful, the median was "Neutral" (Table 2, Q. 8). When asked to rate the priority of proposed features, the median response for "recognize more types of items" was "High Priority" (Table 3, Q. 2).

Participant comments also highlighted the need to recognize more items or at least support a user defined resolution service where participants could input their own information for unrecognized items. Comments included: "It rarely resolved items.

Table 3. Survey respondents' ratings of possible new features for AURA on a scale from 1 (Not Needed), 2 (Very Low Priority), 3 (Low Priority), 4 (Medium), 5 (High Priority), and 6 (Very High Priority)

Potential New Features	Preference by Participant Type (N) Median (SD, Mean)			
	High (3)	Mid (7)	Low (10)	All (20)
1. Improve the offline scanning experience	5 (1, 5)	6 (1, 6)	6 (1, 5)	6 (1, 5)
2. Recognize more types of items	6 (1, 5)	6 (1, 5)	5 (1, 5)	5 (1, 5)
3. Provide additional details about items	6 (1, 6)	5 (1, 5)	5 (1, 5)	5 (1, 5)
4. Expand the number and types of devices that AURA runs on	4 (1, 4)	4 (1, 4)	5 (1, 4)	4 (1, 4)
5. Improve the search option	4 (1, 4)	5 (1, 4)	4 (1, 4)	4 (1, 4)
6. Allow users to provide and edit item information	4 (1, 4)	4 (1, 4)	5 (2, 4)	4 (1, 4)
7. Allow users to organize items by adding category tags and labels	4 (1, 4)	5 (1, 4)	4 (2, 4)	4 (1, 4)
8. Integrate location awareness	4 (1, 4)	4 (1, 3)	4 (1, 4)	4 (1, 4)
9. Allow subscriptions to items scanned by others	3 (1, 3)	4 (1, 3)	4 (1, 4)	4 (1, 4)

Made it fairly useless" and "It [AURA] didn't recognize enough things -- it would have been better if when it didn't recognize it, I could tell it what it was." Allowing users to provide and edit information received a median response of "Medium Priority" on the post-survey (Table 3, Q. 6).

Other challenges in recognizing items observed by the researcher involved locating the barcode to scan initially. Some items have multiple barcodes, other barcodes were out of reach to the user due to the item's position on a display shelf and in other instances the barcodes were on the outer package for a group of items rather than on the single item on display (for example, for bars of soap).

4.3.3 Issues with Connectivity and Offline Mode

Initially we expected participants to primarily use AURA when connected to a wireless network; however on the post-survey the median response was that most participants used AURA "About equally online and offline." This is perhaps a reflection of the frequent use of AURA to create inventories of objects.

During the observations the researcher found that connectivity, whether WiFi or cellular, was not uniformly available or reliable. On the post-survey, when asked how much they were affected by connectivity delays, only one respondent said "Never." Of the other sixteen people who answered this question, six were affected "rarely," four "sometimes," two "often," and four "a lot." Thus, many participants needed to use offline mode. When asked to rate the usefulness of current AURA features on the post-survey, the median response by participants for offline scanning was "Can't live without it," the highest possible response.

Unfortunately, when participants did use offline mode, they found that it lacked several features they wanted including a batch mode for uploading several items together when connectivity was restored, clearer feedback when an item scanned offline had been uploaded to the web portal, and the ability to associate additional information such as categories with items scanned offline. On the post-survey, improving the offline experience received the highest possible median response of "Very High Priority" across all participants (Table 3, Q. 1). When asked to comment on the worst thing about AURA, several participants mentioned the offline experience. Comments included: "missing powerful offline experience," "inability to edit items in offline mode," and "offline: upload is very tedious."

4.3.4 Lack of Value for Low Engagement Objects

We envisioned several different usage scenarios for AURA including retrieving information while shopping for groceries, books, or electronics. Observations in grocery stores and other retail stores made it clear that other scenarios may "fit" better than grocery shopping. In general, AURA did not prove very useful when participants shopped for *low engagement objects* like groceries because most participants purchased the same items and had no interest in researching them.

During the observations participants described features that would potentially make AURA more valuable for them during shopping. Users seemed more likely to use AURA for *high engagement objects* like books or CDs – objects that require users to make fine grain distinctions about exactly which object they are seeking. One user mentioned that she always had trouble remembering the names of her vacuum cleaner refill bags when she goes out shopping and could never remember to write them down. She would like to scan all such items and create a list which she can access when she is in the store. Similarly users also wanted the ability to create personal categories and organizations for their item collections and to create wish lists that they could share with various people.

4.4 Does the Privacy Model Meet Users' Needs?

We implemented what we felt was a conservative privacy model that explicitly asks a user to take two steps to publicly expose information about the objects they are scanning, first uploading item details to the Web application and then making an item public. During the study, one of our research questions centered on whether the privacy model would meet user needs. Other possible privacy models, for example, automatically uploading scanned items or having only public items on the web portal, would require fewer steps for users to make items public and we wondered if users would find the privacy model appropriate or cumbersome.

The data from the post-survey and usage logs suggest that the conservative privacy model worked for our participants. We found during the field study that 17 out of 20 participants chose to explicitly make items public so they could be seen by others rather than leaving all items in their default private state. Overall, 41% of the items uploaded were made public while 59% remained private. Thirteen participants made fewer than 50% of their items public and 7 participants made 50% or more of their items public. Even though participants seemed eager to share at some level, it is clear that many of them thought about what they were willing to make public. On the post-survey the median response across all participants was 'Agree' when asked "I am comfortable with the privacy options provided by AURA." Our experience suggests other object triggered information systems may wish to consider a similarly conservative privacy model.

4.5 How Do People Use the Sharing Features?

One of the goals for the AURA project is to facilitate a community where people can easily share comments and ratings about the items they scan with others. During the field study one of our research questions focused on whether and how our participants used the sharing features provided

When asked about the usefulness of public rating, the median response was "Very Useful" and for public commenting the median response was "Somewhat Useful." We believe that some of the utility of the rating and commenting features suffered from a problem of critical mass, as post-survey comments highlighted that there was not enough shared content to make the comments and rating features useful. As one participant commented, "It needs lots of people using it to make it worth while - I can see the potential, but when there is little overlap of items being scanned & commented it becomes little more than a tool to facilitate googling." Our log data also reflected this lack of overlap in items uploaded by our participants. As general user populations grow or the AURA application is deployed into more cohesive groups with a common annotation task, we believe that public commenting and rating features may become more valuable.

Our system's other sharing options were used very infrequently. The majority of our post-survey respondents (15) told us they had "Never" emailed an item to someone, and publishing an RSS feed of items had a median response of "Not Useful."

5 Discussion

We now discuss the improvements to AURA and similar systems suggested by our field study. We then reflect on our experience and the implications for others that seek to deploy ubiquitous computing applications.

5.1 Realizing the AURA Vision

While our high volume scanners found some value in using AURA, the experiences of our participants highlight a number of considerations for AURA and other object triggered information systems.

Handle Groups of Items: In our original usage scenarios and those of many other similar systems [e.g. 10], users interact with one item at a time, scanning it and then retrieving information. In contrast, participant feedback during the ethnographic observations and on the post-survey stressed the importance of working with groups of items. For example, a participant could scan a number of interesting books and then upload them together to a wish list.

Robust Offline Experience: Our field study experience showed us that even with participants screened for devices with internet connectivity there are times when users may not be able or even wish to connect. To ensure the usability of object triggered information systems, they must provide a reasonably robust offline experience.

Integration with Current Practices: Our observations, particularly in grocery stores, highlighted just how much difficultly the form factor of the handheld device caused when participants were shopping. In addition, the external barcode scanner is bulky and one more thing to remember to carry. The use of certain cell phone cameras by some existing systems [e.g. 9] to recognize barcodes gives us encouragement that the integration of object triggered information system into devices users already carry could lead to widespread adoption of object triggered information systems relatively soon.

User Input for Unrecognized Items: There will always be the potential for unrecognized items in object triggered information systems. So our main focus will be handling unrecognized items more gracefully by providing participants the opportunity to enter their own information. This raises the exciting prospect of encouraging sharing of user defined item information, but also the interesting challenge of handling instances where conflicting information is provided.

Desire for Context: Participant feedback suggested that participants found the information they provided for the experience surveys valuable and wanted the option for AURA to remember this type of context information for all the objects they scanned. It may also be worth exploring whether users find information that could be automatically recorded by the system, such as location, valuable.

End-to-End Support for Applications: We built AURA as a platform to support applications that sense physical objects and then provide related online services and information. While this approach gave AURA the flexibility to be used in a variety of ways, we saw during the field study that participants wanted better end-to-end support for certain applications. The observations of our users suggest that applications for creating inventories and shopping for high engagement objects would be more valuable to our users than applications related to grocery shopping.

5.2 Reflections on Our Experience

While we believe that field studies such as this one are crucial for evaluating potential ubiquitous applications with real people in real settings, they also require a considerable amount of effort. We share reflections about our experience, both positive and negative, with the hope that others may benefit from them.

Provide Hardware: In our study we made a conscious choice to recruit people who already had Pocket PC devices and thus only needed to be provided the barcode scanner. We wanted people to experience AURA on the devices they were already carrying. In retrospect, this decision caused considerable pain for us as we ended up with participants on a variety of platforms. In future studies we plan to provide the entire hardware platform so that we have more control over the usage environment and would recommend that others consider this approach. Note, that cell phone SIM cards offer an interesting option to provide hardware and allow people to keep their phone number and service plan, as Smith et al. [15] did in their study.

Prepare for Connectivity Issues: The vision of ubiquitous access to the internet is becoming more of a reality each day, but what we found still leaves a lot to be desired. Although all our users work on a corporate campus with WiFi, we were aware of potential connectivity challenges and strove to recruit participants who either used the cell network to connect to the Internet and/or had WiFi at home. Had we fully realized the extent to which our users would encounter problems with connectivity we would have also provided users with subscriptions to a variety of WiFi access services and improved offline mode earlier.

Consider Ways of Creating Critical Mass: We had hoped that the tasks we asked the users to complete would lead to an overlap of scanned items and interest in sharing with others. However, for several of AURA's features related to sharing, we believe critical mass was an issue. While it is unlikely that we will be able to deploy in a field study situation with enough users to overcome this problem directly, we are exploring ways to work around this problem by selecting participant populations that already know each other and thus have things in common that may motivate them to share with each other or find each others scanned items interesting. We also plan to call more attention to the lists on the web portal homepage that highlight recent and notable patterns of activity in hopes of generating additional public contribution. We encourage others whose systems contain features that work best with large population of participants to think carefully about ways you might work around this constraint.

Multiple Data Sources Are Valuable: We collected data using multiple methods. Having several sources of data, particularly the ethnographic observations, helped us build a more complete picture of how our participants used AURA. For example, we followed-up on the post-survey about problems we saw in the observations. The agreement between different sources, such as the post-survey and experience survey results also increased our confidence in our results.

6   Concluding Remarks

AURA is one of many systems that connect physical objects to information online. Moving beyond limited usage and demonstrations to deploy AURA in the real world with 20 participants over five weeks shattered several of our usage assumptions and discovered a number of important features and issues that developers of other object triggered information systems may wish to consider. The number of issues we encountered deploying a relatively simple system like AURA highlights the importance of evaluating ubiquitous applications in real world setting to test design assumptions. For AURA, the field study showed us the importance of allowing users to work with groups of items, the necessity of a robust offline experience, and the need to allow users to identify the products they scanned that AURA could not recognize. Despite these issues, several participants did use AURA a fair amount suggesting that with further refinement mobile object triggered information systems are viable ubiquitous computing applications. We are currently addressing the short-comings highlighted by the field study and hope to release the revised client for public download.

Acknowledgements

We gratefully acknowledge our field study participants and the AURA development team: Howard Hwa, Paul Johns, Dany Rouhana, and Jane Wei. We also appreciate the valuable feedback we received from our reviewers and Geraldine Fitzpatrick.

References

1. Barrett, L.F., Barrett D.J.: An Introduction to Computerized Experience Sampling in Psychology. Social Science Computer Review, 19, 2 (2001), 175-185
2. Beeline Shopper, http://www.beelineshopper.com/
3. Bellamy, R.K.E., Brezin, J., Kellogg, W.A., Richards, J.T.: Designing an e-grocery application for a Palm computer: Usability and interface issues. IEEE Personal Communications 8, 4 (2001), 60-64
4. Brody, A., Gottsman, E.: Pocket Bargain Finder: A Handheld Device for Augmented Commerce. Proc. HUC 1999, ACM Press (1999), 44-51
5. Coulouris, G., Kindberg, T., Schiele, B., Schmidt, A., Rehman, K.: What makes for good application-led research in ubiquitous computing. Pervasive 2005 Workshop http://www.cl.cam.ac.uk/~gfc22/ubiappws/
6. CueCat: Digital Convergence, http://www.cuecat.com/
7. Delicious Library: http://www.delicious-monster.com/
8. Fano, Andrew E.: Shopper's Eye: Using Location-based Filtering for a Shopping Agent in the Physical World. Proc. Agents 1998, ACM Press (1998), 416 - 421
9. Gizmodo: Amazon Japan Cell Phone Fancypants Service. http://www.gizmodo.com/gadgets/cellphones/amazon-japan-cell-phone-fancypants-service-026198.php
10. Konomi, S.: QueryLens: Beyond ID-Based Information Access. Proc. Ubicomp 2002, Springer (2002), 210-218
11. Ljungstrand, P., Redström, J., Holmquist, L.E.: Webstickers: Using Physical Tokens to Access, Manage and Share Bookmarks to the Web. Proc. DARE 2000 (2000) 23-31
12. Newcomb, E., Pashley, T., Stasko, J.: Mobile Computing in the Retail Arena. Proc. CHI 2003. ACM Press (2003), 337-344
13. QR Code: Wikipedia, http://en.wikipedia.org/wiki/QR_Code
14. Smith, M., Davenport, D., Hwa, H.: AURA: A mobile platform for object and location annotation. Demo. Ubicomp 2003. Seattle WA
15. Smith I., Consolvo, S., Lamarca, A., Hightower, J., Scott, J., Sohn, T., Hughes, Iachello, G. Abowd, G.: Social Disclosure of Place: From Location Technology to Communication Practices. Pervasive 2005, Lecture Notes in Computer Science, Vol. 3468
16. Socket OrganizerIT: http://www.socketcom.com/product/SW1216-560.asp
17. Want, R., Fishkin, K., Gujar, A. Harrison, B.: Bridging Physical and Virtual Worlds with Electronic Tags. Proc. CHI 1999, ACM Press (1999), 370-377

Abaris: Evaluating Automated Capture Applied to Structured Autism Interventions

Julie A. Kientz,[1] Sebastian Boring,[1,2] Gregory D. Abowd,[1] and Gillian R. Hayes[1]

[1] College of Computing & GVU Center, Georgia Institute of Technology
Atlanta, GA, USA
{julie, abowd, gillian}@cc.gatech.edu

[2] University of Munich
Munich, Germany
boring@cip.ifi.lmu.de

Abstract. We present an example of an automated capture application which provides access to details of discrete trial training, a highly structured intervention therapy often used with developmentally disabled children. This domain presents an interesting case study for capture technology, because of the well-defined practices and the tradition of manual recording and review of materials. There is a strong motivation for therapists to review the rich record of therapy sessions that is made possible by recorded video, but acceptance hinges on minimal intrusion upon the human activities. To achieve that, we leverage several perception technologies that fit with the natural activities of the live experience and allow the creation of meaningful indices. We also critically explore the contribution various perception technologies have on the overall utility of the capture system.

1 Introduction

Despite the increasing popularity of capturing everyday life activities (e.g. [7], [11], [22], [20]), there are still very few published examinations of real use, fueling views that automated capture may not be a compelling capability. Part of the reason for this is the difficulty of finding a domain for which frequent access of captured activity is likely. By identifying a high-need access situation and creating a reliable capture system, exploration of interesting research questions is possible. In this paper, we present an example of a domain with one such high-need access requirement—evidence-based behavioral and academic interventions for developmentally disabled children. We will address how automated capture and access impacts users in this domain, specifically, a team of collaborating therapists. We also determine whether it is worthwhile to employ various perception technologies to understand the captured activity, or whether simpler heuristics for indexing into captured media suffice.

An evidence-based approach to intervention therapy attempts to use empirical data of past performance to inform future decisions. For example, in medicine it is widely acknowledged that such empirical evidence is important for determining progress and

M. Beigl et al. (Eds.): UbiComp 2005, LNCS 3660, pp. 323–339, 2005.
© Springer-Verlag Berlin Heidelberg 2005

guiding treatment decisions, particularly evidence that covers a patient's health outside the doctor's or professional's office. However, there are many situations in education, medicine, and other fields where gathering such evidence is cumbersome, if not impossible. In previous work, researchers explored the potential of automated capture for the specific case of treating children with autism [13]. One example suggested was the support for a team of therapists conducting discrete trial training (DTT), an application of Applied Behavior Analysis methods. An initial capture and access prototype was developed as a technology probe to determine whether practitioners of DTT saw any promise. Based on that feedback, and our own extensive experience over the past year with DTT, we have developed Abaris, a complete capture and access system to support home-based DTT therapy. Our intent is to evaluate the impact of some specific technology decisions on this popular intervention therapy.

This paper presents the design, initial deployment and results, and evaluation of the Abaris system. We pay particular attention to the use of two specific perception technologies during capture, Anoto's digital pen and paper technology [1] and Nexidia's phonetic-based speech detection [3]. These technologies allowed us to create a capture system that was a minimal departure from the existing DTT practice of our team of therapists, increasing the chances for adoption. The choice of each technology is strongly motivated by an understanding of the structure and practice of DTT. Preliminary results show that Abaris has been very well received by our users, and we will discuss why we think it has been successful. More importantly, we will explain whether the perception technologies played a necessary role in that success. The digital pen and paper were critical to the success of the system. While the speech recognition system did provide a useful indexing service to individual segment of therapy sessions, we argue that simpler heuristics would likely have fared just as well.

The structure of the rest of this paper follows. After reviewing relevant related work in automated capture and technology support for DTT, we provide an overview of the specifics of DTT and the structure and communication needs of a therapy team for one child. We then summarize the goals of the initial study to evaluate an automated capture solution to support DTT. We describe Abaris and present the results of a four-month pilot deployment, focusing on the use of Abaris during routine collaborative meetings of the therapists. We then analyze the results of the deployment, with a particular focus on reasons for the success of Abaris and an evaluation of the usefulness of the perception technologies as applied to this domain.

2 Related Work

In Ubiquitous Computing, Abaris falls into the category of automated capture and access applications. Several automated capture and access systems from research have helped explore this area, including applications for the classroom such as eClass/Classroom 2000 [7] and for meeting spaces such as Teamspace [22] and Tivoli [20]. Abaris provides users the ability to access information they already access manually (e.g., notes in the classroom and meeting settings) supplemented with additional information to which they would not normally have access. These applications also focus on low need access situations, whereas Abaris is high need. Like Abaris,

NoteLook [9], NotePals [10], and StuPad [24] all allow asynchronous annotation of videos in a collaborative setting, but are not designed for accessing multiple experiences as a collaborative activity. Abaris also differs from other capture and access systems, such as MyLifeBits [11], the Personal Audio Loop [14], Audio Notebook [23], and MIT's personal memory aid [25] in that these are designed for personal use of unstructured live experiences, rather than group access to a structured activity.

Other examples of technology that support the care of developmentally disabled children are not necessarily automated capture and access technologies. The child interacts directly with many, such as Simone Says for teaching speaking language skills [16] and the Discrete Trial Trainer [2], a commercial product aimed at simulated DTT. A commercial product known as mTrials [19], a PDA based data collection system for DTT, has enjoyed some success but lacks the additional audio and video inputs and collaborative access interface that Abaris provides.

We also relate our work to other ubiquitous computing projects that have focused on the design, authentic use, and/or summative evaluation of full-scale systems. PlantCareLabscape [5], mixed reality games [6], tour guides [8], Tivoli, and the eClass system are all end-to-end solutions to specific domain problems and were deployed for authentic use. Summative evaluation studies were published for all but the first. With the design and evaluation of Abaris, we demonstrate how acceptance and usability are impacted by specific perception technologies, similar to Benford *et al's.* assessment of the value of self-reported positioning in [6].

3 The Domain of Discrete Trial Training

The case study for this paper is based on a popular intervention therapy for children with autism, known as Discrete Trial Training (DTT). Developed in the 1970's by O. Ivar Lovaas [17], DTT has evolved as a specific method from the field of Applied Behavior Analysis (ABA) [4]. Though somewhat different from Lovaas' original conception, DTT is currently a best-practice method for teaching basic skills to children with autism and other developmental disabilities [15]. In DTT therapy, teams of trained therapists do one-on-one sessions with a child to teach basic skills in a structured setting. We outline the basics of DTT and the therapy team below. Although there is variation between different DTT practices, the description below is representative of standard practice, as implemented in a home setting.

The Discrete Trial. Advocates of DTT believe that even children with severe developmental disabilities can learn correct behaviors through controlled and conditioned training. A discrete trial is an example of this learning model. Once the therapist gains the attention of the child, she makes a direct verbal request to the child that requires a well-defined and correct response. If the child responds correctly, he is immediately rewarded with a reinforcing stimulus, such as a piece of candy, a favorite toy, or verbal praise. If the child responds incorrectly, the therapist prompts the child in a way to ensure a correct response. The trial is immediately repeated, with the therapist providing whatever prompt is needed to guarantee a correct response. The therapist records the result of the trial (*I* for an independent or correct response; otherwise, any of seven or eight letters that represent the prompting used by the therapist). If a "correction" trial follows the initial prompted response, the therapist may also record the result of that correction trial.

A DTT Program. The therapy regime for DTT consists of a collection (10 to 20) of programs for which data is collected. Each program consists of a basic skill (*e.g.*, Picture Identification), a target (*e.g.*, picture of a dog), a note further explaining the task (*e.g.*, selection from a field of three pictures), and a specific command (*e.g.*, "Give me the <target_name>.").

A Therapy Session. Each program/target combination is performed a number of times, ideally distributed randomly throughout the 1-2 hour session. All data is recorded on a scoresheet. A graph, as shown in Figure 1, indicating progress for each program is updated at the end of the session to reflect that day's data.

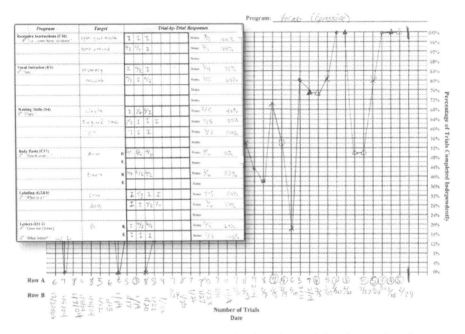

Figure 1: Examples of paper-based forms used by therapists. Left is a therapy data sheet completed during therapy, and right is a graph of the child's progress for a particular skill.

Advancing the Program. A given program/target combination is "mastered" when some pre-defined performance level (*e.g.*, 80% correct responses on a given day) is achieved over some interval of time (*e.g.*, three consecutive days). Once a program/target combination is mastered, the target is changed. When a sufficient variety is mastered for a program, the program is mastered overall. Mastered program/target combinations are practiced (without data collection) throughout a therapy session.

Before a session, a therapist reviews the child's therapy materials. She consults a notebook containing the child's past session data sheets, program progress graphs, mastered skills, and narrative notes from other therapists on the child's progress. She reads over the notes written by other therapists and prepares her session materials, which includes pictures, objects, and writing utensils. After she has prepared everything, she begins the session with the child by playing and interacting with him, and then brings him to the table to rehearse mastered skills and work on target skills.

 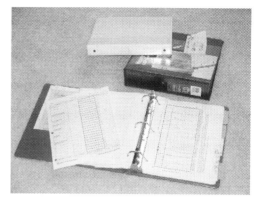

Figure 2: The left image shows a therapist engaged in a therapy session with a child. The right image shows an example of the large amounts of paper required to store all of the data.

Evaluating Progress. The team we studied consisted of a parent (trained in DTT but not practicing), three regular therapists, one lead therapist, and a consultant, all providing therapy to a seven year-old, low-functioning child diagnosed with Autistic Disorder (mild to moderate), using the DTT procedure described above.[1]   The lead therapist has additional tasks of administrative paperwork, such as determination of which program/target combinations are mastered and scheduling new targets and programs for future sessions. The consultant does no direct therapy with the child, but is an expert in behavior analysis. The team typically meets every other week to discuss therapy, analyze data, and make any necessary adjustments to help the child learn the skills more effectively. The consultant leads these meetings and uses the manually recorded data as an agenda to run the meeting (see Figure 1). The consultant looks at the book of graphs and asks the therapists for details on how the child is progressing on each skill. If a certain target skill has been in place for a long time with little improvement, the team may remove the target and replace it with another one, or they may discuss why they do not think he is learning it. Therapists try to remember details of what occurred in their sessions and make hypotheses about what is causing him to perform particularly well or poorly. The consultant will make suggestions with the team generally implementing these within the next two weeks of therapy. After making these changes, the team reviews the progress again at the next meeting.

---

[1] Two members of the team were from the research team reporting this work. All other team members and the child are protected as human subjects under an approved IRB protocol.

4 Research Goals

With a firm understanding of the domain, we now frame the goals of our research into the design and evaluation of Abaris. We begin with two observations:

- The therapy sessions, though fairly fast-paced and flexible, have a well-defined structure that can be leveraged naturally by perception technology, potentially providing a suitably indexed recording for later access.
- The team meetings present a high-need example of access, in which the users who are both capturing and accessing the data absolutely require it to perform their jobs. Furthermore, the meetings consist of a lot of self-reported reflections on past experience between therapist and child, a clear opportunity for improvement with real evidence of what transpired during a therapy session.

Although DTT therapy is a relatively well structured and successful treatment for children with autism, there are some deficiencies in the process that may lead to inaccuracies in the interpretation of the data, making the overall therapy less efficient. Our goals for the Abaris system were to be able to address some of these issues and make therapy a better and more useful experience for the therapists and the child.

Discrete trial training is particularly well suited to the use of automatic capture technologies. Therapists and parents alike are highly motivated to use anything that will save time on laborious paperwork yet does not reduce the quality of the intervention. Additionally, it is a structured activity, with individuals already trained to be cooperative in the process of manually recording data. Because therapists record, calculate, and graph all of the data by hand, there is a high likelihood that the data may be inaccurate due to simple human error. Furthermore, graphing and calculating all of the data using pen and paper is time consuming, often requiring up to one third of the session and taking time away from the child's instruction. By designing a system that automates a lot of this hand analysis and calculation, we can reduce the amount of time spent in paperwork, similar to how others have found that automation can save time in paperwork for Activities for Daily Living (ADLs) [21].

DTT requires a significant amount of improvisation and thus we must design Abaris to be as flexible as possible when capturing data from the therapists. Since pen and paper allows anything to be written anywhere on the page, we feel that keeping the paper for capture is essential. Besides flexibility, we believe that allowing therapists to keep a pen and paper system will have minimal change to existing practice, which will increase the likelihood of acceptance, as noted by Mackay et al. in their study of air traffic controllers [18]. The challenge is to design capture in a way that maximizes the inherent structure of sessions without violating the process, and to provide a nimble access interface that would encourage exploration of the evidence without requiring too much time, effort, and distraction during team meetings.

At current team meetings, therapists speculate about whether a child is responding to prompts in certain ways, how well the child is focused, whether or not the child exhibits some affect, and whether the therapist is conducting each trial correctly. Much of the grading of each trial is subjective, especially in the grading of word pronunciation or letter formation, thus discrepancies in the grading of the child by multiple therapists tend to interfere with measures of progress. These discrepancies can lead to a mismatch in skills taught and the child's abilities, which can be frustrating both for the child and for the therapist. Capture of rich data, such as video, allows therapists to *see* what each of the other therapists is discussing without being present during therapy sessions and to notice things that the therapist herself may not have, ensuring increased consistency and enabling more accurate decisions and advice. Thus, the overall goal for the access interfaces is to provide a means of facilitating discussion amongst groups of therapists about trends in the data using easy access to both empirical and rich data to enable data-based decisions for long-term use.

5 The Abaris System

Abaris contains two major software components—one for *capture* or recording of data, and one for *access* and analysis of data—which are located on the same computer. This computer can act as a network server to allow remote use for certain tasks, like maintaining the programs and viewing the captured sessions. As shown in Figure 3, additional devices supplement the software on the single PC including a high quality printer for augmented datasheets, a web cam for capturing video and audio data, a high-quality wireless microphone for voice recognition, and a digital pen for writing the grades on the specially printed paper.

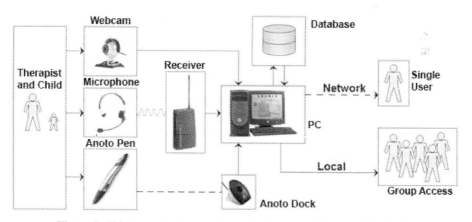

Figure 3: This shows the basic system setup to run and interact with Abaris.

5.1 The Capture Interface

Recorded video from therapy sessions coupled with appropriate indexing allows fast access to particular trials. In current practice, therapists use both a spoken command to indicate the beginning of the trial to the child and a pen to record data after a trial. We leverage these practices to create effective indices into the captured therapy session. Using Nexidia's voice recognition technology (off-the-shelf, phoneme-based speech system), we can retrieve timestamps for a specific command, obtaining estimates for trial beginnings. After trials, therapists record grades on the augmented datasheet using a special pen (see Figure 4, center). Replacing traditional pen and paper with Anoto's digital pen technology affords collection of positions and timestamps of every stroke, while preserving the flexibility inherent to writing.

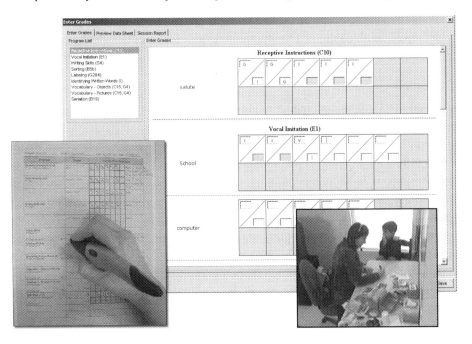

Figure 4: Left is the digital pen and its specially designed paper used for entering trial grades. Center shows the current system does not use any character recognition, instead providing an interface to enter grades. Right is a scene from a therapy session using the Abaris system.

While capturing a session, Abaris records an additional audio file, which is monitored and indexed by Nexidia while recording, including a pattern file that can be searched for speech patterns indicating the beginning of a trial. Within the plain-text XML file generated by the digital pen's interaction with a data sheet, each stroke is stored with its coordinates and associated absolute beginning timestamp. A stroke, by definition, contains at least 6 pixels and more than half of its points inside the 31x20-pixel cell the system is analyzing, preventing erroneous marks on the paper made by therapists signaling trial data. Using data stored from the written records and the patterns in the audio, Abaris reconstructs likely beginning and ending times for particular trials. Further analysis on these timestamps is discussed in the following sections.

5.2 Access Interface

The access interface for Abaris provides therapists with the ability to review sessions as well as to correct grades and timestamps for places where technical or human error created incorrect data. Therapists need to perform these tasks both locally at the site of therapy and remotely from their homes or offices in preparation for team meetings and therapy sessions. Furthermore, they must be able to access Abaris both individually and in a group setting during team meetings. Of course, Abaris must provide at least the same level of functionality as the traditional pen and paper process, including graphing of empirical data and review interfaces for therapist datasheets.

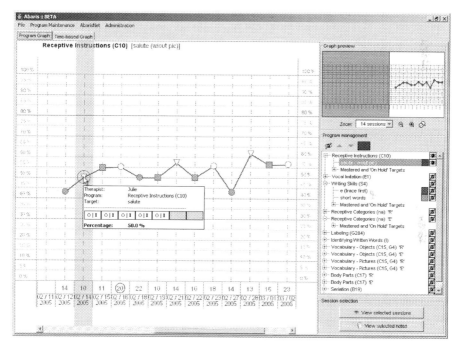

Figure 5: This shows the main access interface displaying a single selected graph on the left, with tool tip indicating information for a specific session. The right shows a view of the entire graph and the list of selectable programs.

Once the access interface is started, the therapist/consultant can choose which programs to view by marking programs and targets to be shown or not. If more than one target is visible the graphs are overlaid in the same view with a displayed legend. Because multiple graphs might become confusing, other visualization techniques facilitate analysis. A tool tip (describing the target and program) appears each time the cursor is near a target's line. Another tool tip shows the data of a target from a particular session when the user hovers near that data point. Figure 5 shows an example of a typical graph with a therapist specific tool tip.

Users can select multiple sessions for which they want to view more details by clicking and highlighting the columns associated with those sessions. This functionality allows the user to review two different sessions quickly to compare procedures. The session browser loads in its own window, with typical video control functions of play, pause, stop, fast forward, and frame seeking functions as well as functions to jump to the next or previous trial of currently visible programs. Along the bottom of the window is a zoomable timeline that shows when trials occurred, using the predictions described above. To the right of the video are the grades for selected programs. Clicking on a grade moves the video to the start time for that trial. If there are several sessions loaded, a user can switch between them by clicking on the timeline of another video or selecting a trial that is not part of the video currently shown. The grades assigned to a trial, as well as the beginning and end times, can be modified. These corrections appear on the graphs immediately after saving the changes. Within the access interface, therapists can also add and edit programs and targets, an activity that happens frequently during the course of a team meeting.

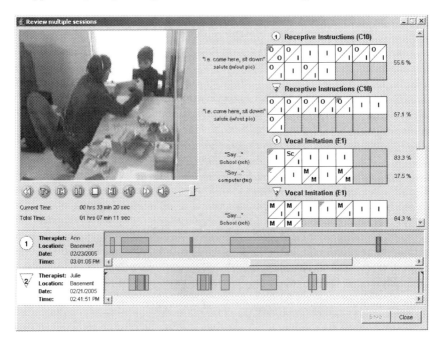

Figure 6: This shows a session browser set up to view two different therapy sessions. The bottom shows the two different timelines, and the left shows the grades for the different trials.

6 Results of Deployment

We deployed the Abaris system described above in one child's home for his team of therapists to use in a pilot study for four months. Meetings to discuss the progress of the child approximately every two weeks for a total of six meetings. We instructed therapists on use of the capture system before deployment, and a researcher was on hand during their first sessions to answer questions. Before the first meeting, we trained the lead therapist and the consultant to use the access interface. During the meetings, researchers were present to answer questions. In the first meeting, one of the researchers controlled the access interface according to therapist requests; at subsequent meetings, the lead therapist controlled the interface.

Our main goals for Abaris were to reduce the amount of paperwork time during sessions, obtain accurate timestamps to allow therapists to index into videos of certain trials, evaluate the use of the perception technologies, determine the usefulness and usability of the Abaris system, and facilitate group meeting discussions.

6.1 Use of Capture System

To date, the team has captured 52 sessions, consisting of 3869 trials and 45.1 hours of recorded data, including every session that has taken place during the study. The capture interface was easy for the therapists to learn, because the digital pen allowed therapists to perform their work in the exact same way they had done it before. Although the interface appeared to be easy for therapists to use, they initially demonstrated skeptical attitudes about its use. Despite this skepticism, participants used Abaris in all of their sessions for which it was available. The only benefit of use at this stage was removing the need for users to "hand graph." This consistent use is remarkable given that at first, all users were contributing to this groupware system while receiving little benefit [12]. We believe this was due in large part to the conscious effort during design to maintain nearly identical work practices that reduce or maintain the same level of effort. At the first meeting that made use of Abaris, participants were then able to experience the benefits of access.

Therapists reported allocation of session time both before and during the deployment. Overall, work time for these hourly employees decreased slightly, but this may be the result of fewer target skills for the child during the time of the deployment due to the child being sick or having a difficult time in school. The percentage of time that therapists spent in paperwork decreased, resulting in more time spent teaching or playing with the child (see Figure 7). Thus, with Abaris, therapists can devote a greater percentage of their paid time to interaction with the child.

Two therapists reported that the clip-on microphone was a bit too heavy for some of their typical clothing and could be uncomfortable. Most preferred to use a head-mounted boom microphone. A few incidents occurred in which the child became fascinated by the microphone and would reach out and play with it, a behavior that typically occurs when therapists wear jewelry the child finds interesting. Although this behavior can be common for some children with autism, it may not happen in all cases. We considered using a room level microphone, but the child often vocalizes during therapy sessions, which affects the accuracy of the voice recognition.

Simple usage errors sometimes had large impact. One of the therapists forgot to press the record button at the beginning of her session, resulting in no video for the session. In one incident, placement of the Anoto paper in the printer backwards resulted in incorrect detection of the timestamps. These errors can be prevented future versions of Abaris, but because of its improvisational nature, we could not predict all of the exceptions to the therapy. For example, the lead therapist wanted to change the success criteria for one type of program, but she had no way of doing this with our current interface. Basing Abaris on pen and paper input allowed for a lot of improvisation, but it was very difficult to plan and address all cases.

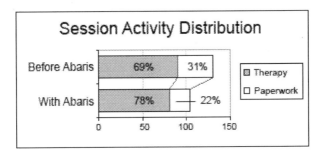

Figure 7: Comparison of the activity makeup of each session before and after deployment.

6.2 Use of Access System

Therapists used the access interface for discussion during two meetings, which lasted 2.5 hours and 1.5 hours, respectively. Each meeting was video recorded and observed, and afterwards we debriefed the therapists on the experience with the system, in which discussion was similar to that of a focus group. Between the first and second meetings, we instrumented the access interface so that we could produce logs of its use providing some empirical evidence of access behaviors. In the second meeting, the team used the access interface to view the video six times, and video viewing took up 20.4 percent of the meeting time. Visualizations of interesting data in these logs are present in Figure 8. The top graph is a typical example of comparing a program across two therapists viewed by the lead therapist before the meeting. The middle graph shows various artifacts in the interface—the timeline and the trial grades—were used to navigate to the desired portion of video. The bottom graph is a detailed version of a portion of the middle graph. That this kind of browsing occurred six times during the meeting is an indication that the team found the value of viewing video outweighed the cost of finding the appropriate session. For 18 months prior to these two meetings with Abaris, the team had access to digital video recordings of the sessions at the site of the meeting, and not once was a segment viewed during a meeting, reportedly because it took too long to find a relevant clip.

Due to the complexity of the data recorded for DTT, therapists reported the access interface to be complicated at first. They received two hours of training before expressing enough comfort to use it on their own. Although ease of use was not as good as we would have liked, therapists reported that the benefits of the system were worth the time it took to learn the access interface. Additionally, the access interface is intended for expert users (*e.g.* the lead therapist and the consultant), allowing them to use the system with all of their clients once they are past this initial learning curve.

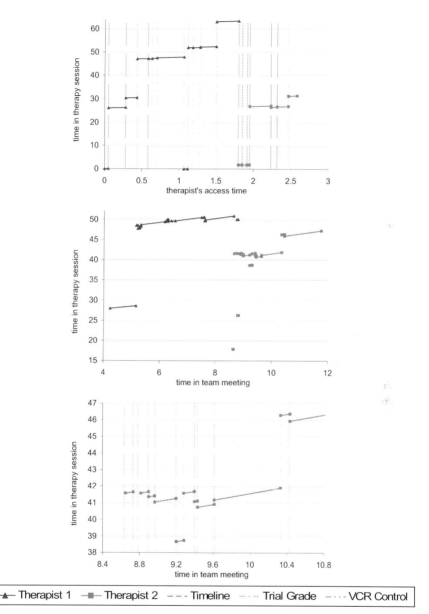

Figure 8: Visualizations from the logs of the second meeting of the team. Top shows access from the lead therapist before the meeting while the center graph shows access to videos during the meeting. The plot with dark, triangle data points shows access to video of one therapist, while the plot with light, square data points shows viewing a different therapist. In the bottom graph, we expand one segment of the top graph (between 8.4-10.4 minutes into the meeting) and show how different artifacts are used to facilitate navigation.

6.3 Overall Therapist Impressions

Though we are still in the process of fully understanding the impact that Abaris had on our team we deployed with, it should be noted that Abaris has been very well received by our team. Through initial post deployment interviews, we have discovered that the only complaints on the capture side were that the microphone was distracting to both the child and to the therapist. Therapists felt that the meetings were more structured and Abaris helped to create an agenda for the meeting. The therapists and the consultant both commented on how helpful it was to see how others did therapy so they could verify that they were doing things correctly. It also allowed them to all see the data, which helped in facilitating the discussion of progress. Aside from the occasional glitches in the code of Abaris, the therapists were very excited about deployment and all of them stated they were sorry that the deployment had to end. We are continuing to assess the impact of the system on the overall therapy sessions and team meetings by observing and analyzing how the team operates post deployment.

7 Discussion: Do Perception Technologies Make a Difference?

The fact that Abaris is considered a useful system by its target user group is encouraging, but as researchers and designers, we want to better understand which features contribute to its usefulness and which do not. The integration of trial time predictions and the recorded video are a reasonable first guess at the success of Abaris. As seen in Figure 8, skimming to an appropriate portion of the video was quick enough to encourage use. End times of trials were equated with the time the grade for that trial was written on the Anoto paper. Beginning trials were estimated based on suggested locations of the appropriate verbal command. We selected four separate therapy sessions, one for each therapist, and used Abaris to create "ground truth" timestamps for the beginning and ending of each trial by manually noting when trials began. Figure 9 shows the error distribution of prediction versus ground truth. A negative error indicates a time prediction earlier than ground truth, and a positive error indicates a prediction after ground truth.

For each of the programs, the error distribution of the Anoto predictions is much narrower than that for Nexidia. The Anoto predictions occurred temporally after the actual end time, as expected, because trials are graded after they occur. The distribution of errors for Nexidia is wider. When viewed grouped by therapist, these error distributions have substantial variation in practice between therapists. Therapst 2's Anoto predictions were very tightly bunched near the actual end of trials. This therapist followed the practice of writing trial grades right after the trial was performed, as opposed to other therapists who ensured delivery of a reinforcing reward first. This is actually considered good practice for DTT, and Abaris benefits from this practice.

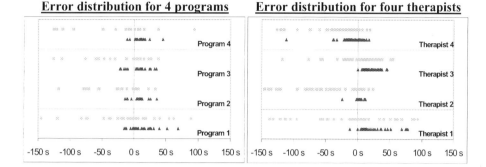

Figure 9: On the left, paired error distributions (in seconds) for Anoto-predicted end of trial (dark triangles) and Nexidia-predicted beginning of trial (light squares) for four of the programs used in the deployment. On the right, error distributions are shown for one session of each of the four therapists (lead and three regulars).

The phoneme-detection of Nexidia, and our accompanying algorithm for assigning assumed beginning of trial times, produced a significant amount of error. Errors are not surprising, given the nature of the therapy, with graded and mastered trials often having the same spoken command and occurring in rapid succession. However, because the interface was still usable, as reported based on use during team meetings and the overwhelming positive reaction of the team of therapists in discussions, this error may not be limiting. If this size of error makes no discernable difference, we hypothesize that speech detection may be unnecessary if we can find an alternative approach that introduces no additional errors.

Unfortunately, voice recognition only provides a best guess for the beginning of a particular trial, because many trials for which grades are not recorded use the same spoken command. For example, a therapist may be grading a child's ability to mimic hand clapping, for which the spoken command is "do this" coupled with the therapist modeling hand clapping. Prior to this trial of interest, a therapist may ask the child to perform any number of other activities with the same command of "do this", and then end with the final request "do this" while hand clapping. Thus, we considered a vision-based solution in which therapists used a simple two-finger gesture on a score sheet to indicate the beginning of a graded trial and the actual grades before and after the trial itself. Though the approach was simple to teach and the vision problem was feasible, we found that therapists could not remember to do the gestures at the correct times, resulting in a loss of grading information. Instead, we developed a simple algorithm for determining the most likely beginning of a trial based on a combination of the time that the trial likely ended (from the Anoto data) and the time that different spoken commands were used.

Considering the narrow distribution of the Anoto errors for trial endings in Figure 9, there are several suggestions for potential temporal heuristics that might produce begin trial estimates at least as good as Nexidia. We have anecdotal evidence that for Therapist 2, a fairly reliable heuristic was a function of the program type and whether or not a correction trial was needed. Our current results give us confidence that we know an upper bound on the error distribution for estimating the start of a trial, and we will experiment with a variety of algorithms to find one that is both accurate and precise enough without impinging on the therapy itself.

8 Conclusions and Future Work

We presented our work on the design, development, and deployment of the Abaris system for supporting therapists who do discrete trial training therapy for children with autism. Our results show that initial therapist reaction is largely positive, which we attribute to the closeness of the system to the therapists current practice. We improved the practice by allowing therapists to spend less time in paperwork and more time in the therapy itself. Also, we evaluated the usefulness of the recognition techniques employed by Abaris by comparing its accuracy with the ability to find the needed video segments. Time stamping using Anoto digital pen technology was useful for this practice, and while the errors were introduced by using Nexidia voice recognition, the indices to the video still were useful in practice. Thus, we hypothesize that you could do just as well as the voice recognition with a trained heuristic based on therapist and program type.

Though our initial results are promising and have lead to some interesting insight, there is still room for exploration with this technology. As of the time of writing, Abaris has just finished the four month deployment, and we are in the beginning stages of analyzing the massive amount of data we have collected beyond what is presented in this study. We plan to take the feedback we've received from the pilot and make final improvements to the system and deploy it with a new team of therapists of which the researchers are not members. Plans for the Abaris system include more visualization of data that otherwise wouldn't be possible with the paper system, using it as a test bed for more recognition, automation, and multimodal interaction techniques and finding ways of sharing a child's therapy information with all those interested in his progress, not just those present at therapy meetings, such as through a web based information portal. Lastly, we are hoping we can use Abaris to contribute to the field of autism interventions by enabling domain experts to analyze the science behind DTT therapy itself and improve on its methods.

Acknowledgments

This work was sponsored in part by the National Science Foundation (ITR grant 0121661), the Aware Home Research Initiative, and the Cure Autism Now foundation. The authors wish to thank Integrated Behavioral Solutions Consulting and our team of therapists for supporting and evaluating us in this work. We also wish to thank Albrecht Schmidt at the University of Munich, Juane Helfin at Georgia State University, Francois Guimbretière and Dave Levin at the University of Maryland, and Georgia Tech's Ubicomp, Autism, and IMTC research groups.

References

1. *Anoto, Inc. Website*, in *http://www.anoto.com*. 2005.
2. *Discrete Trial Trainer (DTT)*, in *http://www.dttrainer.com*. 2004: Columbia, SC.
3. *Nexidia, Inc. Website*, in *http://www.nexidia.com*. 2005.
4. Alberto, P.A. and A.C. Troutman, *Applied Behavior Analysis for Teachers*. 6th ed. 2003: Prentice Hall.
5. Arnstein, L., et al., *Labscape: A Smart Environment for the Cell Biology Laboratory*, in *IEEE Pervasive Computing Magazine*. 2002.
6. Benford, S., et al. *The error of our ways: The experience of self-reported positioning in a location-based game*. in *Ubicomp 2004*. 2004. Nottingham, UK: Springer-Verlag.
7. Brotherton, J.A. and G.D. Abowd, *Lessons learned from eClass: Assessing automated capture and access in the classroom*. ACM Transactions on Computer-Human Interaction, 2003.
8. Cheverst, K., et al. *Developing a context-aware electronic tourist guide: some issues and experiences*. in *SIGCHI conference on Human factors in computing systems*. 2000.
9. Chiu, P.I. *NoteLook: Taking Notes in Meetings with Digital Video and Ink*. in *ACM Multimedia*. 1999. Orlando, FL.
10. Davis, R.C., et al. *NotePals: Lightweight Note Sharing by the Group, for the Group*. in *CHI 1999*. 1999. Pittsburgh, PA.
11. Gemmell, J., et al. *MyLifeBits: Fulfilling the Memex Vision*. in *ACM Multimedia '02*. 2002.
12. Grudin, J., *Groupware and Social Dynamics: Eight Challenges for Developers*. Communications of the ACM, 1994.
13. Hayes, G.R., et al. *Designing Capture Applications to Support the Education of Children with Autism*. in *Ubicomp 2004*. 2004. Nottingham, UK.
14. Hayes, G.R., et al. *The Personal Audio Loop: Designing a Ubiquitous Audio-Based Memory Aid*. in *Mobile HCI 2004*. 2004. Glasgow, Scotland.
15. Heflin, L.J. and R.L. Simpson, *Interventions for Children and Youth with Autism: Prudent Choices in a World of Exaggerated Claims and Empty Promises. Part I: Intervention and Treatment Option Review*. Focus on Autism and Other Developmental Disabilities, 1998. **13**(4): p. 194-211.
16. Lehman, J.F. *Toward the use of speech and natural language technology in intervention for a language-disordered population*. in *Third International ACM Conference on Assistive Technologies*. 1998.
17. Lovaas, O.I., *Teaching Developmentally Disabled Children: The Me Book*. 1981, Austin, Texas: Pro-Ed.
18. Mackay, W.E., et al. *Reinventing the Familiar: Exploring an Augmented Reality Design Space for Air Traffic Control*. in *CHI 1998*. 1998. Los Angeles, CA.
19. Mobile Thinking, I., *mTrials*. 2002: San Diego, CA.
20. Pedersen, E.R., et al. *Tivoli: An Electronic Whiteboard for Informal Workgroup Meetings*. in *ACM INTERCHI 1993*. 1993. Amsterdam, The Netherlands.
21. Philipose, M., et al., *Inferring activities from interactions with objects*, in *IEEE Pervasive Computing*. 2004. p. 50 - 57.
22. Richter, H., et al. *Integrating Meeting Capture within a Collaborative Team Environment*. in *ACM Conference on Ubiquitous Computing*. 2001. Atlanta, GA.
23. Stifelman, L.J., *The Audio Notebook*, in *Media Laboratory, MIT*. 1997.
24. Truong, K.N. and G.D. Abowd. *StuPad: integrating student notes with class lectures*. in *CHI 1999 Extended Abstracts*. 1999.
25. Vemuri, S., et al. *An Audio-Based Personal Memory Aid*. in *Ubicomp 2004*. 2004. Nottingham, UK.

To Frame or Not to Frame: The Role and Design of Frameless Displays in Ubiquitous Applications

Claudio Pinhanez, Mark Podlaseck

IBM Research, T.J. Watson
19 Skyline Drive, Hawthorne, New York 10532, USA
pinhanez@us.ibm.com, podlasec@us.ibm.com

Abstract. A *frameless display* is a display with no perceptible boundaries; it appears to be embodied in the physical world. Frameless displays are created by projecting visual elements on a black background into a physical environment. By considering visual arts and design theory together with our own experience building about a dozen applications, we argue the importance of this technique in creating ubiquitous computer applications that are truly contextualized in the physical world. Nine different examples using frameless displays are described, providing the background for a systematization of frameless displays pros and cons, together with a basic set of usage guidelines. The paper also discusses the differences and constraints on user interaction with visual elements in a frameless display.

1   Introduction

Look again at the title of this paper. What is the impact of framing the first instance of the word "frame" in comparison with its second instance on the title? Does the first instance look detached from the page, as if in its own world? In comparison, the second instance looks completely integrated to the whole page. In fact, as detailed later, that is exactly what visual design theory teaches: a frame creates and indicates spatial disruptions.

This paper examines how the elimination of the frame in visual displays can contribute to the ultimate ubiquitous computing goal of making *"[computer systems] weave themselves into the fabric of everyday life until they are indistinguishable from it."* (from [32], pg. 94). As an example, Figure 1 invites a simple comparison between a framed display (left) and a frameless display (right). The framed advertisement is less integrated in the environment than the character depicted in the frameless display.

Our main hypothesis is that frameless displays connect with the surrounding environment and objects better than framed displays, contextualizing the information presented in them. Of course, frameless displays should be mostly used when this connection or contextualization is needed and avoided otherwise. Given that many ubiquitous applications aim to be contextualized to the user's environment, frameless

M. Beigl et al. (Eds.): UbiComp 2005, LNCS 3660, pp. 340-357, 2005.

Figure 1. A framed (left) and a frameless (right) projected display.

displays have the potential to become an important interface technique and therefore should be understood more thoroughly.

Frameless displays can be easily created through projection systems by simply projecting visual elements surrounded by black pixels, as shown in Figure 2. If the projection system is bright compared to the ambient light (at least 10 times brighter [10]) and has enough contrast to maintain the darkness in the projected black (in the case of LCD projectors), human eyes tend to not perceive the black background of the projected image. Similarly, a head-mounted display, connected to a wearable computer can use the same technique to create personal frameless displays.

There has been a long history of use of frameless displays in the art community (for example [1, 14] and, more recently, in ubiquitous applications [11, 24, 26, 29, 35], among many. A major contribution of this paper is to analyze these applications and our own experience designing and building about a dozen frameless display-based systems and extract rules about when and how to use them.

A more recent trend, however, is to create frameless displays that allow user interaction directly with the visual elements of the display [3, 12, 18, 21, 23, 27, 28, 30, 33]. A typical example is the *Jumping Frog* game-like application we built, where the image of an animated frog is projected on random objects in an environment. Whenever a player tries to catch the frog, the frog jumps to another surface (see Figure 2). As in real life, it is not possible to see the frog during the jump but only when departing from or landing on a surface.

Observations and results of previous studies [22] report that interaction with frameless displays involves different constraints than that with traditional displays. We discuss the possible implications of the studies showing that the interaction with a frameless projected display and its recollection is affected by object(s) in the vicinity of where the interactive element is placed. The impact of this and other issues, and the lessons learned in our own experience with frameless displays are discussed in terms of applicability and guidelines for interactive frameless displays.

Figure 2. (left) Image of a frog (part of an animation sequence) with black background. (right) *Jumping Frog*, a game-like application where participants chase an animated-projected frog that jumps to multiple surfaces in an environment. The black pixels of the image of the left disappear when the image is projected on a normally lit environment.

2   The Use of Frames in Visual Arts and Design

In visual art, *frame* has a number of closely related meanings. In its most general sense, the frame (sometimes called the *visual frame*) refers to the rectangular boundary that separates an image from its surroundings (as defined in [6], pg 11). Visual artists use this frame to orient the viewer's perspective relative to the subject being depicted. In this regard, the visual frame provides a metaphorical window into another world which is disconnected from the viewer in space and/or time.

Over a century ago, visual artists began minimizing the window effect of the visual frame. Paul Cezanne, Pablo Picasso, Piet Mondrian, Kasmir Malevich, and Marcel Duchamp used a number of techniques, such as demolishing the illusion of perspective, to establish that their paintings were not windows into other spaces; rather they were objects that *occupied the same space as the viewer* [19]. Robert Rauschenberg and Jasper Johns further reinforced the physical presence of their paintings by integrating physical objects into the canvas, thereby breaking the visual frame (as in *"Watchman"*, Figure 3, left). Shortly thereafter, artists such as Allan Kaprow [13] and Chris Burden [9] removed the visual frame entirely, creating works embedded in and sometimes indistinguishable from the physical reality of the viewer. For example, Burden's *"Shoot"* (1971) is described by the artist as: *"At 7:45 p.m. I was shot in the left arm by a friend. The bullet was copper jacket 22 long rifle. My friend was standing about fifteen feet from me."* (from [9], pg. 53).

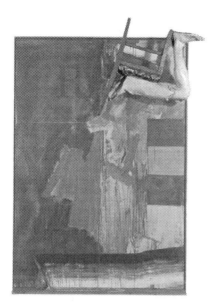 

Figure 3. (left) In Jasper Johns's *"Watchman" (1964)* a three-dimensional chair and human leg extrude from the canvas and break the frame of the painting. (right) A frame from a comic book about comic books, *Understanding Comics [15],* defining itself[1].

By bringing phenomena such as these into the physical space of the viewer, the artists coerced their audiences into becoming emotional and sometimes physical participants, rather than voyeurs gazing through windows at events divorced from their reality. Subsequent theorists in both art [13] and computing [4] have observed that as visual phenomena establish a presence or *embodiment* in the reality of the viewer, their participatory status increases. Furthermore, they note, embodied, and therefore participative, phenomena need not be *physically* present in the time and space of the viewer, as in the works discussed above; they merely need to possess the possibility of occurring in the time and space of the viewer and to be represented as if they did. A prerequisite for this kind of representation is the elimination of the visual frame.

The evolving status of a slightly different kind of frame, the *picture frame*, exemplifies the changing role of the frame in the embodiment of visual phenomena. The picture frame traditionally has served to underline or exaggerate the separation of the image from its immediate environment. Speaking of a lushly carved, 16th-century Venetian frame for a 15th-century Giovanni Bellini painting, a museum curator says: *"This frame actually adds to the illusion that you see Bellini's figures in three-dimensional space with the frame forming a wonderful window."* [17] As modern artists began to emphasize the embodiment of their works in real time and space, picture frames became less substantial and were frequently abandoned altogether.

---

[1] Reprinted with the permission of the author. Copyright 1993.

Frames of an altogether different kind, frames in comic strips and comic books, inherit, magnify, and exploit many of the qualities of visual frames and picture frames. By separating the image inside the frame from the space and time outside the frame (Figure 3, right), comic *frames* (or *panels,* or *boxes*) are able to tell narratives [15]. Comic artists vary the number, shape, and size of their panels in order to establish the rhythm of their stories and to express the passage of time (as detailed in [7], pg. 28). When the box is not drawn explicitly, the *"...non-frame speaks to unlimited space. It has the effect of encompassing unseen but acknowledged background."* (from [7], pg. 45). Here again, the deletion of the frame serves to merge the visual phenomenon with its surroundings, in this case, the rest of the page.

One may even observe an analogous trope in non-visual narratives such as novels. *Metalepsis* is a literary term that refers to the technique of manipulating representational layers. In a metalepsis, the represented begins to take control of the act of representation [16]. When metalepsis occurs in visual narratives such as film, not surprisingly the visual frame of the screen is used to delineate the boundary between the film's story and the viewer's. For example, in Woody Allen's *The Purple Rose of Cairo* (1985), a character in a Hollywood "B" movie (played by Jeff Daniels) notices a repeat viewer in the theater audience (Mia Farrow) and literally climbs out of the film frame to meet/connect with her.

Finally, the windowed panes introduced in the Xerox Star operational system and now ubiquitous in almost all computer interfaces are also an excellent example of using frames to encapsulate space and time. How upset does one get when a web pop-up opens a frameless window occluding the whole desktop, virtually taking over the one's personal workspace?

3   Interactive Frameless Displays

Although the concept of embodied *virtuality* was first articulated by Weiser [32], the powerful effect of the non-frame in interactive displays was perhaps first practically demonstrated by the *DigitalDesk*. [33]. Here, a frameless projection of a computer desktop seamlessly merged with and augmented a physical desktop.

Subsequently, the *I/O Bulb* [30] enabled *"computer-driven graphical constructs to escape the strictures of the rectangular screen and take their place as denizens of real-world architecture."* (from [30], pg. 391) The elimination of the frame (what the authors call *boundarylessness*) is deemed critical to displaying digital imagery that has a *"direct correspondence with pre-existing physical artifacts."* The *Language-Learning Tool* [11] shared a similar approach, labeling physical objects in a room with new words in a foreign language.

Not all frameless digital phenomena are directly associated with physical artifacts. Sometimes the correspondence is symbolic, such as in some versions of *PingPong-Plus* [34], or even poetic, as in the fountain in the *Hall of Ideas* [8]. Occasionally, pragmatic designers acknowledge laptop computers and their displays as physical artifacts and attempt to extend both their physical and virtual properties using localized frameless displays as in the *augmented surfaces* of Rekimoto and Saitoh [26].

User studies in this area are few. Pinhanez et al. [21] anecdotally observed several hundred demonstration attendees successfully pressing "buttons" projected onto neutral surfaces, such as tables. When directed to press a similar "button" projected onto the side of a paint can, the same attendees became confused. This confusion points to open questions about when interactive *physical* and *digital* objects begin to merge (or perhaps collide) within the space of the user. How do users negotiate the overlapping realities? When does one reality assume primacy over the other? How possible is to change the interaction modality of certain objects and surfaces? How does the psychological phenomenon known as *functional fixedness* [5], whereby people are unable to ascribe unfamiliar functions to a familiar object, affect a user's ability to interact with merged spaces?

Two studies trying to uncover how frameless displays affect interaction are briefly reported by Podlaseck et al. in [22]. Subjects were asked to choose the most appealing color from frameless clusters of colored buttons projected onto various objects. Their color choice consistency was then compared to equivalent choices on a desktop monitor to determine whether the projected objects affected the interaction. While the studies demonstrated that (1) the background objects affected the subjects' interactions with the digital objects and that (2) the digital objects affected the subjects' recall of the physical objects, the mechanism of these connections was elusive. For instance, a significant number of subjects in the object group (10%) appear to have been blind to the existence of one of the five background objects, a glass of milk; these subjects never selected colored buttons projected on the milk and did not even recall the presence of the milk when debriefed. These studies indicate that the use of frameless displays and their connections with real-world objects on interface design is anything but straightforward.

4   Examples of Use of Frameless Displays

In spite of the challenges and unknowns in using frameless displays, we have tried to experiment with them in a variety of situations. We have designed and built more than a dozen applications that use frameless displays few years since 2001, including systems that are experienced by new users every day, applications that run in real-world environments without assistance, as well as prototypes designed for and widely demonstrated in trade shows and business meetings. So far we have not used frameless displays to create disruptions in time; all of our applications deal with the spatial effects of using or not frames.

Based on our experience, we structure our presentation of applications that use frameless displays considering two dimensions:

- **Connection type:** a frameless display can be used to embed the application in the environment or to connect it to particular objects that exist in the environment.
- **Interactiveness:** a frameless display can be interactive or not.

Table 1 shows how some of our applications can be classified by their connection type and interactiveness. The top-left quadrant refers to the simplest kind of applica-

Table 1. Classification of the developed applications according to connected type and interactiveness.

	non-interactive	interactive
embedded in environment	Wall Comics Baby Steps Attractor Loop	Jumping Frog Traveling Tic-Tac-Toe Health Food Motivator
connected to objects	Multimedia Diaper Changer Wine Locator	Diaper Selector Interactive Cereal Boxes

tions that are **non-interactive and embedded in the environment**. For example, *Wall Comics* involves comic-strip characters with speech balloons used for advertising purposes (as shown in Figure 1, right). Not using a frame in this case eliminates the spatial separation between the character and the background wall, producing the effect of embedding the character in the physical environment.

Similarly, we developed a visual merchandising system for floor displays which attracts customers to a particular shelf in a store. This application, called the *Baby Steps Attractor Loop*, projects animated baby footsteps on a floor as if a baby is walking towards a shelf (see Figure 4, left). When the steps reach a shelf where diapers are located, a sound of a baby hitting a package is heard and the image of a package of diapers dropping on the floor is seen. In this case, the embedding of the baby steps in the environment naturally provides a direction for the user to follow, without the need for maps. In other words, the frameless display can eliminate the need of an intermediate, symbolic, representation such as a map: it indicates direction by making the "baby" follow the direction itself.

Let's look into another quadrant of the application classification shown in Table 1, the one corresponding to **non-interactive applications connected to objects in the environment**. A straightforward application in this category is the *Multimedia Diaper Changer*. In an advertisement piece created for this application, a video of a crying baby is projected without a frame directly onto the padded surface of a baby changing table. The video is followed by a scrolling text that describes the safety provided by diaper changers and the characteristics and price of that particular model. To increase realism, the baby imagery was captured in a way that the perspective effect was correct for a user standing in front of the diaper changer. The result is the *de facto* integration of the baby imagery and sound with the furniture, almost as if the baby was there, creating a powerful emotional connection with viewers (especially with parents). During a demonstration of this application, we needed to turn off the audio because a number of attendees became emotionally overwhelmed by the exhibit. We doubt that the same video on a traditional monitor would have this kind of effect.

A more interesting but less straightforward example is the *Wine Locator*, an application that has been running since October of 2004 in the Metro Store of the Future in Germany. This application extends a kiosk-based wine recommendation system that had a fundamental problem: after the user had spent many minutes browsing wine information on the kiosk screen, the only way to find the recommended wine was to

 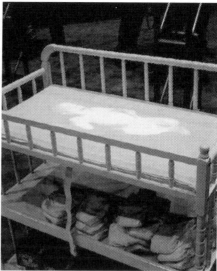

Figure 4. (left) *Baby Steps Attractor Loop*; (right) *Multimedia Diaper Changer*.

look for the selected wine among the 250 wines featured in the wine section, having only the wine's name printed on a sheet of paper. Many times, the customers could not locate the wine and would get extremely frustrated.

Our application adds a "where" button to the kiosk interface (as seen in Figure 5), and uses a steerable interactive projector system similar to [20] to help locate the wine. When the "where" button is pressed, the projector is veered towards the floor space in front of where the selected wine is. It then projects the image, name, and price of the wine, attracting the customer towards that area. The projected image of the wine, as shown in Figure 5, makes it easy for the user to scan the wines on the shelves and find his selection among them. The incorporation of the "where" button has, according to the store manager, increased significantly the use of the kiosk and very likely the volume of wine sales.

Notice, however, that in this application there is an implicit frame created by the projected white background. First, the white background is necessary to increase the visibility of the projected image when the user is still away from the wine, in front of the kiosk. Also, since the wine may be stocked anywhere on the shelf, the frame helps to create some disconnection between the information and the bottommost wine. An alternative could have been to highlight the wine itself by projecting directly onto it (as in [2]). This option was discarded since light can compromise the quality of wine. However, we still consider that this application uses frameless display techniques, especially because the whole floor of wine aisle can be regarded as the actual display area of this application and the projected area simply as a visual pointer to it.

The remaining applications we describe in this section use frameless displays that have interactive elements in them. First, let us examine cases of **interactive applications embedded in the environment**, as listed in the top-right quadrant of Table 1. A good example of this kind of applications is the *Jumping Frog* described earlier in

Figure 5. *Wine Locator.*

this paper (Figure 2). There, the frameless display increases the embedding of the animated frog onto the surface it is projected on, contributing to increase the feeling that the frog inhabits the user environment.

Another of such applications, called *Traveling Tic-Tac-Toe*, has been running since 2003 in the IBM demonstration area of the Epcot Center in Orlando, Florida. It is a variation of the traditional tic-tac-toe game where the game grid is moved after each turn to a random surface in the environment, to walls, cabinet doors, floor, etc. Each player has to find the grid before selecting a square to play (see Figure 6). This demonstration is run many times a day with the assistance of a presenter. The presenters have reported us that it has become one of their most popular attractions and that users are extremely comfortable with the interface and the game concept.

Projecting interactive frameless elements on the floor has been explored in the *Health Food Motivator,* developed for a demonstration of new supermarket technologies for a TV show. The goal here is to motivate people to improve their diet not only by showing them the location of healthier products, but also by engaging them through an active commitment process. Figure 7 shows the application which projects on the floor the message "Take the first step toward" and presents three choices: "lower sodium", "higher fiber", or "low cholesterol". When the user steps on one of these buttons, the application projects footprints on the floor that lead him to the appropriate area.

A frameless display, in this case, is used to embed the projected footsteps in the environment and to intuitively ask the user to follow them. We also believe that projecting the initial message and options without a frame encourages interaction. If a frame was used in this case it could have given the impression to the user that the circles with choices are not to be stepped on. In fact, this demonstration was also shown in an environment where, due to dark lighting conditions, it required the pro-

Figure 6. *Traveling Tic-Tac-Toe.*

jection to be done on a "framed" rug with a white background. In this situation, it was noticed (anecdotally) that people were less willing to step on the "buttons".

The last quadrant to explore on Table 1 corresponds to **interactive applications connected to objects in the environment**. These applications achieve, to some extent, the goal of transforming everyday objects into animated agents able to provide information about them. In the first of such applications, the *Diaper Selector*, a user is presented initially with samples of different types of toddler diapers. We exploit here the user's natural impulse to touch the diaper to feel its texture and volume. When a diaper is touched, it is *spotlighted* and information about it is displayed on the central surface (see Figure 8, right). To further entice users to touch the diapers when nobody is using the interactive display, an inviting message is projected on the central surface and image of hands are projected directly onto the diapers (see Figure 8, left). No frame is used to connect the highlighted diaper and its descriptive text.

This application demonstrates the use of spotlighting as an interface technique available for projected frameless displays connected to objects. As shown in Figure 8, it is possible to illuminate the object as if a spotlight had been directed to it. Spotlighting is another technique to create a reference to the object itself without the need of an intermediary symbol (for instance, an image, thumbnail, or textual description).

These ideas are taken further in the *Interactive Cereal Boxes* application created to complement the *Health Food Motivator* described above. This application transforms a shelf with cereal boxes and a printed panel with nutritional contents information into an interactive informational system. As shown in Figure 9, touching a cereal box makes the system highlight the information panel column of nutritional information corresponding to the box. Also, we use spotlighting to create user feedback so it becomes evident to which type of cereal that information relates. Finally, the system highlights (with a projected red bar) the best features of that particular cereal type compared to others on the shelf. Unlike in the *SearchLight* experiment [31], we focused the design of this application in a more realistic scenario where neither the shelf, the product, nor the user are instrumented directly.

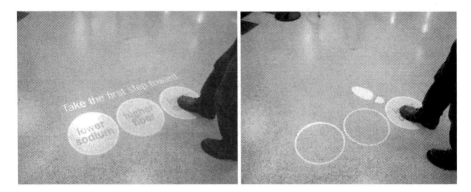

Figure 7. *Health Food Motivator.*

As mentioned, this application has been shown together with the *Health Food Motivator* (see Figure 7). First, the system tries to attract customers to the cereal shelf by inviting them to select a specific diet. After the selection, it leads them with footsteps projected on the floor that lead to the cereal box shelf. As the footsteps approach the shelf, the *Interactive Cereal Boxes* application is started and commanded to spotlight the cereal that is most appropriate for the diet selected by the customer. Since all cereal boxes are interactive, the customer can naturally explore the nutritional content of other types of cereal as described above. Again, the use of a frameless display and the spotlighting technique create a direct connection between the object and the information about it.

Before going ahead, we would like to comment on a complimentary technique used in some of these applications to increase the embedding of the projected display in the environment and the connection to nearby objects. This technique, which we call *real world framing*, involves the use of frame-like elements of the environment or an object to create a visual frame encompassing real world and display elements. This technique is used, for example, in the *Diaper Selector*. As seen in Figure 8, the diapers and the information area are mounted on a white panel bound by the upper and lower shelves. When the application is active, the boundaries of the panel are perceived as a container for the information and interaction, creating a virtual display frame mixing real and virtual objects that has basically the same properties of a traditional framed display. In other words, with the real world framing technique, it is possible to separate part of the real space and transform it into a mixed reality display. We also playfully experimented with this technique in the *Traveling Tic-Tac-Toe* application. Notice that in Figure 6 (right), the grid is projected on a cabinet door, making it less embedded in the environment than when the grid is projected on the wall (Figure 6, left).

5   The Usage of Frameless Displays in Ubiquitous Applications

In all the applications listed above, we were able to gather informal data about the user response, understanding, and acceptance of each application. This feedback,

Figure 8. *Diaper Selector.*

together with ideas from the literature, has allowed us to compile some pros and cons of using frameless displays and to provide basic design guidelines on their usage.

We should emphasize that we are not making a definitive assertion of the validity of the pros, cons, or guidelines, since our evidence is only anecdotal or derived from practical experience. In spite of the possibility, even likelihood, of being incorrect in some cases, as it may be shown by scientific studies in the future, we nonetheless find that this collection of ideas provides a framework to guide practice until better information is available. It also may serve as a draft research agenda for the field.

Let us start with an enumeration of the basic pros and cons of frameless displays.

POSITIVE PROPERTIES OF FRAMELESS DISPLAYS:

- **Embed characters into reality:** in applications embedded in the environment, such as the *Wall Comics* (Figure 1, right) and the *Jumping Frog* (Figure 2) applications, a frameless display seamlessly embeds a flat character into the environment.

- **Connect information to objects:** in applications connected to objects, such as the *Multimedia Diaper Changer* (Figure 4, right) and in [11, 25, 30], positioning information near an object causes immediate, strong associations between the two.

- **Enable the creation of very large virtual displays:** the absence of boundaries removes any reference to where the display actually starts and ends. Therefore if multiple or steerable projectors are used, as in the case of the *Wine Locator* (Figure 5 and in [8]), it is possible to create the sensation of a high-resolution, seamless display area that covers a very large portion of the environment.

- **Create a strong sensation of direction:** projecting arrows or other directional elements in the environment such as in the *Baby Steps Attractor Loop* (Figure 4, left) and in [29], provides an intuitive and, in many cases, unambiguous way of indicating direction. This can be an attractive alternative to maps.

Figure 9. *Interactive Cereal Boxes.*

- **Enable direct pointing to an object:** the *Wine Locator* (Figure 5) illustrates the value of pointing directly to an object in a densely populated environment, eliminating the need for maps and directions.
- **Transform an area or an object into a symbol of itself:** techniques such as spotlighting, used in the *Diaper Selector* (Figure 8), can eliminate the use of intermediate symbols when referring to an object. A display disconnected from the environment — for example, a typical kiosk — uses thumbnails and other visual imagery to help the user connect the displayed information to the concrete object which it refers to. Spotlighting an object, and/or using the object as a trigger, as in the *Interactive Cereal Boxes* (Figure 9), eliminates the "middle-man" symbol from the communication, potentially contributing to increase the association of ideas to the object and possibly enhancing its ability to be remembered.
- **Transform positively the perception of an object:** by illuminating or coloring an object, or displaying appropriate content such as in the *Multimedia Diaper Changer* (Figure 4, right) or in [24], it is possible to make the object(s) more interesting visually. Interaction may induce similar transformation as in the case of the *Jumping Frog* (Figure 2).

CONCERNS WHEN USING FRAMELESS DISPLAYS:

- **Creating undesirable connections between information and objects:** for example, if the animated frog of the *Jumping Frog* (Figure 2) lands on the surface of food (for example, a pizza slice), queasy feelings may be accidentally elicited. Also, designers should be aware that people can find unexpected, frequently undesirable connections between the display content and its surroundings.
- **Making performance and usability of an interface less predictable:** as discussed in Section 3, characteristics of the environment may affect the desirability

to interact with the display. Also, the environmental lighting can render parts or the whole display invisible, unrecognizable, or altered.

- **Invading people's personal space:** in the *Health Food Motivator* (Figure 7), a customer remarked that he thought the buttons displayed on the floor in front of him implied that he needed to diet. Because the connections to the environment, objects, and people are enhanced by a frameless display, it is easier to inadvertently create situations where a user is made self-conscious by the contents of a display.
- **Negatively affecting the perception of object:** in the case of applications connected to objects, as much as the perception of an object can be improved as discussed before, there may be situations where objects negatively affected by the display. For instance, in the *Interactive Cereal Boxes* (Figure 9), the color and the brand legibility of the cereal boxes were somewhat affected by the yellow circle used to spotlight them.
- **Difficulties creating perspective and 3D effects:** the detachment from the environment created by a framed display simplifies the creation of the illusion of 3D through perspective. A frame defines implicitly two candidate horizon lines parallel to its boundaries; in most cases, this hint is sufficient to enable viewers to "parse" the perspective. Conversely, frameless displays lack the ability to create references to anchor the vanishing points that are essential for the perception of perspective, making it harder for the viewer to understand perspective images especially when she is not positioned correctly. For example, the video of the crying baby projected on the padding of the *Multimedia Diaper Changer* (Figure 4, right) only works when the viewer is positioned exactly in front of the diaper changer.
- **Challenging the established vocabulary of design:** as detailed in the next paragraphs, many commonly used techniques in visual design, such as scrolling and sliding content, do not work well in the absence of a frame. For example, the use of a scrolling text in the *Multimedia Diaper Changer* (Figure 4, right) had to be softened by using fading in and out on the top and bottom of the scroll, respectively.

In our experience, the actual practice of creating ubiquitous applications using frameless displays faces a considerable obstacle: it is hard for print- or web-trained visual designers to work with frameless displays. Years of professional experience in composing and transitioning visual elements within a frame are hard for one to immediately abandon. Similarly, narrative devices derived from cinema, such as close-ups, fast editing, or over-the-shoulder shots do not translate well, in our view, to texts and images that are highly connected to the physical world (as observed also by Underkoffler et al. [30]). We have seen in many of our engagements that it takes professional designers many design iterations to start thinking outside the frame.

To support the training of the visual designers, we have been compiling some "rules of engagement" for frameless displays in ubiquitous applications. In reality, *"they are more what you'd call 'guidelines' than actual rules"*[2]. But, nonetheless, here follows a first attempt to capture some of the parameters governing the design of

---

[2] From *Pirates of the Caribbean: The Curse of the Black Pearl* (regarding the pirates' strict code of conduct).

ubiquitous frameless interfaces; notice that some of these guidelines apply primarily to applications that are either embedded in the environment or connected to objects.

DESIGN GUIDELINES FOR FRAMELESS INTERFACES

GENERAL CASE:

- **Use the environment, its objects, and the surface elements as part of the interface:** the best way to connect to the environment is to integrate it to the visual design; frameless displays cannot do it all.
- **Design, if possible, the real world together with the interface:** sometimes it is easier to change an object's position than to fix the visual design. The environment and the objects in the proximity of the display are as integral to the display as the text and graphics.
- **Be aware of the surface being projected on and its effects:** in the case of projected displays, consider and, if possible, use the texture of the surface being projected. For instance, we once obtained a striking effect when we projected a picture of a Monet painting (which originally had a lot of texture) on a white fury carpet. Also, try to use saturated colors to ensure greater contrast.
- **Eliminate the "middle" symbol whenever possible:** as discussed above, one of the most striking properties of frameless displays is the possibility of directly connecting the real with the virtual world and eliminating the need for symbolic reference imagery and text. For instance, if text is projected on the side of an object, there is no need for the image of the object. Similarly, it is possible to indicate directions by showing them directly in the environment, instead of using maps.
- **Avoid implicit frames:** for example, in Figure 1, right, the bottom part of the character profile is cut horizontally, creating an invisible line of reference that implicitly determines a frame. An irregularly shaped cut often works better to keep the display frameless.
- **Be cautious when using cinema-inspired visual techniques:** sliding and panning texts and imagery, fast cutting, close-ups, and over-the-shoulder shots heavily rely on the reference from the frame. When used, they tend to create implicit frames as discussed above. Instead, use fade-in/out, images that expand from and contract to a single point, etc.
- **Avoid using scrolling:** at the heart of this technique is the existence of frame boundaries.
- **Be careful when using navigation mechanisms:** if the interface includes buttons or links that bring additional information or services, check whether the coming information is still connected to the environment or to the object: if not, consider framing it. Similarly, be careful when navigating back from the virtual to the real world.
- **Shoot video against a black background and keep the actors' figures whole:** the background of a video implicitly defines a frame. Also, avoid framing the video subjects, or using close-ups, since they can break the illusion of connection. If cutting the body is absolutely necessary, consider post-editing effects that create irregular or fuzzy boundaries.
- **Be cautious using imagery with perspective:** as discussed in the previous section, the illusion of perspective requires either a framing reference or the correct

positioning of the viewer. This is particularly important when using perspective-based imagery on non-vertical surfaces, since people tend to better parse perspective on vertical imagery (probably from years of exposure of movies and television). Notice that in most cases, photos and videos have implicit perspective.

- **Use sound effects:** whenever possible, use sound effects that increase or soften the connection between the real and the virtual, as needed. For example, in the *Jumping Frog* game (Figure 2), the illusion that the frog jumps is dramatically enhanced by cartoon-like sound effects when it jumps, travels through the air, and lands.

APPLICATIONS EMBEDDED IN THE ENVIRONMENT:

- **Do not use frameless displays when information is disconnected from the environment:** for instance, if the display is showing world news, there is probably no connection with the environment, so the content should be framed.
- **Be careful when jumping from one surface to another surface:** as discussed by Sukaviriya et al. in [29], it can be difficult for users to follow the path of interfaces that jump discontinuously from one surface to another. Be sure, at least, that the surfaces are not too apart.

APPLICATIONS CONNECTED TO OBJECTS:

- **Be careful about the distance from the object to display:** the easiest way to ensure connection between an object and the information on the display is to have them very close to each other. If that is not possible, and if confusion with other objects is likely, consider using soft frames and symbolic imagery to increase the likelihood of the desired connection as used in the *Wine Locator* example.
- **Have mechanisms/sensors to ensure the connected object is there:** if the interface requires the presence of an object to be understood, it is better that the object is there. To be sure, consider the use of sensors or check points that determine the presence of the object. In case the object is not present, or not likely to be present in a specific situation, the system can start operating in a safer mode displaying, for instance, an image of the object.

6   Conclusion

While working together with visual designers and software developers to create the nine applications described in this paper, we often encountered enormous difficulties to communicate our understanding of how frameless displays work. It is very hard for visual designers to stop using the amazing possibilities provided by their lifetime-companion frame, and for software developers to take in account the actual environment the application will live on. Our main goal with this paper is to systematize as much as possible our knowledge about frameless displays in their role and usage in ubiquitous applications so: (1) the communication and discussion with visual designers and software developers becomes easier and based on palpable guidelines; and (2) a possible research agenda in this area is proposed to the ubicomp community.

We believe we convincingly argued that frameless displays increase the connection between the information in the display and the environment and that new possibilities for interface design have become available. For example, the elimination of "middle-man" symbols from the interface, as seen in the *Interactive Cereal Boxes* application, is a good example of a new paradigm that is probably very useful in ubiquitous applications. At the same time, this increased connection is likely to modify some of our ideas of how interaction is addressed in an ubicomp world, given, for instance, how the nature of an object seems to impact the willingness to interact with visual elements rendered on and around it.

We are keenly aware of the need for further refinement and scientific validation of our design guidelines for frameless displays. But, most important, we see them as a portal for an exciting visual design and HCI research agenda. For instance, we just touched in this paper the problem of how to do hotlink-style navigation in a frameless display. The basic question, in this case, seems to be the development of mechanisms to clearly separate information that is contextualized in space from information that is not. Also, although we have focused so far in spatial issues, in future work we plan to experiment with the disruption of time created by framing content.

Finally, understanding the role and design of frameless displays in ubiquitous applications may also help other areas of HCI research. For instance, in applications based on tangible interfaces it is very hard to associate to an object a function or property that is not mapped directly in its natural usage. What is a natural way to ask a cereal box its price? How can a refrigerator in a store connect a customer with the help desk? These and similar problems lead us to believe that creating visual mechanisms to contextualize and decontextualize information is a more fundamental research issue in ubiquitous computing applications than currently understood.

References

1. Anderson, L.: Empty Places. Harper Perennial. New York, New York (1991)
2. Butz, A., et al.: SearchLight - A Lightweight Search Function for Pervasive Environments. In: Proceedings of Pervasive 2004. Vienna, Austria, April 21-23 (2004) pgs. 351-356
3. Chikamori, M., Kunoh, K.: KAGE. In: SIGGRAPH'98 Electronic Art and Animation Catalog. Orlando, Florida, July 19-24 (1998) 14
4. Dourish, P.: Where the Action is : the Foundations of Embodied Interaction. MIT Press. Cambridge, Massachusetts (2001)
5. Duncker, K.: On Problem Solving. Psychological Monographs 270 (1945)
6. Duro, P.: The Rhetoric of the Frame : Essays on the Boundaries of the Artwork. Cambridge University Press. Cambridge, England ; New York, NY, USA (1996)
7. Eisner, W.: Comics & Sequential Art. Poorhouse Press. Guerneville, Calif. (1985)
8. Hall, P.: Starting Small. Metropolis (metropolismag.com). http://www.metropolismag.com/cda/story.php?artid=626 (2004)
9. Henger, S., Kosenko, P.: Chris Burden: A Twenty Year Survey. Newport Harber Art Musuem. (1988)
10. Hoffman, D.: Visual Intelligence: How We Create What We See. W. W. Norton (1998)
11. Intille, S., et al.: Ubiquitous Computing in the Living Room, Concept Sketches and an Implementation of a Persistent User Interface. In: Proc. of the Video Session of UbiComp'03. Seattle, Washington, Oct. 12-15 (2003)
12. Iwai, T.: Composition on the Table. In: SIGGRAPH'99 Electronic Art and Computer Animation Catalog. Los Angeles, California, August, 8-13 (1999) 10

13. Kaprow, A., Kelley, J.: Essays on the Blurring of Art and Life. University of California Press. Berkeley, California (1993)

14. Krueger, M. W.: Artificial Reality II. Addison-Wesley (1990)

15. McCloud, S.: Understanding Comics. Kitchen Sink Press. Northampton, Massachusetts (1993)

16. Meister, J. C.: The Metalepticon: a Computational Approach to Metalepsis. Universität Hamburg. http://www.jcmeister.de/downloads/texts/jcm-metalepticon.html. Sep 3 (2003)

17. Morton, A.: A New Frame of Mind. International Institute for Frame Study. http://www.iifs.org/framehunt.html. Feb 26 (2000)

18. Murata, K., Yamauchi, E.: Fisherman's Cafe. In: SIGGRAPH'99 Electronic Art and Computer Animation Catalog. Los Angeles, California, August, 8-13 (1999) 12

19. Nowlin, S.: Less About Appearances. Skeptical Inquirer (2003) 1-2

20. Pinhanez, C.: The Everywhere Displays Projector: A Device to Create Ubiquitous Graphical Interfaces. In: Proc. of Ubiquitous Computing 2001 (Ubicomp'01). Atlanta, Georgia, September (2001)

21. Pinhanez, C., et al.: Ubiquitous Interactive Graphics. IBM Research Report RC22495 (W0205-143), May 17 (2002)

22. Podlaseck, M., et al.: On Interfaces Projected onto Real-World Objects. In: Proc. of CHI'03 (short papers). Fort Lauderdale, Florida, April 5-10 (2003)

23. Raskar, R., et al.: RFIG Lamps: Interacting With a Self-Describing World via Photosensing Wireless Tags and Projectors. In: Proc. of SIGGRAPH'04. Los Angeles, California, August 8-12 (2004)

24. Raskar, R., et al.: iLamps: Geometrically Aware and Self-Configuring Projectors. In: Proc. of SIGGRAPH'03. San Diego, California, July 27-31 (2003) 809-818

25. Rekimoto, J.: A Multiple Device Approach for Supporting Whiteboard-based Interactions. In: Proc. of CHI'98. Los Angeles, California, April 18-23 (1998) 344-351

26. Rekimoto, J., Saitoh, M.: Augmented Surfaces: A Spatially Continuous Workplace for Hybrid Computing Environments. In: Proc. of CHI'99. Pittsburgh, Pennsylvania, May 15-20 (1999) 378-385

27. Shen, C., et al.: DiamondSpin: An Extensible Toolkit for Around-the-Table Interaction. In: Proc. of CHI'04, April 2004 (2004) 167-174

28. Small, D., White, T.: Stream of Consciouness. In: SIGGRAPH'98 Electronic Art and Animation Catalog. Orlando, Florida, July 19-24 (1998) 50

29. Sukaviriya, N., et al.: Embedding Interactions in a Retail Store Environment: The Design and Lessons Learned. In: Proc. of the Ninth IFIP International Conference on Human-Computer Interaction (INTERACT'03). Zurich, Switzerland, September, 1-5 (2003)

30. Underkoffler, J., et al.: Emancipated Pixels: Real-World Graphics in the Luminous Room. In: Proc. of SIGGRAPH'99. Los Angeles, California, August 8-13 (1999) 385-392

31. Wasinger, R., et al.: Integrating Intra and Extra Gestures into a Mobile and Multimodal Shopping Assistant. In: Proc. of the 3rd International Conference on Pervasive Computing,. Munich, Germany, May 8-13 (2005) pgs 297-314

32. Weiser, M.: The Computer for the Twenty-First Century. Scientific American 265 (3) (1991) 94-100

33. Wellner, P.: Interacting with Paper on the DigitalDesk. Communications of the ACM 36 (7) (1993)

34. Wineski, C., et al.: PingPongPlus: Augmentation and Transformation of Athletic Interpersonal Interaction. In: Proc. of CHI'98. Los Angeles, California (1998) 327-328

35. Yotsukura, T., et al.: Hypermask - Projecting a Talking Head onto a Real Object. The Visual Computer 18 (2) (2002) 111-120

Picking Pockets on the Lawn: The Development of Tactics and Strategies in a Mobile Game

Louise Barkhuus, Matthew Chalmers, Paul Tennent, Malcolm Hall, Marek Bell, Scott Sherwood, and Barry Brown

Department of Computing Science, University of Glasgow,
University Avenue, Glasgow, G12 8QQ, UK
matthew@dcs.gla.ac.uk

Abstract. This paper presents *Treasure*, an outdoor mobile multiplayer game inspired by Weiser's notion of seams, gaps and breaks in different media. Playing Treasure involves movement in and out of a wi-fi network, using PDAs to pick up virtual 'coins' that may be scattered outside network coverage. Coins have to be uploaded to a server to gain game points, and players can collaborate with teammates to double the points given for an upload. Players can also steal coins from opponents. As they move around, players' PDAs sample network signal strength and update coverage maps. Reporting on a study of players taking part in multiple games, we discuss how their tactics and strategies developed as their experience grew with successive games. We suggest that meaningful play arises in just this way, and that repeated play is vital when evaluating such games.

1   Introduction

The study and design of games has added diversity to many areas of ubicomp research. Games are not only a subject worthy of academic attention in themselves [11], they introduce challenges in terms of designing enjoyable experiences. They also lead to technical challenges in implementing distributed ubicomp systems, and players' engagement can lead to new patterns of use that reveal system strengths and weaknesses. For example, *Uncle Roy All Around You* [2] delivered generalisable results concerning positioning systems and the use of self–reporting, and *Real Tournament* [10], a simple 'shooter' game, explored IPv6 and issues such as host mobility, security, content delivery and wireless overlay networks.

In this paper, we present our experiences with *Treasure*, a mobile multiplayer game. Treasure involves both competition and collaboration among players using PDAs with GPS and 802.11 wireless networks. While existing ubicomp games have almost exclusively been trialled in single games, we explored the changing use of game features as players learned about the game through multiple plays. We focus on how their experience of multiple games changed their play and their understanding of the game as well as how the play gives rise to more complex forms of co-operation and competition.

M. Beigl et al. (Eds.): UbiComp 2005, LNCS 3660, pp. 358–374, 2005.

We start the paper by describing the game's motivation, before outlining the technical and design features of the system. We then present our results from the user trials, describing how the tactics and strategies of players changed as game play developed. We then reflect on these trials, and how repeated trials can be used to inform designers of good game experiences. Lastly we outline our ongoing work that builds on Treasure to develop more mobile games with lengthy game playing periods.

2 The Motivation and Design of the Game

Applications may be built to be uniform and 'seamless', but their infrastructure often shows through in interaction, with features such as errors in positioning systems and the limits of 802.11 WiFi coverage becoming apparent in system use [4, 9]. Although this phenomenon is often considered to be negative, we saw the potential to make positive use of it by making the spatial variation of an 802.11 network a central resource in a system design. This infrastructure is a feature presented in the interface, and is also an implicit feature of many interface operations and game actions.

We drew inspiration from Mark Weiser's notions of seams and seamful design [12]. A seam is a break, gap or 'loss in translation' in a number of tools or media, designed for use together as a uniformly and unproblematically experienced whole. Seams often appear when we use different digital systems together, or use a digital system along with the other older media that make up our everyday environment. For example, many applications for mobile computers may be built as if they could be used along with the features of the environment one travels through, e.g. to display web pages about nearby buildings and people. Such applications often assume constant network connectivity, and yet this is not always the case when mobile systems really are mobile: as one walks away from an access point, such systems often crash or become unusable as the wireless connection weakens and then disappears. In urban areas it is likely that there are variations, gaps and overlaps in networks' coverage. The built environment also makes for variations in the accessibility of GPS positioning, due to occlusion and multipath reflections from buildings. Rather than designing the game to be played within one isolated network in an open area, we explored a design in which such features were an explicit and essential part of the game experience.

Although we began with a great variety of game features, devices and roles, an iterative design process led us to progressively simpler designs that concentrated on a small set of simple interactions between players, and a relatively simple map display on PDAs. Earlier designs had other names, including *Seamful Game* and *Bill*. We treated the design process, including the user trials, as exploratory. Designs often changed in response to ongoing findings, which were generally reflections from observational studies of system use. We considered this evaluation approach better suited to our design process than one driven by pre–established formal hypotheses.

Before we outline game play and the underlying system, we note that concepts such as seams and seamful design need not be important for players. Particular seams may be apparent in how players play and discuss a system, but they do not necessarily need or want to analyse these design concepts in abstract terms—just as they do not

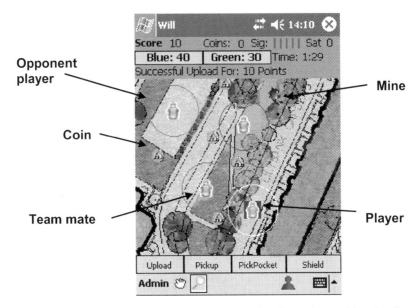

Opponent player

Coin

Team mate

Mine

Player

Fig. 1. The game interface. The map shows players' locations, along with coins that are often positioned outside the network. A semi–transparent map layer of green, yellow and red squares builds up as players move around, revealing network coverage, however for printing reasons these have not been included in this figure.

need to have formal training in the physics of RF propagation or wireless network communication protocols. The way that the game uses or reveals an aspect of ubi-comp infrastructure is not meant to be part of a technical education, even though the technology of the game is clearly an element of its design. We aimed for a game that was fun to play, where play could be observed or recorded in ways that would let us, as researchers, better understand the relationship between game play and the system's design.

2.1   Game Play

The aim of the game is to collect *coins* scattered over an urban area and then get them in to the *treasure chest* (technically, a server). Two teams of two players compete against each other. A clock counts down, and the team with the most coins in their treasure chest at the end wins the game. The coins can only be seen on the map on the players' PDAs (see Fig. 1 for screenshot). Each player's location, the locations of coins and the locations of other players are displayed on his or her map. To pick a coin up, a player has to run over to it and then click the *Pickup* button. Coins are dropped by the server in all parts of the arena, and a player can pick up coins at any time, but a player can only upload coins (with the *Upload* button) when he or she is within the wireless network. The chances of a successful coin upload increase with the strength of the wireless network at that location. To succeed in a game, the player must therefore learn which areas are covered by wireless network and which are not.

The signal strength of the wireless network is shown in the upper right corner of the screen as small bars; when there are few bars and they are red, the signal is low; when there are many bars and they are green, it is high. By moving in and out of areas of network coverage, players also survey the wireless network they are playing with, building up a collective map of signal strength. A high level of signal strength leaves a green trail, a moderate level a yellow trail, and low or no signal colours the area red. In between the coins there are mines, shown as black icons on the PDA map. If a player hits or walks over a mine, he or she loses all the coins on the PDA, and the interface is disabled for 20 seconds, displaying a black countdown screen.

Players can upload coins together and gain double points for their coins. They have to press the *Upload* button at the same time (technically, within three seconds of each other). A player can also pickpocket another player by walking up close and clicking *Pickpocket*; he or she then gets all the coins that the other player has (but not the coins that have already been uploaded). If the player wants to prevent pickpocketing, he/she can raise a shield by clicking *Shield*; this lasts one minute but then has to be recharged. *Upload, Pickpocket* and *Shield* only work inside the network, but the *Pickup* button works anywhere.

2.2   Technical Issues

The trials reported on in this paper involved four HP iPAQ PDAs running Pocket PC, each with a compact flash GPS unit and built-in 802.11. Each runs a C# game client, developed with the .NET Compact Framework. The client's interface is shown in Fig. 1. The system also involves a wireless network access point connected to a PC running the game server (again written in C#). The client and server code is instrumented, with each process building up a log of system events such as GUI actions, new GPS positions and other changes to game state. At the end of the game, when the PDA is on the network, the clients' logs are automatically sent to our server.

At any point during a game, a PDA's network connection can be roughly categorised as disconnected, strongly connected or weakly connected. The last of these is the prevalent state; play often takes place on the edge of the network. As a result, we developed a simple messaging subsystem using the UDP protocol rather than the more common TCP. The server 'heartbeats' the game state, broadcasting all game state information (scores, positions etc.) every second across the network. We have found the messaging system to be robust, but we recognise that it would not scale well to high numbers of clients creating large volumes of state information and net traffic.

Another issue associated with the continuous movement in and out of network by clients is the way that the standard Pocket PC wireless drivers may attempt connections to the nearest network. Also, a GUI window pops up when such a connection happens, with a "New Network Found" notification. Since the movement of players often brings them into range of networks other than our own, we created a custom wireless driver that allowed us to 'lock on' to a particular network SSID and connect only to that. Along with the use of static IP addresses, this allowed data connections to be established very quickly when clients returned to our network, and increased the chance of a successful connection in areas of weak coverage.

3   Related Work

Many mobile multiplayer games have been developed, and several have been run on a large scale in a commercial setting, e.g. Newt Games' *Mogi Mogi* (www.mogimogi.com). However, a game related closely to ours was *Can You See Me Now?* (CYSMN), which linked on-line and street players in a chase game [9]. Street players (*runners*) moved around the game area covered by a game–specific wireless network, and had their positions tracked by GPS. On-line players used arrow keys to move themselves around a 3D view of the same streets, with icons showing the locations of runners. Similarly, online players' positions were shown on the mobile computers carried by runners. Runners chased on-line players through the city, making their GPS positions match the on–line players' positions i.e. 'catching' them. In playing CYSMN, the variable accuracy of GPS caused problems for street players when trying to catch players in areas of bad GPS coverage. However, through repeated plays and their social interaction, runners became more skilled at using their knowledge of good and bad GPS areas, luring online players into areas of good GPS where catching them was easier. In this way the runners took advantage a limitation—a seam—of the game infrastructure, but the game was not designed to make explicit use of this. This shows a benefit of trials of ubicomp systems that take a longer time or involve repeated use: they can reveal the development of deeper understanding and appropriation of system features, most particularly through social interaction.

The *Pirates!* game [8] used RF technology to determine the proximity of players to one another and to static resources. This allowed the game to be played either indoors or outdoors. The game mapped an ocean environment on to the rooms and objects in a conference hall, and players took the role of ship commanders, traveling from island to island, and trading and fighting in order to gain wealth. The underlying RF infrastructure was mapped to specific game events so that when a player came close to a RF beacon representing an island, a game event was triggered. In particular, face–to–face interaction was a key part of the game, encouraging some of the social aspects of gaming that can be lost in some computer game designs. Pirates! was tested at a large conference with 31 users and an average number of players in the game arena of four. An implicit part of the Pirates! game was the range, limits and gaps in RF, but Treasure makes similar infrastructure (802.11) a more explicit part of its design.

Another game that influenced our work was *NodeRunner* (www.noderunner.com), which made use of the wireless network infrastructure existing in a city. As demonstrated at Ubicomp 2003, each team had a PDA equipped with 802.11 and a camera. Teams of players raced against time, logging as many wireless access points as they could and uploading photographic proof of each find to a central server. While NodeRunner made original use of the existing invisible wireless infrastructure, it made no use of the signal beyond the existence of access points.

Numerous other mobile games have been developed, but here we have focused on the games most relevant to our work; other games are based on different infrastructures such as mobile phone networks or focus on other areas such as education. An overview of a number of these systems and related design issues can be found in [3].

4   User Trials

Through our trials we hoped to understand how people used and reacted to a design which makes an element of ubicomp infrastructure an explicit part of an interaction design, a major characteristic of Treasure. We also aimed to apply a lesson from studies of systems such as CYSMN [9], which showed that social interaction often contributes to and reveals how players change and develop new ways of using a system. This occurs as games progress and more experience is gathered and shared. The trials reported here looked at social interaction and multiple plays, with detailed observation intended to reveal the tactics and strategies players developed in the course of multiple games. This point was especially significant to us, as all of our game's earlier trials had been limited to first–time players.

4.1   Participant Recruitment and Trial Structure

The participants were recruited in pairs, and in the end we had nine teams of two. The games were set up so no teams played against each other twice. Nine games were played all together, with four teams playing one game, one team playing two and four teams playing three games. All participants were all compensated equally for their time. The participants were all between the age of 17 and 33 with a mean of 23.5; we recruited a few more females than males, but the teams were mixed as well as same sex. Most were students, from a wide variety of disciplines—including three students of computer science. All participants used computers daily.

We ran the games on a fairly large lawn, its surrounding streets and in part of an adjacent car park. This was a good game arena, in that there was considerable open space, trees to hide behind, and relatively little road traffic. The area was about 7000 square metres (64000 square feet). Roughly half of the area had good wireless network coverage. However, since weather has a significant effect on the strength and reach of 802.11, coverage varied from game to game; hence it is difficult to illustrate a map of average coverage. Generally the right hand side of the map in Fig. 1 had coverage and the left hand side had little or no network coverage. GPS worked well out on the open area of the lawn, but it was difficult to get accurate readings close to the building, adjacent to the lawn, where the 802.11 access point was situated.

Before first-time participants played, they were given a thorough introduction indoors, in a conference room, together with their opponents. One researcher explained the game using a paper prototype of the PDA display for about ten minutes, and then a second researcher entered with the four PDAs. The participants were then given the PDAs, the researchers demonstrated simple manoeuvres such as panning and zooming with the PDA stylus, and then the players demonstrated these same manoeuvres. They were also informed that they would be observed and recorded as they played. When the participants seemed confident with the game, the players and the researchers all walked out into the game arena. Before playing each game, we let the players walk around and pick up coins in a 'pre-game'; they were able to exercise the main game operations such as uploading coins, hitting mines, pickpocketing and using the shield. Players arriving for their second or third games began out on the lawn with a reminder of the game's basics, and then they joined in the 'pre–game'. When we

Fig. 2. The *Replayer* tool is used for analysis of system use. It synchronises multiple video streams (left) and a visualisation of the combined log data from the PDAs and the server, via a VCR–like control panel (bottom right) or a log search tool (centre right).

were sure that everyone understood the scope of the game, we played for 15 minutes. The winning team received a small prize for reasons of motivation.

4.2   Data Collection and Analysis

Data was collected in several ways. First of all, game related data from each game client and from the game server was logged. A tool called *Replayer* was developed for the purpose of combining the log data, and playing it back in a map–like visualisation. Replayer has a graphic interface that illustrates the progress of the game, supports queries of game state, and enables the log data to be synchronized with video streams (Fig. 2). This helped us handle the complex and often inconsistent game state data on each PDA. Potentially, each player's PDA may show a different game state at any given time, because each is based on the player's position and network connectivity, and the PDA will gain updates of game state only when inside the wireless network. Also, if a player moves outside the network, his or her GPS data cannot be sent to the server, and so the server will broadcast the player's last received position until he or she re–enters the network.

Two video streams of each game were also recorded, one from the game arena itself taken by a researcher literally running around, tracing the players and another stream taken from a window above the lawn with a good view of two thirds of the game arena. These were synchronized with the logs by Replayer, enabling analysis where both game play data and video streams were shown on one monitor simultaneously. Another researcher in the arena observed the games, and used a voice recorder to take notes about direct interaction between players. She also provided support if players had technical difficulties. After each game, the participants were interviewed in teams. This was done separately in order to get the individual teams' experiences without the other team listening in. The interviews concentrated on the enjoyment of the game and the collaboration between the teams, and on tactics and strategies that teams used. The interviews were all recorded, and transcribed shortly thereafter for analysis.

Reviewing numerous types of data such as our video recordings, system logs and post-play interviews can be challenging but, by going through each game with Replayer, it was straightforward to find features of particular interest by looking at the two video streams of the game play along with the visualised log data. On observing some feature of interaction in the video, one could check if the game state might have been an influence. Similarly, it was useful to search for certain events such as mines going off, in order to see players' reactions. We also looked for specific patterns in their collection of coins and interaction with each other. After the interviews had been transcribed, both interviews from each game were analysed by categorising topics and comparing the players' actions with game events. Overall the analysis was done on a fine–grained level. For example, the movements and the reactions of the players were described and their social interaction was tightly observed. However, because of the extensive material, we focused on issues relevant to the game experience and the issues described here such as tactics, strategies and collaboration.

5   Results

The games were popular and, after playing, all the participants said that it had been a fun experience. In successive games, teams became competent in the basic mechanics of game play. They became familiar with every game feature, including the more 'seamful' ones, and reported that they did not have as many 'beginners' problems' such as having difficulty finding a network signal or mistakenly thinking that one could pickpocket one's teammate. A number of basic statistics are shown in Fig. 3. When first–time players played against second– or third–time players, the more experienced team generally won. As they became more experienced, they also became more excited, engaged and competitive in the game, and tried hard to excel with a combination of speed and strategies. There were also a number of subtler changes in game play. As players influenced and interacted with each other, they changed how they used individual game features and how they related those features to each other.

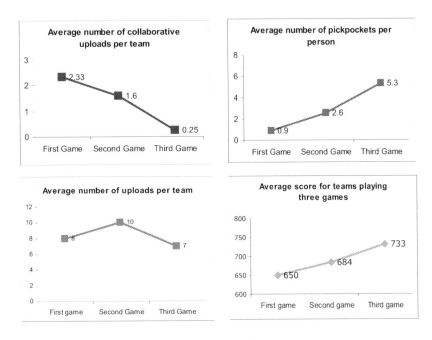

Fig. 3. Scores and trends in the games

Perhaps the most marked trend was that players chose to pickpocket much more often in later games. Second– and third–time players interacted considerably more with each other, not just through pickpocketing but also through talk, gesture and other more general forms of social interaction. We also observed that as one team—often a more experienced team—pickpocketed another heavily, the latter team would respond by using the pickpocket more. As pickpocketing increased, players used shields more and made fewer collaborative uploads. They reported that they felt more confident in their understanding of the game, and became more aware of the risk of having coins stolen. They then preferred to spread out to pick up more coins, and to upload quickly and independently to gain points. To this end, they often hit the *Up-load* button repeatedly and were less careful to be within network; players had learnt that there was no major loss in trying to upload outside the network. Also, on average, players avoided mines better, attempted to upload more frequently and tended to play within a slightly smaller part of the arena as they became more familiar with the game.

We can focus on individual teams and players to give more detail example of how play changed over time. Team B was the only team to win three games, although they never played against a team with more experience than them. In their first game, Team B efficiently used collaborative uploads, succeeding three times, but then they began to change their play. They altered as game play evolved and opponents picked up on features such as pickpocketing. In their later games, their opponents were pickpocketing them so often that they did not upload collaboratively once. The opponents in their second game successfully pickpocketed them three times, and the opponents in their third game succeeded eleven times. Team B pickpocketed in return, succeeding eleven times in their third game also. One of the members of this team commented that their last game had been a 'button-bashing game', which was confirmed by the log data and further comments that echoed the character of this game: "[my team mate] just lost all of her [coins] [...] and I stole them from her who had taken it from [my team mate]...". The team mate interrupted: "We were standing besides each other, trying to upload together and then somebody pickpocketed me and then [my team mate] pickpocketed them back so he ended up with them all. So he uploaded them all instead of a collaborative one".

The trial participants seemed to achieve what Salen and Zimmerman [10] call 'meaningful play' through their experience in that, through multiple plays, the relationships between actions and outcomes were both discernible and integrated into the larger context of the game. For example, one player said after the first game that she did not like the game very much, because it was difficult to find out where the signal was and where she was on the map. After the last game, however, she was asked which one of the three games she had enjoyed the most and replied: "This one [...] because you are more aware of all the things that are going on. You feel more in control of, like, what you are doing rather than just randomly pressing buttons". She and her teammate laughed and chatted as they played and won their third game. They made no collaborative uploads but did pickpocket their opponents ten times, in contrast to the two pickpockets they made in their first game.

Over the course of their games, several teams became more intense and competitive (for example, running more) whereas a few became more relaxed and cheerful. Teammates' interaction with each other appears to have been affected by the type of relationship the team members had. Although we attempted to only pair people who knew each other, two games had one team consisting of participants who did not know each other previously. In these games we observed less interaction among those team members, and only one of these games had a collaborative upload.

We now consider recurrent and significant patterns of use of game features, especially by third time players. Tactics and strategies often characterised particular subgroups of players and, we suggest, largely constituted meaningful play in the game.

5.1   Tactics

Several tactical movements were observed repeatedly during the trials of the game, through direct observation and post–trial video analysis. By tactics we refer to the game–specific movements or short–term actions that players used in the game. Tactics expressed competitiveness and were often used in order to win. Most of them related to the search for coins and uploading, however others were specific to, for example, pickpocketing.

One such game–specific movement was the 180° turn, which we observed three to four times per game. A player walks along, staring down at the PDA and then suddenly, without looking up, turns 180° and walks in the opposite direction as if nothing had happened. When asked why they did this, we found that this was often a reaction to the player's icon passing over a coin without the player managing to pick it up. The player therefore turned around to pass over it again and pick it up.

Fig. 4. A player does a 180° turn while trying to find network connectivity

Because of the lag in GPS, the movement of a player's icon on the PDA was often delayed by several seconds—resulting in problems picking up coins. Most of the players learned this over the course of their games. Another reason for turning around in this way was that a player would suddenly found him– or herself leaving the network. One participant was about to upload with her teammate, but the network connection became weak; she turned 180 degrees to get back into the network (Fig. 4).

Another frequently observed move was the 'spy look'. Since players' eyes were locked to their PDAs for most of the game, and with limited visibility beyond the open lawn, players mostly judged others' position via the map on the PDA. They would stand still for a couple of seconds, look up and then around as if to see who (if anyone) was nearby, then look down and continue walking. The movement was a scanning of the environment, trying to match the information on the screen to the actual positions of the other players. Players were aware that an opposing team member could sneak up on them, without being visible on the screen, and so they would check for this. The contrary also occurred: the screen showed others close to a player and he or she then had to check if they were actually there.

A regular tactic, especially for the first-time players, was a collaborative search for network. Often team members would meet up to do a collaborative upload, but if one or both were outside the network they would walk side by side, staring down at their PDAs to be sure of when they had adequate connectivity to upload. Fig. 5a illustrates this tactic.

Fig. 5a. Two teammates do a collaborative search for network cover

Fig. 5b. Two teammates (right) pickpocket their opponents and then run away

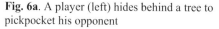

Fig. 6a. A player (left) hides behind a tree to pickpocket his opponent

Fig. 6b. A player tracks his opponents openly, trying to pickpocket them

Another more energetic tactic that was observed several times in first time games consisted of players sneaking up on their opponents, pickpocketing them and then running away, so that the opponents could not steal the coins back (Fig. 5b). Although shields were widely used, the thieves either did not have them charged or thought it more efficient to run. Peculiarly enough, this seemed to be a good strategy even though the lag in GPS updating would make it inefficient. In two instances the runners succeeded and were not pickpocketed back.

A complementary pair of tactics was identified through log analysis and interviews, and related to the players' level of 'sophistication' when picking up coins. Some players would carefully walk towards a coin, pressing *Pickup* only when their icon showed to be on top of the coin or very close to it, whereas other players would constantly and almost aggressively press the pickup button in case they were on top of a coin. Which tactic worked best is hard to say, since the points gained depended only on how many of the coins were uploaded, not how many attempts it took to pick them up. However, use of the former strategy was correlated with higher final scores. It also seemed that the players would use the aggressive technique more often when in a coin saturated area, whereas they would be slower and more careful when few coins were nearby. The interesting issue in this relation is that the range for picking up coins is bigger than 'being on top of it'. If the coin is within 10 meters of the player, according to GPS, it will be picked up—but GPS can jitter and lag. Combining this with the fact that new coins are being dropped constantly during the game can make the more aggressive tactic useful in some situations. The players who highlighted their use of this tactic in the interviews were all third–time players, however, not all of them were the winners of their game.

The combination of GPS inaccuracy and lag, and the game's principle of players moving outside and inside the wireless network, meant that players often experienced an inconsistency between the information on–screen and the environment. Indeed, some players commented on this point after the games, even though they had been told that such inconsistency would occur. However, most of the players quickly learned to cope with this inconsistency between what they saw on–screen and what they saw around them. As a result, some players were quick to utilise it and hide behind a tree to pickpocket innocent opponents on the lawn, or even openly follow the opponents on the path to pickpocket them (as illustrated in Fig. 6). Because some players realised that what was on their screen was not the same as what appeared on the others' screens, they played more boldly, raising their shields and attempting to steal. The games reported as most pleasurable were often the games with high rates of pickpocketing, although high levels of pickpocketing attempts were a winning tactic only if the opposing team did not also attempt to pickpocket frequently.

5.2   Strategies

Strategies are what we call well–considered or even planned ways of playing a game, involving longer–term activity than tactics. As they played more games, players' better understanding of the game rules, experience with the network and the familiarity with the area helped them develop strategies. We uncovered strategies through analysis of log, video and interview data as well as through observation during games. They became easier to identify as the players gained experience, because they were more distinct, the players often consciously decided upon one before the game and they could articulate them in the interviews.

The two main strategies we identified related to how players collected and uploaded coins: players were generally classified as either *hunters* or *gatherers,* and hunting seemed to work better than gathering. Hunters were the players who boldly picked up as many of the coins as they could, often from a wide area, before finding a network connection to upload. They uploaded less frequently and more carefully during the game, making sure that they were inside network coverage and had their shields on before attempting to upload—so they would not be pickpocketed. We identified six players using this strategy in one or more of their games. The trend was that the players would go 'hunting' for coins, taking chances in order to build up a number of coins for a collaborative upload with their teammate. Defined by having less than 20 attempts to upload, along with a high success rate (over 50 percent) as well as many coins for each upload the hunters did very well. In their second game, their average score was 455 while the average over all second games was 325. In their third game, their average score was 480 while the average over all third games was 367. One noteworthy thing is that the hunters did not necessarily occur in the same team: only in one team were both players identified as hunters.

Gatherers, in contrast, uploaded their coins as they picked them up, unless they had to leave the network to pick up coins—and they normally did not go far to do this. This was very much a beginner's strategy, but several players persisted with it throughout their games. Some players, shifted from gathering in the beginning of the game to hunting and collaborative uploads as play progressed and competition increased. Gatherers were very worried about getting pickpocketed, and they hit the *Upload* button frequently as soon as they had picked up a coin or two, attempting to upload their coins quickly. Four players were identified as using this strategy in at least one of their games. Team A serves as an example of gatherers, always trying to upload coins together and rarely going outside the network, even though many coins were located further away. This strategy initially seemed to work; they were inseparable during their third game and won by 290 points against a team of second game players. However, they did not succeed in uploading collaboratively once in that game, but instead used shields frequently and uploaded individually as soon as they had the chance. This game was dominated by an intense level of pickpocketing; team

A managed to pickpocket their opponents ten times, and were pickpocketed eight times.

6   Discussion

The players in the trials of our game enjoyed themselves and, within the limited scope of our trials, they expressed more enjoyment in later games. This is a simple but important point to make when discussing a game, as technical novelty can wear off very quickly. Players became proficient with the basic mechanics of the game, many of which relied on seamful infrastructure features. However, their engagement with the game went beyond that: they developed tactics and strategies that built on their practice and changed their ongoing experience. They created meaningful play; the details of their play show how competitive game features were combined and traded off against collaborative features, for example. To some extent, pickpocketing was the most exciting and influential aspect of game play, and key to players' development of their two predominant strategies, hunting and gathering. The pleasure and fear of pickpocketing changed their attitude towards collaborative uploads. Even though collaborative uploads might produce very high or 'optimal' scores, pickpocketing and defending against pickpocketing were generally seen as more important.

This is just one example of the way that the experience of a game is not only about optimising progress towards a goal. It is also about weighing system features against each other, as well as shaping and reacting to the emerging behavior of opponents and teammates. Although a feature may initially appear useful in one regard, such as collaborative upload, that feature may be perceived and used differently as experience grows and social interaction continues. In many other ubicomp systems, this is also the case. For example, pre–existing infrastructures and the 'old media' environment have been shown to influence new infrastructures in ways that were not anticipated by designers [1, 6]. We take a historical view of context [7], namely that past social interaction, as well as past use of the heterogeneous mix of media, tools and artifacts that make up users' activity, influence users' ongoing interaction. Patterns of use temporally and subjectively combine and interconnect different media. While we do not consider designers to be outside this process, system features used in competitive situations may influence each other in unexpected ways as players accommodate and appropriate those features, i.e. using the designers' system in their context for their uses.

This historical process was, in essence, how players came to interpret and use the new media of the game with the old media of the urban environment. More than other ubicomp systems we are aware of, the game was designed to 'seamfully' reveal 802.11 infrastructure as part of normal use. System use also revealed important features of the game arena, such as difficulty of terrain and likely visibility between players. Objectively speaking, the system affords many possible ways to play, but players' practical understanding of the system and the setting was developed through their experience of interactions with each other as much as their interactions with the system and the space. Through embodied interaction within games, as well as reflective discussion in between games, they shaped each other's interpretation of the space and the technology in a historical and intersubjective way.

Far from being a purely abstract or theoretical issue, we suggest that there are generalisable and practical issues that stem from this point in the areas of evaluation and design of ubicomp systems. One can choose to evaluate a system so as to articulate the detail and degree of change in people's use of it with ongoing activity. A substantial number of papers on ubicomp systems (including some of our own past papers) have relied on one–off plays in short demonstration games, but our experience with *Treasure* has reinforced our opinion that user trials of such games, and of ubicomp systems more generally, should involve repeated use and/or use over a longer time than a single, short session.

Similarly, one can choose to design a system so as to articulate the detail and degree of change in people's use of it with ongoing activity. We see the development of tactics and strategies as something that we should design for in ubicomp. We intend to build on our experience of the *Replayer* tool, which we found to be extremely helpful in our analysis of game play and system use, to make such replays part of the game experience in itself. Many console games, such as EA Games' *Burnout* for example (www.eagames.com), rely on playbacks as key elements of the user experience design. Richly instrumented code on each player's device and on the server, along with support for integrating still images and video, may then support the development of system use and also be part of system use. In other words, recording and replaying system use may aid in developing tactics and strategies for future play, but may also be an important means for players to show each other how they played in the past.

Design that makes the system so starkly open to analysis by users may seem contradictory to the design goal of 'invisibility' or 'transparency' usually associated with ubicomp, but people use past, present and potential activity involving the system in developing their understanding of it, i.e. as a tool they use in making the system transparent. However, Weiser's narrow design focus, concentrating only on transparent use, is at odds with the findings of user studies of how people develop their use of ubicomp systems through experience of both transparent and analytic use, and it clashes with the theory from which the transparency ideal was drawn [7]. Transparent and analytic use are mutually interdependent, with the former unavoidably influenced by analytic activity such as handling 'breakdowns', working on or adapting it, learning about it, teaching others how to use it, considering how to act so that it works better, and considering how to present oneself to others through it. Our ongoing work on making the recording and replay of system use be a resource for users' interaction is motivated by this conceptual point as much as by our experience of deployed ubicomp systems.

Lastly, we are aware of the issue of scaling of game play and system infrastructure. Our game is, at present, relatively constrained in the size of the game arena and the number of players. We have used several access points, with a virtual private network to connect them together, to create a larger game arena, and it is possible that we might be able to scale to still larger areas by using, for example, a campus–wide 802.11 network. However, our system involves a central game server and the broadcasting of all game state in regular 'heartbeat' transmissions. One possible response would be to replicate servers, and to locally partition and prioritise state broadcasts.

However, we are now exploring a different direction and a different set of games that take advantage of the increasingly storage of mobile devices and their ability to set up mobile ad hoc networks. Our new games use peer–to–peer methods to disseminate and access data, and encourage more wide–ranging and opportunistic use of access points in urban areas that afford access to fixed networks as well as direct ad hoc interaction between players (and their PDAs) in the street.

7   Conclusion

In this paper we presented a mobile multiplayer game, Treasure, that uses spatial variation in 802.11 infrastructure as an explicit feature of its design. We set out to find how game play changed in the course of multiple games, as players' experience influenced their tactics and strategies. Mobile multi-user systems can be hard to record and evaluate in detail, and multiple plays can increase evaluation cost and workload, but we found the effort worthwhile. By looking at video of users' behaviour as well as detailed logs of system data, we obtained insights into the emergence and success of different strategies, and how features of the system and the setting were used in players' interaction with each other. As their understanding of the game grew, they used game features in different proportions, combinations and patterns. These changes in their game play did not always result in scoring more points, but they did generally lead to more excitement and engagement in the game. It is important to note that players' development of game play did not stem solely from the space the game was played in, the system design alone, or the space and the system together. Instead, players' use of this mix of old and new media developed through a historical and social process. Over time, people affected and were affected by each other, and system and space served as resources as well as constraints on interaction. This leads us to suggest that system designers may do more to support the development of tactics and strategies by recording data on system use and reusing it within the user experience.

Overall, we believe that our game was successful, in that variations in ubicomp infrastructure were presented and used in ways that were crucial to user engagement and enjoyment. It adds to the evidence that ubicomp infrastructure can or should be considered not only as a technical artifact but as a resource for users' interaction—interaction with the system and interaction with each other. We do not suggest that ubicomp systems should always be designed in seamful ways. Instead, we propose that new design opportunities can be found when researchers and developers consider this approach as an option. Future research may establish whether generalisation of this approach to other application areas than games is fruitful. However, our own plans for future research focus on games, as we consider them to be an area that serves well in demonstrating and generating new design ideas, engaging users in creative and intensive use of new technology, and driving the development of new infrastructure for communication, storage and computation.

References

1   Barkhuus, L., Dourish, P., Everyday Encounters with Context-Aware Computing in a Campus Environment. Proc. Ubicomp (2004) 232–249.
2   Benford, S. et al. The error of our ways: the experience of self-reported position in a location–based game. Proc. Ubicomp (2004) 70–87.
3   Benford, S. et al. Bridging the Physical and Digital in Pervasive Gaming. Communications of the ACM. Vol. 48, issue 3 (2005) 54–57.
4   Brown, B. et al. Lessons from the Lighthouse: Collaboration in a Shared Mixed Reality System. Proc ACM CHI (2003) 577–584.
5   Chalmers, M. et al., Seamful Design: Showing the Seams in Wearable Computing, Proc. IEE Eurowearable (2003) 11-17.
6   Chalmers, M. and Galani, A. Seamful Interweaving: Heterogeneity in the Theory and Design of Interactive Systems. Proc. ACM DIS (2004) 243–252.
7   Chalmers, M. A Historical View of Context. J. CSCW vol. 13 (2004) 223–247.
8   Falk J., Ljungstrand P., Björk S., Hansson R. Pirates: proximity-triggered interaction in a multi-player game. Proc. ACM CHI (2001) 119–120.
9   Flintham M. et al.. Where online meets on the streets: experiences with mobile mixed reality games. Proc. ACM CHI (2003) 569–576.
10 Mitchell M. et al. Six in the city: Introducing *Real Tournament*—a mobile IPv6 based context-aware multiplayer game. In Proc. ACM NETGAMES '03 (2nd workshop on network and system support for games) (2003) 91–100.
11 Salen, K., Zimmerman, E. Rules of Play: Game Design Fundamentals, MIT Press (2004)
12 Weiser, M. Building Invisible Interfaces. Keynote talk, Proc. ACM UIST (1994)

ActiveTheatre – A Collaborative, Event-Based Capture and Access System for the Operating Theatre

Thomas Riisgaard Hansen and Jakob E. Bardram

Centre for Pervasive Healthcare
Department of Computer Science, University of Aarhus
Aabogade 34, DK8200
Aarhus N., Denmark
{thomasr, bardram}@daimi.au.dk

Abstract. Building capture and access (C&A) applications for use in the operation theatre differs greatly from C&A applications built to support other settings e.g. meeting rooms or classrooms. Based on field studies of surgical operations, this paper explores how to design C&A applications for the operation theatre. Based on the findings from our field work, we have built the ActiveTheatre, a C&A prototype. ActiveTheatre is built to support collaboration in and around the operating theatre, to capture events instead of automatically capturing everything, and to be integrated with existing applications already present in the operation theatre. The ActiveTheatre prototype has been developed in close cooperation with surgeons and nurses at a local hospital. The work on the prototype and our initial evaluations have provided an insight into how to design, capture and access applications that are going to be used in other settings than the meeting room.

1. Introduction

Capture and Access (C&A) applications have been an expanding area along with the dawning of ubiquitous computing systems, cheaper storage and the development of new sensor technologies [18]. The increasing focus on C&A systems can be associated with two compelling properties of the C&A systems. Firstly, C&A systems promise to enhance human memory to remember all events. Secondly, C&A systems promise to be able to do time shifting, which for instance could be re-experiencing a meeting, a lecture, a birthday by rewinding the tape and playing the episode with video, sounds, and annotations.

These properties have been explored in a number of applications (see Section 2 on related work). However, the basic workflow in many of them follows the same format. First, there is a preparation phase where information is prepared and handed out before, e.g., a meeting or a class. Then, in the capture phase, a range of media is recorded like video, sound, pen strokes, and slide changes. Then, in the indexing phase, recorded material is structured and annotated either manually or more or less automatically. Finally, in the access phase, captured material can be viewed and navigated. It is characteristic for these systems that they capture and access information in

M. Beigl et al. (Eds.): UbiComp 2005, LNCS 3660, pp. 375–392, 2005.

a continuous flow, making no differentiation between discrete events in the capture phase. Furthermore, many C&A applications have an inherent single-user focus, enabling only individual users to prepare, capture, and access the information which has been recorded earlier.

In this paper we want to draw the attention to other types of work domains where C&A systems are of great value but have to function in a different manner. In contrast to the continuous, single-user 'prepare-record-annotate-access' type of C&A systems, we point to the need for *collaborative and event-based C&A systems*. In such C&A systems, the users and triggers in the usage context help identify, record, and access discrete events of importance in the flow of time and this captured event-based information is immediately available for a collaborative set of users. By doing this, it is the overall goal of this paper to broaden our conceptual understanding of C&A applications to also incorporate collaborative, event-based C&A.

The empirical foundation of our research into C&A is surgical work in operating theaters. The operating theatre differs in a number of ways from meeting rooms or classrooms: it is a highly collaborative environment where skilled surgeons, anesthetists and nurses work together on treating a patient; information is constantly accessed, recorded, and re-accessed in the process of an operation; there are discrete events during an operation where capture is extremely important, but at the same time during large parts of an operation capture is highly irrelevant. Hence, in the design of C&A technology for the operating theatre, it is important to help users capture what is relevant, and share that collaboratively at once, but also to help users in reducing the amount of irrelevant information which would, if captured, make the system useless.

In this project we have worked closely with a range of surgeons, anesthesiologists, and operating nurses. The empirical foundation is described in Section 3. Section 4 discusses the need for C&A technology in the operating theatre and Section 5 presents the design of ActiveTheatre, a C&A application for operating theatres focusing on its support for collaborative, event-based capture and access of critical clinical data. Section 6 presents details of the implementation of ActiveTheatre and section 7 presents our initial evaluation of it done collaboratively with the clinicians participating in the project. Section 8 concludes the paper.

The main contributions of this paper is thus to (i) broaden the understanding of C&A systems for new types of work domains, which is radically different from the meeting room or the classroom, and (ii) to present a concrete implementation of such a collaborative, event-based capture-and-access application.

2. Related Work

Developing systems that are able to automatically capture what is happening in our everyday life and later allow the user of the systems to access these data have been explored in several contexts. As pointed out in the survey chapter of [16] many of the developed projects, however, address a relatively small number of domains and deal with the same kind of problems.

Especially capturing what is going on in meeting rooms or classrooms has been in focus. Even though the two settings are clearly different, the types of interaction going on are in many aspects similar. In many situations one person will give a presentation and the rest of the participants will stay silent and take notes. Occasionally, a subject might be discussed in details by the participants, and in general it is hard to anticipate in advance when something interesting will be said. Furthermore, standard office technology like laptops, PDAs, and tablet PCs are useable in these two settings.

These similarities have resulted in a set of capture and access applications that have a similar structure. First, material is prepared for use in class or at a meeting. Then when the event takes place, everything is captured in order not to miss important information. The captured material is then analyzed and indexed, and finally a uniform access interface is provided to all the potential users of the system. This structure has been used to build capture and access applications for meetings e.g. Coral [11], TeamSpace [14], NoteLook [5] and Dolphin [15], or for building applications for the classroom, e.g. the Classroom 2000 project [1, 12].

When applications move away from capturing the interaction in the meeting room or classroom new requirements that challenge the notion of capture and access arise. Moving automatic capture applications into the home challenges the configuration of these systems to fit into the everyday lives of people at home as pointed out in [17]. Using capture and access to follow the development of children with autism questions how to actually do the capturing of the activities of children who move around in different physical and social settings [6]. Capturing design workspaces questions how to capture unanticipated and collaborative events and how to structure these events optimally to reduce information overload. Arnalonescu et al. [2] investigates capture and access in the design space and uses discrete time-slices instead of continuous streams of data.

We design for a different and rather challenging setting – the operating theatre. The operating theatre resembles some of the above mentioned domains in some aspects, but is clearly different in others. One major difference between the operating theatre and some of the other settings is probably the high degree of collaboration among the various different professions involved. Before the operation many different people have to prepare using different materials, during the operation extensive collaboration is needed, and after the operation many different persons with different backgrounds need to access the data captured in the operating theatre. Even though some projects address collaboration they mainly address the capturing of collaborative activities and not how to support collaborative preparation, capture and access data, and they do not address the same tight collaboration found in e.g. the operation theatre.

In the operation theatre the really important thing to capture is not the entire operation, but small parts of the operation, or when something diverges from what is expected. Because it is almost impossible for an automatic system to index these moments we found capturing systems that support explicit capturing and focus on *events* better suited than automatic capturing applications. In other C&A systems, events are used to index a captured stream of data. The main difference is, however, that in an event-based C&A system the user decides what constitute an event. Because identification of events are done during the capture phase, and not afterwards, data becomes accessible for collaborators immediately. One limitation to this approach is that in some cases, users would only realize an event to be important after it has happened. For example, how can we handle the case when the surgeon indicates that what just happened a few moments ago in the procedure should be recorded for later access? In such cases, buffering techniques like the 'Experience Buffer' [7] may be applied. Finally, Chiu at al. [5] and Arnalonescu et al. [2] suggest systems that support explicit capturing during meetings or design workshops, but those systems only provide limited support for collaboration, and they cannot be directly used in a sterile environment such as an operating theatre.

3. Field Studies

Most people are familiar with how a meeting is structured or what is going on in the classroom, but few people outside the hospital environment actually know what is going on in an operating theatre. In order to understand in details the work taking place while operating on a patient we have undertaken a range of in-depth field studies. Because we are designing technology for operation rooms in general, the main objective of these studies was to study the similarities and differences between a wide range of operational procedures and types of operating rooms. In total more than 20 workdays of observations of patient operations have been done at four different hospitals. We have observed more than 40 unique operations at different departments, ranging from plastic surgery, orthopedic surgery, and obstetric surgery. Some of the departments use an electronic patient record for record keeping, while other departments use a paper-based record.

Relatively few detailed field studies of operating theatres with a technical focus in mind have been made, but as pointed out by Heath et al. [8] an operating theatre is clearly an intense work setting, where life-critical work is being done in close, and often silent, cooperation between extremely skilled persons. One of the main findings from these observations was that in order to make this delicate collaborative work succeed, there was a constant access to clinical and other related information before, during and after the operation. Furthermore, important aspects of the operation were captured and this information was afterward shared collaboratively. Hence, it became interesting to understand what kind of information was accessed and captured, when, by whom, and for what purpose. Our findings are summarized in Table I and are further detailed below.

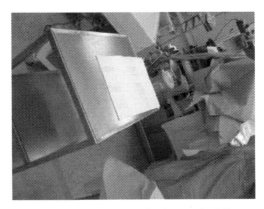

Fig. 1. Using a paper-based medical record while operating

3.1 Information Used During an Operation

We observed that the following types of material were used during an operating.

- **The patient's record** – The paper record or computer based record was always present in the operating theatre and was consulted in different situations (see figure 1 and 2). The surgeon did not have direct access to the record. It was usually situated in one end of the operating room, either as a paper-based record lying on a table or accessible from a desktop PC placed on the table. Often the surgeon would ask the non-sterile nurse to read aloud from the journal. In the operating theatre the record was mainly a single user artifact because it wasn't accessible to the sterile surgeons and nurses.
- **Medical Images** – Medical images were (depending on the operation) used extensively during surgical operations. These images were located in the one end of the operating room together with other kinds of documentation, as can be seen in figure 2.
- **Instructions** – In some situations an operation required the use of some special equipment e.g. an advanced implant or the mixture of some cement. The nurses and doctors used paper instructions and manuals to guide them in the procedure. The manual or instruction was found and placed open on a table nearby. Also anatomy books and charts were used while operating. For example, in one situation some of the blood vessels were crossed in a strange pattern and the surgeon put an anatomy book with a picture of the blood vessel in the leg on a small table next to the patient.

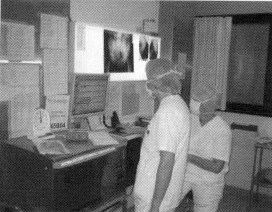

Fig. 2. Accessing medical images and an electronic medical record while operating

In the situations we observed there was a clear need for accessing information during the operation but in all the cases the access to the digital information was problematic and required that external books were brought in, that the nurse had to navigate and read aloud, or that the surgeon had to move away from the patient to access the information.

3.2 Capture During an Operation

Looking closer to the kind of information captured during an operation, the following list contains the more important issues:

- **Notes** – The nurses made notes before, during, and after the operation. In particular, the nurses documented special events from the operation. For example, when the patient was anaesthetized or when the patient was moved into a new position. The surgeon made the description of the operation in the medical record after the operation and depending on the operation, this description was therefore documented between one to sixteen hours after the operation had started.

- **Pictures:** Pictures were used to document some parts of the operation. In one operating theatre cameras were mounted in the operating lamp, the corner of the operating room and below a computer screen. Because it was too complicated to put the pictures in the medical record, such pictures were not used to document the operation. Instead they were printed out and given to the patient. In another operating theatre a normal digital still-picture camera was used by the nurse, who took pictures on request. These pictures were sometimes used to discuss a case at the morning conference or to document what kind of operation a young surgeon had performed.

	Access	*Capture*	*Design*
What	• Patient data • Medical images • Instructions	• Notes • Pictures • Video	The system should support different types of data and integrate with existing systems
When	• Before • During • After	• Before • During	Event-based captured and access Portable information
By whom	• The surgeon • Other doctors and nurses • The patient and relatives	The surgeon and the nurses present at an operation	Support for collaboration and multiple users.
How	• With computers • Pictures on a camera • Browsing notes	• Use of camera • Note taking • Typing in on computers	New ways of interacting with the system

Table 1. Overview of Access and Capture in the operating theatre and the related design issues to consider.

- **Video:** We observed that video recordings were used, especially for operations carried out with an endoscope. The camera was mounted in the endoscope and the video could be streamed to a CD-ROM. However, these video recording were rarely accessed and most of the CDs remained untouched in the surgeon's office, difficult for others to access.

Our conclusion was that even though a lot of data was recorded and there was a need to produce data during the operation, it was difficult to actually record these data and later access them.

3.3 Access of Captured Data

An important question to investigate in the field studies was to ask who actually used the information captured during an operation and for what purpose.

- **Documentation** – Currently, the most used and hence most important piece of information accessed from an operation is the clinical description by the surgeon, which s/he entered in the medical record after the operation. This information is the key to further treatment and care by other fellow clinicians at the hospital and outside. Hence, it was accessed by both doctors and nurses. However, recorded pictures and videos were never used as documentation at this point of time. The software managing the electronic patient record did not support pictures taken during an operation and it was therefore cumbersome to access the pictures.
- **Patient's souvenir:** The pictures were however often shown or given to the patient to keep. The pictures from the operation were shown to the patient on the digital camera and they were often printed out or burnt on a CD-Rom, which was given to the patient.
- **Learning:** In some situations we observed the digital pictures and videos being used as instruments for learning. Some of the captured pictures were shown to and discussed with other doctors at their morning conference.
- **Personal history:** In the plastic surgery department, pictures were used to document different types of operations by younger surgeon.

From what we observed the captured data was used not just in one setting, but in many different settings by many different persons with different background. Using captured data for learning was clearly different from using them for documenting a procedure, which again was completely different from the kind of material the patient received on a CD-Rom. The last column of Table 1 is a summary of the core design requirements coming out of the analysis.

4. Moving Capture and Access into the Operating Theatre

Based on our detailed field studies in operating theatres and our on-going interviews and conversations with surgeons and operating nurses, we are convinced that C&A technology has its purpose in an operating theatre. Such a system would help surgeons and nurses to easily access relevant information at the right time and place, i.e.

while operating and in the operating theatre. Furthermore, C&A technology can help the surgeon and the nurses in making the description of the operation in the medical records immediately during or shortly after the operation, instead of, as it happens now, where it may take hours before it is done.

However, our detailed studies also reveal that there are some fundamental design requirements for C&A technology in the operating theatre, which makes it different from the C&A technology described in Section 2 as designed for, and used in, meeting rooms and classrooms. We need a new type of C&A technology that is better suited for work situations like the operating room, which is characterized as an intense co-located collaborative work environment, with little room for conventional computer technology like desktop PCs, laptops, mouse, and keyboards. It would, for example, be rather difficult for a surgeon to use a normal PC while operating.

More specifically, we found that the notion of *access* was different in our case because it is not something that is separated from the capturing part. In many systems data is first captured e.g. during a meeting and then after the meeting the data is uploaded to a server for access. In the operating theatre, a lot of different information is accessed during the operation at the same time as information is captured. Some of the information accessed is information captured at e.g. operations carried out earlier but it is also information that has been captured during the same operation. Therefore, we found it difficult to maintain a strong division between capturing and accessing data.

Furthermore, the captured information during an operation was not stored in a separate system and accessed through a specific interface afterwards. The captured data was stored in the Electronic Patient Record (EPR), or in Picture Archives and Communication Systems (PACS). In these systems the captured data was integrated with already existing data. The data accessed in relation to an operation would not only be the data captured with a C&A system, but a combination between data captured with the system and data gathered from other systems (e.g. EPR, PACS).

5. ActiveTheatre

Based on the findings from the field studies, we engaged in a user-centered design and development process with a group of doctors, surgeons, nurses, and computer scientists from a company developing PACS systems. We have conducted a future workshop [9], a number of design workshops, and recorded a video prototype in an actual operating theatre [10]. The result is a first version of the ActiveTheatre system which will be presented in this section.

5.1 The Palette Metaphor

ActiveTheatre is designed as an event-based capture and access system, which does not automatically capture everything. Hence, the basic temporal model is *discrete* rather than continuous along an indexed time line. An event can be a text note, a picture or a video clip. To describe the system we have used the metaphor of a palette (resembles [13]). The palette provides a good metaphor because it can hold different types of data, you can put and take things from the palette at any point in time and several users can access the palette. The palette metaphor is illustrated in Figure 3.

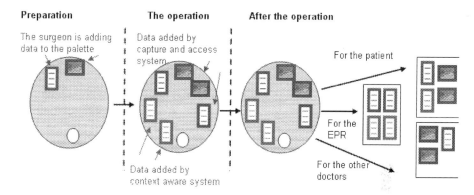

Fig. 3. The palette metaphor describes the ActiveTheatre system

Before an operation the people involved in the event prepare for it. In ActiveTheatre the surgeons and the nurses are able to place digital material on the palette in their offices that should be made easily available for access during the operation.

The surgeon carries the palette to the operating theatre. In the operating theatre the people present are able to access the data on the palette and the palette is coupled to a context-aware system and a capturing system. The context-aware system is able to push relevant data to the palette depending on the situation e.g. some information is only relevant in the first part of the operation; some information depends on the type of operation. The surgeons and nurses are also able to use a capture system in the operating theatre to push data to the palette. The data added to the palette is not a complete video stream of the entire operation, but small video sequences, pictures, or dictated notes that document an important event in the operation.

After the operation the surgeon or a nurse carries the palette to an office where the data on the palette is used to create different kinds of documents depending on who the recipients are. The surgeon can choose a note and two pictures from the palette and add them to the electronic patient record, continue and choose a set of pictures and add them to an operation description for the patient, and he can finally choose some pictures to show e.g. next morning at the morning conference with the other doctors. The palette metaphor incorporates the following design principles (see also Table I):

- **Event-based** – The palette metaphor is an alternative to the timeline metaphor. In the operating theatre there is no need to capture everything, only the important events. During the workshops, this point was stressed several times by the surgeons and nurses; they did not want to produce irrelevant information. The palette metaphor emphasizes that events.
- **Heterogeneous Data and Systems** – Almost all suggested capture and access systems deal with more than one type of data e.g. slides and video or pen strokes and web pages. ActiveTheatre makes no strong distinction between what is accessed and what is captured; both captured and accessed data is added to the pal-

ette. We also wanted the ActiveTheatre to be able to integrate with existing systems present in the hospitals. One of the partners in the project develops PACS software and we wanted to a) propose a design that was able to extract data from these types of systems and add it to the palette and b) be able to store captured data on the palette in PACS and other related systems after the operation.

- **Multiple users and collaboration** – One of the novel issues coming out of the design process was the need for supporting multiple types of uses in a C&A system for operating theatres. Existing C&A systems all provide the same interface for accessing the captured information no matter who uses the system. In the hospital we need multiple representations depending on who is going to access the data. With the palette it is possible to select a number of events and use them to easily generate different representations. For learning and knowledge sharing purposes a lot of detailed pictures from a specific phase of the operation might be relevant, whereas the patient will be interested in only a single picture from that phase. With the palette metaphor the doctor or nurse can use the palette to make the kind of documentation they need depending on who the recipient is.
- **New interaction metaphor** – The palette metaphor also contains a basis for developing new interaction methods in the operating theatre. First of all, the distinction between preparation, operation, and follow-up helps the surgeon to have relevant data available to access, but also to capture things during the operation and save it for later processing. Adding information to the palette during preparation allows the surgeon to look up and prepare information in a quiet environment and not in the interaction-limited and stressful environment of the operating theatre. During operation, a context aware system can identify and add relevant information to the palette with minimal disturbance of the surgeon. The objective of the system is to limit the interaction during the operation when accessing data on the palette and controlling the capturing system, and leave the rest of the interaction to before and after the operation in a richer interaction environment, e.g. with an office computer.

5.2 User Interaction with ActiveTheatre

The ActiveTheatre system offers users a flexible way of preparing, accessing, capturing, and using medical information with regard to a surgical operation based on the 'palette' metaphor. The current user-interface of ActiveTheatre is shown in Figure 4. On the left is a list of data categories, on the right is a list of items captured within the selected category ordered by the time of capture, and in the middle is the data area. Before the operation, a surgeon or nurse can prepare material to access later by selecting and ordering this into groups. The different groups appear as separate items on the left. ActiveTheatre is also coupled with a simple context-aware system, which is able to add extra items and material to the interface depending on the context.

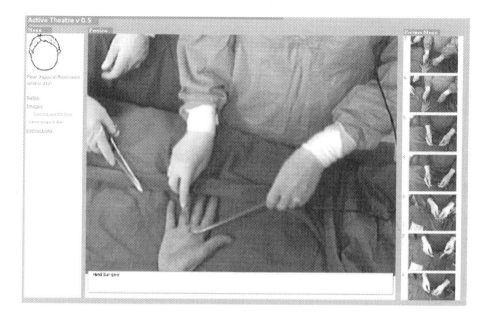

Fig. 4. ActiveTheatre prototype overview

During an operation the users are able to access all the material added to the ActiveTheatre and to capture new material by e.g. taking pictures, recording video or dictating notes. The newly captured material is added to the system, ready for immediate access for all users. ActiveTheatre uses speech-based interaction and zoomable interfaces, thereby allowing the user to access data while using his hands to operate and to view data at a distance.

After the operation, users can select material from the palette and this material can be exported in a number of formats depending on what types of system the data is going to be used in. If the pictures are going to be added to a PACS system one format is used, if it is going to be printed out or put on a CD-ROM another format can be chosen.

5.3 The ActiveTheatre Architecture

The ActiveTheatre is designed and refined to work in an operating theatre, but we wanted to start out with an extensible and modifiable architecture. We wanted the architecture to be flexible enough to also support other contexts e.g. a capture and access system for homes or public places, and modifiability was our main architectural goal [3].

The ActiveTheatre is built around five main components. The input component handles input from external input devices. In the ActiveTheatre we have an external speech component for controlling the application and dictating notes. We use a web cam to capture pictures and video and finally we have a Context Aware sub-system to push information to the system.

Export of used and captured data is handled by the ViewGenerator component, which is able to take selective parts of the model and export it. An XML document is generated that describes the captured data, and how it is stored. An XSLT style sheet can then be combined with the XML document and the exported resources to create a XHTML document viewable in a web browser or another data format suitable for the receiving application. Figure 5 shows an overview of the architecture.

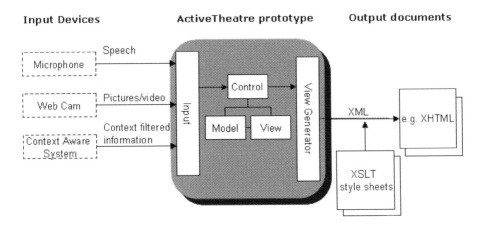

Fig. 5. ActiveTheatre prototype overview

The core of the ActiveTheatre prototype was implemented with a model, view, controller pattern. The model is responsible for handling our different types of media: text, images and video. The view component is responsible for updating our zoomable interface and the controller is responsible for coordinating the communication.

5.4 Context Filtered Information

ActiveTheatre cooperates with a context-awareness subsystem in three ways. First, the context-awareness subsystem is able to suggest digital information to the surgeon based on e.g. the type of operation, instruments used or the patient history. The subsystem monitors the progress of the operation and provide access to relevant data in a timely fashion by knowing the type of operation taking place in an operating theatre and then using this information to fetch relevant data, like surgical instructions. Second, just like users can capture data, changes in the usage context in the operating theatre can trigger data to be added to the palette or removed from it. Finally, the context-awareness sub-system is used to annotate captured data with relevant information, like the id of the patient, the operating surgeon, and the location.

5.5 Speech Interaction and Zoomable Interfaces

To navigate in the system during an operation we used speech commands only. Speech interaction allows the user to use the system while using both hands to do physical work. Speech recognition was also used for creating small notes during the operation. For ActiveTheatre we used Microsoft Speech API (SAPI 5.0). SAPI is a speech recognition and generating system that comes with Microsoft Office XP and it has an API for controlling the speech recognition and generation. The speech engine we used was not trained for clinical practice, but for our proof of concept prototype it was sufficient to demonstrate how the system worked. A range of professional voice recognition systems which are specialized to certain medical terminology exists.

Speech recognition can be used in two different ways. Either it can be used to issue commands, or it can be used to recognize continuous speech. We used a combination of the two techniques. For controlling the system we used command-based speech recognition. For making notes and annotating pictures we needed to recognize continuous speech. We used a specific keyword to switch between dictation and command mode. In dictation mode the system wrote everything the user said except some special commands e.g. "new line". We also used synthesized voice along with animations to give the user feedback about his/her action. This allowed the user to issue commands to the system without having to focus on the screen.

Even though we did not use expensive speech recognition the system worked quite well. The system was able to recognize the different commands even though they were pronounced by different people. However, the speech recognition was more sensitive to the voices who had trained it when trying to recognize continuously speech.

Because the layout of the operating theatre and the position of the people within depend on the type of operation carried out, we did not know in advance how far away the user would be from the screen. This fact combined with the need of sometimes focusing on some small details without moving closer to the screen required a scalable interface. Therefore, most of the interface components in ActiveTheatre are zoomable. We used a modified version of the Piccolo framework to build the zoomable components [4]. Each captured or accessed element, both text and pictures, was placed in a canvas that could be zoomed and panned. With piccolo the user could view even small details without moving away from her/his current position by using speech commands.

5.6 Exporting Data to Other Systems

Accessing the data captured from ActiveTheatre is not done with a special viewer. Depending on the captured data many different systems are able to get, store, and view the captured data. For documentation purposes the captured data is fed to the electronic patient record or a picture archiving system. The patients e.g. prefer to get their data either as a print out or on a CD-ROM; some doctors want to export some of the captured data to web pages that could be used for learning purposes. To integrate ActiveTheatre with these different types of systems the surgeon or nurse is able to mark the resources from the palette they are going to use and then chose a template that specifies how these resources is going to be formatted. ActiveTheatre then exports the selected resources along with an XML document describing the exported resources. With the use of XSLT transformation we implemented several templates for generating web pages from the exported resources, and are currently working on allowing other applications to use the exported data.

6. Preliminary Evaluation / Initial Experience

As a preliminary evaluation of ActiveTheatre, we conducted a scenario-based evaluation workshop in order to assess whether the system supported the need for collaborative, event-based access and capture in an operating theatre. The participants in the evaluation workshop were two surgeons, an anesthesiologist, and two operating nurses. The workshop lasted six hours and took place in a simulated operating theatre at our university. This operating theatre contained an operating table with a 17 inch touch screen on a moveable arm, a large wall-based display in the background, and microphones and loudspeakers. A picture from the workshop is shown in Figure 6. The workshop was divided into a five-hour 'play' part and a one-hour interview part; in the play phase, the clinicians played the scenarios a number of times and in the interview phase a focus group interview was done. We video recorded the whole workshop and have subsequently analyzed the tapes.

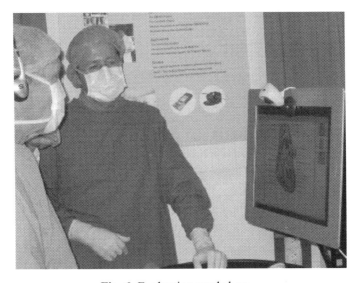

Fig. 6. Evaluation workshop

The main purpose was to get early feedback on the system and its interface in the workshop, and even though we wanted to address several aspects of the system in the evaluation we focused on two main questions:

- Does the event-based 'palette' metaphor in ActiveTheatre suit the work done in an operating theatre?
- Does ActiveTheatre support collaboration and multiple users?

The main flow of the enacted scenario was: (i) a surgeon prepares for an operation in an office on a standard PC with keyboard and mouse; (ii) the surgeon goes to the simulated operating theatre and pretends to perform an operation in this setting with the help of an assisting surgeon, a scrub nurse, and a non-sterile nurse; (iii) after the operation the surgeon prepares different views, again in an office. The main findings are summarized below.

6.1 Event Based Capture and Access

One of our main points we wanted to clarify was if the use of explicit capturing focusing on events was able to support the work done in the operating theatre. All the participants had a strong bias towards event-based capturing in contrast to continuous capturing. Their arguments were that it was seldom more than a couple of isolated events that were interesting to capture. Further, they found it important to only capture the important events. A problem with hospital work is not always the lack of information, but sometimes too much available information. Being able to explicitly capture data allows the surgeon or nurse to only capture what they find important, and even in these situations they also find it important to be able to further sort the captured data after the operation, which is illustrated by the following quote.

Anesthesiologist: *"If pictures are captured then there is someone who is going to judge if these pictures are going to be stored. Someone should be able to look at a sequence of pictures and decide if these pictures are relevant for the patient record. If this is not the case it should be possible to delete the pictures right away".*

Following this discussion, the participants also talked about how to best capture or document an event. In some situations one surgeon actually found that a precise textual description of an event was more valuable than a picture. It was commented that the value of a picture greatly depends on the type of operation carried out. The participants however agreed that if it was really easy to interact with a capturing system it would be relevant to capture pictures, video clips and texts. They also foresaw that these types of capturing systems could be used to require new and better ways of documenting operations illustrated by the following quote:

Orthopedic surgeon: *"If, with the help of the technology, it is possible to take pictures and videos it is probably going to be a requirement that you take pictures of different events during an operation"*

All the participants found speech to be an easy way to access capturing and access systems, but pointed out that it was really important that the system recognized correctly if it should be pleasant to use.

Finally, we discussed if dictated notes would be relevant to capture, because dictating a note to some degree removes focus from the work at hand. In general the participants did not think that it was possible to generate a complete description of the operation while operating, but that a speech recognition system would be valuable in creating a draft of the operation description or making small reminders. It was especially mentioned as being valuable for long operations, or if an operation differs a lot from what is originally expected. After the operation the surgeon will be able to correct the mistakes in the draft and create the final version, as the following quote illustrates:

Head surgeon: *"That is what I imagine. The part about generating the text can easily be done during the last part of the operation, but I think correcting the small details need to be done in a quite place. I think it is interesting to generate a draft of the text before you are carried away by the coffee table".*

6.2 Collaboration and Multiple Users

The second issue we wanted to evaluate was how our system supported collaborative work. Support for collaboration was an issue from the beginning of the evaluation workshop. When a surgeon prepared for an operation the prepared data should not only be accessible by the surgeon, but by all the people involved in the team like the scrub nurse pointed out:

Scrub Nurse: *"For me it is logical. When John prepares the information for the operation the data is attached to the operation and not his login. If this is the case we will be able to access the pictures without John having to login all the time".*

What she is pointing out is that it is not just the surgeon that prepares for an operation, but the entire team. The nurses are, for example, responsible for finding both the instruments and related digital material. Therefore she especially liked the idea that the nurses would be able to add things to the palette both before and during the operation.

ActiveTheatre is designed to work on a shared display and allows all users to access the system simultaneously. However, during an operation a lot of parallel events are going on at the same time. The nurse might look at some instructions she needs while the surgeon is documenting the operation with pictures. The participants suggested that we somehow addressed this problem of parallel activities by e.g. providing several screens but at the same time should pay attention to the difference between public and private information and displays.

Integrating the capturing system with other already present systems in the hospital was also mentioned as central to a C&A application. The participants complained that it was too difficult (and sometimes impossible) to transfer data from one application to another. As illustrated in the quote below, it was, for example, especially complicated to attach digital images to the patient record:

Surgeon: *"It is seldom I put the pictures in the journal. It is too complicated. Instead I give them to the patient"*

It is the easy integration between the different systems that is seen as the biggest obstacle if captured data is going to be used in the electronic patient record, enhanced documentation, patient souvenirs, for learning, or as part of a surgeons personal diary.

7. Conclusion and Future Work

We found that building capture and access systems for the operating theatre led to new design requirements not previously addressed by related systems. ActiveTheatre is a prototype of a novel system that addresses these challenges:

- ActiveTheatre supports highly collaborative environments by allowing several users to work with the system before, during, and after an operation.
- It is built around the idea of focusing on events structured with a palette metaphor.
- ActiveTheatre is not designed as a monolith system, but built to be part of a network of applications that exchange data.
- The prototype shows how speech and zoomable interfaces can be useful interaction techniques for capture and access applications.

The next main target for the ActiveTheatre application is a pilot deployment for four to six weeks in an operating theatre in the hospital we cooperate with (scheduled October 2005). In order to meet this target, we are currently working on how to improve our system to better support parallel activities in the operating theatre as discussed in the evaluation. We are also working on integrating our system with some of the existing systems provided by our commercial partners in the project in order to use real data in the pilot deployment.

Though our research mainly have been based and focused on supporting medical work in relation to the operating theatre, some of our findings can also be used in other settings where events are more important than timelines, where collaboration is important, where new interfaces are needed, or where an application needs to work with a network of other applications. Exploring other areas is another issue we would like to pursue.

References

1. Abowd, G., Atkeson, C., Brotherton, J., Enqvist, T., Gulley, P., LeMon, J.: Investigating the Capture, Integration and Access Problem of Ubiquitous Computing in an Educational Setting. Proceedings of CHI (1998) 440 - 447.
2. Arnalonescu, W., Neeley, L., Winograd, T.: Where the Wild Things Work: Capturing Shared Physical Design Workspaces. Proceedings of CSCW (2004) 533-541.
3. Bass, L., Clements, P., Kazman, R.: Software Architecture in Practice. Addison-Wesley Professional, 2. edition (2003).
4. Bederson, B. B., Grosjean, J., & Meyer, J.: Toolkit Design for Interactive Structured Graphics. IEEE Transactions on Software Engineering, vol. 30 nr. 8 (2004) 535-546.
5. Chiu, P., Kapuskar, A., Reitmeier, S., Wilcox, L.: NoteLook: Taking Notes in Meetings with Digital Video and Ink. Proceedings of ACM Multimedia (1999) 1-10.
6. Hayes, G., Kientz, J., Truong, K., White, D., Abowd, G., Pering, T.: Designing Capture Applications to Support the Education of Children with Autism. Proceedings of UbiComp, LNCS 3205 (2004) 161-178.
7. Hayes, G., Truong, K, Abowd, G., Pering, T: Experience Buffers: A Socially Appropriate, Selective Archiving Tool for Evidence-Based Care. Proceeding of CHI, Extended Abstracts (2005) 1435-1438.

8. Heath, C. Lehn, D., Hindmarsh, J., Svensson, M., Sanchez, Luff, P.: Configuring Awareness. Computer Supported Cooperative Work vol.11 nr.3-4 (2002) 317–347.
9. Kensing, F. and Madsen. K. H.: Generating Visions: Future Workshops and Metaphorical
   Design. In J. Greenbaum and M. Kyng, editors, Design at Work: Cooperative Design of
   Computer Systems, Lawrence Erlbaum Associates, Hillsdale, NJ (1991) 155–168.
10. Mackay, W. E., Ratzer, A., Janecek, P.: Video Artifacts for design: bridging the Gap be-
    tween abstraction and detail, Proceedings of the conference on Designing Interactive Sys-
    tems DIS, ACM (2002) 72-82.
11. Minneman, S., Harrison, S., Janssen, B., Moran, T., Kurtenbach, G., Smith, I.: A Confed-
    eration of Tools for Capturing and Accessing Collaborative Activity. Proceedings of ACM
    Multimedia (1995) 1 - 21.
12. Pimentel, M., Abowd, G., Ishiguro, Y.: Linking by Interacting: a Paradigm for Authoring
    Hypertext. Proceedings of Hypertext (2000) 39-48.
13. Rekimoto, J.: Pick-and-Drop: A Direct Manipulation Technique for Multiple Computer
    Environments, Proceedings of UIST (1997) 31-39.
14. Richter, H., Abowd, G., Geyer, W., Fuchs, L., Daijavad, S., Poltrock, S.: Integrating Meet-
    ing Capture within a Collaborative Team Environment. Proceedings of UbiComp (2001)
    123 - 138.
15. Streitz, N., Geissler, J., Haake, J., Hol, J.: DOLPHIN: Integrated Meeting Support across
    LiveBoards, Local and Remote Desktop Environments. Proceedings of CSCW 1994 (1994)
    345 - 358.
16. Truong, K., Abowd, G., Brotherton, J., Who, What, When, Where, How: Design Issues of
    Capture and Access Applications, Proceedings of UbiComp, LNCS 2201 (2001) 209-224.
17. Truong, K., Huang, E., Abowd, G., CAMP: A Magnetic Poetry Interface for End-User
    Programming of Capture Applications for the Home. Proceedings of UbiComp, LNCS 3205
    (2004), 143-160.
18. Weiser, M.: The Computer for the 21st Century. Scientific America (1991).

Author Index

Lecture Notes in Computer Science

For information about Vols. 1–3560

please contact your bookseller or Springer

Vol. 3611: L. Wang, K. Chen, Y. S. Ong (Eds.), Advances in Natural Computation, Part II. LXI, 1292 pages. 2005.

Vol. 3610: L. Wang, K. Chen, Y. S. Ong (Eds.), Advances in Natural Computation, Part I. LXI, 1302 pages. 2005.

Vol. 3608: F. Dehne, A. López-Ortiz, J.-R. Sack (Eds.), Algorithms and Data Structures. XIV, 446 pages. 2005.

Vol. 3607: J.-D. Zucker, L. Saitta (Eds.), Abstraction, Reformulation and Approximation. XII, 376 pages. 2005. (Subseries LNAI).

Vol. 3606: V. Malyshkin (Ed.), Parallel Computing Technologies. XII, 470 pages. 2005.

Vol. 3604: R. Martin, H. Bez, M. Sabin (Eds.), Mathematics of Surfaces XI. IX, 473 pages. 2005.

Vol. 3603: J. Hurd, T. Melham (Eds.), Theorem Proving in Higher Order Logics. IX, 409 pages. 2005.

Vol. 3602: R. Eigenmann, Z. Li, S.P. Midkiff (Eds.), Languages and Compilers for High Performance Computing. IX, 486 pages. 2005.

Vol. 3599: U. Aßmann, M. Aksit, A. Rensink (Eds.), Model Driven Architecture. X, 235 pages. 2005.

Vol. 3598: H. Murakami, H. Nakashima, H. Tokuda, M. Yasumura, Ubiquitous Computing Systems. XIII, 275 pages. 2005.

Vol. 3597: S. Shimojo, S. Ichii, T.W. Ling, K.-H. Song (Eds.), Web and Communication Technologies and Internet-Related Social Issues - HSI 2005. XIX, 368 pages. 2005.

Vol. 3596: F. Dau, M.-L. Mugnier, G. Stumme (Eds.), Conceptual Structures: Common Semantics for Sharing Knowledge. XI, 467 pages. 2005. (Subseries LNAI).

Vol. 3595: L. Wang (Ed.), Computing and Combinatorics. XVI, 995 pages. 2005.

Vol. 3594: J.C. Setubal, S. Verjovski-Almeida (Eds.), Advances in Bioinformatics and Computational Biology. XIV, 258 pages. 2005. (Subseries LNBI).

Vol. 3593: V. Mařík, R. W. Brennan, M. Pěchouček (Eds.), Holonic and Multi-Agent Systems for Manufacturing. XI, 269 pages. 2005. (Subseries LNAI).

Vol. 3592: S. Katsikas, J. Lopez, G. Pernul (Eds.), Trust, Privacy and Security in Digital Business. XII, 332 pages. 2005.

Vol. 3591: M.A. Wimmer, R. Traunmüller, Å. Grönlund, K.V. Andersen (Eds.), Electronic Government. XIII, 317 pages. 2005.

Vol. 3590: K. Bauknecht, B. Pröll, H. Werthner (Eds.), E-Commerce and Web Technologies. XIV, 380 pages. 2005.

Vol. 3589: A M. Tjoa, J. Trujillo (Eds.), Data Warehousing and Knowledge Discovery. XVI, 538 pages. 2005.

Vol. 3588: K.V. Andersen, J. Debenham, R. Wagner (Eds.), Database and Expert Systems Applications. XX, 955 pages. 2005.

Vol. 3587: P. Perner, A. Imiya (Eds.), Machine Learning and Data Mining in Pattern Recognition. XVII, 695 pages. 2005. (Subseries LNAI).

Vol. 3586: A.P. Black (Ed.), ECOOP 2005 - Object-Oriented Programming. XVII, 631 pages. 2005.

Vol. 3584: X. Li, S. Wang, Z.Y. Dong (Eds.), Advanced Data Mining and Applications. XIX, 835 pages. 2005. (Subseries LNAI).

Vol. 3583: R.W. H. Lau, Q. Li, R. Cheung, W. Liu (Eds.), Advances in Web-Based Learning – ICWL 2005. XIV, 420 pages. 2005.

Vol. 3582: J. Fitzgerald, I.J. Hayes, A. Tarlecki (Eds.), FM 2005: Formal Methods. XIV, 558 pages. 2005.

Vol. 3581: S. Miksch, J. Hunter, E. Keravnou (Eds.), Artificial Intelligence in Medicine. XVII, 547 pages. 2005. (Subseries LNAI).

Vol. 3580: L. Caires, G.F. Italiano, L. Monteiro, C. Palamidessi, M. Yung (Eds.), Automata, Languages and Programming. XXV, 1477 pages. 2005.

Vol. 3579: D. Lowe, M. Gaedke (Eds.), Web Engineering. XXII, 633 pages. 2005.

Vol. 3578: M. Gallagher, J. Hogan, F. Maire (Eds.), Intelligent Data Engineering and Automated Learning - IDEAL 2005. XVI, 599 pages. 2005.

Vol. 3577: R. Falcone, S. Barber, J. Sabater-Mir, M.P. Singh (Eds.), Trusting Agents for Trusting Electronic Societies. VIII, 235 pages. 2005. (Subseries LNAI).

Vol. 3576: K. Etessami, S.K. Rajamani (Eds.), Computer Aided Verification. XV, 564 pages. 2005.

Vol. 3575: S. Wermter, G. Palm, M. Elshaw (Eds.), Biomimetic Neural Learning for Intelligent Robots. IX, 383 pages. 2005. (Subseries LNAI).

Vol. 3574: C. Boyd, J.M. González Nieto (Eds.), Information Security and Privacy. XIII, 586 pages. 2005.

Vol. 3573: S. Etalle (Ed.), Logic Based Program Synthesis and Transformation. VIII, 279 pages. 2005.

Vol. 3572: C. De Felice, A. Restivo (Eds.), Developments in Language Theory. XI, 409 pages. 2005.

Vol. 3571: L. Godo (Ed.), Symbolic and Quantitative Approaches to Reasoning with Uncertainty. XVI, 1028 pages. 2005. (Subseries LNAI).

Vol. 3570: A. S. Patrick, M. Yung (Eds.), Financial Cryptography and Data Security. XII, 376 pages. 2005.

Vol. 3569: F. Bacchus, T. Walsh (Eds.), Theory and Applications of Satisfiability Testing. XII, 492 pages. 2005.

Vol. 3568: W.-K. Leow, M.S. Lew, T.-S. Chua, W.-Y. Ma, L. Chaisorn, E.M. Bakker (Eds.), Image and Video Retrieval. XVII, 672 pages. 2005.

Vol. 3567: M. Jackson, D. Nelson, S. Stirk (Eds.), Database: Enterprise, Skills and Innovation. XII, 185 pages. 2005.

Vol. 3566: J.-P. Banâtre, P. Fradet, J.-L. Giavitto, O. Michel (Eds.), Unconventional Programming Paradigms. XI, 367 pages. 2005.

Vol. 3565: G.E. Christensen, M. Sonka (Eds.), Information Processing in Medical Imaging. XXI, 777 pages. 2005.

Vol. 3564: N. Eisinger, J. Małuszyński (Eds.), Reasoning Web. IX, 319 pages. 2005.

Vol. 3562: J. Mira, J.R. Álvarez (Eds.), Artificial Intelligence and Knowledge Engineering Applications: A Bioinspired Approach, Part II. XXIV, 636 pages. 2005.

Vol. 3561: J. Mira, J.R. Álvarez (Eds.), Mechanisms, Symbols, and Models Underlying Cognition, Part I. XXIV, 532 pages. 2005.

ates